The Reflective Heart

The Reflective Heart

Discovering Spiritual Intelligence
in Ibn 'Arabī's *Meccan Illuminations*

by James Winston Morris

FONS VITAE

First published in 2005 by
Fons Vitae
49 Mockingbird Valley Drive
Louisville, KY 40207
http://www.fonsvitae.com

Copyright Fons Vitae 2005

Library of Congress Control Number: 2005927161

ISBN 1-887752-67-6

This book was typeset by Neville Blakemore, Jr.

Cover photograph "Teign Valley, Dartmoor"
copyright Corinna Merriman-Morris 2005

Printed in Canada.

To those teachers who first introduced me to Ibn 'Arabi:

Henry Corbin, Toshihiko Izutsu,
Seyyed Hossein Nasr, and Michel Chodkiewicz

And for all those colleagues, friends and students who
have continued to share in these discoveries

TABLE OF CONTENTS

Ibn 'Arabī's distinctive elucidation of Islamic tradition has presented daunting challenges to commentators from that same tradition ever since he lived and wrote—1165-1240. And James Morris exhibits a familiarity with that literature, but spares us its parry and thrust. He is rather intent, as his title underscores, to present the master's explorations in such a way as to develop the reflective dimensions of our hearts. So rather than offer us a commentary, he gifts us with a presentation of Ibn 'Arabī's unique manner of eliciting our awareness of the reality of our self with the universe it mirrors. As we follow Morris' manner of presenting his master, he will initiate us into Ibn 'Arabī's own way of allowing the Qur'an to be his master. In this way, both Muslims and other-believers are offered ways of appropriating the scriptures given to us in our respective traditions. In short, Morris' presentation teaches us how to become apprentices to a spiritual master—in this case, Ibn 'Arabī—in the very way in which Morris exhibits his apprenticeship to Ibn 'Arabī. Put simply, if Ibn 'Arabī develops a reflective heart by assiduous meditation on his revelational source, the Qur'an, Morris' extensive and intensive penetration of this voluminous work of Ibn 'Arabī exhibits for us the fruit we may expect from meditation on our own scriptures. Morris' way of teaching mirrors that of the "great teacher."

We may be disposed to such comparative results once we reflect that each of the Abrahamic faiths avows a free creator of the universe, leaving to inquirers in each tradition to try to penetrate the unique relation which must then obtain between creatures and their creator. Unique because we creatures cannot persist outside the presence of this One who creates us, who cannot be another item in the created universe. How then may we attempt to think of this One, and of ourselves in relation to that One whose presence constitutes us? This challenge has been taken up by philosophers and theologians alike, yet Ibn 'Arabī's work reminds us that at this exalted level of inquiry, the differences tend to collapse. Indeed, one can say the same for Meister Eckhart and John of the Cross in the Christian tradition (whose probings of the heart Ibn 'Arabī appears to echo) and portions of Moses Maimonides in the Jewish tradition. For each of these traditions begins with a distinctive mode of revelation, yet the One who is revealed cannot be other than the free creator of the universe, lest that revelation compete with created voices. Put philosophically, without free creation there can be no revelation; put more theologically, the manner of revelation and our response to it will be shaped by our realizing how that revelation can only be the creating word addressing our very being.

In this way, as Morris presents them, Ibn 'Arabī's Meccan Illuminations intend to initiate us into the mystery of being creatures. Yet creaturehood is also an everyday fact about us, so these reflections will have to employ literary strategies designed to move us from the unusual to the ordinary. Now Ibn 'Arabī's poignant examples (from his own life) of the divine presence in our midst can be strikingly unusual, so Morris must show us how his deftly his master can employ the striking and bizarre to bring us to recognize that same presence in our "ordinary" life. And he does this precisely by mirroring Ibn 'Arabī's complex strategies, so the working of a master is presented to us through the skilled outworking of a practiced apprentice, thereby offering us the opportunity to become apprentices in turn. Therein lies the beauty and the challenge of these reflections.

David B. Burrell, C.S.C.
Hesburgh Professor
   in Philosophy and Theology
University of Notre Dame

ACKNOWLEDGEMENTS

Each chapter of this book has its own history of discovery, sharing, and gradual refinement. In each case, the initial impetus came through invitations to deliver public lectures: as a visiting professor at the École Pratique des Hautes Études (Paris, 2003), at Columbia University (Nour Foundation, New York), the Book Foundation, and at Oxford and the University of California at Berkeley, for the international Symposia sponsored by the Muhyiddīn Ibn 'Arabī Society. So special thanks are due, to begin with, to those responsible for creating and organizing those seminal events, as well as to all the original participants at each occasion.

Subsequently those thoughts and accompanying translations have been continually re-shaped, refined and transformed—and repeatedly illuminated in so many invaluably revealing ways—by the reactions of my students at the University of Exeter and Oberlin, and by the feedback from even more numerous adult participants in dozens of workshops and seminars on various dimensions of spiritual intelligence held throughout Europe, America, and many different regions of the Islamic world in recent years. My confidence in the universal value and accessibility of these teachings and insights—despite all the challenges of translation and communication so particular to the works of Ibn 'Arabī—is deeply rooted in, and profoundly indebted to, the experiences of all those who have so movingly shared, on one or another of those many occasions, in this ongoing process of remembrance and realization. In particular, the initial suggestion for the fitting title of this book first came from one of them, my dear friend S. Brand.

The final completion of this volume was aided by a research grant from the Arts and Humanities Research Board (AHRB) and research leave from the University of Exeter.

Every attempt to list the names of all those friends, colleagues, students and collaborators alluded to above has only highlighted the far greater number of those participants in this project whose contributions might thereby be left out. Here I can only mention the indispensable roles of Gray Henry in kindly arranging for this publication, of Kabir and Camille Helminski in so graciously providing the circumstances that made that possible—and above all, of the constantly supportive and illuminating reflections of my wife, Corey.

James W. Morris
University of Exeter

THE REFLECTIVE HEART:
THE PROCESS OF SPIRITUAL INTELLIGENCE

For almost eight centuries, Ibn 'Arabī has enjoyed a well-deserved reputation as a difficult writer—but also as an incomparable teacher whose works are as rewarding as they are often supremely challenging. And the intrinsic, intentional difficulties of his distinctive way of writing are only compounded for modern audiences who are necessarily far removed from the cultural contexts and presuppositions, all the complex symbolic languages of his own time.[1] Readers who come to this volume after having encountered his monumental *Meccan Illuminations* in earlier translations and studies will already have acquired their own skills for exploring and appreciating the depths of that work.[2] So the following introductory remarks are intended instead for those other readers who may be approaching these *Futūhāt* for the first time, or with little previous background in the specific religious and cultural traditions assumed throughout Ibn 'Arabī's work. These indications are based on many years of practical experience in presenting and introducing his writings not simply in university classrooms, but as part of workshops and seminars for diverse adult audiences in many countries and languages, from radically different cultural and religious backgrounds.

In fact, nothing could be more familiar to any of us than the actual process of spiritual intelligence, since that universal process includes and engages every aspect of our lives—concretely, individually, constantly and inescapably. What may actually be unfamiliar, and thereby accounts for

1

so much of the initial difficulty of Ibn 'Arabī's writing, is above all the matter of names—the challenge of connecting initially unfamiliar symbols and technical terms with their properly corresponding reference-points in each reader's own experience. The very title of this book is one revealing example, since the "Heart" in question here has rather different and broader meanings from what that word ordinarily suggests in English. In all these selections from Ibn 'Arabī's writings, reflecting their constant implicit references to the teachings of the Qur'an and hadith, the Heart of the theomorphic, fully realized human being (*qalb al-insān*), is understood as the locus of every conceivable form and dimension of human experience, of all the infinite, ever-renewed divine Signs or theophanies that constitute the ever-renewed creation.

Thus the heart's distinctive activity of "reflection" mentioned in the title refers to two equally indispensable aspects of that universal process of spiritual intelligence. First, it points to the complex intellectual and spiritual processes of "remembering God" (*dhikr Allāh*)—to what the Qur'an variously refers to, on every page, as our seeking, looking, probing, thinking, understanding, pondering, contemplating, recalling—all so that we might come to recognize the divine Source and meaning of those phenomena, that task which is our distinctively human capacity, finality and responsibility. Secondly, it alludes to the ongoing practical processes and actions of purification and spiritual discipline, to the often painful task of polishing the mirror of the heart, so that through these trials and lessons it can eventually become a true and effective reflection of each of the divine qualities, of the "Most Beautiful Names."[3] Now with time, practice and increasing familiarity, that essential inner process of connection and specification, of moving from the familiar scriptural symbols to the spiritual intuition of their corresponding experiential realities, becomes reflexive and almost instinctive. But most readers today, like students working with their masters in the past, initially need a good deal of help and guidance—an unavoidable practical requirement which helps explain the formidable apparatus of footnotes, excurses, commentaries and introductions to be found in every serious translation of any of Ibn 'Arabī's writings.

To return from those names to reality, the complex processes of spiritual intelligence can be reduced conceptually to three equally universal elements, all summed up in the title: experience; reflection; and right practice. Ibn 'Arabī's highly distinctive rhetoric is carefully designed first to illuminate each of those three constitutive dimensions of our experience, to reveal them clearly to our awareness, as the essential bases for further refinement and discernment. And then to help us integrate them dynamically in true right action, so that we can begin to consciously, effectively cooperate—at once for ourselves and increasingly in our relations with others—with all the many teachers in this cosmic school of spiritual perfection. How this actually happens in Ibn 'Arabī's writings is best discovered through actual practice, but the concluding Chapter Five below explores the different dimensions of that process in greater detail.

Each of the following Chapters carefully follows Ibn 'Arabī's consecutive development of these three inseparable facets of spiritual intelligence, in relation to a particular spiritual theme, as he slowly unveils the different dimensions of that selected theme in the course of his magnum opus, *The Meccan Illuminations*.[4] I have sought throughout to convey that gradual intellectual and spiritual development as much as possible in his own words. Such selectivity and focus, of course, necessarily simplifies the far more complex process of actually exploring and reading these "*Openings*" integrally, in their original form.[5] But that ideal task remains daunting even for lifelong students of this teacher, while the unfolding of these five thematic essays can already fairly suggest something of both the richness and the distinctive challenges of the underlying work as a whole. And for those who have been enticed into further exploration of the *Futūhāt*, the long concluding Chapter Five here is intended to serve as a helpful bridge to the useful study of the longer, more complete translations from that work which have slowly begun to appear, in several languages, in recent years.

Each of these studies begins with a summary introduction to the specific spiritual themes and symbols in the Qur'an and the hadith (the traditions relating the teachings of the Prophet Muhammad) which are normally presupposed as the literary and rhetorical basis for all of Ibn 'Arabī's—and his original readers'—own developments and interpretations. Ibn 'Arabī regularly assumes in his readers a profound familiarity with the most detailed forms and literal details of that immense body of earlier Islamic tradition, and above all with the expressly universal metaphysical and spiritual teachings it was understood to convey. So there is no real shortcut or practical substitute for some initial familiarity with that basic scriptural and cultural background.

The next essential step in the spiritually effective reading of these selections—i.e., in approaching Ibn 'Arabī's words in the way that he certainly meant for them to be read and pondered—is for readers to identify those particular passages in which they can recognize unmistakably the specific, concrete mirroring of some of their own corresponding spiritual experiences. For all the lasting spiritual effectiveness and unique appeal of these *Openings* over the centuries—just as with their equivalents among the great world masterpieces of classical Sufi poetry—has depended on Ibn 'Arabī's remarkable provision of this extraordinarily inclusive "mirror of the soul." For this immense work, taken as a whole, provides a vast phenomenology of the spirit—perhaps the most far-reaching in all the world's religious literatures—through the vehicle of outwardly disparate phenomenological descriptions drawn from all the different facets of the spiritual life. The intention behind all of those constantly shifting accounts and distinctive rhetorical devices is to evoke in each reader a heightened or renewed awareness of the ultimately spiritual dimensions of what we ordinarily, unreflectively tend to ignore or pass over as the apparently unproblematic phenomena of everyday life. The actual literary forms of Ibn 'Arabī's ongoing mirror are extraordinarily diverse, and thus often not immediately recognizable as such: they include scriptural verses and stories, elaborate discussions of divine Names, key events in the lives of Muhammad and other prophets, the sayings and teachings of Sufi saints and other spiritual figures both known and unknown, short proverbs and wise sayings, on to extraordinary firsthand accounts of the author's own spiritual experiences and encounters, the remarkable autobiographical dimension that is so powerfully highlighted in the very title of his work.[6]

Now the discursive elaboration required today to explain or properly contextualize and translate so many of those unfamiliar allusions naturally moves the reader in a purely intellectual and conceptual direction quite removed from the original rhetorical purpose of such passages as immediately effective spiritual mirrors. That is why it is practically quite essential, in the course of reading and carefully meditating on each of the following studies, to identify quite consciously those particular short selections which *do* succeed in evoking one's memories of one's own corresponding spiritual states and experiences. In each Chapter of this book, I have carefully extracted and highlighted—in relation to the corresponding theme—some of the particularly accessible and moving illustrations of this spiritual mirroring phenomenon, in a way that at least approximates the more active intervention, questioning and verification that was possible in those more forcefully interactive settings (such as teacher and student, or master and disciple) that were presupposed among Ibn 'Arabī's original audiences. To take one particularly accessible and widespread example, Ibn 'Arabī's descriptions of the profound spiritual significance of our encounters with wilderness and primordial nature—near the end of the Chapter One (on spiritual Journeying) below—refer directly to familiar spiritual realities which should speak immediately to almost all readers today. Similarly evocative and immediately accessible passages will be found scattered throughout each of the following Chapters.

In each such case, once we as readers have identified our own uniquely personal experience of the actual spiritual phenomena Ibn 'Arabī is briefly evoking, the essential practical relevance of his ongoing discussion and elaboration of the manifold related elements of spiritual practice and reflection normally becomes immediately, and quite concretely, apparent.[7] From that point onward, the revelatory interaction of these three constituent elements of spiritual intelligence—of experience, reflection, and right action—gradually unfolds with an almost magical spontaneity and effectiveness, through our now awakened reflection on the spiritual laws and realities revealed through the in-

6

teractions of our experience with both right and *wrong* actions (the most lastingly effective and memorable teachers).[8] In other words, in each of these translated selections, that proper connection of Ibn 'Arabī's mirroring evocations with the reader's own corresponding experience—wherever and however that connection may be discovered—is an indispensable doorway which, to use the key expression of his own title, suddenly and unexpectedly opens up (the literal sense of *futūh*) immense spiritual prospects and ongoing insights. In contrast, the failure to identify at least some of those indispensable spiritual correspondences quickly condemns his less engaged readers to an ultimately sterile, mystifying maze of purely conceptual distinctions or opaque practical allusions and exhortations: a host of understandable dead-ends only too familiar to scholarly students of this author's earlier heritage and range of historical interpreters and influences.[9]

The broad thematic titles given to each of the following Chapters can be understood in two complementary ways. On the one hand, those themes can be seen as highlighting successive steps or essential phases in a cyclical process of spiritual realization and self-discovery. Following Ibn 'Arabī's own account of the natural order of spiritual development, we begin here with the initial stages of the spiritual quest and Journeying (Chapter One), culminating—through grace—in the attainment of contemplative quietude and peace. At that point, the purification of the Heart begins to focus on the active refinement of our inner spiritual Listening and inspiration (Chapter Two). Then that awakened love and inspired awareness of divine Beauty, the fruit of effective spiritual listening, must be transformed through spiritual Seeing and inspired insight into our uniquely personal, creative manifestations of right and beautiful action

7

(*ihsān*)—that active culmination of spiritual life eventually leading on to the realization of the beatific Vision of God (Chapter Three). Yet that active, realized Discernment of all the dimensions of spiritual communication and creativity, Ibn 'Arabī insists—echoing all those prophets and messengers who are his own guides—turns out to be not the end of each soul's journeying, but the opening up of further, ever wider responsibilities and challenges (Chapter Four). Finally, as always with Ibn 'Arabī, that realized awareness of our wider spiritual responsibility, of our intrinsically human servanthood, culminates in our growing recognition of the inner meanings of the eschatological symbolism of Islamic tradition: of that Garden, he insists, which is *already* visibly present in each theophanic reflection of the polished Heart, in each act of the divine "shadow-Play" of our existence (Chapter Five, on the two-fold Return). In this cyclical perspective, each of these developments leads naturally to the next, and—here on earth, at least—we are always unavoidably caught up in each of these facets of that journey.

At the same time, though, Ibn 'Arabī also persistently emphasizes that this more visible cycle of spiritual intelligence is also ultimately—or at least potentially—one of *ascension*. Thus each of these essays also traces, for its chosen theme, his careful elaboration of the slowly unfolding revelation of ever-larger circles of responsibility, right action and spiritual vision, already typified and concretely symbolized in the spiraling ascension (*mi'rāj*)—and epochal returning—of the Prophet's own archetypal Night-journey.[10] And here again, his distinctive language constantly challenges his readers to relate that initially theoretical elevation to their own unique journey of discovery.

Powerful as these short selections from *The Meccan Illuminations* often are, such brief tastes and allusions are no substitute for the real thing. Hopefully they will awaken the desire and motivation to go beyond these initial thematic approaches, while also suitably preparing those readers who may wish to continue and deepen these preliminary explorations.

Finally, I must mention another distinct set of interconnected themes and considerations that are woven throughout these essays, although they are raised most explicitly and comprehensively in the concluding Chapter Five. That is the carefully illustrated exploration of the nature, function and wide range of intentions underlying Ibn ʿArabī's uniquely complex and demanding spiritual language and its typical rhetorical structures and assumptions. On one hand, this may at first seem like a relatively technical, scholarly concern, relevant only to academic specialists—since it is certainly indispensable, all the same, for any serious and accurate appreciation of this Shaykh's own works. But it also has a profound potential importance for two much wider audiences and related fields of study that are likely to be of interest to almost all of Ibn ʿArabī's readers today.

First, because Ibn ʿArabī's language itself arises out of such an extraordinarily penetrating and revealing awareness of the deeper structures and meanings of the Qurʾan (and hadith), it turns out to provide constantly illuminating keys to understanding and appreciating the inspirations, forms and intentions of a vast range of masterworks—and not simply in poetry and literature—by the greatest creative figures throughout all the related fields of the Islamic humanities, who were themselves shaped and inspired by the lifelong penetration of those same scriptural sources. The perspectives and principles involved here are equally

9

central and indispensable for an informed appreciation of those artistic and spiritual masterpieces, and for any lastingly effective and spiritually grounded revival or reconstruction of authentically Islamic thought.

Secondly, spiritual intelligence is of course something that is only learned by practice. In the traditional language of the Sufi paths, this basic reality was expressed above all in the untranslatable expression of *suhba*, referring to each seeker's indispensable "learning-through-companionship" with the spiritual guide or master. So readers of these essays, without even focusing explicitly on those underlying literary, analytical and structural (indeed even political) dimensions of the following discussions, should find—like so many earlier students of the *shaykh al-akbar*—that the effects of Ibn 'Arabī's lessons and insights do carry over into an ever-deepening appreciation and more penetrating understanding of cognate literatures, as well as other forms of spiritual communication, from any and all of the world's other great religious and civilizational traditions.

JOURNEYING

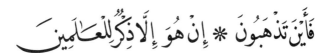

So where then are you all going?
Surely this is only a Reminder to all the worlds...

Sūrat al-Takwīr, 81:26-27

فَأَفْلَمْ يَسِيرُواْ فِى ٱلْأَرْضِ فَتَكُونَ لَهُمْ قُلُوبٌ يَعْقِلُونَ بِهَآ
أَوْ ءَاذَانٌ يَسْمَعُونَ بِهَاۖ فَإِنَّهَا لَا تَعْمَى ٱلْأَبْصَـٰرُ
وَلَـٰكِن تَعْمَى ٱلْقُلُوبُ ٱلَّتِى فِى ٱلصُّدُورِ

Have they not traveled in the Earth, so that they have Hearts
with which they understand or ears with which they hear?!
For it is not the eyes that are blind, but the hearts in the
breasts which are blind!

Sūrat al-Hajj, 22:46

11

CHAPTER ONE

JOURNEYING: WANDERING AND ASCENT

He is the one who causes you all to move on the dry land and the sea until, when you all were in the ship, and they sail with them, with a good wind, and they rejoiced in it: there came to them a stormy wind and there came to them a wave from everywhere and they thought that they were surrounded by them: (then) they called upon God, making the Religion purely for Him—(saying) "Surely if You rescue us from this we will certainly be among those who are thankful!"

But when He saved them—suddenly they are rebelling in the earth without any right!...

Sura of Jonah, 10:22-23

The broad theme of spiritual voyaging, travel and pilgrimage is woven throughout the Qur'an—and through so many key aspects of Islamic ritual and later tradition, including the writings of Ibn 'Arabī—in ways that are so pervasive and yet so taken for granted that, paradoxically, the original Qur'anic texts sometimes seem to have become almost invisible. As always, Ibn 'Arabī's revealing treatment of this subject is intimately tied to his gradual illumination of the detailed wording and actual contexts of the many Qur'anic verses relating to this theme, so we must begin here (in section I below) by recalling some of those key scriptural passages and expressions. In particular, these remarkable verses from the story of Jonah placed at the very beginning of this Chapter—with their pointedly explicit insistence on God's guiding role in every stage of the soul's growth, on the *dry land* of our actions and *at sea* in all the waves of our inner and outer experience, and with their revealing hesitation between "you" and "they"—most completely encompass all the manifold dimensions of the spiritual journey in the Shaykh's teaching.

The following section II then traces Ibn 'Arabī's initial development of this set of distinctive thematic leitmotifs in the opening *Fasl al-Ma'ārif* (chapters 1-72) of the *Meccan Illuminations*, while section III focuses specifically on some of his fascinating elaborations of this theme throughout the long chapters on the basic Islamic acts of worship (the *'ibādāt*, chapters 69-72). Finally, the concluding section IV includes translations of extended passages from two of the three entire chapters explicitly devoted to spiritual journeying (chapters 173-175). And all of these discussions in the *Futūhāt* can be understood as a sort of extended commentary on Ibn 'Arabī's earlier, rhapsodic (and often quite enigmatic) treatment of this same subject in his earlier *Book of Unveiling of the Results of the Spiritual Journeys*[1]—a work which is often very helpful in understanding the allusions to this theme in the *Futūhāt*.[2]

I. JOURNEYING IN THE QUR'AN

If we set aside the special theme of the Hajj and pilgrimage, which has such a central role in the genesis and structure of Ibn 'Arabī's *Meccan Illuminations*,[3] the most prominent Qur'anic roots referring to notions of spiritual journeying are four, which are briefly summarized here in order of their frequency of appearance in the Qur'an—although it quickly becomes obvious that frequency of rep-

13

etition is by itself no special indicator of their importance in Ibn 'Arabī's own understanding and explanation of these ideas. What is readily apparent, however, as soon as we begin to look at the Qur'anic use of these key terms, is the typical way that Ibn 'Arabī's usage constantly returns to the actual, detailed contextual development of these themes and Arabic roots within the scripture itself, leaving aside for the most part the often very different technical usage of these same terms in later Sufism and other traditionally Islamic, but extra-Qur'anic historical contexts.

(1) *Sāra/sayr*: "GOING" OR "MOVING" IN GENERAL

The forms of this Arabic root—the same word referred to in the title and epigraph (verse 10:22) of this Chapter—are by far the most common expression for traveling or journeying in the Qur'an, appearing some twenty-seven times. Significantly, at least for Ibn 'Arabī, this particular root often appears in passages (such as this opening verse from the Sura of Jonah) referring specifically to *God's* directly causing things, as well as people, to move or to be transformed, as in the many descriptions of His eschatological "moving" of the mountains on the Last Day.

To begin with the most common cases, the longer formulaic phrase *"travel through the earth, and regard/reflect..."* itself recurs in very similar forms on fourteen occasions. In an interesting illustration of Qur'anic parallelism, seven of those verses are in the imperative, while seven others express simultaneous reproach and questioning, in almost identical phrasing: *Have they not traveled through the earth, that they might regard how was the ultimate end of those who were before them?!* (12:109, etc.). In both instances, however, these verses are broadly similar in phrasing and meaning, referring to the need for reflection and eventual recognition of the deeper spiritual laws and patterns of divine punishment regarding earlier peoples and groups who did wrong to prophets and others. While most of those verses are not more directly connected with spiritual journeying, three of them do stand out as obvious inspirations for many of Ibn 'Arabī's own discussions of this theme in the *Futūhāt*.

The most notable of these passages makes clear the essential inner connection between spiritual traveling and the perceptions of the human Heart (*qalb*), the ultimate locus of all the spiritual senses in the Qur'an: *Have they not traveled in the Earth, so that they have hearts with which they understand and ears with which they hear?! For it is not the eyes that are blind, but the hearts in the breasts which are blind!* (22:46).

The second passage (at 29:19-20) alludes to many of the most central themes in Ibn 'Arabī's spiritual teaching. In this particular context, it suggests above all what will be discussed below as the "vertical," metaphysical dimension of the spiritual journey, the movement inward—or upward—toward a deeper awareness of the Ground or Source underlying all the moments of the soul's ever-renewed awareness of the endless procession and manifestation of the divine Names: *Have they not seen how God begins the creation, and then He renews it? Surely that is easy for God. / Say: "Travel through the Earth and regard how He began the creation; next God brings forth the plane of the other world (nash'at al-ākhira), and verily God is Capable of every thing!"*

Finally, the following verses (at 30:41-42) allude to one of Ibn 'Arabī's favorite paradoxes regarding the absolute universality of this journeying and the way it actually comes into being for each soul and continues to develop, con-

15

sciously or not, through the ongoing totality of all our human actions and experiences—including the temptations and apparent successes of the Shaytān, and all the infernal "fires" and "winds" (mentioned in the Qur'an and hadith) flowing from those encounters. It is the same comprehensive vision of our human destiny, no doubt inspired by the same Qur'anic sources, that is so memorably summarized in 'Attār's celebrated image of the "thirty birds" (*sī murgh*) and their troubled quest for that mysterious divine King (the *Sīmurgh*) who turns out in the end to be reflected in their own transformed and purified Image: *Corruption has appeared on the dry land and the sea through what people's hands have acquired, so that He might have them taste some of what they (themselves) did—so that they might return. / Say: "travel through the Earth and regard how was the ultimate result for those before...."*

(2) *Safara/safar*: "Traveling" or Journeying toward a particular Goal

Interestingly enough, this particular Arabic root, which later became the classical Islamic expression for the spiritual journey (in Sufism as well as other Muslim contemplative traditions), occurs only twelve times in the Qur'an. And in fact, only eight of those verses actually refer to traveling,[4] in five cases with regard to religio-legal questions such as the obligation of fasting for those who are on a journey. One distinctive feature of this Qur'anic usage, which also helps to explain Ibn 'Arabī's relative reluctance to use this term, is that (unlike either the *sāra* or *salaka* roots) it always refers primarily to something that human beings do by themselves, to the result of their own limited purposes and intentionality. For as we shall see, the particular semantic focus of this term on our conscious goals and intentions, even in supposedly spiritual contexts, sharply limits its appropriateness for expressing the metaphysical ideas and deeper kinds of spiritual awareness that Ibn 'Arabī is usually seeking to communicate in his discussions of the spiritual journey.

(3) *Salaka/sulūk*: "TRAVELING A ROAD"—NOT ALWAYS
IN THE RIGHT DIRECTION

This Arabic root also occurs twelve times in the Qur'an, frequently in forms that highlight God's active and ultimately guiding role in the directions and destinies of human beings. Equally important, it is also used several times in specific reference to wrongdoers, and to the forces leading them to their perdition or punishment—a usage again dramatically opposed to the much broader standard application of this term, throughout later Sufi tradition, to the spiritual path and the voyagers following it.

(4) *Sāha/siyāha*: "WANDERING" AND
SOLITARY DEVOTIONS[5]

Forms of this root occur only three times in the Qur'an, but in each case in prominent—and somewhat mysterious—contexts that may help to explain its centrality in Ibn 'Arabī's own discussions of spiritual journeying. At verse 9:112, the active practice of this spiritual virtue, however it may be understood, is part of a famous long list of epithets describing that rare spiritual elite who have achieved "the Supreme Attainment" (*al-fawz al-'azīm*). And at 66:5, in the feminine, the active participle form is again used in a distinctive description of the spiritually ideal woman. Together, those two compelling contexts already strongly suggest a rare, highly distinctive spiritual quality and activity that is far more profound (and demanding) than the simple meaning of "fasting" suggested by many classical Qur'an commentators.

Finally, there is the active imperative form of this verb used at 9:2: *So wander in the earth for four months, and know that you all cannot get away from God...!* This verse—if one understands it (as Ibn 'Arabī often does) not just in reference to a particular historical group of miscreants, but to all human beings—strongly suggests some of the key themes in his own elaborate development of this term outlined below. In particular, one may note the implication that this initial solitary wandering is only the beginning stage (perhaps the first third?) of a much longer process; and the Shaykh's stress that the actual realized discovery of the divine Presence, in all its universality, is ultimately dependent on this initially inescapable—and only apparently solitary—phase of apparent "wandering through the earth." As is so often the case, here a single, initially unpromising Qur'anic verse turns out to summarize and contain implicitly all the manifold practical and metaphysical lessons that Ibn 'Arabī goes on to unfold throughout these opening chapters of the *Futūhāt*.

II. WANDERING TOWARD GOD: AUTOBIOGRAPHY AND ADVICE

One of the most distinctive features of Ibn 'Arabī's unique rhetorical style is his constant mixing of unforgettable anecdotal, often autobiographical illustrations of his spiritual themes with more abstractly conceptual, theological or allusive scriptural treatments of the same metaphysical subjects. That characteristically phenomenological method is particularly evident in his gradual development of the notion of spiritual journeying in the long opening Section (chapters 1-73) of the *Futūhāt*. His first explicit mention of the spiritual journey, using any of the four major Qur'anic expressions just discussed,[6] comes surprisingly late in the *Futūhāt*, in a famous passage of chapter 29 devoted to the mysterious spiritual figure of al-Khadir, where Ibn 'Arabī mentions his own early experiences of "solitary wandering" (*siyāha*) during his youth in Andalusia. This was apparently the same period of nearly constant journeying, throughout the wider Maghrib, that gave rise to many of the significant spiritual encounters with memorable saintly personalities later recorded in his *Rūh al-Quds*.[7] After describing his second personal encounter with al-Khadir, in the harbor of Tunis, the Shaykh continues:

Then after that date I left to begin wandering along the shores of the Mediterranean, accompanied by a man who denied the miraculous powers of the saints. One day we entered an isolated and ruined mosque, intending to pray the noon prayer there. Suddenly a group of the "wanderers seeking solitude" (*al-sā'ihūn al-munqati'ūn*) came in after us, also desiring to pray, as we had, in that mosque. Among them was that man who spoke to me while walking on the sea (in Tunis), who I was told was al-Khadir, and another man of lofty rank, even greater than him in station, with whom I was already acquainted and bound by friendship.[8] ... Now when we had finished the prayer..., I got up to speak (with my friend) at the door of the mosque, overlooking the Mediterranean, and just then the man whom I called al-Khadir took the prayer mat that was in the mihrab of the mosque, spread it out in the air about five yards above the ground, and stood upon that mat, up there in the air, performing his supplementary prayers....

After the man had finished praying, I went over and greeted him, and he said to me: "I only did what you see for the sake of this person who denies (such things)"—and he pointed to my companion who had denied miracles, who was now sitting in the middle of the mosque looking up at him— "so that he might know that God does whatever He wills with whomever He wills!"

Ibn 'Arabī's next reference to spiritual journeying (in this case to *sulūk* and *safar*) comes later in the same chapter 29, in a passage where he begins by noting the practically fundamental distinction between our universal or metaphysical closeness to God—which he illustrates here with the famous Qur'anic verses *We are closer to him than his jugular vein* (50:16) and *We are closer to him than you all are, yet you all do not see!* (56:85)—and that "special closeness" or actively realized spiritual proximity (*qurb makhsūs*) of certain rare individuals which is so beautifully described in the famous divine saying: "...If (My) servant comes close to Me by a hand's breadth, I will approach him by an arm's length; and if he approaches Me by an arm's length, I will come nearer to him by a mile; and if he comes to Me walking, I will come to him running."[9]

"This special closeness," Ibn 'Arabī goes on to explain, "refers to all those actions and states through which people seek to draw closer to God." So the rest of the *Futūhāt* is concerned above all with this necessarily individual spiritual journeying that comes about through following the divine revealed Pathway (*sharī'a*) in both its equally essential and inseparable dimensions of true faith and right action, which Ibn 'Arabī finds symbolized together in the "dry land and sea" mentioned in several Qur'anic verses, including the famous passage (10:22) on the *journey through the dry land and the sea* cited at the beginning of this Chapter.

> ...Now since this proximity (to God) is through traveling and voyaging toward Him, that (comes about) through His Attribute of being *The Light* (*al-nūr*), so that we might be guided along the path. For as He said (6:97): *He placed the stars for you, so that you might be guided by them in the shadows of the earth*—which is the external journey through the actions of the body—*and of the sea*—which is the inner spiritual journeying through the actions of the soul.

Soon afterwards in chapter 29—in the context of Ibn 'Arabī's famous autobiographical discussion of his own distinctive spiritual state as an "absolute servant" of God (*'abd mahd*)—he returns to the topic of the solitary wanderers (the *sā'ihūn*) who are at the very beginning of their spiritual journey. What drives them to their lonely wandering, he explains, is their initially exteriorized search for a state of absolute devotion to God, a condition that they at first mistakenly—but quite understandably—associate with a withdrawal from *human* company. For in reality that spiritual condition of true servanthood ultimately can only be attained, as he makes clear in many later passages, through a much more difficult inner transformation and absolute conformity to the true and ongoing divine revealing:

> Now with every servant of God whose attention is turned to any of the creatures who has a right over him: that servant's servanthood (to God, *'ubūda*) is diminished in proportion to that right (held by another). Because that other creature is seeking the fulfillment of that right from (this servant), and has

21

a certain authority (*sultān*) over him, so that he cannot be a pure servant, purely devoted to God.

This is what motivated those who isolate themselves for God to seek solitude from other creatures, what led them to take up wandering (*siyāha*) in the wastelands and seashore, and to flee from other people.... For they are seeking liberation (*hurrīya*) from all created things. And I myself met a large group of those solitaries in the days of my own Wandering. During the time when I was in this spiritual station, I did not possess any living thing at all, indeed not even the clothing I was wearing!

STILLNESS AND THE "ABANDONMENT OF JOURNEYING"

In contrast to the highly visible ascetic effort and striving of those who are in the initial stage of outward wandering, chapter 31[10] introduces the higher, culminating state which Ibn 'Arabī will later describe as "abandoning the (illusion of) traveling" (*tark al-safar*: see the later chapter on that spiritual condition translated in section IV below):

...For they knew that (the assertion of) "motion" (i.e., by their own will and power) involved a pretense (i.e., that they, and not God, were the true movers), while stillness (*sukūn*) was not corrupted by such pretense. (So they said:) "Now God has ordered us to cross these great spiritual expanses and these dangerous deserts in order to reach Him. But if we were to cross them by ourselves (or through our own egoistic souls: *bi-nufusinā*), we could not be sure that our souls wouldn't take pride in that once they arrived—for they are by nature given to self-importance, desire for precedence and love of

22

praise. And in that case we would be among those
who fall short in that station...."

Thus these very special voyagers, Ibn 'Arabī concludes, took
as their *hijjīr*, their spiritual motto and symbolic formula of
dhikr, the *hawqala*:

> "...There is no power *except through God*," because
> that expression is specifically connected to actions,
> whether in deed or speech, outwardly or inwardly.
> Because actions are what they have been ordered to
> do—and indeed the journey is (only) action, with
> heart and body, the spirit and the senses.

THE TWO DIMENSIONS OF SPIRITUAL JOURNEYING

Considerably later, in chapter 47, Ibn 'Arabī returns to
emphasize what makes "spiritual journeying" (*sulūk*) so
particular and inseparable from the human condition: it is
the particular opportunity, and burden, of moral choice and
responsibility. Human voyaging—along with that of the
jinn—is unique in all creation in that it takes place simultaneously in *two* dimensions:

> For they are called (by God) to this journeying, and
> therefore they journey both upward (*'uluwwan*: or
> "on the higher, spiritual planes"), by responding to
> the Call given through divinely revealed prescrip-
> tion (*al-da'wa al-mashrū'a*, which is the *amr taklīfī*,
> the divine "command to spiritual responsibility");
> and downward, through their responding to the (di-
> vine) "existentiating Command" (the *amr irādī* or
> *takwīnī*). And they do so without knowing (their
> ultimate destiny and station) until after the divine
> Will has been fulfilled.

Therefore the traveling of every individual person among the jinn and humans ends up at their *station known* (by God) (37:164) for which that individual was created—*both the blessed and the tormented among them* (11:105). But every being except for them is already created in its station (and therefore cannot really be said to "journey" to it)....

THE SOLITARY WANDERERS AND
THE INVOCATIONS OF ALL CREATURES

A little further on, in chapters 51 (on the "people of spiritual scrupulousness," *ahl al-wara‘*) and 53 (on the spiritual disciplines that the seeker should follow even before discovering a master), Ibn ‘Arabī returns to some other motives that can push certain people to seek out solitude (*‘uzla* or *khalwa*) and greater proximity to God through solitary wandering (*siyāha*) in uninhabited areas. There is a surprisingly contemporary tone to some of his descriptions here. In the case of the people of spiritual scrupulousness, who seek to avoid inner entanglement in social relations, gossip and other preoccupations that do not really concern them, he explains:

> Some of them, or indeed most of them, are unable to keep people from meddling and speaking of what does not concern them. So this burden drove them to avoid people, preferring solitude and isolation from people through spiritual retreats—locking their doors against the intrusion of people. Still others (have sought) isolation through wandering in the mountains and gorges, seashores and canyons. There God relieves and comforts them with His Name *the All-Compassionate* in various ways of

24

intimate communion with Him that are granted to them by this "Breath of the All-Compassionate" (*nafas al-Rahmān*).

So he causes them to hear the spiritual invocations (*dhikr*) of the rocks and stones, the murmurs of the rippling waters, the whistling of the stormy winds, the conversations of the birds, the praises and glorifications of each community among the creatures, and their greetings and conversations among them. Thus these wanderers do find companionship with (those creatures), instead of their (original) loneliness, and they return to community and other creatures.[11]

As for those who are only starting out on the path, before they have even found a spiritual guide, Ibn 'Arabī notes (in chapter 53) that they must begin with an inner as well as an outer "isolation" (*'uzla*), the inner one being the concentration of the heart on its own states during the process of *dhikr* or recollection of the divine presence.

As for the outward, sensible isolation, at the very beginning of (the spiritual seeker's) state, that is their withdrawing from people and their company, either within their own house, or else through wandering through God's earth…, frequenting the mountains and seashores and other places far from people.

Ibn 'Arabī then goes on to warn those beginning this period of solitary wandering to avoid as well the company of the wild animals—"even if God should make them speak to you and keep you company!"—instead "desiring only God and not being distracted by anything else," so that they can focus entirely on their states of *dhikr* in their hearts.

III. The Inner Secrets of Traveling Through the Prescribed Acts of Worship

In the five long chapters of the *Futūhāt* devoted to the "secrets" or inner spiritual meanings (*asrār*) of the foundational acts of worship (chapters 69-72, on the *'ibādāt*: purification, ritual prayer, fasting in Ramadan, charity and the pilgrimage), Ibn 'Arabī actually offers what is undoubtedly one of the most complete phenomenologies of the recurrent forms and manifestations of the spiritual life to be found in Islamic tradition, and perhaps even more widely. In fact almost all of these chapters, which would amount to many volumes if properly translated and explained, are intimately concerned with the journey of the Heart. Here Ibn 'Arabī's explanations—outwardly following the traditional issues and terminology of legal disputes (*ikhtilāf*) about the application of Qur'an, hadith and tradition to the proper performance of these acts of worship—explicitly take up the notion of traveling (*safar*) throughout the dozens of sub-sections concerning the fulfillment of these basic religious obligations by the traveler (*musāfir*). These discussions are especially prominent in connection with the religious duties of ritual prayer, fasting, and pilgrimage. However, since we cannot begin to explore all of those extensive passages in detail, this chapter will mention but a few highlights of Ibn 'Arabī's commentaries.

In the chapter on the Hajj (chapter 72), one of his most evocative and memorable discussions, to which we can all immediately relate, is the passage where Ibn 'Arabī talks of the earthly—and at times seemingly quite infernal—journeying that every human being must undertake in order to understand the true reality of God's all-encompassing Loving Compassion (*rahma*), not through lip-service or outward belief (*taqlīd*), but rather by actual personal experience (*dhawq*: "tasting") painfully and slowly acquired through the course of life's revealing trials and situations of spiritual testing. After recalling the famous hadith stating that "the House of God"—the ultimate goal of the Hajj pilgrimage—"is the heart of His faithful servant," Ibn 'Arabī goes on to clarify how totally demanding and rare are the two fundamental conditions for that pilgrimage of true faith (*īmān*) and servanthood (*'ubūdiyya*):

> The stages (of the spiritual journey) between the (unenlightened) heart and the divine Throne, are between the divine Name "God" (*Allāh*) and the divine Name "the All-Compassionate" (*al-Rahmān*).[12] And even though (the Qur'an affirms that) *By whatsoever (Name) you all call, His are the Most Beautiful Names*,[13] still no one denies (some ultimate reality of) God. But (people) do deny the All-Compassionate, since (those lacking true faith) said *"Who is al-Rahmān?"*[14] For the station of witnessing of godhood is more universal, because of its affirming the totality (of existence), since it clearly includes both suffering and mercy, since both of those are found in existence, as no one would deny.
>
> But the station of immediately witnessing God's "Absolute-Compassion" (*rahmāniyya*) is only known and recognized by those who have received the compassionate blessing of Faith (*al-marhūmūn bi-l-īmān*). So no one denies that except those who are deprived (of that true faith), insofar as they are not aware that they have been blessed by faith. Because God's Absolute-Compassion contains nothing but Forgiveness and Absolute Good!

27

So God[15] is truly known through (each individual's experience of the corresponding inner) states: *Allāh ma'rūf bi-l-ḥāl*. So the All-Compassionate (*al-Raḥmān*) is also denied (because) of (certain people's apparently opposing) states. Therefore when it is said to them "*By Whatsoever Name you call, His are the Most Beautiful Names*," the people of painful trials (*ahl al-balā'*) only know that through outward lip-service (*taqlīd*), through God's having informed (them) of that from behind the veil of their tribulations.

So understand this! For I have pointed you toward things which, if you only travel according to them, will reveal to you aspects of the Knowledge of God whose extent can only be determined by God. Because the true spiritual Knower ('*ārif*) who knows through immediate personal experience of the full extent of the Knowing of God that we have just mentioned is exceedingly rare today!

THE GUIDING ROLES OF GRACE, INTELLECT, AND THE REVEALED PATHWAY

Ibn 'Arabi's next discussion of the spiritual journey comes up a little later in the same chapter 72, when he takes up the traditional legal question whether a woman pilgrim needs a male guardian or family companion. For him, that raises the recurrent practical question of the roles of spiritual guidance and grace in each soul's journeying. As he observes there:

Every soul desires the Pilgrimage to God, which is seeing and reflecting on the inner awareness of God that comes from direct witnessing (*shuhūd*). But can the *murīd*, the spiritual seeker, set out on that Pilgrimage by himself? Or can he only set out with the aid of a guide (*murshid*), which is either a comprehensive intelligence... or knowledge of the revealed Pathway (*shar'*, in its root sense)? The right answer is that this seeker must be either "desired and pulled" (directly by God: *murād majdhūb*), in which case it is the divine Grace and providential Caring (*'ināya*) that accompanies the seeker, so that he does not need a human guide—which is extraordinarily rare. Or if the seeker is not drawn directly by God, then he must necessarily set out with the help of a guide, which is either his intellect or the revealed Pathway.

Now even the most perfect human intellect, Ibn 'Arabī goes on to explain, can only lead the pilgrim so far, to that "first spiritual knowing" (*ma'rifat al-ūlā*) which is the inner confirmation of the truth of the divinely revealed Pathway, the *shar'*. Then "in the second stage he must be accompanied by the *shar'*, which takes his hand in traveling and leads him to confirmation of the Truly Real (*ithbāt al-Haqq*)." But both stages together are necessary to the full journey: for "the intellect is together with the revealed Pathway in this question."

JOURNEYING, OR "BEING CARRIED"?

Somewhat later in chapter 72, Ibn 'Arabī goes on to explain that those distinctions of grace and individual effort we have just noted only concern the beginning stages of the spiritual pilgrimage: nearer to the end, every traveler—not just the divinely favored *majdhūb*—eventually discovers that

29

we are all being carried along (or "*made* to journey," as our opening verse has it):

> The people of God (*rijāl Allāh*) are of two sorts: those who actually see that they are being "made to journey" (*musayyarūn*); and those who see (or imagine) that they are themselves doing the voyaging.... So the person who sees that they are being carried along (by God) must keep in a state of sacred purity (*ihrām*) in every state (since they know that they are already in the divine Presence). But those who think that they alone are doing the traveling are in a spiritual state according with what has motivated them on this journey.[16]

This is a crucial point which the Shaykh goes on to elaborate in much greater detail in chapter 175 ("On the Spiritual Station of Giving Up Traveling"), partially translated at the end of section IV below—as he had already done in his earlier, highly condensed poetic discussions of the spiritual journeys of Muhammad and other Biblical prophets in his *Treatise Unveiling the Results of the Spiritual Travels*, and indeed in his even earlier, autobiographical *K. al-Isrā'*.

PRAYER AND THE GOAL OF ALL JOURNEYING

In his chapter on the inner secrets of the ritual prayer (*salāt*: chapter 69), Ibn 'Arabī has dozens of fascinating observations regarding the spiritual journey. Here one can only mention a few passages where he makes clear the full universality—i.e., practically, as well as metaphysically or ontologically—of the process of spiritual purification and transformation to which he is alluding throughout all his observations about the traveler's religious obligations.

Taking as his starting point the traditional legal question as to what particular types of travel require a shortening or abridgement of the required ritual prayers, Ibn 'Arabī begins by pointing out the divine insistence that all beings or entities and every single state "comes back to God." Quoting such recurrent Qur'anic verses as *To Him you all are returned* (2:28, etc.) and *All things return to God* (2:210, etc.), he indicates that:

> All of these Signs/verses (*āyāt*) and their like indicate that the journey of (every) human being is (only) to God…since God is the Goal of every traveler. (This is so) whether he be journeying away from God, or through the existence of his own soul, or from one created being to another [i.e., through all the more normal states of most people], or in and through God, or in the Names of his Lord. For the Truly Real (*al-Haqq*) is the Goal of all the paths, whether or not those paths are ones that are (intentionally) sought out or not!

Here, as Ibn 'Arabī goes on to consider the paths of those who are sinning, as well as those who consciously seek proximity to God, we find him formulating one of his typically paradoxical, yet profoundly thought-provoking insights:

> Now what is the goal of the *sālik*, the spiritual voyager? As for the voyager who travels in a state of sin (or a "disobedient act," *ma'siya*), he can only be determined to be "disobedient" if at the same time he also has faith…! For he is someone who mixes good deeds together with bad, and that is a traveler (*musāfir*).

Those who fail to see how this traveler is faithful by the very fact that he is disobedient (don't realize) that he is still in a state of willing obedience (*tā'a*) in that he has pleased God *by the fact that he does have faith* that what he has done was disobedient. So the traveler's faith, in regard to his state, is stronger than that particular deed which is called a "sin."

THE FOUR SPIRITUAL JOURNEYS

A little earlier in this same chapter, Ibn 'Arabī even more bluntly highlights the universality of this process of spiritual journeying:

Traveling (*safar*) is an intrinsically necessary state for everything other than God…indeed for everything that can be said to exist! And this (realization) is the journey of the greatest ones among the people of God (*akābiru rijāl Allāh*)....

Their journey (has four dimensions): the journey (in and with God) through Knowing and Realization (*'ilm* and *tahaqquq*); the journey through the divine Names by taking on their attributes and qualities (*takhalluq*), which is the journey of their state descending from that first state; a third journey through the created things, by seeing the lessons contained within them (*i'tibār*), which is a separate state from the first two states; and a comprehensive journey that integrates all these three journeys in their states—which is the most prodigious of the journeys through the created things, although the first journey (in and with God) is the most immense and sublime journey of all![17]

Spiritual Knowing as the Fruit of Right Actions

Chapter 71, on the inner secrets of Fasting (during Ramadan), has the most detailed and frequent allusions to the mysteries of the spiritual journey—many of which are so mysterious and complex that their discussion must be reserved for another occasion. Perhaps the most immediately interesting of those allusions, in this context, is Ibn 'Arabī's insistence—which he reiterates in a number of other places in the *Futūhāt*—that the necessity, for almost all advanced voyagers, of traveling according to the divinely revealed Pathways (the *shar'*) does not mean that each spiritual traveler must have some kind of scholarly (or even conscious!) formal knowledge of the original, outwardly revealed scriptural authorities. For him, what is practically essential—indeed indispensable, even (or especially?) for the religiously learned—is to act in accordance with the real meaning and intention of those revelations, which is a "knowing" of an entirely different order.

Ibn 'Arabī's starting point for this discussion is a potentially ambiguous saying of the early—and self-consciously pious and strictly observant—Sufi teacher, al-Junayd, that: "this knowing of ours is limited by the Book (the Qur'an) and the Sunna (tradition of the Prophet)!" While such a saying could readily be understood, especially by Islamic religious scholars, in historicist ways that would radically limit both the legitimate sources and the potential expressions of spiritual awareness and praxis, Ibn 'Arabī explains it in a very different, far more open light. For him, "this saying means that (this distinctive spiritual knowing) is the result of the divinely prescribed action—by which Junayd meant to distinguish it from what is arrived at by

33

those who rely on their intellects." As the Ibn 'Arabī goes on to elaborate:

> We only took our proof from action according to those two (divine guidelines), without (necessarily) having to come across the traditional transmission (*naql*, of the related scripture) that supports the person who has reached this spiritual station....
>
> We have seen that (inspired knowing flowing directly from the spiritually appropriate actions) in a great many of our companions—who even take their (scriptural) proofs from the Qur'an without ever having learned the Qur'an or Sunna, as was reported of Abū Yazīd al-Bastāmī [who was supposed to have come to know the entire Qur'an without ever having memorized the Arabic text]. And if the traveler is not given (such immediate spiritual knowledge of the scriptures), then he still shouldn't either accept or reject (someone's spiritual claims from that standpoint)—just as we do when the Peoples of the Book inform us about something or another from their scriptures.

Spiritual Unveiling and the Denial of Chance

One final, particularly striking allusion to the mysteries of the spiritual journey, is a remarkable section (also in chapter 71 on the fasting of Ramadan) concerning those Friends or (future) martyrs who are inwardly informed by God of sins that they have yet to commit—along with their subsequent repentance—even *before* they actually live through those later outward events!:

34

This sort of experience is only a little whiff of the sort of spiritual unveiling that actually belongs to souls, and of their being informed about the unseen world without (the person's conscious mind) actually being aware of this. The reason for this is that the soul is really from the unseen world: although the bodily dimension is its mother, the divine Spirit is its father, so it is actually informed (of the spiritual world) from behind a subtle veil. Indeed this is so much so that when the person who has this ability enters the path of the People of God [the spiritual elect], that person races along it with all sorts of spiritual unveiling, because of their preparedness and predisposition for that (direct spiritual experience).

These are the sorts of things that are ordinarily called "chance coincidences" (*ittifāqāt*)—although in our opinion nothing "coincidental" (or "accidental," the other meaning of *ittifāq*) actually exists! For the whole Affair (of creation) belongs to God, and God does not bring anything into being "by accident": He only brings something to pass on the basis of His sound Knowledge and intentional Will and secret Decree and His (existentiating) Determination.

The deeper secret of this twofold inner state and mystery of the human soul—which constantly underlies Ibn 'Arabī's discussions of our common, universal journey—is beautifully summed up in a far-reaching imagined dialogue between God and the rebellious Iblis:

So God said to Iblīs: "*Why* did you refuse to bow down in worship (to Adam)?" And he said: "O my

35

Lord, if you wanted me to bow down, I would have bowed down!" Then God said to him: "*When* did you know that I didn't want you to bow down, after you had refused and opposed Me, or before that?" Then Iblis answered: "O my Lord, I only knew after my refusal happened." And God replied: "Then I only punished you because of that!"

Like Ibn 'Arabī's earlier remark about "the distance between the Heart and the Throne" (from chapter 72, n. 12 above), the whole span of the soul's spiritual itinerary is contained within this brief exchange.

IV. FROM WANDERING TO REPOSE: THE "VERTICAL" JOURNEY

Hopefully these few key passages from the earlier chapters of the *Futūhāt* have been sufficient to suggest that Ibn 'Arabī's discussions of spiritual journeying, in this and other works, continually move back and forth between two very different—but complementary and simultaneous—perspectives. On the one hand, there is what we might call the "horizontal" axis, deployed on the level of our individual experience of (linear) time and (inner and outer) movement, a perspective which follows many earlier and later Sufi writings in its detailed phenomenological attention to all the complex shifts and transformations of that apparently linear movement through the unfolding experiences of each soul's inner life. Like those earlier writings, Ibn 'Arabī's account in this respect often adopts the language and imagery of a pilgrimage caravan (or the nostalgic, solitary retracings of the pre-Islamic poets), moving through its stages, stopping-places, and stations along a single common path.

However alternatively, but also simultaneously, Ibn 'Arabī constantly draws his reader's attention back to another, more "vertical" dimension of our spiritual journeying—this time inspired in its imagery by the hadith on the Prophet's Ascension and Night-journey[18]—in which his focus is instead on the metaphysical transformation and elevation of perspective that takes place as the voyager's focus of identity shifts from the lower, basharic soul (and its taken-for-granted worlds of society, space and time), through the radically different planes of imagination and Spirit, toward its paradoxical reunion with the divine Beloved.

Much of the remainder of the *Futūhāt* can be viewed as an ever more detailed examination of those two contrasting, yet always simultaneous, perspectives on this single journey of the soul. Those two complementary points of view are beautifully summarized in the following two closely connected chapters from the second broad division of the *Futūhāt*, the *Fasl al-muʿāmalāt* (chapters 74-189, on the "spiritual inter-actions" of the soul and God).[19] The first of these chapters has the additional interest of evoking and analyzing in considerable detail familiar spiritual dimensions of our experience of the world of primordial wilderness—as a specially privileged mirror of the divine Presence—which are, to the best of our knowledge, rarely mentioned explicitly in pre-modern writings from the Islamic tradition. Rooted in the too often neglected natural emphases of the Qur'an itself, this chapter is an extraordinarily articulate witness to the deeper spiritual dimensions of "environmental consciousness" and our transforming experience of the natural world, from within the heart of classical Islamic tradition.

37

CHAPTER 173: ON THE INNER KNOWING
OF THE STATION OF WANDERING AND ITS SECRETS

God described the people of God as *"wandering"* (*sā'ihūn,* at 9:112). Now "wandering" means roaming about the earth by way of seeking spiritual insight (*i'tibār*) and closeness to God, because of the essential loneliness (or "estrangement")[20] that comes from keeping company with the (human) creatures! For you must know that the people of God have only sought out this wandering through the earth and the accompanying poverty, and the shores of the seas, because of (the state) that has overcome them through their keeping company with (other people).... That is because although (that socializing looks) outwardly like intimacy and familiarity, inwardly it is really a feeling of loneliness and alienation—although the person who goes off seeking that wandering is unaware of that: he doesn't realize that it was only this inner estrangement that led him to that until *after* he has discovered what that wandering brings about within him.

This is because God created the fully Human being (*insān*)—who is Adam and every other *khalīfa* ("steward" of God)—in His own image. Yet (God) denied the possibility of likening anything to Him, in His saying *there is nothing like Him/like His likeness* (at 42:11); and He secreted the mystery of this divine Reality within the Human being. So when someone turns toward God and repents, his soul becomes aware of that (spiritual) level—I mean of the denial of any "likeness" (to God). Then when he looks at those like him among the people, he is jealous that there should be anyone like him—just as God (al-Haqq) is jealous that there should be anyone else attributing godhood to themselves.[21] And as a result, he feels estranged from those people and seeks to be alone with his own essence, away from all others like him, so that he is intimate with nothing but his own essence. Therefore he flees with his soul/self to those deserted places where he sees no one like himself, frequenting the mountains and the depths of gorges. And this is the spiritual state of "solitary wandering" (siyāha).

Then this wandering begins to disclose[22] to him what he was seeking, so that he becomes intimate (or "keeps company") with his own essence. [...] For there is no longer any pretender there laying claim to godhood (ulūhīya). And likewise, for this person, in the state of poverty (faqr) in which he now finds himself, there is no one else there like himself to be called a human being, except for the wild animals. For the wild animals and other species than his own are in the same relation to him as the world is to God. This is why such a person chooses the "disclosing-journey" (safar)—i.e., the reality that makes manifest what we have mentioned (i.e., of the divine Names and Attributes only revealed through creation and our experience of it).

And this Reality is what (the famous early Sufi) Shiblī was alluding to when he passed the night with one of his (Sufi) brothers and stayed up talking with him through the night. Then Shiblī's companion said to him: "O Shiblī, stand up so we can worship together." And Shiblī replied: "Worship can't be shared (*shirka*: i.e., between anyone but the Lord and servant)!"

And neither can Lordship (*rubūbīya*) be shared. Thus it is as a result of that (divine) Form according to which Human being was created that (the wanderer) seeks to flee from other people, rather than any of the other creatures. For not a single one of the other creatures has ever claimed godhood, except for this human species. So it is because of this that the wanderer doesn't want to see his like (among other people). This is the spiritual station of *this* journey. ...and this is the wandering of the elite (*khusūs*) among the People of God.

As for the wandering of the commonality (*al-'umūm*) among them, the occasion for their wandering is God's saying (29:56): *O My servants who have faith—surely My Earth is vast: so let them worship Me!* So they began to reflect on what was "*God's* Earth," and they concluded that it was all the unoccupied earth (*'ard mawāt*, in legal terms) without any owner but God. For that land, far from any cultivated and civilized places, is especially God's; it is attributed solely to Him, without any (human) associate. [...] And the land far from civilization is free from (human encroachment). Therefore those (God-seekers) said: "The earth in which God ordered us to worship must have some special characteristic—and the only characteristic of this (wild) land is that there is not a soul (or a 'breath': *nafs/nafas*) in it, except for the Breath of the All-Compassionate!"

So when a human being worships his Lord in (wild) land like this, he finds that intimacy and companionship, and with it relief from that loneliness he felt back in civilization! And he finds pleasure and a blissful feeling in his heart, in his being all alone. All of that is from the influence of that Breath of the All-Compassionate through which God "breathes out" and reveals of Himself (*naffasa bihi 'anhu*) these (states) which that person could not find among the suffering and anguish and distress of the earth that is shared (with other humans).

So this is what led the common folk among the people of God to take up Wandering. Then (once they had started) they saw in this (wild) earth Signs and wonders and lessons which called them to reflect on what might be due to the King/Owner of this earth. So God illumined their hearts with the Lights of inspired knowing. And He opened up for them, in their reflection on these Signs and Indications [...] a Prophetic inheritance from His saying (at the beginning of Sūrat al-Isrā'): *Praise be to the One who took His servant by night [...] so that We might cause him to see among Our Signs* (17:1). (Like the Prophet in his Ascension), the wanderers among the servants of God directly witness among God's Signs and Prodigies things that increase them in the strength of their faith and their souls, and in their inner awareness of God and His Relations and His Lovingmercy and Compassion for His creatures:

Thus when they see the peak of a towering mountain they are reminded of their own (spiritual) dignity and sublimity, such that they do not seek from God anything but the "Breaths," which means being alone with Him, withdrawn (in spiritual re-

41

treat, *khalwa*) from their fellows so as to avoid being distracted from those (inspired divine) Breaths.

And when they are in the depths of a gorge or in one of the canyons, that reminds them of their servanthood and humbleness beneath the omnipotent Might of their Creator's Rule. So they are humble by themselves, and they recognize their true extent and come to know that whatever eminence they reach is only through *God's* Grace and providential Caring—not through anything they deserve.

Then when they stand by the ocean's shore, the sea reminds them of the infinite extent of God's Knowing and His Majesty and Lovingmercy. And when they regard, standing next to that immensity, the way the winds cause the waves to crash and play, that reminds them—in regard to God—of the contrast and interplay and interconnections of the various divine Names.... Thus God opens up and reveals to them, in their innermost selves, ways of knowing Him that they could only attain through their witnessing of that ocean during their Wandering. And this greatly increases their glorification and praises of God!

Finally, there are the marvelous things that happen to them with regard to the wild animals seeking out their company and growing close to them. So among them are those who speak to the animals in their own language, and those who understand the animals' communication and who can see how they are worshipping God. All that only increases their own eagerness and efforts to follow and serve their Lord. There are a great many stories of that in the books of the Sufis, and if this book were not focused on divine secrets and forms of knowing, we would have mentioned some of the stories and marvelous happenings we ourselves witnessed during (the period of) our own wandering and associating with these people....

Ibn 'Arabī's following chapter on "Giving up the (illusion of self-directed) Traveling" (*tark al-safar*) is dramatically shorter, indeed one of the briefest chapters in the entire *Futūhāt*—but its length is clearly not a measure of its significance. Rather, its very brevity seems to suggest something of the dramatic clarity and transformed perspective that is revealed by moving upward through what one might call the "vertical" axis of this spiritual voyage, toward re-union and immediate witnessing of the true nature of all our traveling:

CHAPTER 175: ON THE SPIRITUAL KNOWLEDGE
OF THE STATION OF ABANDONING TRAVELING

...God said: *He is with you all wherever you are* (57:4), so traversing distances involves extra trouble, indeed a particular effort. For nothing is moving me except for my seeking Him: if I did not make Him my goal and the object of my seeking through this wandering and this journey, then I wouldn't be seeking Him. But He has already informed me that He is with me in the state of my motions and changes, just as He is with me in the state of my standing still.... Why should I roam about—when moving in order to attain Him is a sign that one hasn't yet found Him in stillness?

Therefore I seek His Face in the place where I am standing![23] And when I have recognized Him there...His Names seek me, instead of me seeking them; and the Lights (of His presence) take me as their goal—I don't (have to) aim for them.... For remaining still is preferable to (or "comes before": *awlā min*) moving.... God did not order us (at 73:9) to *take Him as (our) Agent!* (*wakīl*: i.e., as someone to act in our place) except so that *we* might remain still, while He is the One who takes care of the affair of His servant, bringing in full measure everything He has destined to befall us. So even if what befalls the servant is traveling and moving, let *God* be the one who bears him on the litter of divine Caring—while the servant remains in that condition of stillness where he is. Then he will not even experience any tiring movement, being in repose, shaded and served (by God)! This is the journey of the one who has abandoned traveling, even when he is destined to journey!

Now we have tasted both those states, and we have seen that stillness is preferable to movement—and greater in the awareness (of God) that comes from the shifting of the states coming over us at every breath/instant. For there is no escaping that shifting (of the states) within us: that is a path that is always bringing something new, in which we are led, rather than making our own way....

...[Therefore] moving toward Him is the very essence of not knowing Him, and stillness with Him is the very essence of knowing Him! So *be*, according to what befalls you!

LISTENING

وَٱللَّهُ أَخْرَجَكُم مِّنۢ بُطُونِ أُمَّهَٰتِكُمْ لَا تَعْلَمُونَ شَيْـًٔا

وَجَعَلَ لَكُمُ ٱلسَّمْعَ وَٱلْأَبْصَٰرَ وَٱلْأَفْـِٔدَةَ لَعَلَّكُمْ تَشْكُرُونَ

*And God brought you all out of the wombs of your mothers,
understanding nothing, and He gave you all hearing and
eyes and hearts—that perhaps you might give thanks.*

Sūrat al-Nahl, 16:78

إِنَّ فِى ذَٰلِكَ لَأَيَٰتٍ لِّقَوْمٍ يَسْمَعُونَ

*...Surely in that are Signs for the people who are (truly)
hearing!*

(10:67, 16:65, 30:23)

وَإِذَا سَمِعُوا۟ مَآ أُنزِلَ إِلَى ٱلرَّسُولِ تَرَىٰٓ أَعْيُنَهُمْ

تَفِيضُ مِنَ ٱلدَّمْعِ مِمَّا عَرَفُوا۟ مِنَ ٱلْحَقِّ

*And when they hear what has been sent down to the Mes-
senger, you see their eyes filling with tears, because of what
they have recognized of the Truth/ from the Truly Real (al-
Haqq)....*

Sūrat al-Mā'ida, 5:83

45

CHAPTER TWO

LISTENING: CONTEMPLATION AND THE PURIFIED HEART

Surely there is a Reminder in that for whoever has a heart, or listens attentively, while he/He is witnessing...

Sūra Qāf, 50:37

This Qur'anic verse beautifully summarizes a sort of recurrent paradox that has puzzled every student of Ibn 'Arabī from time to time. One need only recall, for example, his classic discussion of the "Wisdom of the Heart" of the true spiritual Knowers (the *'urafā'*) in the central chapter on Shu'ayb in his *Fusūs al-Hikam*, where this same verse figures so prominently.[1] If, from the wider Qur'anic metaphysical point of view so well illustrated in that famous chapter, it may be true that all human perception and all experience is ultimately theophany,[2] it is even more indisputably true—as his distinction in that chapter between the rare enlightened Knowers and the rest of humanity pointedly acknowledges—that we don't usually experience things that way, that for many of us there is a noticeable gulf in our lives between rare moments of true contemplative prayer and our ordinary states of perception. And that gulf often seems too much to bridge by our own efforts, whether of prayer or other forms of spiritual practice: if we have some intuition of what the inner life of the Shaykh's enlightened Knowers might be like, it is probably based on a few special moments of grace, on a memorable but ephemeral state (*ḥāl*), not a lasting, fully realized spiritual station (*maqām*).

Put simply, then, what is it about this heart—or rather, *how* is it?—that can so miraculously transform perception into contemplation, everyday experience into theophany, the words and movements of ritual into the ineffable reality of prayer? As the Qur'an repeatedly insists, each of us surely has "had a heart"—but what is it that so rarely and unforgettably makes that heart truly "witnessing" (*shahīd*), actively and consciously contemplating the Truly Real, so that our transient awareness is transformed into true prayer and remembrance of God? That transformation of everyday experience into realized theophany, whenever and however it occurs, is always a mysterious divine "opening" (*fath*) or illumination, so it is not surprising that Ibn 'Arabī's most detailed and effective discussions of that central question of spiritual practice are scattered throughout the immense record of his own personal "Meccan Openings" (*al-Futūḥāt al-Makkiyya*).

Before beginning to explore his unfolding discussion of the secrets of prayer and the heart in the opening chapters of the *Futūḥāt*, however, it is necessary to summarize a few essential features of the broader development of this problem in the Qur'an and the hadith, since that basic scriptural background, as always, is presumed throughout the Shaykh's own teachings.

I. The Heart in the Qur'an and Hadith

To begin with, it would be difficult to exaggerate either the centrality or the complexity of the Qur'anic references to the "Heart" in this extended metaphysical and epistemological sense, as the locus of our awareness—and even more frequently of our ignorance—of the divine Presence. The

Arabic noun, *al-qalb*, appears some 132 times (only two or three of these possibly referring to the bodily organ), far more than such closely related terms as *fu'ād* or *lubb/albāb* (both occurring sixteen times). The contrast between the Qur'anic treatment of the heart and the discussion of any number of closely related terms or roots—such as *sadr* ("breast"), *'aql* ("intellect" or "understanding"), *nafs* (in the sense of "soul"), *sarīra* ("innermost self"), etc.—only serves to highlight the epistemological comprehensiveness and peculiarly *divine* focus or connection associated with this particular Qur'anic expression. Typically enough, Ibn 'Arabī's own widely scattered discussions of the heart, when we look at them more closely, turn out to be dictated not so much by various earlier Islamic traditions (which had quickly developed multiple technical meanings for each of these different terms) as by his own profound reflection and meditation on the full complexities of this original Qur'anic usage. Here we must focus on only a few central features of the Qur'anic discussions of the heart that are directly related to the problem with which we began, and which are usually assumed each time Ibn 'Arabī brings up that term.

1) The Qur'an repeatedly emphasizes God's extraordinary closeness and proximity to the human heart (e.g., at 8:24, *He passes between the man and his heart*), as well as the uniquely all-encompassing divine knowledge of *what is in their hearts* (4:66, 33:51, etc.).

2) That divine awareness of what is in the heart extends in particular to people's innermost intentions—especially in contrast to their words and ostensible actions. That is one important indicator, along with each of the following points, that considerably more than abstract epistemology is involved here: from the Qur'anic perspective, a spiritually crucial dimension of the human heart is the integral

involvement—together with God—of our own individual will and intimate intentions, which are portrayed as somehow inseparable from the degree and nature of our awareness of the divine. In consequence, the Qur'an can even speak of the heart (as more commonly of the soul, *al-nafs*) as the enduring individual self or ongoing seat of our moral and spiritual responsibility, as at 2:225: ...*He will call you to account for what your hearts have earned.*

3) Perhaps most obvious of all in the Qur'an is the consistent stress on the *divine* responsibility, indeed the ongoing divine Activity, expressed in all the different states of our hearts, including especially our recurrent failures to remember God. In this respect, as those familiar with the Qur'an will recognize, the larger metaphysical paradox which opened this discussion is certainly not, to begin with, Ibn 'Arabī's own invention: almost half of the Qur'anic references to the heart directly mention God's responsibility for the heart's changing states, often without any explicit reference to the shared role of the human "actor."

4) In several famous Qur'anic passages, repeated throughout Sufi literature and related expressions of popular piety, the enlightened or divinely supported heart (whether in this world or the next) is said to be the locus of true Remembrance of God (*dhikr Allāh*, at 13:28) and the grace of divinely bestowed Peace and Tranquility, as well as the receptacle for the sending down of the Spirit, Gabriel and other special acts of divine support.[3] But the Qur'anic references to these special states of enlightened hearts are limited to what in context usually seems like a very small and elect group: Muhammad and other divine prophets, certain of their disciples or saints, or some of the blessed in the Gardens of Paradise.

49

5) With far greater frequency, the Qur'an refers instead to God's sealing, veiling, hardening, locking, binding, closing, or frightening hearts—to hearts that as a result (of their own misdeeds or the divine reaction) are "sick" or "blind" and "suffering." Typical of this disproportionate emphasis are the many Qur'anic references to hearts that "fail to understand" (*lā yafqahūn*), far more frequently than to those who do properly perceive the divine Signs, whose hearts are "understanding" (*'āqilūn*). In the Qur'an, therefore, the starkly contrasting dimensions and potentialities of the human heart with which we began are, if anything, even more predominant and vividly drawn. The Qur'anic account of the heart and its situation is repeatedly cast in an intensely dramatic and unavoidably existential form. That intrinsic inner drama is certainly presupposed in each of Ibn 'Arabī's own discussions of the heart, whatever the particular language or context of each discussion.

6) Against that sharply drawn dramatic backdrop, the Qur'anic verses that indicate the actual ways or conditions for us to move from these "negative" or perverse states of the human heart to full awareness of God and the corresponding divine Peace and understanding are relatively few, but certainly all the more worth noting: these practically decisive verses include references to the "softening" and "humbling" or "purification" and "strengthening" of hearts, to the necessity of a "sound" or "repentant" or "mindful" heart (*qalb salīm* or *munīb*), and so on.[4]

7) Finally, as can be seen quite clearly in the numerous Qur'anic verses referring to the creation or divine bestowing of the human spiritual faculties of hearing (*sam'*), vision (*basar*) and the "knowing heart" (*fu'ād*, the locus of true understanding)—including verse 16:78 in the epigraph to this Chapter, and many other similar verses—it is note-

worthy, at least for Ibn 'Arabī, that the Qur'an typically lists hearing *first*, even before sight or understanding . For Ibn 'Arabī, at least, this seems to allude above all to the central Qur'anic theme of the primordial divine covenant and questioning of all human spirits, at their very creation, before their being sent down to bodily existence (the famous *Am I not your Lord?*, at 7:172). Thus in his extraordinary account of the beatific state of the souls entering the Garden (in chapter 65 of the *Futūhāt*), "listening"—in the sense of pure spiritual perception and receptivity—is again their essential innermost state:

> For He began His creating us by Speaking, when He said "*Be!*". Hence the first thing that was ours from Him was (our) listening (*samā'*). And so He concluded with (this beatific) listening—which is of these Good-tidings!

HADITH ON THE HEART

Unlike the case with many topics in the *Futūhāt*, the Prophetic sayings or hadith favored by Ibn 'Arabī in his discussions of the heart are short and to the point. (This is partly because, as we shall see, the Shaykh's allusions to the purification of the heart frequently occur in connection with more concrete, practical aspects of Islamic worship and ritual.) As readers of any of the Shaykh's works are well aware, each of these hadith typically serves as a highly condensed, pedagogically pointed summary of many related verses and concepts in the Qur'an. Almost all of these particular hadith were already widely used within earlier Sufi tradition, and several of them should already be familiar to readers of the *Fusūs* and other English translations of Ibn 'Arabī's writings. However, reflecting on the inner connections of those sayings when they are viewed together, in the following summary, helps to highlight not only their thematic density and mnemonic effectiveness, but also their relatively greater emphasis (compared with the above-mentioned Qur'anic verses about the heart) on the crucial dimensions of spiritual practice and realization.

• *"The heart of the person of faith is between two of God's Fingers."* This canonical hadith is depicted as the response to Aisha's asking the Prophet whether he was ever afraid. This beautifully succinct image concretely pulls together dozens of the Qur'anic verses just mentioned, powerfully representing the constant ups-and-downs of our inner experience, the contrasting roles of the different divine Names of Majesty and Beauty (*Jalāl* and *Jamāl*) expressed and realized through that experience, the "ever-renewed theophanies" (*tajalliyāt*) of those contrasting divine attributes, and the reality of God's ultimate control of that panoply of ever-changing inner states.

• Perhaps the most frequently cited saying about the heart in all of the Shaykh's works is the famous canonical *hadīth qudsī* ("divine saying": one in which the divine Voice speaks in the first person, as in the Qur'an): *"My earth and My heaven do not encompass Me, but the heart of My servant who has faith does encompass Me."* (Often this was summarized by various Sufis in the briefer formula, "The heart of the person of faith is the Throne of the All-Merciful": *qalb al-mu'min 'arsh al-Rahmān*.) Ibn 'Arabī's own understanding of either of these

52

sayings is of course inseparably related to the equally famous hadith that figures so prominently in the opening chapter of the *Fusūs* and throughout the Shaykh's writings, describing Adam's having been created "according to the form of the All-Merciful" (*'alā sūrat al-Rahmān*).

• "Hearts rust like iron,[5] and their polishing is through remembrance of God (*dhikr Allāh*) and recitation of the Qur'an."

• "Were it not for the excess of your talking and the turmoil in your hearts, you would see what I see and hear what I hear!"

• "O Transformer of hearts (*yā muqallib al-qulūb*), keep my heart firm in Your Religion."

• "My eyes are sleeping, but my heart is awake."

• "(True spiritual) Knowing is a light that God projects into the heart of the Knower."

• "Seek the guidance (*istaftī*: 'ask for the *fatwā*') of your heart, whatever opinion others may give."

II. THE OPENING OF THE HEART IN *THE MECCAN ILLUMINATIONS*

Ibn 'Arabī's gradual unveiling of his own realization and understanding of the heart in the opening sections of the *Meccan Illuminations* is a beautiful illustration of his unique methods of spiritual pedagogy in that work—methods that are consciously based on his own understanding of the nature and divine underpinnings of that reality of the heart which literally makes us what we are: for the heart, as he simply puts it, "is *insān*," is the very inner reality of fully realized human being. His method of teaching there is not the elaboration of a single theory or system that could somehow be adequately summarized, but rather the intentionally poignant and revelatory scattering of allusions to that one Reality in a way that closely mirrors the actual process of spiritual experience and growth in each of our lives.[6] The key to that process of discovery, in each succeeding chapter of his *Futūhāt*, is not so much the development of new concepts (since his underlying metaphysical perspectives are always present and constantly repeated), but rather the new meanings that each attentive reader constantly discovers through our mysteriously activated awareness of the ever-renewed reflections of what Ibn 'Arabī (and the Qur'an and hadith) are talking about within the changing forms of our own experience, moment by moment.[7]

For that reason we shall follow the unfolding of that teaching very much in the order that references to the heart actually appear in the *Futūhāt*, beginning—as Ibn 'Arabī himself does—with his evocation of his own revelatory experiences of this reality that underlie this and all his writings, and with some of his more abstract references to that contemplative and divinely inspired dimension of spiritual experience. The language of those opening discussions may at first seem impossibly far removed from anything we could possibly encounter ourselves; yet the Shaykh gradually moves on to deeper and deeper phenomenological allusions (*ishārāt*) that begin to awaken our intuitive awareness of a kind of knowledge and understanding that in fact is constitutive of all that gives meaning to our lives in this world.

54

As we shall see, those more phenomenological, even anecdotal, passages are often remarkably reminiscent of classical discussions of spiritual experience—whether in poetry, prose or scripture—familiar in the works of mystics and artists who were working within other religious traditions.

IBN 'ARABĪ'S BEGINNING: "THERE WAS NO KNOWING IN OUR HEART OF ANYTHING BUT GOD."

The first mention of the heart in the *Futūhāt* is in a key autobiographical poem at the very beginning of the book, part of Ibn 'Arabī's famous opening letter to his Tunisian Sufi friend, the shaykh 'Azīz al-Mahdawī, explaining the spiritual circumstances and motives for composing this work. As that famous passage (at I, 71) makes clear, when the Shaykh speaks of the heart in this work, he is speaking from his own direct experience: *everything* in this immense book, he insists, comes from a single revelatory experience, when after

> continually knocking at God's gate (of the heart), closely attentive (*murāqib*: a key term throughout all his discussions of the heart), not being distracted…, there appeared to my eye (and "my essence" or "self": *'aynī*) the splendors of His Face, until nothing was there but that Essence, so that I encompassed a knowing of Being in which there was no knowing in our heart of anything but God.

Then follows a remarkable, almost outrageously boastful invitation for each reader to plunge into the rest of this book: "If those people, who are so strange (*al-khalq al-gharīb*), would follow my Way, the angels would not ask you about the Realities (of the divine Names), what they are!"[8]

CHAPTER 1: THE HEART AS THE "HOUSE OF GOD" AND "HEART OF BEING"

In the opening poetic lines of the very first chapter (I, 215), Ibn 'Arabī calls on his reader to "Look at that House (of God),[9] whose unveiled Light is resplendent to purified hearts, to those who see It/Him through/with God (billāh), without any veil...." Returning to the openly autobiographical plane, that opening poem introduces Ibn 'Arabī's celebrated conversation at this inner "House" or Temple of the Heart between his earthly self and the image of his true Self, a mysterious divine "youth" (fatā) who reveals to him all the spiritual secrets to be recorded in these many volumes of spiritual Openings. Having "turned the face of his heart toward his Lord," Ibn 'Arabī is told by this divine Person (at I, 226-27):

This Kaaba of Mine is the Heart of being, and My Throne (the whole universe) is a limited body for this Heart. Neither of them encompasses Me...but My House which does encompass Me is your heart,[10] which is the sought-for Goal (al-maqsūd), deposited in your visible body. So those circling around your heart are the mysteries/secrets (of the divine Names), who resemble your (human) bodies circumambulating these rocks (of the earthly Kaaba)....

So just as one who knows those Secrets—who are circling about the Heart which encompasses Me—is in the loftiest and most resplendent of stations, so you (human beings) have precedence over those (angels) circling the all-encompassing divine

56

Throne. For you all are circling the Heart of the
Being of the world: you are in the station of the secrets of those who know.... For none but you (human beings) encompass Me, and I have not revealed
Myself in the Form of Perfection to any but *your*
inner Realities. So realize the full extent of what I
have freely bestowed on you from the supernal Dignity....

You are the receptacle (*anta al-inā'*), and I am I
(*wa anā anā*). So do not seek Me in yourself, lest
you suffer and toil; and do not seek Me outside yourself, or you will have no pleasure. Never stop seeking Me, or you will suffer torment. So do seek Me
until you find Me, and then ascend! But follow the
right *adab*[11] in your seeking, and be ever-present
(with Me) as you set out on your way of going (toward Me).

"THESE (WORDS) ARE ONLY HEARTS
INTENT UPON THE DOOR OF THE DIVINE PRESENCE"

In the following chapter 2, which concerns the metaphysical mysteries conveyed by the esoteric "science of letters,"
Ibn 'Arabī's references to the heart almost always occur in
the course of epistemological discussions where he is trying to explain the special nature of that divinely inspired
knowing which is the original source of this arcane discipline. Here one can only quote a few key passages from
those initial discussions (at I, 250-51), which necessarily
appear somewhat abstract or mysterious at this early point
and in this explicitly autobiographical context:

Now it is the Real (*al-Haqq*) from Whom we take
this knowledge, by emptying our hearts of thinking

57

and by preparing them to receive the divine inspirations (*wāridāt*). It is He who gives us this matter from its very Source, without any summarizing or confusion (as in poetic or intellectual inspiration), so that we know the Realities as they really are, whether they be individual Realities (of the divine Names), or ones that come into existence in combinations, or the divine Realities: and we do not have any doubt about anything concerning them. Our knowledge comes from There, and the Real (*al-Haqq*) is our teacher—through inheritance from the prophets, preserved and protected from error or generality or (confusion with) external form.... And our share of that is in proportion to the purity of the place (of our heart) and our receptivity and awareness of God.

A little later in the same chapter (I, 255-58), however, the Shaykh goes on to highlight the relevance of this inspiration to all his readers:

Our aim in this book is to reveal the glimmers and allusions and intimations from the secrets of Being. For if we were to speak fully and openly about the inner secrets of these letters and what is demanded by their realities..., (our work would never come to an end), since they are among those "Words of God" of which He has said: *If the sea were ink for the Words of My Lord, the sea would be dried up before the Words of My Lord would be exhausted....* (18:109).

This kind of inspired knowing, as he points out,

contains a secret mystery and a remarkable allusion for whoever reflects deeply on it and comes across these divine Words. Because if these kinds of knowing were the result of thinking and reflection, human being (*insān*) could be circumscribed in a short period. But instead, these acts of knowing arrive from the Truly Real (*al-Haqq*), continually flowing into the heart of the (true) servant: they are His devoted spirits descending upon the servant from the world of His Unseen, through His Lovingmercy...and *from His Presence* (18:65). For God is perpetually bestowing them and continually flowing forth with them, and the "place" (of the heart) is likewise continually receiving—either knowing or ignorance. So if the servant (of God) is prepared and receptive, and has polished and purified the mirror of their heart, then they realize that divine Giving continually and they receive in a single instant what could never be bounded within time....

"I have recorded these inspirations in accordance with the command of my Lord that I received," Ibn 'Arabī continues (I, 264-65):

For I do not speak about anything except by way of (reporting) what I have heard (from God)—just as I will stop (writing) whenever I am directed to do so. For our compositions—this book and all the others—are not like other books; we do not follow the procedure of (ordinary) writers... (who follow their own aims and desires, or what is required by a knowledge they want to communicate, at their own discretion). No, we are not like that in our writings. They are only hearts intent upon the Door of the divine Presence[12], carefully attending to what is opened up to them through that Door, needy (*faqīra*) and empty of all knowledge (of their own)....

So sometimes there appears to them from behind that curtain a particular matter that they hasten to obey in the way that was defined for them in that Command. And sometimes they receive things that are unlike anything ordinarily found by custom or thinking or reflection in outward knowledge..., because of a hidden correspondence that is only perceived by the people of spiritual unveiling.

Indeed sometimes it is even stranger than that: for things are given to this heart that it is ordered to communicate, although the person doesn't understand them at this time, because of a divine Wisdom which is hidden from the people. Therefore every person who composes according to this "receiving" from God is not restricted to understanding that about which they are speaking....

THE PURIFIED HEART AND SPIRITUAL UNVEILING

Not surprisingly, for Ibn 'Arabī the process of true spiritual understanding and interpretation of Scripture or other forms of revelation requires a very similar kind of preparedness and receptivity of the heart. Thus somewhat later in the same chapter 2 (II, 73-75), in a discussion of how one should properly go about discovering the intended meanings of apparently obscure or anthropomorphic expressions in revealed Scripture, Ibn 'Arabī again stresses the indispensable role of the heart in the practical methods adopted by the "people of unveiling and realization" for spiritually understanding such problematic or mysterious divine sayings:

We empty our hearts of reflective thinking, and we sit together with the Real (*al-Haqq*) on the carpet of *adab* and spiritual attentiveness (*murāqaba*) and presence and readiness to receive whatever comes to us from Him—so that it is God who takes care of teaching us by means of unveiling and spiritual realization. So when they have focused their hearts and their spiritual aspirations (*himam*) on God and have truly taken refuge with Him—giving up any reliance on the claims of reflection and investigation and intellectual results—then their hearts are purified and open. Once they have this inner receptivity, God manifests Himself to them, teaching them and informing them through the direct vision of the inner meanings of those (obscure scriptural) words and reports, in a single instant. This is one of the kinds of spiritual unveiling.

…(Through it) they limit (the meanings of these scriptural or prophetic expressions) to *what (God) actually intended by them*—even if that very same expression occurs in another report (with an entirely different intended meaning). For there (these identical words) have another meaning, among those sacred dimensions of meaning, which is specified in that specific act of witnessing.

However this relatively common and familiar type of unveiling of the proper spiritual meanings of scripture or revelation within the purified and receptive heart, Ibn 'Arabī cautions, is quite distinct from the relatively rarer divine "Addressing" (*khitāb*) of new words or writing or other inspired messages intended for others (beyond the initial re-

61

cipient), such as those particular divine openings Ibn 'Arabī has been ordered to set down throughout the *Futūhāt* itself.

"ALL OF THE HEART IS A FACE": UNVEILING THE DIVINE PRESENCES

If all this still seems distant indeed from our usual forms of knowledge and awareness, the failure to realize this kind of true communication and transforming proximity to God, Ibn 'Arabī insists (at II, 82-85), is definitely not the fault of the heart itself:

> You should know that the heart is a polished mirror, that all of it is a face, and that it never rusts. For if it has been said to "rust" (as in the famous hadith that "hearts rust like iron..."..., that expression only refers to when the heart becomes connected and pre-occupied with (seeking) knowledge of worldly matters (*asbāb*), and thereby distracted from its knowing of and through God. In that case its connection with what is other than God does obscure the face of the heart, because it prevents God's Self-manifestations (*tajalliyāt*) from reaching the heart, because the divine Presence is continually manifesting Itself, and one could not imagine any "veil" for that Self-manifestation. But when this heart fails to receive that Manifestation in the prescribed and praiseworthy way, because it has received something other than God instead, then that receiving of something else is what is referred to as the "rust" and "veils" and "lock" and "blindness" and the like (all mentioned in the Qur'anic verses on the heart).

Here (at II, 84) Ibn 'Arabī goes on to explain in very abstract and schematic terms, using his distinctive, theological-sounding technical terminology, some of the underlying grounds for the apparent paradox with which we began—that is, the obvious and undeniable qualitative differences between most of our ordinary experience and anything that we might even remotely call moments of theophany. His explanation is that although the Heart in itself is by its very nature nothing but the timeless "place" of the divine Self-manifestation, those same experiences and phenomena can be subjectively perceived at four different levels of increasing relative distance from God. It is essential to keep in mind that Shaykh's technical distinctions in this passage are meant to describe the possible ways we can actually perceive or contextualize the same "objects" of our experience—in their perceived connection (or lack thereof) with God—and not different kinds or classes of phenomena in themselves.

> For the hearts are eternally and unceasingly, by their very primordial nature, polished and pure and resplendent (mirrors of God). Therefore every heart in which the Presence of God is manifest insofar as the theophany of the divine Essence (*al-tajalli al-dhātī*), or (what the mystics call) "the Red Ruby", is the heart of the perfected human being, the (true) Knower (of and with God), the (pure) contemplator (of God)—and there is no other theophany higher than that. Beneath that is the theophany of the divine Attributes (in which the heart immediately grasps and comes to know the various divine Names manifest in its experience). And beneath both of those (higher levels of theophany) is the theophany

of the divine Activities—but (in which those actions are) still perceived as being the Presence of God. As for anyone who does not (perceive all the happenings of their experience) as Self-manifestations flowing from the Presence of God, that is the heart of a person who is heedless of God, banished from the proximity of God.

The unfolding discussions of the heart scattered throughout the rest of the *Futūhāt* are essentially a vast phenomenological amplification of what Ibn 'Arabī has so briefly summarized here, designed to bring out the essential connections or "harmonic correspondences" (*munāsabāt*) between the underlying Realities of these divine Attributes and Activities, and their actual exemplifications in each reader's own experience—and thereby to initiate the transforming movement from veiled states of heedlessness to the unveiling of the heart's own innate knowing and spiritual perfection.

III. UNVEILING THE HEART (CHAPTERS 3-54)

In chapter 3 (II, 105-107), in his first discussion of the famous hadith of "God's Two Fingers" and the related prayer of the Prophet for the "Transformer of hearts" to "fix my heart in Your Religion," Ibn 'Arabī takes up a kind of inspiration and awareness of the heart that, if much less spectacular, is also much closer to the actual reality of our moment-by-moment experience: namely, the universal human awareness of *moral* realities, and the resulting conflicts, judgments, and "tests" (to use the recurrent Qur'anic expression) that continually occupy the divine theater of the Heart.

...God's *"turning over"* (*taqlīb*) of the hearts (6:110) is His creating in them our concern with good and our concern with evil. So whenever the human being perceives the conflict of these opposing inclinations (*khawātir*) in the heart, that is an expression of God's *turning over* the heart—and this is a kind of knowing that the human being cannot keep from having.

Ibn 'Arabī goes on to explain that the allusion to God's "Two Fingers" holding the heart, in the well known hadith, refers "to the speed of its turning over between faith and rejection (of God), with all that implies," and that the duality of the *two* Fingers here likewise refers to the opposing "inclinations toward good and evil." However, he hastens to add that a particular spiritual "unveiling" reveals (in ways he only explains considerably later[13]) that these mysterious "Two Fingers" are related to the famous hadith concerning "*both* of God's Hands being 'Right' Hands," since all the divine Attributes are ultimately instruments of the all-encompassing divine Love and Compassion (*Rahma*).

The Heart's Sensitivity to Spiritual Places and Influences

In chapter 4, in the context of praising the special spiritual blessings and influences of Mecca, Ibn 'Arabī goes on to mention (at II, 120-24) a kind of contemplation and inspired knowledge of the heart that is a bit less mundane, but still a remarkably powerful and widespread experience for many individuals who today are often unaware of its deeper religious roots and significance—i.e., the question of our sensitivity to the spiritual power of sacred places:

One of the conditions for the person who knows through direct vision, who is master of the stages and modes of witnessing the Unseen spiritual realities (*mashāhid al-ghayb*), is that he is aware that places have an influence on sensitive hearts.... (As he goes on to explain here, only the individual entirely under the influence of his own perturbed inner states, the *sāhib al-hāl*, could fail to perceive this powerful difference in the spiritual intensity of being associated with different places.) ...But as for the perfected person, the master of this spiritual stage (*sāhib al-maqām*), he is able to discern this difference in the power of places, just as God differentiates between them.... What a difference there is between a city most of whose buildings are the carnal passions (*shahawāt*) and a city most of whose buildings are (divine) Signs and Miracles!

Here Ibn 'Arabī seems to be alluding more specifically to the "cities" or spiritual communities of human hearts. He then goes on to address directly his close spiritual friend in Tunis, the Shaykh Mahdawī (for whom the entire corpus of the *Futūhāt* was originally composed), and to remind him of his inexplicable preference for spiritual retreat at a particular place in a cemetery of Tunis, where he felt closer to the presence of al-Khadir—and eventually encountered that ageless initiatic figure.

...Now my friend knows that this (power of spiritual places) is due to those who inhabit that place, either in the present, such as some of the noble angels or the pious spirits (*jinn*), or else through the spiritual intentions (*himma*) of those who used to inhabit them and have passed on, such as (...the

66

house of Abū Yazīd al-Bastāmī, the prayer-room of
al-Junayd, etc.) and the places of the Righteous (the
Sālihīn) who have left behind this abode, but whose
influences have remained behind them, so that sensitive hearts are influenced by them. This is also
the cause for the influences that different places of
prayer have on the intensity of presence (*wujūd*) of
the heart—not the number of their bricks! ... So
whoever doesn't notice this difference in the spiritual presence of their heart between the marketplace
and the place of prayer is under the influence of
their passing *hāl*, not the master of this spiritual station.

...Indeed your intensity of presence (*wujūd*) is
according to your companions (*julasā'*), for the spiritual aspirations (*himam*) of one's companions have
a tremendous influence on the heart of the one who
is there with them—and their intentions are according to their spiritual ranks.

...So for us, the awareness of this matter, I mean
the knowledge of the spiritual influence of places
and the sensitivity to its greater or lesser presence,
is part of the completion of the mastery of the
Knower and the high dignity of that station, of the
Knower's responsibility for things and his faculty
of spiritual discernment.

Of course this particular case is only one small part of the
larger question of the spiritual presence or awareness of the
heart, and in chapter 12 (II, 346) Ibn 'Arabī alludes to the
spiritual exemplar whose words and presence lie behind so
much of his own teaching:

Now (Muhammad) alluded to something which the people of God have put into practice and found to be sound, and that is his saying: "If it were not for your speaking too much and the turmoil in your hearts, then you would have seen what I see and would have heard what I hear." For he was singled out for the rank of perfection (*kamāl*) in all things, including perfection in servanthood, so that he was the absolute servant (of God).

...And Aisha said: "the Messenger of God used to remember God in all of his states," and we have had an abundant inheritance from that. Now this (constant presence with God) is a matter that specifically involves the inner dimension of the fully human being and our speech (*qawl*), although things (apparently) contradicting that may appear in our actions, as we have realized and verified with regard to this spiritual station—even if that appears puzzling to someone who has no knowledge of the spiritual states.

Fortunately, although many of the forms or degrees of prayer and contemplation evoked by Ibn 'Arabī might appear at first glance to lie beyond the usual range of our experience, or in some cases, even beyond our most ambitious aspirations, he is also a master in evoking and suggesting the fundamental role of the divine activity and the providential divine Caring that constantly underlies every stage of this individual process of realization. And he does this not just in abstract, metaphysical terms, but often, especially in these *Meccan Illuminations*, in subtly practical ways whose relevance and meaning only become clear to readers who are willing to approach this work slowly and attentively in terms of its subtle echoes and implications in their own experience. His language for describing the phenomena of grace and the human-divine interactions, in all their richness, is surely most fully developed in the hundreds of later chapters of the *Futūhāt* on the various spiritual states, stations, and waystations, but already chapter 24 (III, 178-79) marks one of his first allusions to this practically central dimension of the problem that concerns us here:

> As for those hearts who are passionately in love (*muta'ashshiqa*) with the (divine) Breaths, since the treasuries of the animating spirits (of human souls) are in love with the Breaths of the All-Merciful— because of this inner connection and correspondence (between the divine Spirit and our human spirits)— the Messenger of God said: "The Breath of the All-Merciful is coming to me from the Yemen." This is because the animating Spirit (that gives life to our soul) is a (divine) Breath, and the Source of those breaths, for the hearts that are in love with them, is the Breath of the All-Merciful which is from the "Yemen,"[14] for whoever has been taken from their true Homeland, separated from their home and resting place. Therefore (that divine Breath) contains release from (the hearts') oppression and the removal of misfortunes. Which is why the Messenger also said: "surely God has fragrant breaths (or 'breezes', *nafahāt*), so go toward the fragrant breaths of your Lord!"

THE LISTENING HEART AND THE "PEOPLE OF THE NIGHT"

One of the Shaykh's most powerfully moving evocations of the soul's state of true prayer and awareness of God is in his chapter 41, on the "People of the Night"—the "Night" in question (based on complex allusions to a number of hadith and Qur'anic verses, as well as classical Arabic love-poetry) being conceived here as the inner state of mutual intimacy and awareness between the human lover and the divine Beloved, however and whenever that contemplative state might occur. In this remarkable intimate, speechless dialogue within the heart, it is the *divine* Voice that is speaking at first here (IV, 41-43), describing the inner reality of these "nocturnal" prayers, of the fully realized state of recollection of God (*dhikr*):

> So *I* am the One reciting[15] *My* Book to the person praying, through his tongue—and he is the one who is listening, for that is My "nighttime conversation" (*musāmiratī*). And that servant is the one who is taking pleasure in My Speaking—such that if he stopped (to ponder) the meanings (of what I am saying) he would be taken away from Me by his thinking and reflection.
>
> For what is essential for the servant here is to listen attentively to Me, to devote his hearing entirely to what I am saying, until the point where *I* am actually the One in that reciting—as though I were reciting it to him and making him listen to it—until I *am* the One explaining My words to him, translating its inner meaning to him. That is My nocturnal conversing with the servant, so that he takes his knowing directly from Me, not from his own thinking or considerations.
>
> For (the true spiritual Knower) is not distracted (from total attention to Me) by the mentioning of the Garden or of the Fire, of the Accounting and

Reviewing (of our works at the Judgment), or of this world or the next. For that (accomplished Knower) does not reflect on each verse with his intellect or investigate it with his own thinking. Instead he only *listens attentively* (alluding to the key verse at 50:37 with which we began) to what I am saying to him, *while he is witnessing* (Me), present with Me, while I take upon Myself the responsibility for teaching him.... In that way the Knower realizes with complete certainty knowings which did not come from within himself, since It was from Me that he heard the Qur'an, from Me that he heard Its explanation and the commentary on Its meanings, what *I* meant by this or that particular verse or chapter.

That is the Knower's proper *adab* with me, his carefully listening and paying heed to Me. So if I seek him out for a nocturnal conversation concerning something, he answers Me immediately with his presence and readiness, and his immediate witnessing.

...Indeed if the dawn comes along and I have ascended upon the Throne[16]..., My servant goes off to his livelihood and the company of his fellows. But I have already opened up a "Door" for him among My creatures, a Door between Myself and him through which My servant sees Me and through which I see him—although the others don't notice that. So I converse with My servant through *his* tongue, without his being aware of that. And My servant receives (that spiritual instruction) from Me *upon clear insight* (12:108), although those people don't know that and think that they are the ones who

71

are talking to him, even though (in reality) no one is speaking other than Me! They imagine that My servant is answering them, when they are actually replying to no one but Me!

The final paragraph here of course recalls some of the metaphysical teachings most commonly associated with Ibn 'Arabī and his later interpreters, ideas which he most often develops in connection with the hadith of the divine "transformation through the forms (of the creatures)" and the celebrated hadith of Gabriel in which the spiritual virtue of *ihsān* ("right-and-beautiful-action"), the ultimate aim of Religion, is defined as "serving God as though you see Him." But this extraordinary divine speech from chapter 41, with its open identification of the heart as the open Door linking God and the soul—and thus of even the most mundane incidents of each person's everyday life as priceless, entirely individual "private lessons" from God—throws a very different, less mystical and much more practical and instructive light on that same spiritual teaching.

THE "TRUE BALANCE" OF THE HEART
AND THE HIDDEN SAINTS

Ibn 'Arabī's next discussion of the enlightened Heart, in chapter 43 (IV, 78-82) on the "people of inner spiritual scrupulousness" (*wara'*), emphasizes even more strongly the importance of carrying out this spiritual practice of realizing the divine Presence within all the testing demands of social life in this world, but in complete secrecy, without leaving any opening for the multiple forms of inner hypocrisy and potential corruption that are usually tied up, in any culture, with any overt or distinctive personal focus on ostensibly spiritual activities. And in fact the Prophetic advice regarding this state that Ibn 'Arabī quotes here, if one puts it into practice, is likely to lead in directions somewhat different from any society's public expectations of religiosity:

> Now since this was the inner state of the people of *wara'*, they followed in their (daily) matters and activities the ways of the common people, not letting them know that this (inner scrupulousness and attentiveness) distinguished them from them, concealing themselves behind the conventional arrangements in the world so that no special praise is accorded the person who takes on those ways.

Here the Shaykh goes on to explain that "the people of God carefully avoid anything like" what would cause them to be singled out for their piety or asceticism or good nature and the like. He then asks his reader to:

> Ponder what (the Prophet) said about this spiritual station, teaching his intimates how they should act in regard to it: "stop doing whatever disturbs you, and turn to what does not disturb you!" And his saying: "Seek the guidance of your heart (*istaftī qalbaka*), no matter what the opinion of others."

These two hadith, which could certainly be interpreted (if taken in isolation) in order to justify some of the notorious ways of the *malāmiyya* or the nonconformist attitudes associated with the ideal of the *"rend"* (the true spiritual Knower) in Hafez's poetry, in fact offer some of the most useful and straightforward—if also incredibly demanding and challenging—practical spiritual guidance one could find anywhere in the *Futūhāt:*

> Thus (the Prophet) pointed them in the direction of their own hearts, because of what he knew their

hearts contained of the secret/mystery of God (*sirr Allāh*), what their hearts included (of that Secret) that is essential to realizing this spiritual station. For in the hearts there is a special divine Care and Protection[17] that is not perceived by any but the people of attentive awareness (*ahl al-murāqaba*), concealed for them there (in the heart).

The people of this *Pure Religion* (39:3), Ibn 'Arabī admits, almost inevitably become recognized eventually as somehow peculiar—although most people do not at all suspect just *why* they are so mysteriously special. The particular example he chooses to give here, of the remarkable conscientiousness of an anonymous sister of the famous early Baghdadi Sufi Bishr al-Hāfī, revealed in a question she brought to the learned jurist Ahmad Ibn Hanbal, is a telling illustration of the outwardly modest way of life the Shaykh has in mind. The key to this highest level of conscientious spiritual practice, he again insists, is simply to begin applying these two utterly straightforward sayings of the Prophet:

> For he gave us the True Balance (*al-mīzān*) in our hearts, so that our station might be concealed from others, wholly devoted to God, in complete purity and sincerity, not known by any but God and then His trusted companion. *Is not the Pure Religion (wholly) God's?!* (39:3)—since any other form of religion is inevitably corrupted either by the promptings of the egoistic self (the *nafs*) or its concern with social proprieties.
>
> ...So when the people of this spiritual station saw the Prophet's careful attention to what is realized within the heart of the servant, what he said about it and what he pointed out that the human be-

ing should do and should avoid by seeking to remain concealed: (when they saw all that), they put
it into practice in order to realize that (station), they
followed that path, and they knew that the salvation
we seek from the Bringer of the revealed Pathway
is only possible through concealing our spiritual
state. So he bestowed upon them (the duty) to act
according to that and to actively realize it.

Therefore the people of this station realized that
this (earthly) abode is an abode of concealment (for
us just as it is for God), and why God was not content in describing (His) religion until He had qualified it as the *Pure and Sincere (Religion)* (39:3). So
they sought a way in which they would not be corrupted by any form of associating (any worldly motives with the pure service of God), so that they might
apply themselves to this place (i.e., life in this world)
with just what it deserves, from the point of view of
proper *adab*, wisdom, and observing and following
the revealed Pathway. Hence they veiled themselves
from the ordinary people through the veils of scru-
pulous piety, which those people don't even notice,
since (for them) that is the outward aspect of religion (*zāhir al-dīn*) and the received forms of knowledge. For if the people of this spiritual station followed outwardly anything other than the commonly
received forms of religion they would stand out—
and thereby end up accomplishing the opposite of
what they were seeking.

Yet if "the common people only notice these (anonymous
Friends of God) according to the usual motives they have

concerning them," he concludes, those who have actually realized this high spiritual station are *already*

> being praised by God, by the holy divine Names, by the angels, by the prophets and messengers, and by the animals and plants and minerals and every-thing that sings God's praises. It is only the jinn and human beings (*al-thaqalayn*) who are entirely unaware of them, except for those individuals to whom God may reveal their identity.

This emphatic allusion to the necessary anonymity of the "Friends of God" (the *awliyā'*) is of course a central theme in Ibn 'Arabī's spiritual teaching, and one that is marvel-ously illustrated by his anecdotes about his own personal encounters with such hidden saints throughout the Islamic world, whether scattered in the *Futūhāt* or, more accessibly in English, in the stories of his own early teachers and com-panions translated in *Sufis of Andalusia*.[18] However, from a practical point of view, it might be even more revealing to connect what Ibn 'Arabī has said about such hidden saints, whether in those collected stories or here in chapter 43, with his lesson on God's instruction of the heart (and His mun-dane instruments of that teaching) in the immediately pre-ceding excerpts from chapter 41. The special spiritual ef-fectiveness, and the deeper fascination, of this strangely powerful book—mirroring life itself—lies in just such jux-tapositions and hidden connections.

THE HEART'S PRAYER AS LIGHT AND PRESENCE: *"THOSE DRAWN NEAR TO GOD"*

Now since the external, visible path of these true "people of the Heart," for Ibn 'Arabī, ordinarily comprises above all the "outward aspect of Religion" (*zāhir al-Dīn*), it is not surprising if much of the rest of this opening section of the *Futūhāt* [19] is devoted to the inner secrets or spiritual mysteries (*asrār*)—the "heart-dimension"—of the obligatory religious duties, and especially of the ritual prayer (*salāt*). As the Shaykh points out in his next discussion of the heart, in chapter 47 (IV, 134-37):

> Now there is no act of worship or devotion (*'ibāda*) that God has prescribed for His servants that does not have a special connection with a divine Name, or a divine Reality implicit in that Name, which gives to (the person carrying out) that devotion what it gives to the heart in this world...and in the other world. ...(For in this world, those corresponding gifts of each divine Name to the heart include its distinctive) stations and forms of knowing and awareness, and the divine Signs and manifestations of Grace (*karamāt*) included in its specific spiritual states.
>
> ...Now God says that He converses intimately with the person praying [alluding to the selections from chapter 41 above], and that *He is Light* (24:35), so He confides (in His servant's heart in prayer) through His Name "The Light" (*al-Nūr*) and no other. And just as Light drives away all darkness, so the ritual prayer cuts off every other preoccupation, unlike the other acts (of devotion), which do not involve letting go of everything other than God, as the ritual prayer does. This is why prayer is called "a light" [in the famous hadith "Prayer is a light"], because in that way God gives (the servant) the Good News that if he confides in God and entrusts himself to Him through His Name "*The Light*," then He

77

is alone with the servant and removes every transient thing (*kawn*) in the servant's act of witnessing Him during their intimate conversation.

...Therefore every servant who is (outwardly) praying, but whose act of prayer does not remove them from everything (other than God), is not truly praying, and that act of prayer is not a Light for them. And anyone who is reciting (the verses of the Qur'an) inwardly, within their soul, but who does not directly witness *God's remembering them within Himself,* has not...really remembered God within their soul, because of the lack of the right inner correspondence (between God and the receptive soul), due to what is present there of the things of this world, such as family and children and friends, or of the other world, such as the presence of the angels in his thoughts.... The inward state (of pure presence and unimpeded receptivity) of the servant praying must be such that none but their Lord is intimately addressing them in their prayer and recitation, in their praises and petitions (to God).

Then Ibn 'Arabī goes on here to multiply at length the inner conditions for experiencing the true reality of the ritual prayer. For as he points out, "Among the acts of devotion and worship (*'ibādat*), there is none that brings the servant closer to the angelic spiritual stations of *those drawn near to God* (the *muqarrabūn*, at 56:11, etc.), which is the highest station of the Friends of God—whether of angel or Messenger or prophet or Friend or person of faith—than the act of prayer." Lest one despair of ever realizing—at least as something more than a memorable momentary state—such a true inner condition of prayer, the Shaykh immediately

78

follows this description with another remarkable imagined speech of God to His angels, a compelling speech which underlines the extraordinary dignity and rarity of every human achievement in this realm of prayer:

> ...For I have placed between this servant of Mine and the "station of Proximity (to Me)" (*maqām al-qurba*) many veils and immense obstacles, including the goals of the carnal soul; sensual desires and passions; taking care of other people, property, family, servants and friends; and terrible fears. Yet (My servant) has cut through all that and continued to strive until he has prostrated himself and drawn near (to Me) and has become one of *those brought near* (the *muqarrabūn*). So look, O My angels, at how specially favored you are and at the superiority of your rank, although I did not test you with these obstacles nor obligate you to undergo their pains. And then realize the special rank of this (human) servant, and give him all that he is due for everything that he has undergone and suffered on his path (toward Me), for My sake!

OPENING THE HEART'S DOOR TO DIVINE BEWILDERMENT

In chapter 50, on the "people of spiritual bewilderment" (*hayra*)—one of the highest spiritual stations, for Ibn 'Arabī—he returns to an even closer phenomenological description of this state of the truly open and purified heart, in an account whose unexpected conclusion recalls some of the most celebrated poems of John of the Cross. The first part of that long description (IV, 218-25), though, simply summarizes the process by which any of the "people of spiritual unveiling"—as opposed to the followers of intellectual reflection or of mere formal belief and obedience (*taqlīd*)—set out to discover the right *divine* answer to their religious questions, arising from the recurrent fundamental problem of applying or interpreting scriptural tradition:

> So this group apply themselves vigorously to ac-quiring (the reality concerning) something that has come down in the divine reports from the side of the Real (*al-Haqq*), and they begin by "polishing their hearts through acts of *dhikr* and the recitation of the Qur'an" (as specified in the famous hadith), by emptying the receptacle (of their hearts) from all inquiry about contingent things, and through the presence of careful attentiveness (to the inner state of their hearts, *murāqaba*)—along with observing the purity of their outward action through follow-ing the limits set by revelation.... (Such a person seeking sound inspiration) turns their thoughts com-pletely from their self (*nafs*), since that (turning away) disperses their worries, and remains alone carefully attending to their heart, at the Door of their Lord.
>
> Then when God opens up this Door for the pos-sessor of such a heart, they realize a divine Self-manifestation (or theophany: *tajalli*) that is in ac-cordance with their inner condition. And through that (inspiration they realize) the relation of some-thing to God that they would never have dared to risk relating to God before and would never have even attributed to God...[unless that were already reported by the divine prophets, in which case they still could only have accepted it on faith]. But now that person applies that (newly revealed aspect of

the divine) to God as verified and realized knowing, because of what was revealed to them through
that divine Self-manifestation.

But this sort of extra-ordinary experience of divine illumination is only the first step toward the deeper spiritual state
of ongoing "Bewilderment" (*hayra*):

> For after the first such Self-manifestation (the per-
> son experiencing such an unexpected revelation of
> God's nature or activity in the world) imagines that
> they have reached their goal and accomplished the
> matter, and that there is nothing to be sought be-
> yond that except for that (new revelatory state) to
> continue. But then another Self-manifestation oc-
> curs to them, with still another quality and implica-
> tion unlike that of the first—even though the (di-
> vine Reality) manifesting Itself is undoubtedly the
> same, in the same position as in the first case. After
> that still other divine Self-manifestations follow one
> another for that person, with their different impli-
> cations, so that through this (ongoing spiritual un-
> veiling) that person comes to know that this matter
> has no end at which it might stop. Only then do
> they realize that they have not perceived (or "at-
> tained") the divine Ipseity, and that the divine Es-
> sence (*huwīya*) cannot be made manifest to them,
> *in that it is the Spirit* (the *rūh*) *of every theophany.*
>
> So that person's "bewilderment" increases, but
> there is great pleasure in it...[which, Ibn 'Arabī has-
> tens to add, is totally unlike that radically different,
> normally quite frustrating "perplexity" of our intel-
> lect that is called by the same name]. People like
> this have been raised above the contingent things,

so that they witness nothing but (God), and He is the object of their witnessing.... . Their state of "bewilderment" only grows more intense, and (because of the intensity of the satisfaction associated with it) they only seek to continue experiencing those successive Self-manifestations.

THE "HEART'S LANGUAGE" OF THE TRUE SEEKERS

Perhaps such a description, as is not infrequently the case with Ibn 'Arabī, may seem to apply to a state of the contemplating heart almost inconceivably beyond anything we might consider possible in our own experience. But as always, the Shaykh returns to this subject from another perspective which may suggest that the fruits of such inspiration are in fact not so far removed from things we have already realized, if we can only make the essential connection between his concepts here and the corresponding spiritual phenomena. His next extended discussion of the Heart, in chapter 54 (IV, 268-77) on the symbolic "allusions" (*ishārāt*) and technical vocabulary of the Sufis, is a striking illustration of that kind of unexpected connection—and of the fundamental role of individual preparedness and (humanly) inexplicable spiritual aptitudes in the realization of everything discussed in the *Futūhāt*:

> One of the most astonishing things about this path (of the people of God), and something that is only found here, is the fact that there is no other group bearing a kind of knowledge—whether the logicians, grammarians, mathematicians, geometricians, theologians or philosophers—who do not also have a technical vocabulary that the novice among them

82

does not know except by frequenting a master or another one of them: that is necessarily the case.

Except for the unique case of the people of this path, when a sincere seeker (*murīd*) enters among them who does not know anything at all about their technical terminology: indeed this phenomenon is precisely what allows them to recognize that person's inner spiritual sincerity (*sidq*). For if God has already opened the eye of that seeker's understanding and that person has (truly) taken the beginning of their spiritual "tasting" from God, then that person will sit down among them and speak with them using their terminology in the special way that no one else knows but them—even though that person knew nothing before about the special expressions of the people of God!

For that sincere spiritual seeker understands everything that they are talking about, just as though that person were actually the one who had decided upon those technical expressions; and that seeker (immediately) joins them in using that language, without feeling any strangeness about doing so— indeed that person feels that the knowledge of these expressions is immediately self-evident and unavoidable. *It is as though he had always known that language, without knowing how he ever came to acquire it.*

Ibn 'Arabī's allusion here to the vast extent of the unconscious or ordinarily unarticulated spiritual knowing and awareness of the heart that is often taken for granted precisely by those who most obviously possess it is a phenomenon that everyone has probably encountered at one time or another, and not only in the study of religion.

IV. THE SECRETS OF PURIFICATION

The next discussions of the Heart in the *Futūhāt* are in the lengthy chapter 68 on the inner spiritual meanings or "secrets of Purification" (*asrār al-tahāra*), where dimensions of the heart's spiritual purification are raised more than twenty times, usually in implicit or explicit connection with the ritual prayer (the subject of the even longer following chapter 69). Many of Ibn 'Arabī's points there about realizing the contemplative potential of the heart are both brief and exceedingly practical even for the uninitiated reader, while others are astonishingly subtle and far-reaching in their implications. The limits of this Chapter only allow us to highlight a few of the most important of those passages.

THE HEART'S INTUITIVE DISCERNMENT
OF DIVINE INSPIRATION (AND ITS CONTRARIES)

To begin with, Ibn 'Arabī points out (at V, 148-49) that:

the divine knowing received directly from God's Presence through revelation (*'ilm ladunnī ilāhī mashrū'*) has a single taste—even if the places where it is drunk[20] may differ, they do not differ in being good: and whether it is good or better, it is all pure, without any corruption.... For the prophets and Friends and everyone who informs us from God all say the same thing of God..., not differing among themselves, and confirming one another—just as the pure rain from the sky is not different when it falls.

So let the foundation of your purification of your heart be with water like this—with nothing but knowledge known through divinely revealed prescribing (*shar'*), which has been likened to rainwater. ...For then your own essence and your purifi-

84

cation (of it) will be like that spring from which water flows forth. And if you should differentiate sweetness or saltiness (in what is claimed to be "re-vealed" rainwater), then know that your perceptions are sound! This is a topic to which I have not found anyone alluding. And yet the person who eats sugar knows its sweetness like that, and knows that there is something wrong with the bitterness of aloes: they don't need a "rational proof" (*dalīl 'aqlī*) (to recognize the difference)! Now I have definitely pointed this out to you, so take my indication to heart—and watch out!

Now that that is established, my friend, start employing the forms of knowledge given by the divine revealing (*shar'*) in (purifying) your own essence; and use the knowings of the Friends and the true Knowers who took them from God in your own spiritual exercises and spiritual efforts and exertions, refraining from the excesses of the bodily members and the promptings of the egoistic self (the *nafs*). For if you cannot distinguish between those waters (i.e., which ones are truly pure and divinely revealed, and which polluted by human interference), then know that something is wrong with your nature, that it has somehow been corrupted. In that case we can do nothing for you, except that God may help you, through His Lovingmercy.

PURIFYING THE HEART: THE UNIVERSAL DUTY

It should not be necessary to underline the continued practical relevance of his remarks here, or the way they apply equally to every sound religious tradition. This innate hu-

man awareness of the right course of spiritual action, Ibn
'Arabī continues (V, 165-71), is a purification that is religiously obligatory

> ...for every responsible-rational person (every '*āqil*,
> in the legal sense of that term). For that person is
> the one who understands *from God* ('*an Allāh*) what
> they are ordered and prohibited, and what God gives
> to them in their innermost being; they are the per-
> son who is able to distinguish, among the inner
> promptings of their heart, what comes from God
> and what from their egoistic self (*nafs*), what from
> the touch of an angel or the touch of a devil: *and
> that is the fully human being* (*al-insān*)! So if some-
> one reaches that degree in their spiritual awareness
> (*ma'rifa*) and their discernment, and understands
> from God what He wants from them, and truly hears
> God's saying (in the famous divine saying) that "the
> heart of My servant encompasses Me": then it is
> obligatory for that person in this situation to use this
> (awareness) in purifying his heart and every other
> member connected with it, in the way God intends.

Therefore, the Shaykh concludes (at V, 166), this inner purification and discernment are an obligation for every single
responsible human being, whether or not they've even heard
of the historical forms of religion:

> Our own way of proceeding (our *madhhab*) is that
> all people in general—whether they are among the
> people of faith, or of the rejection of God, or inner
> hypocrites—are "addressed" (*mukhātabūn*: spoken
> to directly by God in their hearts) regarding the
> Sources of the divine Pathway (the *sharī'a*, in its

root sense) and its branches, and that therefore they are all held responsible at the Day of the Rising.

"For us," he explains further on (V, 320-22), *"purification itself is an independent act of worship and devotion (ʿibāda)."* Indeed for Ibn ʿArabī, as we have already seen, it is in a way the ultimate root and aim of every act of worship. From the traditional legal point of view, of course:

> It may also be the condition for properly performing another act of worship and devotion, either an obligatory condition or one necessary for its proper performance, while for another act of devotion it may be only preferable or part of the Prophet's personal example (*mustahabb* or *sunna*).
>
> The inner spiritual grounds (*hukm al-bātin*) for that is that the purification of the heart is a precondition for our intimate converse (*munājat*) with God or for our contemplating Him—a condition that is at once both obligatory (or "essential": *wājib*) and necessary for the proper realization (of that spiritual intimacy and true contemplation).
>
> …Sometimes, (the Shaykh continues), spiritual knowing may be an essential condition for the soundness of our faith in a matter. And sometimes faith in turn may be an obligatory condition as well as a necessary condition for assuring the soundness of our knowing through experiential unveiling. However in faith there is the purification of the heart from being veiled (from God's presence), while (true spiritual) knowing purifies the heart from ignorance and doubt and pretension. So *purify your heart with both of those purifications* (of faith and of knowl-

edge): you will rise high, through that, in both the worlds, and through it you will attain the knowledge of the "Two Handfuls" (in the hadith image of human souls destined either to suffering or bliss).

As for the inner spiritual judgment (*hukm al-bātin*) concerning all of this, we say that every prescribed religious action that is not preceded by this purification through faith is unsound because of this lack of faith. Therefore (true) faith is necessary for every religious action.

The Process of the Heart's Purification

In his ensuing discussion (V, 341-44) of the purifications appropriate to the pilgrim visiting the Kaaba—whether that "pilgrimage" be inward or outward—Ibn 'Arabī makes two points that are very simple, but practically of the utmost importance. The first concerns the proper inner attitude to have in our relations with all the other creatures, which is the full realization of the virtue of *ihsān*—of "seeing God" and the divine Presence through and with all things:

> Now spiritual purification (*tahārat al-bātin*)—which is (purification of) the heart—is through liberating ourselves (from all attachments other than God), in order to seek (His) friendship. And there is no (true) friendship and closeness with God except through freeing yourself from the creatures, insofar as you used to consider them (only) in light of their relation to yourself (to your ego or *nafs*) and not through God (and the realization of *His* aims in their regard).

The Shaykh's second point is made in regard to the spiritual experience of the pilgrim with regard to the "treasure" and blessing and guidance that the Prophet has mentioned as being reserved for those visiting the "House (or Temple: *al-bayt*) of God":

> So consider the one who comes to circumambulate (the Kaaba), when he has turned to his heart after going around (the House). If he finds an increase in his awareness of his Lord and a *"clear indication"* (from God) that he did not have before, then he knows from that that he has properly carried out his purification for entering Mecca.
>
> But if he finds none of that (in his heart), then he knows that he has failed to purify himself, did not come to his Lord, and so did not (truly) go around His House. For it is impossible that anyone should come to stay with a noble and wealthy host, entering into his house, and yet not experience his hospitality! ...So if such a person comes close (to God's House), he comes close to the rocks, not to the Essence (or the Source: *al-'ayn*)—May God place us among the possessors of hearts, the people of God and those close to Him!

This process of inner purification obligatory for all real, effective worship and devotion, Ibn 'Arabī constantly reiterates, is always changing and always essential (V, 349):

> The purification of the heart (is obligatory) so that it may be joined with its Lord, and so that its spiritual aspiration may be joined in intimate converse (*munājāt*) with Him through the raising of the veil from (the servant's heart). ...So it is necessary for anyone who is seeking this state (of the heart's intrinsic intimacy with God) to purify themselves with

a special purification. Indeed I say that *every* state of the servant with God requires its own special purification.

THE SECRETS OF PURIFICATION: THE "TOUCH OF SATAN" AND THE "ANGEL'S TOUCH"

At this point (V, 346-47) Ibn 'Arabī adds a special warning, but one which also highlights his typical reliance on the actual consequences of spiritual effort—and the sensitivity of each individual's heart—in overcoming these recurrent dangers of the path:

> Now the guardians (the *bawwābs* of the heart) may sometimes be sleeping or distracted, so that the secret promptings (*khawātir*) of the carnal souls and the devils find nothing to keep them from entering that person's heart. In that case, when that person says *"Labbayk!"* ["Here I am, Lord!," the traditional pilgrim's call] with their tongue, imagining that they are coming in response to the call of their Lord, they are only responding to the prompting of their own *nafs* or of a devil calling to them in their heart.

And Ibn 'Arabī goes on to describe the glee of that ever-present impostor in thus fooling the deluded seeker: "So *If it were not for the Generosity of God and His Lovingmercy*—through the tongue of our inner spiritual state (*lisān al-bātin wa-l-hāl*) and the spiritual intention preceding that event," such a person who was imperfectly purified would surely encounter the *dire suffering* mentioned in that same verse (24:14). But in reality, as he insists in another extraordinary passage of this same chapter, it is necessary to take a much more comprehensive view of the providential divine

Caring (*'ināya*) and "Outwitting" (*makar*), with respect to Iblīs and all the Satans, for that providential Caring is in reality a proof of God's Mercy and Grace that is ultimately manifested precisely through eventual consequences of the multitude of such memorable spiritual mishaps and delusions that each person inevitably experiences over time.

This is why, Ibn 'Arabī explains (V, 354-56), "it is necessary to purify the heart from the 'touch of Satan'"—which he has elsewhere identified with the passion of blind anger (*sakht*)—"when it descends on the heart and touches the inner being of a person." And that purification of the heart is itself accomplished through the "touch of the angel," which is the manifestation of God's providential Caring for the heart at that point.

"Now if the hadith of God's 'Two Fingers' alluded to that (mysterious working of Grace and divine Providence)," Ibn 'Arabī continues, then:

> *both* of those Fingers are Lovingmercy (*rahma*)...since if it were not for God's Lovingmercy for His servant through that touch of the devil, the servant would never receive their reward for countering that prompting (of the devil) and turning away from it to the work of the angel's touch (i.e., the experience of repentance and divine Grace), so that the servant acquires two rewards (first for their inner struggle, then for their eventual repentance and right action). And that is why we say that God attributed both (of those "Two Fingers") to the Divine Name *the All-Compassionate* (*al-Rahmān*).

This profound spiritual observation, which has often been treated as paradoxical or even heretical by later Islamic critics of the Shaykh, in fact could not be more central to Ibn

'Arabī's comprehensive awareness of the processes of spiritual growth and transformation, on both the individual and larger cosmic levels. Indeed in a key passage so long that it can only be summarized here, Ibn 'Arabī carefully points out how the devil always ends up accomplishing the exact opposite of what he intended, as the ultimate results of his deception eventually push the servant first to regret—"the greatest of the pillars of repentance and return to God," as the Shaykh calls it—and then to true repentance and returning to God (*tawba*). Thus he points out that the apparent "victim" of Satan:

> has the reward of the *shahīd* [here not so much martyr, as the literal *"witness"* of God's Love and Mercy] because of the occurrence of that act (of turning to God) in him. And the *shahīd* [as confirmed both by Qur'an, in the famous verses 2:154 and 3:169, and by many hadith] is *alive*, not dead—for what life could be greater than the Life of hearts together with God, in whatever activity that may be?! For the presence (of the heart) with faith, in the face of the opposition (of Satan), renders that action alive with the Life of the (divine) Presence.

So this, Ibn 'Arabī concludes (V, 356) , is again why *both* divine "Fingers"—although they appear to us, in terms of our own dualistic feelings and judgments of our experience, as diametrically opposed—are in fact equally essential spiritual instruments of God's Love and Mercy:

> If (the devil) knew that God was blessing the servant, through the (devil's) touch, with a special sort of happiness, then he wouldn't have done any of that. But this is the divine Cunning (*makar Allāh*)

through which He fools Iblīs, and I have not seen anyone else allude to that. And indeed were it not for my knowing Iblīs and being aware of his ignorance and his compulsion that drives him to counter (God), I too would not have alluded to this... But this is what encouraged me to mention this, because the devil can never stop at those occasions (for temptation) because of his veil, through his compulsion to make the servant suffer and his ignorance that God is (always) turning (to forgive) the servant. For God always cunningly deceives someone in such a way that they themselves fail to notice it, even if others are able to see what is really happening!

PURIFICATION AND THE HEART'S CONSTANT ATTENTIVENESS

The preceding discussion highlights one of the active principles of spiritual life underlying one of Ibn 'Arabī's most straightforward and illuminating pieces of practical advice (V, 359-60) regarding this ongoing purification of the heart and the way it transforms every single event of our life, inner or outer, into a further occasion for discovering the secrets of our relationship with God:

Now the Knower finds in one of his spiritual states a contraction or expansion whose immediate cause he does not know. And for the people of the path this is (always) a significant matter. For he knows that this (uncertainty as to the meaning of this experience) is due to his unconsciousness or heedlessness with regard to carefully observing his heart and his spiritual intention—and to his lack of inspired spiritual insight in grasping the inner correspondence of that state with the matter which that (divine) Attribute caused him to experience. In that case, what is incumbent on (the Knower) is to inwardly surrender (*taslīm*) to the eventual effects of the (divine) Decree, until he sees what that gives rise to in the future.

But if the Knower recognizes (the inner reason for that particular experience), then he should purify himself through being completely present with God in his knowledge of those correspondences, so that he does not become unaware of what has come to him from God through these "sanctifying spiritual experiences" (*wāridāt al-taqdīs*)—so that he is not unaware of which (divine) Name became (real) to him through that experience, and which Name came to be through him, and which Name is actually influencing him at that instant, causing him to call out for that experience.

Thus these (spiritually educational dimensions of our experience realized by the Knower, sooner or later) are *three*: the Name that is calling (to the Knower), the Name that is called (into being) through him, and the Name that is (at this instant) coming over him. Of course there is no possible correspondence (of this sort) through which God, in His Essence, might be (ultimately) circumscribed to us or through us....

But through His Names we are connected (with Him), through those Names we take on His qualities,[21] and through them we become realized (or "come to realize what is Real": *natahaqqaq*)—and God makes this possible!

The "Total Ablution of the Heart"

The next set of allusions to the heart's purification in this chapter (V, 363-366) stands out in every possible way from the discussions that surround it. The passage itself is almost certainly an illustration of that quintessential spiritual teaching destined for the "elite of the elite" which Ibn 'Arabī, in a key passage of his Introduction, claims to have intentionally scattered throughout the *Futūhāt*.[22] An adequate translation and commentary of these pages would require a separate study, but the real difficulty, as one might expect of such a complex spiritual lesson, has nothing at all to do with its linguistic expression. The essential point of this particular teaching clearly has something to do with overcoming spiritual dualism—but at a fundamental level of depth and subtlety, and of necessarily personal and nearly ineffable intensity, considerably more profound than in the passages just discussed.

This singular section begins with a discussion of certain distinctive spiritual qualities that, according to Ibn 'Arabī, require a complete bodily ablution (*ghusl*)—an act of purification that Islamic ritual typically requires for very different types and circumstances of major impurity. Ibn 'Arabī's movement here beyond the received forms of Islamic worship, which serve as at least the ostensible point of departure for all of his other discussions of spiritual purification in the remainder of chapter 68, is already a dramatic sign of the unique spiritual character of this particular exposition. The largest part of the passage, however, is a strange and in some ways metaphysically comprehensive catalogue of a wide range of human spiritual or ontological states and qualities.

This extraordinary sub-chapter (or "Door")[23] opens as follows:

> Now we have already established that *janāba* (the technical legal term for a major ritual impurity requiring the total bodily ablution) is *ghurba* (a state of "exile," estrangement, or removal from one's rightful place). And here that is the exile of the servant from his rightful homeland which he deserves—and that is nothing but the state of pure servanthood (*'ubūdiyya*). Or that (impurity) is the estrangement of an attribute of Lordship from its rightful homeland (with God), so that someone (wrongfully) ascribes it to himself or uses it to describe some contingent creature or another. Now there is no disputing that one must be purified from this question.
>
> So you must know that this single total ablution mentioned here in this chapter branches out into 150 spiritual states, and that *the servant, in his heart, must be completely purified from every single one of those states.* So we will mention to you the essence (*'ayn*) of each one of them, if God wills, in ten sections, each section containing fifteen states, so that you will recognize how you (should) meet them when they occur to the heart of the servant. Because they must inevitably occur to every heart, both of ordinary people and of the (spiritual) elite[24]— and God gives support and inspiration, there is no power but through Him!

While the adequate translation of this strange catalogue of spiritual states would be very long, we can at least note that it includes a number of what would ordinarily be viewed as inherently "opposite" or contrary states (at least partially reminiscent of the paired lists of polarities among the divine Names in the hadith and elsewhere): e.g., this world and the other world, life and death, mercy and anger, and so on, although the vast majority are of what would ordinarily be taken as positive and even rarely achieved spiritual virtues. This long catalogue of spiritual conditions, with no other explanation or amplification, is followed by the following remarks:

> You must know—may God support us and You with a Spirit from Him!—that according to the school (*madhhab*) of the people of God and His elite among the people of spiritual unveiling, it is obligatory for every human being to completely purify their heart and their inner being from everything that we have mentioned in these (ten) sections, as well as everything else each of these spiritual states includes which we did not mention, for fear of being too long, There is no dispute among the people of immediate spiritual experience ("tastings") concerning that. But those who seek to purify themselves from most of them will need an abundance of difficult[25] knowledge concerning the proper ways to become purified from what we have mentioned. And some of these states may serve as purifications from others!

Later in this same chapter, Ibn 'Arabī's explanation of the proper times for purification also begins to move more openly beyond the ritual or legal contexts that are the usual occasion for such discussions in this chapter, as in the following passage (V, 374):

Now the purification of all things is with and through the Real (*bi-l-Haqq*). So if someone becomes heedless of the (heart's primordial) witnessing (of God) and instead see his self (or ego, the *nafs*) taking the different kinds of knowing that the Real is (always) causing to descend on the heart, then he must be purified because of his seeing his own ego-self (rather than God).

In the same way, if we should happen to encounter another person in a matter in such a way that we teach them, either through our state or our words, and if that teaching flows from our presence (with the Real), then no purification is necessary, for we have not left our state of purity (with God). But if we should notice our own self (our *nafs*) in the process of teaching another person through our words or our state, then purification is absolutely obligatory for us, because of our noticing our self. For the people of God in this path do everything that they do with and through God, out of their witnessing and unveiling of and from Him.

Of course the very awareness of this hidden egoistic corruption or unconscious hypocrisy, and our corresponding need for purification, is itself a kind of gift of divine Grace, as Ibn 'Arabī recalls in this phenomenologically precise summary (V, 435):

Therefore the proper "time" or moment of purification in the spiritual sense, for us, is whenever one has specifically realized the (eternally unfolding) connection between the divine address to the person obligated by it (the *mukallaf*) regarding what is incumbent on them both inwardly and outwardly.

98

In spiritual terms, that is a divine Self-manifestation that suddenly comes over their heart, which is called in the path a "surprise attack."

And finally, near the very end of this chapter (at V, 499), Ibn 'Arabī restates everything above as simply as possible:

> For God sees nothing of the human being (*al-insān*) but the heart. So it is incumbent on the servant that his heart should always and continually be pure, because it is the place God sees in him.

V. Listening For God

By now we have followed Ibn 'Arabī's lessons on the heart and contemplation as far as his monumental chapter on the inner spiritual meanings of the ritual prayer (*salāt*: chapter 69), which would require several lengthy volumes to translate adequately into English. So it is fitting to conclude this introductory essay with what he says there (VI, 217-219) about that puzzling Qur'anic verse (50:37) with which we began this Chapter, in his discussion of the prescribed moments of *silence* during the ritual prayer:

> ...So it is obligatory for the servant, when he has finished reciting the verse (in prayer), to *listen attentively, while he/He is witnessing* (50:37). Therefore (the person praying) becomes silent, so that he can see what God is saying to him concerning that, as is only the spiritually appropriate behavior (*adab*) with God. For we must not interrupt someone who is speaking to us, since that is only proper etiquette even in ordinary conversations—and God is far more deserving that we should be that way with Him!

...That is how this matter remains between the listener and the One speaking to him, so that the listener might gain benefit (from that silent pure receiving in prayer). For you must know that kings do not take a person without proper *adab* to sit with them, nor to converse with them at night, nor to be their intimate companion.

SEEING

وَفِى ٱلْأَرْضِ ءَايَتٌ لِّلْمُوقِنِينَ ۞ وَفِىٓ أَنفُسِكُمْ أَفَلَا تُبْصِرُونَ

Now in the earth are Signs for those of assured faith, and in your own souls: So then why do you all not see ?!

Sūrat al-Dhāriyyāt, 51:20-21

لَّا تُدْرِكُهُ ٱلْأَبْصَٰرُ وَهُوَ يُدْرِكُ ٱلْأَبْصَٰرَ وَهُوَ ٱللَّطِيفُ ٱلْخَبِيرُ
قَدْ جَآءَكُم بَصَآئِرُ مِن رَّبِّكُمْ فَمَنْ أَبْصَرَ فَلِنَفْسِهِۦ وَمَنْ عَمِىَ فَعَلَيْهَا
وَمَآ أَنَا۠ عَلَيْكُم بِحَفِيظٍ

(Their) seeing does not perceive Him, while He encompasses (all their) seeing, for He is the Most-Subtle, the All-Aware. There have already come to you all spiritual insights from your Lord: so whoever was seeing, that is for (the good of) his soul; and whoever was blind, that is against it—and I am not a keeper for you all!

Sūrat al-An'ām, 6:103-104

CHAPTER THREE

SEEING: SPIRITUAL VISION AND THE MYSTERIES OF *Ihsān*

And God's is the place-of-shining-forth and the place-of-darkening: so wherever you all may turn, there is the Face of God!

Sūrat al-Baqara, 2:115

O Friend/Beloved, through Love we are conjoined with You:
Wherever You put Your foot, we are the ground for You.

In this school/path of Loving, how can it possibly be
That we see the world through You—and yet we don't see You?

Rumi, quatrain[1]

The theme of the beatific vision of God, for anyone familiar with the Qur'an, would almost automatically recall the last part of the famous Qur'anic passage (2:115) translated above. For few Qur'anic verses could more concisely convey the enduring popular images of Ibn 'Arabī and the school of his subsequent philosophic interpreters in Islamic culture. Indeed it would scarcely be an exaggeration to say that all the writings of Ibn 'Arabī and his subsequent generations of commentators, with their complex ontological schemas of divine Self-Manifestations, Apparitions, and Presences (*tajalliyāt, mazāhir, hadarāt*), could be viewed as a sort of vast, ongoing commentary on that single Qur'anic verse.

But in the end, the intellectual brilliance and philosophical fascination of the all-encompassing metaphysical systems elaborated by that later tradition cannot quite conceal a more difficult and troubling question, an unavoidable dilemma that is so beautifully expressed in Rumi's own short comment on that same verse. What practical difference, ultimately, does that bold Qur'anic statement—or its complex elaborations in later Islamic thought—really make in the life we actually live? Even assuming all human beings have some inherent sense of what true theophany and vision of God might involve—if only in our deepest memories of what the Qur'an portrays (7:172) as the primordial Covenant between each soul and its Creator (the "Last Night" memorialized by all the Islamic mystical poets)— that mysterious awareness itself only seems to highlight, as Rumi's poem suggests, the poignant distance between such rare moments of spiritual realization and our ordinary mundane existence. However one might imagine the divine Face, skeptics and believers alike would probably agree that our days are more often spent, if not in complete blindness, then at least in profound heedlessness of that state of true Vision. And other Islamic interpreters have of course attempted to defuse the dramatic existential challenge posed by this verse, with its radical immediacy and unequivocal universality, by relegating the whole problem to that vague eschatological "next world" and some yet-to-arrive point in earthly time where they would prefer to situate all the powerful scriptural allusions to that vision of God's Face.

Fortunately there is another, less well known Ibn 'Arabī whose teachings are in fact centrally focused on precisely the sort of recurrent existential questions and fundamental

issues of spiritual practice that are raised—and illuminated—by deeper reflection on verses such as this. Nowhere is that more clearly the case than in his magnum opus,
the immense *Meccan Illuminations (al-Futūhāt
al-Makkīya)*. Indeed it is probably the much wider popular
influence of this "second" Ibn 'Arabī, whose insights have
been continually borrowed and (usually tacitly) quoted and
applied by many generations of Muslim preachers, theologians, Sufi masters, jurists and artists down to the present
day, that eventually won for him the widespread honorific
title of *al-Shaykh al-Akbar*, "the Greatest Master."[2] One
reason for the paradox of the relative anonymity and yet
near-universal influence of this particularly wide-ranging
spiritual and hermeneutical aspect of Ibn 'Arabī's work in
later Islamic culture, of course, may be precisely the emi-
nently practical focus of such writing and the usual occasions for studying or teaching it: one usually consults a
pharmacopoeia to find the right effective treatment for this
or that specific illness, not to add a learned commentary.

However, a more profound and fundamental reason for
this characteristic anonymity and pervasiveness of Ibn
'Arabī's enduring cultural and spiritual influence is the
unique role of Islamic scripture—both Qur'an and hadith—
in the distinctive composition and rhetorical forms of the
Futūhāt itself.[3] Virtually every line of that monumental
work, even where there is no explicit reference to a specific
hadith or passage of the Qur'an, in fact constitutes a kind of
complex spiritual hologram, simultaneously interweaving
deeper allusions to dozens of Qur'anic verses and hadith
(as well as many later Islamic religious disciplines), that is
designed to awaken the engaged reader's awareness of the
underlying realities or recurrent spiritual meanings (*ma'ānī*)
connecting those scriptural teachings, along with his or her

104

indispensable recognition of the corresponding concrete exemplification or active "descent" of those particular divine
Names within this particular unique situation and personal
experience.[4] Only the masterpieces of Islamic mystical
poetry in Persian and other eastern Islamicate languages,
using very different literary forms, can approach something
of the same density of expression and scriptural allusiveness, and the same effective power of transformation. And
one unintended result, in both those cases, is that any attempt at a continuous, adequate translation for modern audiences is almost inevitably overwhelmed by the massive
annotation needed to detail the underlying context of allusions and the web of symbolic interconnections and resonances originally presupposed by this kind of writing.[5]

Ibn 'Arabī's discussion of the divine "Face"—and of
the corresponding human possibilities of theophanic perception—in the long opening section of the *Futūhāt* (chapters 1-73) provides an illuminating case-study of his distinctive methods of rhetoric and spiritual pedagogy throughout that work. Given his characteristic reliance on scriptural allusions and interpretation, this Chapter begins (in
section I) by outlining the many Qur'anic passages on the
divine Face and the corresponding right "orientation" of
human action and intention that can mysteriously transform
our ordinary experience into the realization of theophany—
or of desperate estrangement from God's Regard. Section
II then summarizes the particular hadith concerning
theophanic vision which are the primary vehicle for Ibn
'Arabī's teaching about this problem throughout the
Futūhāt. However, the actual imagery and specific language
of those Prophetic sayings, some of them fairly long, are so
important in this context that those relevant hadith have been
translated in full in a separate section placed at the end of
this Chapter.

Following this essential scriptural background, the
Shaykh's own discussion of the human meaning of the "vision of God" in these initial chapters of the *Futūhāt* naturally falls into four successive divisions, which become increasingly explicit and more practical in their focus as his
teaching unfolds. Not surprisingly, bringing together these
related facets of a common problem from so many separate
chapters beautifully illustrates Ibn 'Arabī's typical pedagogical method of intentionally scattering his most profound
spiritual teachings throughout this book, a distinctive approach he describes to his readers—while also explaining
the underlying motives for this literary procedure—in several key passages of his Introduction.[6]

The first explicit allusion to this problem of theophany
in the *Futūhāt* is to be found in Ibn 'Arabī's decisive, openly
autobiographical remarks indicating the experiential source
and context for all the rest of his account, a confession rooted
in his own unforgettable unitive vision of "the Splendor of
God's Face" (section III below). Secondly, in a number of
early passages summarized here in section IV, he gradually
introduces some basic terminological allusions (*ishārāt*) and
premises, both practical and metaphysical, which provide
the intellectual foundations for his later, more elaborate
symbolic developments of this theme based on the Qur'an
and hadith. The next and richest stage of his discussion
here is a complex phenomenological survey (in chapters
61-65, section V below) of the full range of actual human
awareness of—or blindness to—the divine Face, conveyed
in the elaborate symbolic language of Qur'anic (and hadith)
eschatology, moving from the sufferings of Gehenna to the
beatific vision of the blessed during the "Day of the Visit"
with God in Paradise. And finally (section VI), Ibn 'Arabī
turns to some more practical spiritual advice on how we

106

can actually begin to move from the sufferings of the Fire to the joys of the Gardens and its revelatory theophanic vision, in his long phenomenological discussions of the "inner spiritual meanings" (*asrār*) of the basic forms of Islamic worship.[7]

I. THE "*FACE OF GOD*" AND HUMAN FACES: THE QUR'ANIC SOURCES

The symbol of the divine and human face (*wajh*) is a central one in the Qur'an, occurring more than seventy times, and at least sixty of those passages use that key Arabic term in extended or metaphorical senses directly related to the practical spiritual problem of theophany, to our need for seeking and properly "facing" the ever-present illumination of the divine Face. As is so often the case, the metaphysical and practical allusiveness of the Qur'anic usage greatly depends on the multiple, overlapping meanings of the original Arabic root. To mention only the most important elements of that semantic field in this particular context, the word *wajh* itself can refer not only to the physical face and the emotions conveyed by its expressions, or to the "front" and visible appearance of something, as in English—but also to a direction or orientation; an intention, aim or goal; a way or manner of proceeding; a particular meaning or sense; a perspective or point of view; and particularly to the true substance or essential reality of something. All of these meanings are already present to varying degrees in the relevant Qur'anic passages, and the interrelations of these themes in that scriptural context are constantly mirrored in Ibn 'Arabī's own subsequent development of the interrelated metaphysical and practical spiritual dimensions of our awareness of God.

The scattered Qur'anic references to the Face of God and human faces clearly fall into five groups: there are (1) the celebrated ontological references to the eternity of the divine Face Itself; (2) passages prescribing the "seeking" or "desiring" of God's Face as an essential inner condition for spiritually effective action; (3) verses enjoining the proper orientation of each individual's face toward the right "direction" of prayer and true Religion; (4) similar references to the "surrender" of one's face or innermost intention to God; and (5) a host of vividly symbolic eschatological descriptions of the vivid blessings, or torments, of the "faces" of human beings in their contrasting states after the final Judgment.

Surprisingly enough, considering the prominence given to this particular opening verses (at 2:115) in later Islamic intellectual and mystical traditions, there are only three Qur'anic passages actually focusing on the divine Face "in Itself," so to speak, rather than as the ultimate or ideal object of human striving. In addition to that opening verse, the other two, almost equally famous instances are ...*every thing is perishing except for His Face*...[8] (28:88); and *Everyone who is upon it is passing away, but the Face of your Lord remains (forever)*... (55:26-27). The unequivocal emphasis in each of these three passages on the absolute permanence and omnipresence of the divine Presence only serves to heighten the apparent paradox posed by so much apparent human indifference to this ultimate reality of things, by the perverse spiritual "blindness" (or deafness, incomprehension, forgetfulness, and heedlessness) repeatedly condemned throughout the Qur'an.

The essential practical connection between our own actions and intentions and our corresponding degree of realization or actual awareness of theophany already begins to

108

emerge as soon as we turn to the eight Qur'anic passages that speak of our *"seeking* (or *'desiring')* *God's Face."* To begin with, in each of those cases this special state of spiritual intention is specifically connected to corresponding actions such as *expending* (one's efforts or possessions) *for the good* (2:272, 13:22) and *giving in charity* to those who are needy (30: 38-39), of continually *calling upon God* in prayer (*morning and night*: at 6:52; 18:28; 13:22), and of obliging one's soul to *persevere* in each of these activities (13:22, 18:28). An especially revealing and memorable passage—in light of the connections Ibn 'Arabī repeatedly draws to the famous divine saying concerning the discovery of God's Presence through helping the hungry, thirsty and sick—is the description (at 76:8-9) of the true *servants of God* who *...provide food to feed, for the love of God, the one who is sick, the orphan and the prisoner, (saying): "We are only feeding you all for the Face of God; we do not desire from you any reward or thanks!"*.

The second major point tying together this set of Qur'anic passages is their common stress, either explicitly (as in the passage just quoted) or implicitly, on the dimension of spiritual psychology: i.e., on this special state of purely God-centered motivation as an essential precondition for the effective spiritual impact or (to use the most common Qur'anic expression) the ultimate "recompense" of those particular outward actions—a demanding prerequisite that strongly suggests the manifold dangers of hypocrisy and worldly social aims (or of more subtle inner psychic compensation and self-gratification) often accompanying and underlying such outwardly pious activity. Indeed many of these verses on "seeking God's Face," in their wider Qur'anic context, are actually parts of longer descriptions of the ultimate fate of the blessed in the hereafter. This third, eschatological dimension of the problem, which also provides the dramatic setting for several of the key hadith on the beatific vision used by Ibn 'Arabī (section II below), is quite explicit in the memorable Qur'anic verses which most radically insist on the absolute spiritual necessity of acting *only* "for God's Face": *And there is no one (who has) with him any blessing as a reward, except only for seeking the Face of his Lord the Most-High!* (92:19-20).

The inner, spiritual nature of this special state of receptivity and openness to the divine Presence is especially emphasized by the first group of verses on the individual human "face," which offer a vivid contrast between the special, near-prophetic condition of those who truly *"surrender their face"* (in the sense of their will, intention, honor, true self, etc.) to God, and the fearful state of those who are *"crouched over their face"* or who have *"turned their back on their face."*[9] Especially telling here, given the essential inner connection that both Ibn 'Arabī and the famous hadith of Gabriel—discussed and translated in detail below—make between the highest, all-encompassing spiritual virtue of *ihsān* ("right and beautiful action") and the theophanic awareness of God, is the way the Qur'an itself links this condition of *"surrendering one's face to God"* to the rare and difficult state of "being *muhsin* (the person who practices *ihsān*)" at 31:22.

The second group of Qur'anic verses referring to the individual human face, those enjoining the "turning" or "raising up" of our faces toward the object of prayer or the true primordial Religion, continue to stress the same essential connection between the outward and inner, intentional aspects of religious action. Thus the many references to the proper direction or *qibla* of the ritual prayer (six times at 2:144-150) are followed by the celebrated insistence at

2:177 that *true piety is not that you turn your faces toward the east and the west...* , and by the even more explicit and all-encompassing injunction at 7:29 to *raise up your faces in every place of prayer and call upon Him, keeping Religion totally sincere for Him....* The model for this inner transformation (at 6:79) is Abraham's exclamation that *I have turned my face toward the Creator of the heavens and the earth, in pure faith (hanīfan)*, which is echoed in the three other passages calling on the Prophet (or each addressee of the Qur'an) to *raise up your face to Religion, in pure faith* (10:105, 30:30) or *to The Eternal Religion (al-dīn al-qayyim*, at 30:43).

The ultimate—or inner—consequences of this proper "turning" and "surrender" of the soul's face, and of our frequent failures to do so, are described in more dramatic terms in some thirty verses that include many of the most vivid and unforgettable eschatological descriptions in the Qur'an. Although the beatific *vision* of God is not mentioned explicitly in most of those passages (in contrast to the several long eschatological hadith discussed in the following section), the "*faces*" of the blessed are consistently described there as "*glowing*," "*radiant*," "*shining*," and resplendent with grace and laughter and joy—all terms that could readily be understood as a kind of mirrored reflection of the supernal Light of the divine Face.[10] In contrast, the faces of the suffering ones are often described, among other torments, as "*darkened*" or "*dust-covered*" or "*blackened*" and covered over by the consuming Fire of Gehenna. Even before taking up the hadith referring more openly to the vision of God, one effect of this dramatic eschatological symbolism of the Qur'an, combined with the recurrence of the face as an apparent synonym for the human soul in so many of these passages, is to suggest quite powerfully the sort of profound inner connection between the problem of theophany and human suffering which becomes so prominent in Ibn 'Arabī's own interpretation of these passages.

Often the practical spiritual meaning of otherwise mysterious terms and concepts in the Qur'an is revealed most strikingly in the symbolic tales (*qisas*) of earlier prophets and holy figures, stories which—like the hadith discussed in the following section—more dramatically point to the recurrent testing circumstances and human dilemmas in which those spiritual realities are actually realized in peoples' lives. Certainly this is true for the problem of theophany and "seeking God's Face" in the two passages where the Qur'an employs the active, verbal forms of this same root (*w-j-h*) to speak of particular prophets' "turning their faces" toward God. For one of those passages begins with Moses (at 28:22), *When he turned his face toward Midian and said: "Perhaps my Lord will guide me in the right way"*—and continues through the very end of that chapter to detail *"The* Story" (the title of this particular Sura) of Moses' search, intertwined with its significance for Muhammad's own prophetic mission, in terms which constantly evoke the perennial difficulties and challenges encountered in seeking, recognizing, and then acting upon our awareness of the divine Presence. The second passage, more condensed and directly focused on the symbolism of theophanic vision, describes, in its own terms: *How We cause Abraham to see the (divine) Sovereignty of the heavens and the earth, so that he might be among those-knowing-with-certainty* (6:75). Indeed all of Ibn 'Arabī's own more phenomenological discussions of the problem of realizing or recognizing theophany (and many of the related hadith discussed and translated below) reflect and presuppose that telling symbolic account of the divinely guided process of spiritual pedagogy by which Abraham successively takes as *"my Lord"* the apparitions of a planet, the moon, and the sun until, finally enlightened by their eventual passing, he is able to exclaim: *Now I am liberated from what you-all are associating (with God); indeed I have faced my face toward the One Who Creates the heavens and the earth, in pure faith...!* (6:79).

II. THEOPHANY AND RIGHT ACTION: THE HADITH ON THE VISION OF GOD

Surprisingly enough, given the prominence and profusion of these richly symbolic Qur'anic references to the problem of theophanic vision, Ibn 'Arabī's own elaborate treatment of the vision of God's Face and the practical ways to its realization throughout the opening chapters of the *Meccan Illuminations*[11] initially proceeds with almost no explicit discussion of these Qur'anic verses, relying instead on repeated allusions to a selected handful of extraordinary Prophetic sayings, including several divine sayings in which Muhammad reports teachings that are ultimately referred back (sometimes through the angel Gabriel or earlier prophets) to a divine Speaker expressed directly in the first person. Now these particular eschatological hadith are almost all included in the canonical Sunni collections (especially the *Sahīh* volumes of both Muslim and Bukhārī) and were therefore quite familiar, at least in their general outlines, to the vast majority of Ibn 'Arabī's originally intended readers. In addition, two or three of these hadith have such a basic doctrinal importance for Ibn 'Arabī's own ideas and perspectives, as often for Sufism and Islamic spirituality in general, that allusions to them can be found on virtually every page of his major works.[12] And like many of the other well-known hadith, each of these sayings artfully summarizes and draws together, in dramatically memorable literary form, references to all those Qur'anic themes just discussed, as well as a great many other related scriptural topics and passages. In that respect, these particular hadith beautifully illustrate one of Ibn 'Arabī's most characteristic metaphysical and practical doctrines, an insight fundamental to his own understanding of the problem of theophany: the decisive, irreducible importance of the divinely rooted creative Imagination (*khiyāl*) in virtually all spiritual experience and teaching. Thus we can at least surmise that his strict reliance on these hadith (rather than on the corresponding Qur'anic verses) in presenting this subject is itself meant to be a visible application of the key spiritual virtue of *adab*, of truly appropriate action and insightful respect for the Prophet's own inspired example in relying on these particular stories to teach his Companions how to go about properly "seeking God's Face."

The most important of these hadith on the vision of God for Ibn 'Arabī's own development of this topic include the following sayings, which are briefly summarized here in order of their relative length. Since the exact wording and dramatic sequence of these hadith, as well as their implicit references to the Qur'an, are often critically important for Ibn 'Arabī's exposition, full literal translations of the relevant sections, with some further explanations, have been provided in a longer separate section at the very end of this Chapter. The names given in quotation marks at the beginning of these summaries (and in the concluding translation section) reflect the shorter Arabic titles or catch-phrases which Ibn 'Arabī himself sometimes uses as an abbreviated reference to each of these hadith.

• The "hadith of the Veils" is short enough to quote in its entirety (according to the most commonly cited version, from Ibn Māja): *"God has seventy thousand veils of light and darkness: if He were to remove them, the radiant splendors of His Face would burn up whoever* (or *'whatever creature'*) *was reached by His Gaze."*[13] In order to grasp the importance of this image for the question of theophanic vision, especially from Ibn 'Arabī's perspective, it is essential to emphasize that, in accordance with the underlying Arabic term,[14] the divine veils must be understood here not as total barriers or obstacles to any sort of perception, but rather—as in fact is so often the case with a cloth curtain or veil—as allowing us to *see through* partially to the underlying reality, as much as is appropriate or indeed safely possible. Indeed Ibn 'Arabī's entire understanding of the metaphysical teaching of the Qur'an could be simply described as a "theology of trans-parition" (*transparaître*).

• In the famous divine saying of "the supererogatory works of devotion,"[15] the immediately relevant section is God's statement that: "... *My servant continues to come nearer to Me through the further acts of devotion until I love him. Then when I love him I am* [or: '(already) *was'*] *his hearing with which he hears, his sight with which he sees, his hand with which he holds, and his foot with which he walks....*" From the point of view of the spiritual problem of actually realizing theophany, the fundamental points in this hadith, for Ibn 'Arabī, are first of all its insistence on the essential interplay between the individual human effort of devotion and worship, initially grounded in the universal religious obligations, and the wider transforming power of divine Grace and Love. The second essential point, which is characteristic of Ibn 'Arabī's metaphysical teachings and concretely illustrated in his autobiographical descriptions of his own decisive experience of enlightenment (in section III below), is the resulting emphasis on the active *divine* role in the theophanic experience of spiritual "vision" (or "hearing," etc.)—i.e., on the soul's becoming (or existentially realizing) what in reality already was, and always is, the case.

• The divine saying that Ibn 'Arabī even more frequently cites to illuminate the necessary interplay of spiritual realization and right action is the famous "hadith of the Questioning" at the Resurrection, beginning with the divine reproach (to an overly confident pious soul at the Judgment) that "*I was sick, but you did not visit Me....*" While this hadith of course closely parallels a familiar section of the gospel of Matthew (25:41-45), two further reminders may be helpful for readers unfamiliar with this type of literature in its specifically Islamic context. First, in its original context this particular hadith immediately recalls a multitude of Qur'anic verses exhorting the feeding of the hungry (thirsty, travelers, etc.) and closely related acts of charity and sacrifice, as well as the often overtly symbolic and considerably more extensive *spiritual* nature of the "hunger," "thirst," and "illness" mentioned in so many Qur'anic passages. Likewise, it is important to know that the dramatic usage of the eschatological setting in this hadith (and several others translated below) to convey the sense of a revelatory unveiling and making-visible of what is in fact *already* the underlying spiritual reality of things is considerably more compatible with the actual literal Arabic language and likely meanings of the corresponding Qur'anic eschatological passages than either available English Qur'an translations or prevailing modern habits of thought (typically reflected in those inadequate translations) might otherwise suggest.

• The celebrated hadith describing Gabriel's questioning of Muhammad regarding the three dimensions of Religion (*al-dīn*), as *islām*, *īmān*, and *ihsān*, has a prominent place in the two *Sahīh* collections of Muslim and Bukhārī, and has long been widely used in popular religious instruction throughout the Islamic world. The problematic interrelation between "acting rightly" or "doing good" (the everyday meaning of *ihsān*) and the fully realized vision or awareness of God is of course already clearly highlighted in the Prophet's description of *ihsān* there—following the usual understanding, rather than the more revealing readings sometimes adopted by Ibn 'Arabī[16]—as "*That you worship/serve God as though you see Him; for even if you don't see Him, surely He sees you.*" At least equally important, though, for Ibn 'Arabī's understanding of the wider significance of this teaching about theophany and spiritual perception, is the dramatic exemplification of that spiritual lesson in the telling "punchline" of this famous story, where only the Prophet is

117

actually able to recognize this mysterious white-clad stranger (outwardly visible to all his Companions there, including 'Umar) as in fact the angel Gabriel, the divine emissary "come to teach the people their Religion."

• The Prophet's long lesson recounted by Abū Hurayra, commonly known as the "hadith of the Visit" (of the blessed with God) or of the "Dune of Musk" (referring to the symbolic locality mentioned in that saying), with its explicitly eschatological setting, is one of the classic Islamic scriptural accounts of the beatific vision and is also included in most of the major Sunni hadith collections. Even without entering into the enigmatic complexities introduced by the different "platforms of Light" and gem-like "pedestals" distinguishing the different ranks of the messengers, prophets and saints[17]—with their suggestive symbolic parallels to the visionary circles of Dante's *Paradisio* or later Buddhist soteriological teachings—the most basic images in this saying of the "unclouded sun" (blinding in itself, like the divine Face in the hadith of the Veils above) or of the "full moon" immediately evoke, for any Muslim audience, a whole intricate network of mysterious, presumably symbolic allusions to the sun and the moon in many celebrated Qur'anic passages, including the famous episode of the testing (or revelation) of Abraham's faith already mentioned above. At the same time, the implicit application to the problem of theophany of the wider natural symbolism of both these heavenly luminaries, including the radically shifting phases of the moon and the "beclouding" and cyclical "setting" of the sun (already alluded to in the verse 2:118 opening this Chapter), immediately suggests a more immediate, this-worldly spiritual relevance of this hadith, an interpretive stance that concords with that underlying Qur'anic usage and is clearly assumed in many of Ibn 'Arabī's own references to this saying. Finally, the powerful stress in this hadith—and perhaps even more so in the following "hadith of the Intercession"—on the continuous workings and awareness of divine Grace, Love and Forgiveness as essential preconditions not only for any vision of God, but even for effectively undertaking the sort of human spiritual actions eventually leading to that realized vision, points to one of the primary scriptural sources for the characteristically dominant role of the divine Creative Compassion or absolute Lovingmercy (*rahma*) in virtually all the distinctive aspects of Ibn 'Arabī's own spiritual teaching.

• The "hadith of the Transformation through the Forms" and the "hadith of the Intercession" are actually names (referring respectively to incidents at the beginning and end of each report) for different sections of two long and closely related eschatological hadith, ascribed respectively to Abū Hurayra and Abū Sa'īd al-Khudrī and recorded in several versions in the canonical collections of both Muslim and Bukhārī, which open in each case with virtually the same question as in the preceding hadith, regarding the certainty of our vision of God after death, and with the same Prophetic compari-

119

son to our viewing of the full moon or of the un-clouded sun in this life.

• The next section, introduced as a kind of amplifi-cation of that initial response, is perhaps the most frequently cited hadith passage (usually in the form of implicit allusions) in all of Ibn 'Arabī's work. It describes the testing of "this Community" with re-gard to their true ultimate objects of worship on the Day of the Resurrection. According to this account, God will present Himself to those pious souls "in a form other than (or: 'farthest from') what they know, and He will say to them: *'I am your Lord!'*." But the "hypocrites" among them—who, for Ibn 'Arabī, ultimately include most of mankind with the excep-tion of the rare Friends and "true servants of God"—will repeatedly fail to recognize the divine Presence, or even turn away from It, until God finally appears to them in the particular form they have already imagined and expected, according to their inner beliefs and unconscious cultural programming (*taqlīd*) in this world. The connections between this particular story and the preceding "hadith of the Questioning," and their far-reaching practical spiri-tual implications, are especially obvious.

• The final, much longer section of this same hadith details in openly symbolic terms the vast cosmic process of universal redemption by which the ac-tivities of "intercession" of the angels, prophets, and people of faith—and finally of God, *The Most-Merciful and Compassionate of all* (12:64, 92)—gradually draw out of the Fire even the worst

120

and most complete sinners, "who have done no good at all!" This extraordinary hadith, with its all-encompassing soteriological scope and remarkable wealth of allusions to the Qur'an (as well as many other hadith), compresses into a single coherent and dramatically compelling vision the inner meaning and ultimate conclusion of the entire course of all human existence. It is no exaggeration to state that the entire *Futūhāt*, and indeed the rest of Ibn 'Arabī's writings as well, can all be read as a detailed (if often implicit) commentary on the implications of this particular hadith, including of course the multitude of corresponding Qur'anic passages. Yet given the repeated, overwhelming stress on the all-encompassing saving power of the divine Love and Forgiveness throughout this hadith, it is also not difficult to imagine why it has not been the subject of much more open discussion and commentary.

• Although it is not recorded in the standard, earlier Sunni hadith collections, the long hadith of "The Stages of the Rising," which Ibn 'Arabī cites according to oral chains of transmission going back from his own personal source in Mecca to either Muhammad or Ali, can be read as a more detailed commentary on the symbolic implications and scriptural associations of the preceding hadith. Almost as long as a short book, this strictly eschatological divine saying contains several allusions to the beatific vision at its conclusion. It is quoted in its entirety in the concluding eschatological chapters (64-65) of the *Futūhāt*, where it provides the extended symbolic groundwork for Ibn 'Arabī's presentation

121

there of the wider process of human ethical and spiritual perfection.[18]

As we turn in the following sections to the ways Ibn 'Arabī actually uses these scriptural themes in the *Futūhāt* to illuminate the different practical, intellectual and theological dimensions of the problem of theophany, it is extremely important to keep in mind the way those underlying scriptural sources are actually evoked and were originally intended to operate on his readers.[19] We have to place ourselves, at least imaginatively, back within the lengthy process of self-discovery and realization that Ibn 'Arabī consciously intended for his original readers to pass through as they gradually pieced together, over many months of reading, reflection, prayer and contemplation, his widely scattered allusions to this theme (or any of this book's many other related topics), in the necessary light of their own spiritual intentions, motivations and accompanying experiences.

As the Shaykh explains in his Introduction to these *Meccan Illuminations*—and as readers of that vast work in any case quickly discover for themselves—his allusions to these hadith (or to the underlying Qur'anic verses) are rarely presented as the objects of an intellectual, discursive commentary or explanation in their own right. Instead, he typically presumes a profound familiarity with all these hadith— and all the more so with the entire Qur'an—and therefore inserts these scriptural allusions as the potent occasions for evoking each reader's own concrete and quite particular corresponding experiences of spiritual realities that those sayings can only suggest. His aim is that intimate process of self-recognition, necessarily both reflective and spiritual, which Su'ād al-Hakīm[20] has so aptly described as *mi'rāj al-kalima*: "the spiritual ascension of the Word," as the inspired symbols of these hadith (or Qur'anic verses) gradually begin to interpenetrate, coalesce and eventually become illuminated by the corresponding realities in the reader's own experience.

Another, possibly simpler way of describing this procedure of spiritual pedagogy is to note that Ibn 'Arabī obliges each of his readers, in the *Futūhāt*, to pass through something like the actual inner process—at once imaginative, experiential and intellectual—that connccts the scattered verses of the Qur'an with their dramatically and pedagogically effective re-expression in the hadith. But one cannot successfully complete that process without at the same time spontaneously coming to recognize the contemporary, more immediate expressions of both those scriptural sources in all the particular concrete forms (cultural, literary, social and religious) of one's own experience. This is a kind of teaching meant to generate teachers.

III. THE PERSONAL STARTING POINT: "THE SPLENDOR OF HIS FACE"

Among the spiritually significant dreams that Ibn 'Arabī recorded in his short (and undated) *"Epistle of Good Tidings"*[21] is his brief description of a litany or formula of *dhikr* which God gave to him during one such visionary incident:

> I saw while I was sleeping as though God were calling out to me, saying to me: "O My servant, if you want to be close to Me, honored and enjoying delight with Me, then constantly say: *'My Lord, cause me to see, so that I might look upon You!'* Repeat that for Me many times."

We cannot know for sure whether the bestowal of this particular *dhikr* actually preceded the Shaykh's own transforming vision of the divine Face, or whether this dream itself simply expresses the central importance which the quest for that spiritual realization eventually came to have in his own teaching and religious experience. But in either case, Ibn 'Arabī does clearly state that the *Futūhāt* itself grows out of his own very personal experiences of "learning to see," and that dramatically autobiographical dimension continues to underlie even his most abstract metaphysical and theological formulations of those revelatory lessons.

Ibn 'Arabī's first mention of the divine Face comes at a decisive moment at the very beginning of the *Futūhāt*, in the short autobiographical poem at the end of the introductory Epistle (*risāla*) to his Tunisian Sufi friend 'Abd al-'Azīz al-Mahdawī[22] in which he explains his motives for composing this immense book:

Now when I persisted in knocking on God's Door
    I was always attentive, nor was I distracted,

Until there appeared to my eye[23] "*the Splendors of His Face*"
    until—O wonder!—there was nothing [or "you were
                      nothing"] but It.[24]

So I encompassed in knowing (all) Being—nor did we
    know in our heart any other than God.

SEEING "WITH THE EYE OF THE REAL": THE BEAUTY OF ALL CREATION

Somewhat later, in chapter 36,[25] Ibn 'Arabī explains that the "vision of the divine Face" granted him at this moment was the source of everything expounded in the *Futūhāt*— and that the special theophanic awareness he discovered in that moment of inspiration has since been never-ceasing:

Thus God bestowed on us—through this state-of-arising (*nash'a*) in which God constituted us in this path—the Face of the Truly Real (*wajh al-Haqq*) in every thing. So for us, in our vision, there is nothing existing in the world but that we directly witness it with the Eye of the Truly Real (*shuhūd 'ayn Haqq*), through which we are glorifying Him. So we do not blame anything at all in the world of being!

As we shall see (in section V below), the connection between that transforming theophanic vision of the divine Presence in all things and Ibn 'Arabī's final remark here about his consequent inability to blame or accuse God (of any fault or imperfection in His Creation) will be essential to his later explanation of the inner distance between the spiritual states of the Fire (*al-nār*) and the beatific bliss (*na'īm*) of those who have reached the paradisiac state of "surrender-to-peace" in the Garden.

But already this brief autobiographical description suggests a very practical touchstone that helps to eliminate certain misconceptions about what we might otherwise take as theophanic states, while suggesting that the possibility and reality of this sort of experience (at least as a momentary revelatory spiritual "state" or *hāl*) is something much more widely shared than we might at first expect. This is brought out more openly in another, longer passage, much later in the *Futūhāt*,[26] which seems to describe key aspects (or spiritual consequences) of the same transforming experience that are alluded to in more eschatological language in the passages translated in section V below:

In this (spiritual stage) there is a knowing which removes the burden of anguish[27] from the soul of the person who knows it. For when one looks at what is ordinarily the case with (peoples') souls, the way that all the things happening to them cause them such anguish and distress, (it is enough) to make a person want to kill himself[28] because of what he sees. This knowing is called the "knowing of blissful repose" (*'ilm al-rāha*), because it is the knowing of the People of the Garden (of paradise) in particular. So whenever God reveals this knowing to one of the people of this world (already) in this world, that person has received in advance the blissful repose of eternity—although the person with this quality (in this world) still continues to respect the appropriate courtesy (*adab*) (towards God) concerning the commandment of what is right and the prohibition of what is wrong, according to his rank.

And in this spiritual stage is the knowing that what God made manifest to vision in the bodies (of all things in this world) is an adornment for those bodies; (the knowing) of why it is that some of what appears (in the world) seems ugly to a particular person, when that person regards it as ugly; and (the knowing) of *which* eye it is that a person sees with when they see the whole world as beautiful, when they *do* see it, so that they respond to it spontaneously with beautiful actions.[29] Now this knowing is one of the most beautiful (or "best") and most beneficial forms of knowing about the world, and it (corresponds to) what some of the theologians say about this: that "there is no Actor but God, and all of His Acts are beautiful."

The Heart as the True "Face" of Each Person

The second mention of Ibn 'Arabī's vision of the Face comes considerably later in chapter 1 (I, 222-23), during the Shaykh's famous opening dialogue with the mysterious "eternal Youth" (*fatā*) who is at once God, His personal "Lord" (*rabb*), the inner Reality of the Kaaba (the primordial Temple and "House of God"), and Ibn 'Arabī's own deepest self and true essence (*'ayn*). Here already he makes the essential practical connection between the different degrees of theophanic vision symbolized in the hadith of God's "transformation through the forms (of the creatures)" and the actual accomplishment—at once spiritual, aesthetic, ethical and intellectual—of the crucial virtue of *ihsān* ("right-and-beautiful-action") as the fully realized fruit of faith (*īmān*) and devotion. At the same time he also brings out clearly the endlessly varied individual ways through which that realization and enlightened vision is forever coming to be:

> I said (to the divine Youth): "Know... that when I had arrived with Him through faith and had settled down with Him in the spiritual Presence of *ihsān*, He brought me to rest in His sacred places and acquainted me with His innermost sanctuaries."
>
> And (the Youth) replied: "The rituals (of pilgrimage) are only so many out of the desire (for the pilgrims) to seek the Connection (with God): so if you hadn't found Me here, you would have found Me there! If I had been veiled from you at one station, I would have revealed Myself to you in another. However (in reality)—as I have taught you in many of your spiritual stopping-places and indicated to you many times in some of your inner states—even though I have veiled Myself (from most

127

people), I do have a Self-manifestation that not every Knower recognizes, except for whoever has encompassed in knowing the spiritual awarenesses you have encompassed.

Don't you see Me revealing Myself to them, in the Rising,[30] in a form other than the form and distinctive sign that they recognize. So they deny My Lordship and seek refuge from that form—even though they are actually seeking refuge with it, *except that they don't realize it* (2:12)! Yet they keep on saying to that theophanic form of manifestation: 'We take refuge from you with God! For here we are, waiting for our Lord!' So then I appear before them in the form that they were waiting for, and they all affirm My lordship and their own servanthood.

But they are really worshipping and serving their own 'totem' (of divinity, *'alāma*), witnessing (only) the image (of God) that has become established among them! So whoever among them says that he is worshipping Me is *saying a lie* (58:2) and has absolutely amazed Me! For how could that be true of him, since when I revealed Myself to him he denied Me!? Indeed whoever restricts Me to one form rather than another is really only worshipping what they themselves have imagined!"

Given the special attention so many modern commentators have often given to the central role of imagination in Ibn 'Arabī's thought, it is important to note as well the spiritually decisive distinction he draws here between each individual's ego-centered, "self-deluding imagination" (*takhayyul* or *wahm*) and the ongoing cosmic divine "Imaging-forth" (*khiyāl*) underlying all of manifest creation.

All the practical and religious dimensions of the Shaykh's teaching depend on acknowledging the profound reality of this basic distinction—and the corresponding spiritual necessity for human beings to begin to discover and eventually conform to the forms of the *divine* Imagination, rather than following the self-imposed "idols" and unconscious images alluded to in that famous divine saying this mysterious divine Youth is so memorably restating here.

> [The divine Youth continues:] That "imaginary image" (*takhayyul*) is the reality that person has secretly established and given power in their heart. So they imagine they are worshipping Me, while they are actually denying Me! But as for the true Knowers (of God), I cannot possibly be hidden from their regard, because they are absent from created things and their own inner selves (in their complete absorption with Me). So that for them, nothing appears to them other than Me, and they understand nothing of the existent things but My Names. Thus whatever thing appears to them and manifests Itself (*tajallā*), they say: "*You* are the Praised One, the Most-High!"
>
> So the (two inner conditions) are not at all alike. But most people are (in a state) between witnessing and being heedless, except that for them it is all one thing!

A few lines later in the same conversation with this divine Youth (I, 226), Ibn 'Arabī adds one further essential clarification, when he speaks of "turning away *the face of my Heart*." This important understanding of the essential reality of the human "face" is greatly amplified in a later passage in chapter 69 (on "the inner secrets of Purification," V,

188), where Ibn 'Arabī is explaining the spiritual lessons to be drawn from the prescribed ritual ablution of the face:

> Therefore the human being should pay close attention to his actions and inactions, both outwardly and inwardly, and should attentively observe the influences of his Lord in his heart. Because the face of his *heart* is what is essential here. For the "face" of the human being—or of anything else—is its true reality and its essence and its unique individuality (*'ayn*). Hence when someone speaks of the *wajh* ("face," or essential aspect) of a thing or a question or a legal judgment, they mean the intrinsic reality or essence or concrete specificity of the thing to which they're referring.
>
> God said: *Faces that Day glowing with light, gazing toward their Lord! And faces that Day scowling, suspecting something disastrous is befalling them.* (75:22-25). Now the "faces" located on the front of human beings are not described as "suspecting"; for the act of suspecting or supposing only comes from the inner reality of the human being.

This interpretation of the Heart of the human being[31] as the true inner "face" and spiritual reality of each person is consistently presupposed throughout the rest of the *Futūhāt*. As the Shaykh's allusion in the above passage indicates, it also opens up important perspectives for understanding and interpreting the many Qur'anic passages concerning the human "face" that were briefly introduced earlier in this Chapter (section I).

130

IV. "*SURPRISED* BY HIS FACE":
POLISHING THE MIRROR OF THE HEART

The real nature of that human "face"—or rather of the divine "Eye" and spiritual Essence (*'ayn*) of the Spirit that is the primordial Heart of each human being[32]—and therefore of the many Qur'anic references to the "turning" of one's face toward or away from God, is further elaborated in the following chapter 2 (II, 82-83), where Ibn 'Arabī explains:

> So know that the heart is a polished mirror—*all* of it is a face—that does not (itself) ever "rust." So if someone should say about it that it rusts—as in the (Prophet's) saying: "Certainly hearts tarnish like iron," in the hadith that concludes "the polishing of the heart is through remembrance of God and recitation of the Qur'an..."—that is because the heart has become preoccupied with knowing the secondary causes (*al-asbāb*), the apparent workings of this world), instead of with knowing God. So its attachment to what is other than God has "rusted over" the face of the heart, in that it blocks the Self-manifestation (*tajalli*) of the Truly Real in that heart.
>
> For the divine Presence is perpetually manifesting Itself, and one could never imagine Its ever veiling Itself from us. So when this heart fails to receive that (divine Self-manifestation) from the direction of the praiseworthy and revelatory divine "addressing"[33] (speaking to us), because it has received something else instead, then its act of receiving that something other (than God) is what is referred to (in the scriptures) as "tarnishing," "*veils*," "*locking*," "*blindness*," "*rust*" and the like.[34] For in fact the Truly Real Himself is (perpetually) bestow-

ing this knowing on you in the heart, except that (your heart) is (preoccupied with) knowing something other than God—although the Knowers of-and-through God[35] know that in reality (that distracted heart) too is actually knowing of and through God.

SEEING AND ILLUSION: THE SHIFTING REGARD OF THE HEART

As Ibn 'Arabī goes on to explain in a revealing passage in chapter 17 (III, 51-53), this uniquely human possibility of turning away from the ongoing Self-revelation and vision of God explains why most people are ordinarily "surprised" by the sight of God's Face, often when they least expect it: For there is no change or transformation (*taqallub*), whether it be in the higher or lower worlds, but that it proceeds from God's Intending (or "Facing": *tawajjuh ilāhī*) of a special Theophany (*bi-tajall^{in} khāss*) to this particular eye (or individual: *'ayn*), according to its preparedness for that Theophany which is given by its own inner reality.

> ...Now the outward form of this shifting [of the heart's attention between the divine "Face" and particular created things] is that a human being happens to be seeking, to begin with, the knowledge of some existent thing (*kawn*) or another, or some sign pointing to what he is seeking, which is also a particular existent thing. But when he attains what he was seeking, suddenly the Face of the Real (*wajh al-Haqq*) appears to him in that thing, even though he wasn't seeking that Face.[36] Once the seeker becomes connected with that (particular theophany), they forget about what they were originally seeking, and that Knowing shifts (them) to seeking what is bestowed on them by that (divine) Face.

Now among them are those (Knowers) who are aware of that shifting [between the particular forms they perceive or seek and the divine "Face" of the Real lying behind them], while others are actually in that state, but are unaware of what it actually is (that their own spiritual attention) is shifting from or toward.

The "others" here, Ibn 'Arabī concludes—in a reference to his central metaphysical thesis of the "perpetually renewed creation" (*khalq jadīd*) and related metaphysical conceptions familiar to all readers of his *Fusūs al-Hikam*—are ultimately anyone who imagines that the world is constituted of discrete and self-subsistent "things," without noticing what—or rather Who—is actually sustaining all those recurrent appearances:

Does what is bestowed by the (divine) Realities remain in the same state for even one breath, or one instant of time—so that the Activity of the Divinity with regard to (sustaining) those things becomes useless!? This is inconceivable... since this perpetual shifting concerns the "likenesses" of things (*amthāl*), so that there is this shifting from the thing to its likeness at every instant. ... It is like our saying "So-and-so never stopped walking all day and didn't sit down"—although without a doubt that walking consists of a great many repeated motions, none of which is exactly the same as any other, although they are "alike." So your knowing shifts with the constant changes of those (created likenesses of things).

IHSĀN AND THE PURIFIED VISION OF THE FRIENDS OF GOD

Soon after, in chapter 5 (II, 143), Ibn ʿArabī begins to explain the practical spiritual secret of those rare Knowers (*'urafā'*) who are able to maintain that transformed spiritual state of immediate theophanic vision. The absolute importance of this subject is aptly indicated by his insistence there that "this knowing is the spiritual station of the Inheritors (from the prophets), and there is no higher station than this one, because it is an unchanging direct witnessing (of God)." The secret of those special Friends of God, it turns out, is nothing but the inner meaning of Muhammad's already remarkable teaching about the reality of *ihsān*, in the famous hadith of Gabriel on the three dimensions of Religion:

> And this is the station in which the states of the spiritual voyagers are dissolved and the stations of the spiritual travelers disappear, until [in the words of a famous Sufi saying] "The one who was not vanishes, and He Who always is remains."[37] (For them) there is no "other" to affirm His Self-revealing (*zuhūr*), and no darkness remains with His Light. [So according to the Prophet's famous explanation of *ihsān*]: "...*If you are not*, then you do see Him!" Recognize the true reality of "if you are not," and (then) you yourself are the (divine existentiating Command) "*Be!*".[38]

The initial shock of Ibn ʿArabī's playfully creative (and grammatically justifiable) reading of the well known concluding phrase from this hadith defining *ihsān*—which is ordinarily read simply as "Even if you do not see Him"—should not obscure the fact that the spiritual reality he is

134

pointing to here is nothing other than the more familiar and fundamental Qur'anic conception of *islām*, of the inner "surrender" or disappearance of the ego-self (the "you" of this hadith) within the all-encompassing divine Will. However, this is not the only place where Ibn 'Arabī reads the same description of *ihsān* in this remarkably complex[39] and spiritually revealing fashion: this revelatory experience of the "disappearance (of the ego-self) in the act of witnessing (God's Presence)" is analyzed at much greater length in his short popular treatise of the same title.[40] And the centrality of this particular Prophetic teaching in his own spiritual perspective is especially evident in his later discussion of the same famous hadith in chapter 36,[41] where he points out the special role of the injunction to worship God "as though you see Him" already in the Qur'anic account of Jesus and his teachings, and by extension in the spiritual awareness of all those spiritual "heirs" among the Friends of God who are intrinsically "Jesus-like" in their religious aptitudes and capacities. Therefore, he concludes there:

> You should know that what is ours through a divine revealing (*shar'*) other than that of Jesus—Peace be with him!—is (the Prophet's) saying: "For if you are not, then you do see Him; and certainly He sees you." For this is one of the fundamental principles (of his true followers).

The "Solitary Ones" Absorbed in their Vision of the Real

In chapter 23 (III, 154-55), "on the inner knowing of the spiritual 'Poles' (among the Friends) and their secrets," Ibn 'Arabī goes on to explain that the full realization of this theophanic vision is limited to those especially accom-

plished spiritual figures he often calls "the Solitary ones,"
the *Afrād*.[42] These rare individuals who truly exemplify the
realized state of *ihsān* are described there in the following
terms drawn from another famous divine saying:

> They are not known for their miracles or prodigies
> (*karamāt*), nor singled out for praise, nor are they
> pointed out for their "sound piety" (*salāh*), at least
> as that is commonly understood by most people,
> although there is nothing corrupt about them. They
> are the hidden ones, the innocent ones, (God's) trust-
> ees in the world, concealed among the people. As
> God's Messenger reported from His Lord: "For Me,
> the most blessed of My Friends (*awliyā'ī*) is the
> person of faith who is unburdened (by attachments),
> who takes pleasure in prayer, who has truly realized
> the state of *ihsān* in devotion to his Lord and ea-
> gerly served Him both in secret and openly. And
> that person was concealed among the people."[43]

As Ibn 'Arabī goes on to explain, what inwardly distinguishes those Friends who have realized this highest spiritual station is above all the constant attentive "turning" of
their face toward God, their sincere and direct recognition
of *all* their experience as theophany. If an earlier Sufi,
emphasizing the paradoxical secrecy and necessarily hidden nature of this realization, went so far as to say that these
individuals were "blackened of face[44] in this world and the
next," the Shaykh explains that such an expression—"if it
was intended to refer to the spiritual states of this group"—
means simply that:

All of their moments, both in this world and in the other, are completely absorbed in (contemplating) God's Self-manifestations to them. For in our view, a human being sees in the mirror of the Truly Real, when He manifests Himself to that person, nothing but his own soul/self and his spiritual station, which is one of the existing (created) things (*akwān*). And an existent thing (*kawn*), in the Light of the Truly Real, is darkness (or "shadow," *zulma*): therefore that person witnesses nothing but their own "blackness."

For the "face" (*wajh*) of a thing is its essence and its true reality. So only for this group, in particular, is the divine Self-manifestation perpetual and never ending, *since they are always with the Real* (*al-Haqq*), in this world and in the other world, through that ongoing divine Self-manifestation we mentioned. For these are the Solitary ones, the *Afrād*.

SELF-GIVING AND SPIRITUAL PERSEVERANCE AS POLISHING TOOLS

All of this is intriguing enough, but also—at least for those readers who have not yet consciously realized such a spiritual state—still expressed in fairly abstract and theoretical terms. Only in chapter 47 (IV, 140-41) does Ibn 'Arabī begin to develop the more accessible, spiritually practical dimensions of this problem, in what might at first appear to be a quite unrelated context, his explanation of the enigmatic hadith that "*voluntary self-giving (sadaqa) is a Proof (from/of God)*":[45]

As for this connection between the (divine) "Proof"
and voluntary self-giving, it comes from the fact that
God made human beings selfish (*shuhh*: "greedy"
or "miserly") by their natural[46] disposition...in the
very source of their created constitution (*nash'a*)....
Now the root of this (divine Proof exemplified in
true acts of charity) is that human beings take their
very being from God, so that they have been given
the natural disposition to take advantage (from others), not to be helpful to them. Hence their natural
reality (*haqīqa*) does not in itself explain their voluntarily giving of themselves. Therefore when
someone does *voluntarily* give of himself, his voluntary charity is a proof that he has overcome the
inherent selfishness and greed of his egoistic self
(*nafs*) that was implanted in him by God. So this is
why the Prophet said "Voluntary self-giving is a
(divine) Proof."

The inner connection of this overcoming of the ego-self to
the realization of theophanic vision, for Ibn 'Arabī, is just
as allusively suggested in another, equally succinct section
of the same hadith: "Spiritual perseverance is a radiance
(*al-sabr diyā'*)." As he goes on to explain, by drawing a
connection between this "radiant light" and the famous
hadith about the "70,000 veils of light and darkness" concealing the divine Face:

Spiritual unveiling is only possible through the illuminating radiance of (God's) Light, not through the
Light itself. Because it is the property of Light that
it can only obliterate the darkness, while unveiling

actually takes place through the Light's (illuminating) "radiance." So (in that sense) the Light is also a veil, just as the darkness is a veil, as the Messenger of God said, in regard to his Lord, that "His veil is the Light" and his saying that "God has seventy— or 70,000—veils of Light and darkness."

Therefore he called spiritual perseverance,[47] which is (exemplified in) fasting and the pilgrimage, "a radiance." That is, if you clothe yourself in *sabr*, through it will be revealed the spiritual perception of those things that are bestowed by the inner reality of its radiance.

SELF-PRETENTIOUSNESS AS THE ESSENCE OF SPIRITUAL SICKNESS

Finally, in chapter 54 (IV, 263), on the understanding of spiritual allusions (*ishārāt*), Ibn 'Arabī reminds his readers of the deeper dangers of failing to pursue this essential unveiling, dangers that will be more amply discussed in the following section on Gehenna and the sufferings of the Fire. At the same time, of course, this brief reminder is itself a profound allusion to the deeper functions and transforming spiritual role of human suffering within the all-encompassing, cosmic framework of divine spiritual pedagogy that the Shaykh finds expressed throughout all the eschatological language of the Qur'an (section V below).

> Whoever is unaware of the Face of God (*wajh al-Haqq*) in all the things is overcome and mastered by (unconscious) pretensions.[48] And that ego-pretentiousness is the very essence of (spiritual) sickness (*'ayn al-marad*). But the people of spiritual Realization (the *muhaqqiqūn*) have established that there is nothing in being but God. As for us,

139

although we do exist, still our being is only through Him. And the (intrinsic) state of someone whose being is through another is non-existence (*'adam*).

Of course Ibn 'Arabī's concluding words here are themselves an obvious allusion to his own earlier spiritual reading of the Prophet's definition of *iḥsān* as an essential condition for the realized vision of God's Face: "If *you are not*, then you see Him." But there is another, subtler allusion here, in his identification of our manifold unconscious pretensions to some kind of ultimate "divinity" (the inner state of *da'wā*) as the very "essence of sickness." The full importance of that aside will only come into perspective when we have made the further essential connection with the famous divine saying that begins "I was sick, yet you did not visit Me...," and with Ibn 'Arabī's even more extraordinary claim that those divine Words themselves express the ultimate source and essence of Hell.

V. Lifting the Veils: From Gehenna to the Beatific Vision

Ibn 'Arabī's extended discussion of the scriptural symbols of Islamic eschatology in chapters 61-65 of the *Meccan Illuminations*—especially when it is supplemented by essential explanations from many other parts of that immense work—turns out to be a truly awe-inspiring, panoramic perspective on all the stages and forms of human spiritual realization, from both the individual and the divine, supratemporal and macrocosmic points of view. Thus it is highly significant that in his opening eschatological chapter 61 (IV, 366), entitled "On the inner knowing of Gehenna, *where most of the creatures are, with respect to their suffering*"—

a place which he later openly identifies with the entire material cosmos—he begins (IV, 369-370) by explaining that:

> And God created (Gehenna) from the Self-manifestation of His saying—in the (divine) new-Speaking (recorded in the collection) of Muslim: *"I was hungry, yet you didn't feed Me! And I was thirsty, yet you didn't give Me to drink! And I was sick, yet you didn't visit Me!"* This is the most prodigious of the descents through which the Real descended to His servants in His Gracious-Kindness toward them. Therefore Gehenna—may God preserve us and you all from It!—was created from this Reality.

Surely few phrases could be more typical of Ibn 'Arabī's distinctive rhetoric, or of the remarkable demands it places on each serious reader. When one encounters such a passage for the first time, what is immediately and inevitably highlighted are all the normally implicit, far from monotheistic, dualisms (of Creator and created, Attributes of Beauty and Majesty, "self" and "other," heaven and hell, fear and hope, and so on) that in fact—as the hadith itself was intended to point out—continue to govern each individual's initial unconscious patterns of striving and action in the world. In a very theoretical and abstract way, of course, those apparent oppositions are resolved for readers more familiar with Ibn 'Arabī's metaphysics of the divine Names and Self-manifestations (*tajalliyāt*); but the consolations of such a purely philosophic understanding are necessarily rather limited.

A more spiritually effective commentary on this particular passage might be provided by today's headlines or evening news, or by the latest conflict at work or home: in any case, those are the mundane particular objects of contemplation that must be faced, again and again, in the course of everyday life in order for the full reality and implications of what Ibn 'Arabī is saying here to begin to sink in. Everything else in his long chapters on eschatology, including his extraordinary musical descriptions of paradise and the beatific Vision, is only a sort of extended commentary on the theophanic blindness—but also the corresponding possibility of true and revelatory "seeing"—implied in this outwardly simple hadith:

> For all the pains that are created there (in Gehenna) and which are found by those who enter there— [and Ibn 'Arabī later, following the Qur'an (at 19:71), pointedly insists that there is *no one* who does not first enter Gehenna before moving to the higher spiritual states of the Rising]—come from the attribute of the divine "Anger."[49] Those pains only come to be there through the creatures, human beings and jinn, who enter there, when they enter there.

Citing the Qur'anic exhortation (at 20:81) ... *and do not overstep* (My limits) *regarding this, lest My Anger settle upon you all—for whoever My Anger settles upon has surely fallen down!*, Ibn 'Arabī explains that this means that:

> In other words, "My Anger descends *through you.*" For God ascribed this Anger to Himself, so that when It (or "He") descends with those people, they are the "resting-place" for It/Him. *So they themselves are the resting-place of the Anger, while He/It is what descends through them.* So the Anger, here, is precisely the pain itself!

However, Ibn 'Arabī quickly goes on to point out here (IV, 377-378) and in subsequent chapters that the very same "place" (of the Heart) is also the potential locus of manifestation for all the positive qualities of the absolute divine Compassion or Lovingmercy (*al-rahma*), since:

> God created for Gehenna *seven doors, for each door of them a separate portion* (15:44) of the world and of suffering. Each of these seven doors is also open (to one of the Gardens), but Gehenna has an eighth door in it that is locked and does not open: that is the door of being-veiled (*bāb al-hijāb*) from the Vision of God.

In the context of the preceding hadith, of course, it is clear that that ultimate, impenetrable veil is precisely our ignorance—or refusal—to *recognize* in reality and in practice the divine Face in all the suffering that surrounds us. At the same time, Ibn 'Arabī's allusion here to the possible lifting or rending of that veil takes us back to that autobiographical poem about his own transforming theophanic Vision and his persistent "knocking on God's Door," from the very beginning of the *Meccan Illuminations*, with which this Chapter began (section III above).

THE THEOPHANIC "EYE" AND LIGHT OF THE IMAGINATION

However, the Shaykh's first more explicit discussion of the other, more hopeful aspect of this problem, about opening that essential Door to the beatific vision, only occurs much later, near the end of chapter 64, "on the spiritual 'Stopping-places' of the Resurrection." There (IV, 465), after pointing out that "the ultimate sources of the seven gates of the Fire are (the same) for the seven gates of the Garden," he hastens to add that:

There is also an eighth gate, which opens onto the Garden of the Vision (of God, the highest of the Gardens of paradise). And that is the *same* locked gate that is in the Fire, which is the Door of being-veiled (from God): for it is never opened (for the residents of Gehenna as long as they are there), since the people of the Fire are veiled from their Lord.

But Ibn ʿArabī is not content simply to point out how, in the divine scheme of things, the soul's ultimate "punishment" is always simultaneous with—if indeed it does not often inwardly precede—its more visible "crimes." He is also concerned with clarifying, more profoundly, how this painful inner veiling is itself a necessary, purifying prelude to the full appreciation and eventual realization of theophanic vision of the Real. Thus in his discussion at the very end of chapter 64 (IV, 472) of the eschatological "Bridge"[50] over the Fire which every soul must eventually traverse on its way to paradise, he explains:

Now since the Bridge is through the Fire (of Gehenna)—and there is no way to the Garden except by crossing It—God said: *There is not one of you-all but that they are entering (the Fire)! That is certain and decreed with your Lord!* (19:71). So whoever truly knows the meaning of this saying recognizes the place of Gehenna and what it is.

If we all necessarily know very well, as Ibn ʿArabī boldly implies here, just where Gehenna is, we all have an equally understandable and pressing personal interest in finding this saving "Bridge" and in learning how to cross it. Part of his answer concerning its identity, at least, was already suggested in the very title of his chapter 63, "concerning the inner knowing of the abiding of humanity in the *barzakh*," the "connecting boundary" between this world and the "other world" of the Rising. One of the fundamental principles of the Shaykh's thought, already familiar to all readers of the *Fusūs al-Hikam*, is of course the identity of that *barzakh* with the cosmic, divine creative Imagination (*khiyāl*, not our often dangerously illusory individual *takhayyul*).

As he exclaims in the opening poem of that chapter (63), "Were it not for the *Khiyāl*, today we would be in nothingness!" And that divine "Imagination," he continues there (at IV, 406-7), is none other than the secret of the hadith of *ihsān* and the true Door to the realized vision of God's Face:

> The Dominion of Imagination (*sultān al-khiyāl*) is
> the very essence of the "*as-though* (you saw Him),"
> and it is the real meaning of (the Prophet's) saying
> (in explaining *ihsān*) "worship/serve God as though
> you saw Him."

This chapter (at IV, 412-413) is also where Ibn 'Arabī first quite openly makes the essential inner connection between the spiritual practice of *ihsān* and the powerful hadith of God's "transformation through the forms." The secret of actually recognizing the divine Presence behind each of its Self-manifestations, he indicates, is suggested by the very words of that saying:

> This is how you may understand what is mentioned
> in that sound report (from the Prophet) concerning
> the Creator's "Manifesting Himself (to the souls at
> the Rising) in a form farthest from the one in which
> they (normally) saw Him," and concerning His trans-
> forming Himself into "a form that they recognize
> (as something other than God)"—while they have
> denied that form and taken refuge with Him from
> it.

145

So you must know with *which* "eye" you see Him! For I have already taught you that the (universal cosmic) Imagination is perceived through Itself—I mean through the eye of the Imagination (or "through the divine Imagination itself": *'ayn al-khiyāl*)—or it may be perceived through (merely physical) sight (*al-basar*). So which of those two "eyes" is the sound one that we can rely on?

Now we have said in that regard:

> When my Beloved reveals Himself
> > With which eye do you see Him?

> With *His* eye, not with my eye
> > For no one sees Him but Him.

(We only said this poem) to exalt His station and to confirm His Words, since He said (at 6:103-104): (their) *eyesight does not perceive Him...* [51] And He did not specify one particular abode [for this theophanic spiritual insight, such as this world, as opposed to paradise]. Instead He sent these Words as an absolutely valid Sign/verse (*āya mutlaqa*) and a matter that is completely specific and fully verified! Therefore no one perceives Him but Him. And it is with *His* eye that I see Him—(as God says) in the sound report:[52] "*I was his eye with which he saw....*"

So wake up, you heedless sleeper, from being (veiled) like this, and take this to heart! For I have opened up for you a Door to the forms of awareness (of God) that thinking cannot even reach—even though intellects can at least come to accept it—either through providential divine Caring [i.e., through a spiritually enlightening state of Grace] or (as it says in another hadith) "by polishing the hearts with Remembrance (of God) and recitation of the Qur'an."

A few pages later (IV, 417-418) in this same remarkably dense chapter—which carefully sets out the essence of Ibn 'Arabī's understanding not so much of any particular religion, as of the essential spiritual dimension of all the arts and humanities—he underlines even more explicitly this central theophanic role of the divine Imagination:

> For it was in regard to this (divine *khiyāl*), from its Presence, that the Prophet says (in his explanation of *ihsān*), "Worship God *as though* you see him" and (in another hadith) "God is in the *qibla* of the person praying." That is to say: "imagine Him before you during prayer, while you are facing Him, so that you will feel His Regard upon you and be humble before Him. And observe the appropriate inner attitude (*adab*) with Him in your praying...."
>
> For if the revealer of the Way (*al-shārīᶜ*) had not known that within you there is a reality called "Imagination" which has this quality, he would not have said to you "as though you see him" with your eyesight (*basar*)...since the (physical) eyesight doesn't perceive anything (during prayer) but the wall (in front of you)! Yet we know that the revealer of the Way addressed you (telling you) to *imagine* that you are facing God directly before you in prayer, making it incumbent on you to accept that. And God says: ... *So wherever you all turn, then there is the Face of God!* (2:115).[53] For the "face" of something is its true reality and its essence (or "eye": *'ayn*).

Then Ibn 'Arabī goes on (at IV, 419) to explain the inner connection between this divine reality of Imagination and the infinitely varied individual experiences of theophanic "recognition" of God's Face:

> For light is an outward condition for unveiling and manifestation, since if there is no light, the physical eyesight (*basar*) doesn't perceive anything. So God made this Imagination a light through which is perceived the bringing-into-forms[54] of every thing, whatever it may be. Thus His Light penetrates the absolute non-existence and transforms and shapes it into the forms of being (*yusawwiruhu wujūdan*). Thus the (divine) Imagination is more deserving of the Name "*the Light*" (24: 35) than all the created things that are (usually) described as luminous, since His Light (of the cosmic Imagination) does not resemble the (created) lights. And through It the theophanies are perceived.

BEATIFIC VISION: UNVEILED COMMUNION— AND THE ILLUMINED FACES IN THE "RETURN"

In chapter 65, on the inner understanding of Paradise, Ibn 'Arabī moves on to his most extended poetic description of the ultimate vision of the divine Face, described here in the context of the "Visit" of the blessed with God at the "Dune of the (beatific) Vision" that was mentioned in the famous eschatological hadith (see section II and the full translation at the end of this Chapter below). Here we can cite only some of the most relevant highlights of this dramatic, emotionally charged word-painting—a complex set of images, largely drawn from the eschatological symbolism of the Qur'an (and related hadith), which is at the same time clearly

148

intended as a poetic description of the whole course of human existence. That account begins (V, 78) with a divine messenger (*rasūl*, the same term applied by the Qur'an to the prophets who bring the different revelations, and to certain angels):

> Then a messenger comes to them from God and says: "Prepare yourselves for the vision of your Lord!"— and already He is there, revealing Himself to them! Then they begin to get ready. So God[55] is revealing Himself, and there are three veils between Him and His creatures: the veils of His Glory, Majesty and Immensity. But they are not even able to look upon those veils.
>
> So He says to the greatest of His chamberlains[56] in His Presence: "Lift up the veils between My servants and Me, so that they can see Me." Then the veils are raised up, and God reveals Himself to their vision from behind a *single* veil, whose Name is "The Most Beautiful, the Most Subtle-and-Gracious" (*al-jamīl al-latīf*)—and all of them are a single act-of-vision!
>
> Then He pours out upon them a Light that flows invisibly[57] through their innermost essences, so that through It they all become completely Hearing (*sam'*), and they are completely overwhelmed by the Beauty of the Lord. Their innermost essences are completely illuminated by the Light of that Supernal Beauty.

Next, quoting the Prophet's own description in the final section of the long hadith of the fifty "Halting-places of the Resurrection"[58]—the saying which provides the framework for Ibn 'Arabī's entire narrative of humanity's spiritual per-

149

fection in these concluding eschatological chapters of the *Futūhāt*—the Shaykh describes a scene[59] where God addresses the people of Paradise directly:

> O My servants who have surrendered (to Peace: *muslimūn*): You have surrendered to Peace, and I am Peace (*anā al-salām*), and My Dwelling place is the Abode of Peace (*dār al-salām*, 10:25). *Now I shall show you all My Face*, just as you have heard My Speech. So when I have revealed Myself to you and I have removed the veils from My Face, then praise Me! And enter, all of you, into My Abode, no longer veiled from Me, entering in Peace and Faith. Now enter in upon Me and sit down around Me, so that you are all gazing upon Me and so you are seeing Me up close!
>
> …I am your Lord: you were all worshipping Me, and loving Me and fearing Me—even though you did not see Me! …Truly I am most Pleased with you all, and I love you, and I love what you love. With Me there is for you whatever your souls desire and whatever gives pleasure to your eyes (or: 'essences'). With Me there is for you whatever you have claim to, and whatever you may wish—and whatever you wish, I also wish! So just ask Me— and do not be ashamed or timid or feel left alone!
>
> This is My Dwelling place where I have brought you all to live, My Garden where I have lodged you, and My Self which I have caused you all to see…. I am gazing upon you all, never turning My Sight away from you. So ask Me for whatever you wish and whatever you desire. Already I kept close to you with My Self (or: 'My Breath')—and I am your

closest Companion and most intimate Friend! So after this there is no need, nor any lack; no sorrow, no poverty, no sickness, no decrepitude, no resentment, no anxiety, no loss—forever and eternally ever after!

Then, after completing the elaborate description of the inexhaustible blessings of Paradise in this same long hadith, Ibn 'Arabī concludes (V, 82-83) with his own personal, more original description of the Vision of God's Face and its ongoing consequences (a panorama that is itself based on the long canonical "hadith of the Intercession"):

Then God (*al-Haqq*), after telling them that, lifts up the Veil and reveals Himself to His servants—and *they all bow down in prayer* (17:7).[60] But He says to them: "Lift up your heads! This is not the right place for bowing down! O My servants, I only invited you all here so that you might take delight in witnessing Me!"[61] Then there overcomes them in that (witnessing) whatever God wills.

Next He says to them all: "Is there anything else for you (that you still desire) after this?"

And they answer: "O our Lord, what thing could yet remain, when you have rescued us from the Fire and brought us into the Abode of Your Contentment, settled us in Your Proximity, clothed us in the garments of Your Grace, and caused us to see Your Face?!"

Then God says: "But there is something more for you…My everlasting Contentment (*ridā'ī*) with you all: never will I ever be angry with you!"

151

"What sweeter words could there be!," Ibn 'Arabī remarks
at this point:

> For He created us with His Speech, when He said
> "*Be!*,"[62] so that the very first thing we ever had from
> Him was Hearing (*al-samā‘*, alluding also to 7:172).
> And now He concludes with that with which He
> began. For He said this address (in Paradise), and
> then He concluded with the Hearing—which is pre-
> cisely this Good News (*bushrā*)! And the people
> differ greatly in the degree of their seeing him (as
> described symbolically in the hadith of the "Dune
> of Vision"),[63] and there is an immense difference
> among them in this respect, according to their re-
> spective degrees of knowing (God): so among them
> (are the higher and the lower).

Ibn 'Arabī's following remarks here (V, 84-85) about the
visibility and expanding "reflections" of the inner lights of
this event—even among those who were *not* there to see
for themselves—as the blessed return from their unforgettable Vision (and "Audition") of the divine Face, are worth
pondering again and again:

> Then He says to the angels: "return them to their
> palaces (in the Gardens of paradise)!" (That is be-
> cause) they no longer know the way back, as a re-
> sult of two things: the drunkenness that has over-
> come them from the Vision (of God), and because
> of the greater Good which has increased for them
> through their path (to God), so that they no longer
> recognize that (earlier) way.[64] So if it were not for
> the angels guiding them, they would not even rec-
> ognize their own homes!

Then when they reach their dwellings and their people are there before them, the young maidens and the young men, they see that all they possess has become enrobed in the resplendent light and beauty and radiance from their faces, flowing forth upon what they possess with an essential radiance.[65] So they say to their people: "But you have increased in light and beauty and radiance! We did not leave you like this!"

And their people answer them back: "But the same thing has happened to *you*! You have increased in radiance and beauty, quite unlike how you were when you first left us!" And they all delight in each other.

Those acquainted with Ibn 'Arabī's writings and his complex understanding of the ongoing cosmic role of the prophets and Friends of God will recognize here a clear allusion to his many descriptions of the special function of those highest saints or Friends of God, including the prophets, who continue to "return back" (*al-rājiʿūn*) from their own enlightenment and realized proximity with God in order to support and further the spiritual realization of all their fellow human beings.[66] And even readers unfamiliar with Ibn 'Arabī's own ideas on this subject, or with the complex symbolism of Qur'anic eschatology, will recognize the extraordinarily detailed and powerful evocation of everything he has just described here in the remarkable spiritual film, *Bagdad Cafe*.[67]

His concluding words here again evoke the mysterious providential interplay of divine "Anger" and all-encompassing Compassion and Lovingmercy that gradually leads each soul toward this realized Vision of God's Face:

So know that Rest and Loving-Compassion (*rāha wa rahma*) are absolute throughout all of the Garden.[68] And even though (the divine) Compassion is not itself an existent "thing" (*amr wujūdī*)—but rather an expression for whatever gives rise to pleasure and joy and delight in the (human) object of that Loving-Compassion—still those (actual manifestations and occasions of that divine joy and delight) *are* existent things.

So everyone in the Garden is filled with delight. And everything in It is joyful bliss (*na'īm*)!

VI. Learning to Look: The Secrets of Realization

If it is tempting to stop here with Ibn 'Arabī's dramatic eschatological descriptions of the beatific Vision, more inquisitive and demanding readers cannot help but notice that he has hardly begun to speak of the just *how* that ultimate spiritual station might be fully realized and lastingly attained. Not surprisingly, all the rest of these *Futūhāt* quite literally is made up of his ever more complex answer to that basic existential question. But it is also worth noting that his lengthy practical answer essentially begins with his discussion, in the immediately following chapters, of the spiritual "mysteries" or "inner meanings" (*asrār*) of the obligatory acts of worship (the *'ibādāt*).

One of his most striking and metaphysically comprehensive allusions to the practical spiritual process of "seeking God's Face" is the following passage from chapter 69, on the inner secrets of the ritual prayer. Here the Shaykh weaves together the hadith of the 70,000 divine veils with a memorable section in the long hadith of the Intercession describing how the ashes of those souls "who had never done anything good at all" are nevertheless washed in the

"River of Life" and mysteriously transformed by that divine Compassion and Lovingmercy into beautiful "Pearls" in the Gardens of paradise. In Ibn 'Arabī's far-reaching interpretation (at VI, 351), these poetic symbols become a powerful description of the ways the self-imposed torments of all those who have momentarily estranged themselves from God are themselves the ultimate, if unintended, means to their own painful spiritual purification:

> But the divine Presence is described as being "Jealously solicitous"[69] about Its Being, with respect to the (unwarranted) claim of this pretentious claimant (to divine status).[70] So if the pretense (of divinity) had not originated with this person, that (divine Jealousy) would not have overwhelmed them. For it is inevitable that with the lifting of the veils (to quote the hadith): "the Splendors (of God's Face) will burn up whatever created thing (*al-khalq*) is encompassed by (His) Gaze"—meaning (by "created thing") whatever belongs to the bodily nature. Because the World of the (divine) Command is (purely spiritual) "lights" that are not burned up, but rather are harmoniously included within the Greatest Light—and the World of the Command has no pretensions within it!
>
> So the world of created things *does* burn up and become "ashes," and the very non-existence inherent in (its being created) does remain ashes, without any more pretense (to self-subsistent being). Therefore nothing is reduced to non-existence but those pretensions themselves, through the transformation of that individual essence (or "eye": *'ayn*), whose innate predispositions had given it its pre-

155

tensions, into an essence/eye without those pretensions.

Further on in chapter 69 (VI, 172-74), Ibn 'Arabī makes it clear that the essential practical key to more fruitfully and self-consciously—and less painfully—"seeking God's Face" is contained above all in the second, humanly active part of the divine saying that begins "I was sick and you did not visit Me..."—the same hadith whose opening words, as he had earlier explained (in chapter 61), were the ultimate Source and description of Gehenna. In other words, for him the rest of this saying also alludes to the ultimate "cure" of that all too visible affliction of the human condition, but in a way that is far from immediately obvious to most of those who encounter this divine prescription:

> The inner meaning of that is that it is incumbent on every person of (true spiritual) intelligence to veil the divine Secret, because unveiling It might drive whoever is neither (spiritually) knowing nor intelligent to a lack of proper respect for the divine Majesty....
>
> Likewise, it is essential for the (spiritual) Knower to conceal from the ignorant the inner secrets of the Real (*asrār al-Haqq*) in things like His Saying: *"There is no meeting of three but that He is the fourth of them...,"*[71] and His Saying *"and We are closer to him than the jugular vein"* (50:16), and His saying (in the *hadīth al-nawāfil*): *"I was* (already the purified servant's) *sight and hearing and tongue..."* For if the ignorant person heard that, it might lead them to a prohibited misunderstanding of divine incarnation (*hulūl*) or to an undue restriction (of God's infinite Manifestations).

So likewise with the divine saying "I was hungry and you did not feed Me....":

> (The Knower) should veil his awareness of the inner meaning of this from the ignorant and not add anything beyond the explanation that the (divine) Speaker Himself gave, just as God veiled (that Secret) in His Saying: *"And as for so-and-so, He was sick, and if you had visited him, you would have found Me with him..."* For this (divine explanation) is more difficult than the first part (of that same hadith)!
>
> Yet for those who know through God (*al-'ulamā' bi-llāh*: the Shaykh's usual term for the highest state of spiritual realization), with this explanation He granted them another awareness of Him that they had not yet possessed.

As we might expect, Ibn 'Arabī again cannot resist giving some further hints about that second, deeper spiritual understanding of this hadith—the simple practical secret of theophanic Vision—somewhat later in chapter 69 (VII, 203):

> Now the "divine Prosternation" (*al-sujūd al-ilāhī*) is the greatest of the divine Acts-of-Descent through which the Truly Real makes Himself come down to the level of His servant. And it is (expressed in) His Saying: *"I was sick, but you did not visit Me; and I was hungry, but you did not feed Me; and I was thirsty, but you did not give me drink."* There could be no divine Descent greater than that! Then God goes on to explain that (by saying) that "So-and-so was sick, and so-and-so was hungry, and so-and-so was thirsty," and He caused Himself to descend to

their levels through *their* states and connected all that to Himself through his describing Himself by those states.

So whoever perceives that, all of it, on the part of the Truly Real during their Prayer has indeed perceived the "Divine Cycle of Prayer,"[72] through having the Truly Real as their Imām! And the (true) servant responds to that (direct revelation of God's Presence) with the thankfulness this gracious divine Favor deserves.

Ibn 'Arabī is even more explicit in his summary of this "secret" later in chapter 70 (VIII, 360), on the inner mysteries of charity, of "purifying self-giving" (*zakāt*). Here he openly brings out the inner connections between the hadith on the true realization of *ihsān* ("if *you are not*, then you see Him") and the deeper mysteries of this remarkable divine saying:

So if the servant is with his Master like this [i.e., fully realizing his intrinsic "servanthood," *'ubūdiyya*], then the servant vanishes and it is the Master who appears. For the very source of manifestation is pretension (to self-subsistent "Lordship," *rubūbīya*). Therefore the Master, in this state, takes on the attribute of the servant in this other (person), as an honor to the servant. And this (is expressed in) His saying: "I was sick and you did not visit Me, I was hungry and you did not feed Me," since both hunger and sickness are among the attributes of the servants.

And likewise God said in His reply (to the pious hypocrites' protests): "So-and-so was sick, but you didn't visit them; for if you had visited them, you would have found Me with them!"

Now *God is with the servant who is like this,* and the servant whose attribute is like this—[i.e., who does respond actively and appropriately to that theophanic "illness, thirst and hunger," at all the levels of being]—*was already* with their Lord. So understand!

Finally, all these threads of Ibn 'Arabī's argument are brought together in his description of the "truly sincere lover" (*al-muhibb al-sādiq*) in chapter 276 (II, 596):

Now the truly sincere lover is the person who changes to (take on) the attributes of the beloved, not someone who brings the beloved down to their own attributes. Don't you see that God, the Truly Real, out of His Love for us, descended to us through His hidden subtle-acts-of-Grace (*altāfuhu al-khafīya*), which are appropriate to us? [And He does all this out of Love] even though His Majesty and Greatness are exalted far above that. Hence He descended to "smiling happily" with us (as described in another eschatological hadith) when we come to His House seeking intimate conversation with Him. And (He descended) to "being filled with joy" at our repenting and returning to Him after we have turned away from Him. And (He descended) to His taking our place in our being hungry and thirsty and sick, to making Himself descend to our level and taking our place whenever one of His servants is ill, so that He said to some of them "*I was sick, and you did not visit Me....*"

For these are the fruits of (His) Love when He descended among us. And that is why we said that true sincerity in love makes the lover take on the attributes of the beloved. So the sincere servant (of God) is like that in their love for their Lord, in "taking on as their character the qualities"[73] of His Names.

Therefore they take on the (divine) qualities of "being independent" of everything other than God, of "being strong" for God, of "giving bountifully" with God's Hand, and of *safeguarding the Eye of God* ... because of their love for Him.

VII. ACTIVE CONTEMPLATION: PRACTICING *Ihsān*

This much, then, the Shaykh tells us about the beatific vision of God's Face in the opening sections of his *Meccan Illuminations*: what it really is; how it is even possible; why we ordinarily fail to realize it; what that spiritual perception is actually like (whether or not we initially recognize such theophanic Seeing and Hearing); and finally, how—and *with whom*—we can truly begin to "seek His Face." In each case, the practical key to that realization of theophany turns out to be *ihsān*—and *ihsān* in the comprehensive etymological, root sense of that extraordinarily fertile Arabic term: first coming to perceive and know, and then creating and putting into action, all that is truly good and beautiful. In other words, without that real—and necessarily individual and spontaneous—inspired awareness of divine Presence clearly reflected in each instant of our lives, without that active contemplation of that divine Beauty so accurately described in the Prophet's answer to Gabriel's question, what we usually conceive of as *ihsān*, as simply "doing good," is at best only a secondhand, socially and culturally conditioned imitation of the one real thing.

Therefore it is not surprising that in one of Ibn ʿArabī's longer dramatic accounts of his own personal spiritual ascension, in chapter 367 of the *Futūhāt*, his enlightened awareness of the full extent of the spiritual fruits of *ihsān* described in all the Qur'anic accounts of paradise only comes at the very climax of his journey,[74] when his voyage has passed beyond the cosmic Temple and entered the "Garden of Proximity (to God)" (*jannat al-ma'wā*) that immediately precedes his culminating experience of unitive Vision:

> So when I had left (the celestial Temple), I came to *the Lotus-Tree of the Limit*[75] (53:14), and I halted amongst Its lowest and its loftiest branches. Now *it was enveloped* (53:16) in the lights of (right) actions, and in the shelter of Its branches were singing the birds of the spirits of those who perform those actions, *since that Tree is in the form of Human Being*.[76]

Obviously Ibn 'Arabī was not seeking philosophic, logical proofs for such revelations or for the scriptures which were his inspiration in this and all his other undertakings. Instead, one might say that his method is one of using the sacred Imagination—in the sense of the archetypal images and stories provided by his own religious tradition—to awaken each reader's individual spiritual imagination, to illuminate and reveal the recurrent "reflections" of those scriptural likenesses in the "ever-renewed creation" of his readers' own unique spiritual experiences. For him, those archetypes—like all the divine Names—can *only* be discovered through their own realized and ever-renewed images. With that method, and that aim, it is not really surprising if Ibn 'Arabī's writings came to provide the favorite theoretical explanation, and theological justification, for the quintessential theophanic endeavors of so many subsequent artists and master-creators in all the Islamic humanities (poets, mystics, musicians, and their audiences) throughout the following centuries. Nor is it very surprising if a Sufi poet like Rumi, in the memorable quatrain which opened this Chapter, could manage to evoke in those few Persian words what is so endlessly elaborated throughout the pages of the *Futūhāt*.

Yet the lasting fascination, and the peculiar persuasive claims, of Ibn 'Arabī's own understanding of the theophanic Imagination are brought out with a special intensity whenever one encounters its workings and its description in more distant and outwardly alien settings: such memorable discoveries are always a potent example of what he so beautifully described (in section IV above) as being "surprised" by God's Face. One dramatic illustration of that sort of revelation can be found in the following familiar verses, whose underlying question so closely mirrors Rumi's quatrain. This more recent poet's words, like all of Ibn 'Arabī's, invoke "... *Presences,/ That passion, piety or affection knows, and that all heavenly glory symbolize.*"[77] And what this poet here calls "labour" beautifully conveys everything that Ibn 'Arabī also sought to teach about the mysteries of *ihsān*:

> Labour is blossoming or dancing where
> The body is not bruised to pleasure soul,
> Nor beauty born out of its own despair,
> Nor blear-eyed wisdom out of midnight oil.
> O chestnut-tree, great-rooted blossomer,
> Are you the leaf, the blossom or the bole?
> Oh body swayed to music, O brightening glance,
> How can we know the dancer from the dance?

HADITH ON THE VISION OF GOD

The following translations, given without the entire chain of transmitters (*isnād*) included in the canonical collections, are based on popular, uncritical editions of each hadith (compared here with the Arabic texts of these divine sayings given in the study by W. Graham, and in the translations of Ibn 'Arabī's own famous collection, the *Mishkāt al-Anwār*). These English versions and notes should be sufficient for illustrating the general themes alluded to in Ibn 'Arabī's often implicit and unacknowledged references to these sayings, but they are in no way intended as an adequate critical study of each hadith. (Often there are several significantly different versions of each saying, with different chains of transmission, contained within a single hadith collection; and the differences among versions of the same basic report appearing in several different collections are typically even greater).

Readers without Arabic interested in exploring Ibn 'Arabī's own use of these hadith, as well as related divine sayings and eschatological hadith (including the long "Halting-places of the Resurrection"), will find indications of his characteristic use of these allusions in the notes to *The Bezels of Wisdom* (translation by R. Austin) and in the selected translations from *The Meccan Revelations* (tr. by J. Morris and W. Chittick, Pir Press, 2002), as well as in William Chittick's extensive translations from the *Futūhāt* in *The Sufi Path of Knowledge* and *The Self-Disclosures of God*, which include more useful detailed indexes and lists of hadith and related sayings. Especially interesting is Ibn

'Arabī's own personal collection of 101 divine sayings, the *Mishkāt al-Anwār* (translated by M. Valsān, *La Niche des Lumières*, Paris, 1983; English translation and critical Arabic edition by S. Hirtenstein and M. Tiernan, Oxford, Anqa Publishers, 2004). Most of the divine sayings included in Ibn 'Arabī's *Mishkāt* which are taken from the standard early Sunni collections are also translated and extensively annotated in the concluding section of William Graham's *Divine Word and Prophetic Word in Early Islam*, Mouton/ Paris, 1977.

The "Hadith of the Veils"[78]

"God has seventy [or 700/70,000] veils of light and darkness: if He were to remove them, the radiant splendors of His Face would burn up whoever[79] was reached by His Gaze."

The "Hadith of the Supererogatory Works"[80]

The Messenger of God said that God said: "Whoever opposes a Friend (*walī*) of Mine, I declare war on them. And My servant does not come near to Me with anything more lovable (*ahabb*) to Me than what I have made a duty[81] for him.

And My servant continues to come nearer to Me through the further acts of devotion[82] until I love[83] him. Then when I love him I *am*[84] his hearing with which he hears, his sight with which he sees, his hand with which he holds, and his foot with which he walks.

And if he asks Me, I most surely give to him. And if he seeks My help, I surely help him. I have never hesitated about anything I do as I hesitate about (taking) the soul of the person of faith who dislikes death, since I dislike hurting him."

THE "HADITH OF THE QUESTIONING" (AT THE RESURRECTION)[85]

God says on the Day of the Rising: "O son of Adam, I was sick and you didn't visit Me."

He said: "O my Lord, how could I visit You, and You are Lord of the worlds?!"

God said: "Didn't you know that My servant so-and-so was sick, yet you didn't visit him? Or didn't you know that if you had visited him *you would have found Me with him*?"

[Then God says:] "O son of Adam, did I not ask you for food, but you refused to feed Me?"

He said: "O my Lord, how could I feed You, and You are Lord of the Worlds!?"

God said: "Now didn't you know that my servant so-and-so asked you for food, but you didn't feed him? And didn't you know that if you had fed him *you would have found that with Me*?"[86]

[Then God says:] "O son of Adam, I asked you for a drink, but you didn't give Me anything to drink."

He said: "O my Lord, how could I give You a drink, and You are Lord of the Worlds!?"

God said: "My servant so-and-so asked you for a drink, but you didn't give him any. But if you had given him a drink *you would have found that with Me*."

THE "HADITH OF GABRIEL"[87]

The Prophet came out for the people (to meet him) one day, and a man came up to him who said: "What is faith (*īmān*)?"

He replied: "Faith (means) that you have faith in God, His angels, His Books, in (your) meeting Him, in His messengers, and that you have faith in the Rising."[88]

165

Then he asked: "What is *islām*?"[89]

He answered: "*Islām* is that you worship God and don't associate (anything) with Him, that you perform the prayer (*salāt*), give in charity,[90] and fast during the month of Ramadan."[91]

Then he asked: "What is *ihsān*?"[92]

He replied: "To worship God as though you see Him. And even if you don't see Him, surely He sees you." [The last sentence could also be translated more artfully, as it is in some of Ibn 'Arabī's interpretations quoted earlier in this Chapter, as "*And if you are not, you see Him*; and surely He sees you.*"]

Then he went off, and (the Prophet) said: "bring him back." But they couldn't see anything. Then he said: "This is Gabriel, who came to teach the people their Religion (*dīn*)."

THE "HADITH OF THE VISIT" OR "HADITH OF THE DUNE"[93]

Abū Hurayra said to Sa'īd: "I ask God to bring you and me together in the Market of Paradise!"

And Sa'īd asked: "You mean there's a Market there?"

Abū Hurayra replied: "Yes, the Messenger of God informed me that:

'When the people of the Garden (of Paradise) enter it, they settle down in it according to the excellence of their actions. After that, during the period corresponding to the Day of Reunion[94] among the days of this world, they are called and they visit their Lord: He shows them His Throne, and He manifests Himself to them in one of the meadows of the Garden.

Then there are set up for them platforms ("*minbars*") of Light and pearl and ruby and emerald and gold and silver.[95] The lowest ones of them and those among them who are

beneath them take their seats on dunes of musk and cam-
phor. And those sitting down do not see that those who are
on the pedestals have more excellent seats than them'."

I asked the Messenger of God: "Do we see our Lord?"

And he replied: "Yes indeed! Do you all have any doubt
about (your) seeing the sun, or the moon when it is full?"

"No," I said.

[He replied]: "So likewise you all do not have any doubt
about seeing your Lord! Now there does not remain a single
person in that gathering but that God is present and conversing with him so intimately that He will say to (each)
one of you:

> *'Don't you remember so-and-so to whom
> you did such and such?'*—and He re-
> minds that person of some of their (acts
> of) treachery and deceit in this world.

> Then that person says: 'O Lord, didn't
> You forgive me?'

> And He says: *'Indeed it was through the
> vastness of My Forgiveness that you have
> reached your station here.'*

> And while they are together like that
> clouds will form above them and perfume
> will rain down upon them, sweeter and
> more fragrant than anything they have
> ever experienced.

> Then He says: *'Rise up, all of you, to that
> which I have readied for you from My
> Grace, and take what you desired!'*"

[The Prophet] said: "So we are brought a Market that
has been enclosed and surrounded by the angels, contain-

ing that whose like 'no eyes have seen, ears have not heard, and has not occurred to hearts.'"[96]

He said: "Then whatever we desired is brought to us. There is no selling in it, nor any buying there. And in that Market the people of the Garden encounter one another. So if a person who has a higher station meets someone who is below them—yet there is no lowly place there—and that (second) person is delighted with the garment (the first one) is wearing, even before they have finished speaking a garment even more beautiful than that appears[97] to them upon that person. And that is because there must not be any sorrow there."

[He continued:] "Then we return to our stations and meet our spouses,[98] who say: 'Welcome back! But now that you've come back your beauty and your fragrance are much finer than when you left us!'

And we answer: 'This Day we gathered in the company of our Lord, and He gave us the right to come back transformed[99] the way we are!'."

THE "HADITH OF THE TRANSFORMATION
THROUGH THE FORMS"[100]

This entire hadīth can be understood in part as a sort of extended commentary on the Qur'anic verses at 39:42-75, especially the following ones:

God receives and greets[101] the souls at the moment of their death and those which haven't died in their sleeping.[102] So He takes those for which He decreed death and He sends[103] the others until a named limit. Indeed there is a Sign in that for a people who reflect and penetrate deeply! (39:42)

...Say: "O My servants who have gone to excess against their (own) souls, do not despair of the Lovingmercy of God!" Surely God forgives the sins altogether! Indeed He is the All-Forgiving, the All-Merciful/All-Loving. (39:53)

...And they did not conceive of God according to the Truth/Reality of His Qadr[104]*...on the Day of the Rising....* (39:67).

* * *

[...By 'Atā' ibn Yazīd, from Abū Hurayra, who reported that:]

Some people said to the Messenger of God, "O Messenger of God, do we see our Lord[105] on the Day of the Rising?"

Then the Messenger of God replied: "Do you have any trouble[106] in seeing the moon on the night when it is full?"

"No, O Messenger of God," they said.

"Do you have any trouble," he said, "about (seeing) the sun when there are no clouds beneath it?"

"No, O Messenger of God," they said.

"Then surely you do see Him[107] just like that!," he replied.

[The Prophet continued:] "God brings together the people[108] on the Day of Rising and says: '*Let whoever was worshipping something pursue that.*'

So whoever was worshipping the sun pursues that, whoever was worshipping the moon pursues that, whoever was worshipping the *Tāghūts*[109] pursues them, and there remains this Community (*umma*), including its 'hypocrites' (*munāfiqūn*).

Then God comes to them in a form other than His form that they recognize (or 'know'), and He says: '*I am your Lord!*'

And they say: 'We take refuge with God from you! This is our place until our Lord comes to us. And when our Lord does come, we'll recognize him (immediately)!'

Then God comes to them in His form that they do recognize and He says: '*I am your Lord!*'

Then they say: 'You are our Lord,' and they pursue (that form).

And the 'Bridge' (*al-sirāt*) is set up over the two sides of Gehenna, and I and my community are the first to cross. No one speaks that Day but the Messengers, and their petition (to God) that Day is: 'O My God, grant (them) salvation, grant salvation!...'[110]

Then the people are seized by the 'Hooks' (of the Fire) according to their *actions*: among them is the person of faith who remains behind because of his (bad) actions, and among them the one who receives his recompense (of a limited punishment) until he is saved.

(This process proceeds) until when God has finished judging the servants and wished, in His Loving-Compassion, to bring out those whom He wishes among the people of the Fire, He ordered[111] the angels to bring out of the Fire those—among those on whom God wishes to show Loving-Compassion—who did not associate anything with God, among those who say 'There is no god but God.'

For the angels do recognize them in the Fire. They know them by the effect of their praying,[112] for the Fire eats up everything of the descendants of Adam but the effect of their praying. Because God has forbidden the Fire to consume the effect of praying.

So they are brought out of the Fire, all scraped and torn apart. And the Water of Life is poured over them, so that through it they spring back to life just like the seedling carried along in the silt by the flood.

Next, God finishes judging among the servants, and still there remains a man whose *face* is turned looking toward the Fire, who is the last of the people of the Garden to enter the Garden.

Now that person says: 'O My Lord, turn my face away from the Fire! For its wind (or: "smell") was hurting me and its flames were burning me up!' So that person calls upon God and asks Him for what God had wished that person would ask of Him.

Then God says: *'Wouldn't you want to ask for something else, if I did that for you?'*

And that person says: 'I'm not asking you for *anything* else!' And he gives his Lord all sorts of pledges and promises (not to ask for anything more), as God wishes.

Then God turns his face away from the Fire, and when He has brought that person close to the Garden and he has seen It, he is silent (or: 'becomes calm'), as (long as) God wishes for him to be silent.

So then that person says: 'O my Lord, bring me close to the Door of the Garden!'

And God says to him: *'But didn't you just give all your pledges and promises that you wouldn't ask Me for anything but what I'd given you?! Woe unto you, O son of Adam—look how untrustworthy you are!'*

So that person says: 'O my Lord!,' and he keeps on praying and pleading with God until He says to him: *'Now won't you want to ask for something else again, if I grant you that?'*

And that person replies: 'No, by Your Majesty!,' and he gives his Lord all the pledges and promises that God may wish.

Then God brings him up to the Door of the Garden, and when he is standing next to the Door of the Garden, Para-

171

dise is opened up to him, so that he sees all the good and the joyful pleasures It contains.

Now that person will be silent and calm as long as God wishes for him to be so, and then he says: 'My Lord, bring me into the Garden!'

So God says to him: *'Didn't you give Me all your pledges and promises that you wouldn't ask Me for anything more than what I'd given you!? Woe to you, O son of Adam, how untrustworthy you are!'*

Then that person says: 'O my Lord, don't make me the most wretched of Your creatures!' And he keeps on praying and calling on God until *God laughs* because of him!

So when God laughs because of him, He says: *'Go on, enter the Garden!'* And when He had caused that person to enter Paradise, God said to him: *'Wish (for whatever you desire)!'*

So that person keeps on asking his Lord and wishing as long as God keeps pointing out to him (all sorts of things), reminding him first of this and then of that...until, when all his wishes and desires are quite exhausted, God says to him: *'All that is yours, and its like along with it!'*."

So 'Atā' ibn Yazīd [the reporter of the whole hadith] continued:

Now Abū Sa'īd al-Khudrī was with Abū Hurayra all along, and he didn't correct him about anything in it until Abū Hurayra mentioned that God had said to that man "...and *its like* along with it."

Abū Sa'īd said: "(No, he said) 'And *ten times as much* like it, along with it!,' O Abū Hurayra."

Abū Hurayra said: "I only remembered His saying *'All that, and its like along with it!'*."

Abū Sa'īd said: "I swear that I learned it by heart exactly from the Messenger of God, that he said: *'That, and ten times as much like it!'*."

Abū Hurayra concluded: "And that man was the last of the people of the Garden to enter the Garden."

THE "HADITH OF THE INTERCESSION"[113]

[... from Abū Sa'īd al-Khudrī, who said:] Some people during the time of the Messenger of God asked him: "O Messenger of God, do we see our Lord on the Day of the Rising?"

The Messenger of God said: "Yes! Do you have any trouble seeing the sun at noon, on a bright clear day when there are no clouds? Or do you have any trouble seeing the full moon on a clear and cloudless night?"

"No, O Messenger of God!," they replied.

He said: "You will have no more trouble in seeing God on the Day of the Rising than you have in seeing either of them!"

[The Prophet continued:]

Now when it is the Day of the Rising, a Caller called out "Let every *Umma*[114] follow what it was worshipping!" Then there is not a one of those who were worshipping idols or graven images other than God, but that they all go on falling into the Fire, one by one. (This continued) until none remained but those who were worshipping God, both the pious and the sinners, among the People of the (revealed) Book who lived long ago... [But most of them also turn out to have "associated" others in their worship of God, so that their "thirst" is recompensed by the painful "mirages" of the Fire.]

(This continued) until none remained but those who are worshipping God (alone), both the pious and the sinners. The Lord of the Worlds came to

173

them in the form farthest from the one in which they imagined ("saw") Him. He said (to them): *"What are you-all waiting for?! Every Umma is pursuing what they used to worship!"*

"O our Lord," they replied, "we kept away from *those* people[115] (while we were) in the world,[116] no matter how much we were in need of them, and we had nothing to do with them!"

So He says (to them): *"(But) I am your Lord!"*

"We take refuge with God from you!," they say. "We don't associate anything with God!" (And they keep on saying this) two or three times, until some of them are just about to turn around and go away.

Then He says: *"Is there any Sign (āya) between you all and Him by which you would recognize Him?"*

And they say: "Yes."

Then *(the True Reality) is revealed...,*[117] and the only ones who remain, whom God allows to pray, are those who used to bow down to God spontaneously, out of their soul's own desire. As for all of those who used to bow down in prayer out of social conformity and to protect their reputation (out of fear of what others might say or do), God makes them entirely into 'backs', so that whenever they want to bow down in prayer, instead they keep falling back on their backs!

Then they will raise up their heads (from prayer), and He will already have been transformed (back) into His form in which they saw Him the first time (i.e., in this world).

Then after that He said: *"I am your Lord!"*— and they are saying: "(Yes indeed), *You* are our Lord!"

Then after that the Bridge (*al-jisr*) is set up over Gehenna, and the Intercession takes place and they are all saying: "O my God, protect (us), protect!"[118]

Then someone says: "O Messenger of God, what is this 'Bridge'?"

He said:

It is a slippery, precarious toehold, covered with hooks and spikes and thorns like a bush in the desert they call "*al-sa'dān*." The people of faith pass over it as quickly as the glance of an eye, or like lightning, the wind, birds, fast horses or camels. Some escape untouched; some are scratched and torn, but manage to get away; while others tumble into the Fire of Gehenna. (And this continues) until the people of faith are safely free from the Fire.

Now by Him Who holds my soul in His Hand, not one of you could implore and beseech (someone) in seeking to gain what is (your) right and due any more intensely than the people of faith plead with God, on the Day of the Rising, on behalf of their friends who are in the Fire!

They are saying: "O our Lord, those (friends of ours) used to fast with us, and they were praying and they were loving!"

Then it is said to them: "Bring out whoever you all knew (among them)!" So their forms are kept protected from the Fire, and they bring out a great many people whom the fire had already consumed halfway up their legs, or to the knee.

Next they say: "O our Lord, there does not remain in the Fire a single one of those whom You ordered us (to bring out)."

175

So He says: *"Return, all of you, and bring out anyone in whose heart you find even a dinar's weight*[119] *of good!"*

So they bring out a great many people, and then they say: "O our Lord, we did not leave in the Fire a single one of those whom You ordered us (to bring out)."

Next He says: *"Return, all of you, and bring out anyone in whose heart you find even half a dinar's weight of good!"*

So they bring out a great many people, and then they say: "O our Lord, we did not leave in the Fire a single one of those You ordered us (to bring out)."

Next He says: *"Return, all of you, and bring out anyone in whose heart you find even 'an atom's-weight of good'!"*[120]

So they bring out a great many people, and then they say: "O our Lord, we didn't leave in the Fire any good at all!"

Now Abū Saʿīd al-Khudrī was saying (as he recounted what the Prophet said): "If you all don't believe what I'm recounting in this hadith, then read, if you will, (the Qurʾanic verse) *Surely God does not do even an atom's weight of wrong, and if it be a good-and-beautiful (action), He multiplies it many times, and He brings from His Presence an immense Reward!* (4:40)."

[To resume Abū Saʿīd's recounting of the Prophet's original story:]

Then God says: *"The angels have interceded; and the prophets*[121] *have interceded; the people of faith have interceded. Now none remains but the Most Loving and Compassionate of all."*[122]

176

Then He grasps a handful from the Fire, and He brings out of It a group of people who never did any good at all, who have already returned to charred ashes. Then He throws them into a river in one of the openings of the Garden, a river that is called "the River of Life." And they come out of (that River) like a seed that grows out of the muddy silt carried along by the flood: haven't you seen how it grows up next to a rock or a tree, green on the side facing the sun, and paler on the shady side?

He continued: They will come out like pearls, with seal-rings on their necks. Then the people of the Garden recognize them: "These are those who have been set free by the All-Compassionate, Who has admitted them into the Garden without any (good) deed that they did or sent before them."

Then He says: *Enter the Garden* (cf. 89:30)—*whatever you see there is yours!*"

They say: "O Lord, You have granted us blessings which you did not grant to anyone else in the world!"

And He says: *"There is with Me (a blessing and favor) better than this."*

And they reply: "O our Lord, what could possibly be better than this?"

He answers: *"My absolute Love-and-Satisfaction:*[123] *I will never be angry with you after this!"*

THE HADITH OF "THE HALTING-PLACES
OF THE RESURRECTION"[124]

This extremely long hadith, which is not recorded in the early Sunni collections, is quoted in full by Ibn 'Arabī in the course of the key eschatological chapters 64 and 65 of the *Futūhāt*, describing the Gardens (of paradise) and the events of the Rising and the final Judgment. Near the beginning of chapter 64 (IV, 436-37), and again at the end of his own hadith collection, the *Mishkāt al-Anwār*,[125] he explains that he studied it personally with "our shaykh (the *sharīf*) al-Qassār," in front of the Kaaba at Mecca in the year 599 A.H. (the same year he wrote the *Mishkāt al-Anwār*), and he gives the full *isnād* going back to 'Abdullāh ibn Mas'ūd, who heard it "from 'Alī b. Abī Tālib, surrounded by a number of the Companions of God's Messenger"—a picture evidently intended to emphasize both its great importance and the public reliability of the transmission.

The hadith itself begins (IV, 437): "There are fifty Halting-places (*mawāqif*) in the Rising, and each of them is for a thousand years,[126] after the people have left their tombs...." The first forty-nine stages or tests, concluding with seven "bridges" constituting the famous "Bridge" (*al-sirāt*) over the Fire of Gehenna, are discussed in the sections quoted in chapter 64 (IV, 437-442). Most of these stages involve the description of a complex spiritual or moral virtue—beginning with faith (*īmān*)—which is said to immediately "save" (from the ensuing tests and sufferings) those souls who fully realize that particular virtue. The final halting-place consists of a detailed, highly poetic portrayal of God's welcoming of the blessed in Paradise (V, 78-82), including several of the shorter selections translated in section V of this Chapter—most of which are also recorded as separate divine sayings in the *Mishkāt al-Anwār*.

DISCERNING

قُلْ هَلْ يَسْتَوِى ٱلَّذِينَ يَعْلَمُونَ وَٱلَّذِينَ لَا يَعْلَمُونَ إِنَّمَا يَتَذَكَّرُ أُوْلُوا ٱلْأَلْبَـٰبِ

... Say: "Are those who know and those who do not know on the same level?!" Only the people of knowing-hearts are (truly) remembering.

فَبَشِّرْ عِبَادِ ٭ ٱلَّذِينَ يَسْتَمِعُونَ ٱلْقَوْلَ فَيَتَّبِعُونَ أَحْسَنَهُۥ أُوْلَـٰٓئِكَ ٱلَّذِينَ هَدَىٰهُمُ ٱللَّهُ وَأُوْلَـٰٓئِكَ هُمْ أُوْلُوا ٱلْأَلْبَـٰبِ

... So give good news to My servants who listen attentively to the Word, and then they follow the best/most beautiful of It: Those are the ones whom God has rightly guided, and those, they are the people of knowing-hearts!

Sūrat al-Zumar, 39:9 and 17-18

179

CHAPTER FOUR

DISCERNING:
LEARNING TO "TRANSLATE FROM GOD"

And it was not for any ordinary person (bashar) that
God should speak to him except through inspira-
tion, or from behind a veil, or He sends a messen-
ger to reveal—with His permission—whatever He
wishes. Surely He is Exalted, All-Wise!

Sūrat al-Shūrā, 42:51

This spiritual waystation also includes the knowing
of what God has placed in the world as (a subject
of) wonder—and the "wondrous" (as people ordinarily understand it) is only what breaks with their
habitual perception of reality. But for those who
comprehend things from the divine perspective, *ev-*
ery thing in this habitual course of things is itself a
subject of wonder—whereas the people of habits
only marvel at what departs from that habitual
course.

— *al-Futūhāt al-Makkiyya*, chapter 366.

The subject of this Chapter, the effective exercise of realized spiritual intelligence, brings together all the multi-faceted considerations and insights that we have begun to explore in the three preceding Chapters. For the act and expression of spiritual discernment involves a constant inter-

play of seeking, then of receptivity and contemplation ("listening"), reflection, appropriate action, and then further observation and reflection on the consequences of that action and the challenges of the next destined situation of testing and learning—and so on, in a never-ending, yet never identically repeated ascending spiral. And this process is not something mysterious and esoteric, but something that we necessarily constantly practice, from infancy onward—most obviously and subtly, perhaps, in our intimate daily interactions with all the other souls around us. Thus to speak at all of this process of "discerning," in any area of life, constantly raises the essential paradox that Ibn 'Arabī has so succinctly expressed in the brief epigraph above, taken from the very end of that section of the *Meccan Illuminations* which is our primary focus and illustration in this Chapter.

As he suggests in that short passage, one of the constant and most unavoidable obstacles to the actual spiritual perception of our experience—indeed of all things and all experiences, as the Qur'an constantly insists—as theophanies or divine Signs (*āyāt*) is our vast array of unconscious, unexamined, socially reinforced assumptions about what is or isn't somehow "spiritual." The usually overwhelming authority and familiarity of our customary, habitual perception of things means that we naturally tend to think that only extra-ordinary, extreme or bizarrely unusual occurrences and awarenesses could somehow qualify as being spiritual, inspired or otherwise particularly significant. And the ways those unconscious, normally invisible veils of embedded custom and habit can be raised by sudden unexpected shifts in our surroundings or circumstances (immersion in an unfamiliar language or culture, catastrophic illness or other dramatic life-changes, and the

like), revealing unexpected insights and dramatically different perspectives, are of course both a recurrent feature
of our spiritual experience and a fundamental element
throughout literature and many other arts. Indeed as Ibn
'Arabī himself points out in several key passages already
highlighted in the preceding Chapters, every conscious spiritual journey begins with our somehow being fundamentally
"surprised by God," by the freshly awakened revelation of
one or another of the divine qualities or Names.

This same essential paradox of the human condition also
underlies the constant necessity of renewal, creativity, diversity and shifting forms of expression for any effective
form of spiritual teaching and communication—and even a
moment's reflection on those necessities immediately highlights the unavoidable intrinsic limitations, restrictions and
pitfalls of language, especially of writing, in this particular
domain. So it is only fitting that section I of this Chapter
begins with the introduction of a few of the characteristic
features of Ibn 'Arabī's own distinctive and extraordinarily
demanding style of spiritual writing, of his distinctive rhetoric of realization—a discussion that is taken up and illustrated at greater length in Chapter Five below.

The remainder of this Chapter is devoted to Ibn 'Arabī's
influential brief presentation of the essential facets of discernment, or of active, fully realized spiritual intelligence,
that is included in chapter 366 of the *Meccan Illuminations*.
Section II introduces and contextualizes that chapter and
the issues it takes up, while the following two longer sections focus respectively on the initial receptive dimensions
of spiritual discernment, and then on their outwardly active
manifestations in effective communication and right and
beautiful action. Section V then returns to the special spiritual (and rhetorical) role of specific human examples and

exemplars in these discussions—and by extension, throughout Ibn 'Arabī's writings and a host of related traditions of the Islamic humanities. That theme continues in the following, concluding Chapter, which takes up at many levels the deeper connections, parallels and resonances between Ibn 'Arabī's Qur'an-inspired language and the more familiar (at least in translation) poetic masterworks of Rumi, Hafez and 'Attār.

I. DISCERNMENT AND DECONSTRUCTION:
LANGUAGE AND EXAMPLE

The implications for effective spiritual communication of the fundamental paradox quoted at the beginning of this Chapter can be explained schematically in very simple terms. Practically overcoming them, however, is not nearly so simple. If someone trying to teach about spiritual intelligence starts directly with examples and illustrations drawn from the familiar domains of everyday life, it is very hard for the recipients of that teaching to perceive what lies beyond their own determinant mental categories, assumptions, beliefs or—to use Ibn 'Arabī's own favorite expression—their "veils." And if they cannot make that transition to their own inner, spiritually autonomous and authentic, unveiled perception of the actual realities and deeper aims to which their teacher is referring, those students will almost inevitably perceive and apply that teaching in terms of their own already familiar ends and categories—a kind of potent natural spiritual reductionism whose manifestations, dangers and limitations are of course widely apparent everywhere around us in our own (and probably every other) time. At best, such a procedure means that any far-reaching spiritual aims will almost immediately be mis-conceived as a kind of narrowly restrictive, albeit familiar, effort of out-

183

ward ethical purification or mere moral preaching. And more fundamentally, the particular pre-existing individual psychological motivations that must be aroused and utilized if one starts from such worldly appeals are likely either to be quickly exhausted (whenever that limited set of immediate psychic aims is even briefly realized), or else to become powerful intrinsic barriers to any ongoing spiritual development that requires the surrender or contradiction of those initial aims.

Given those formidable and recurrent obstacles, which seem to arise in every human situation, it is fairly obvious why most spiritual teachers—no doubt including Ibn 'Arabī himself—find that the most effective initial rhetorical means are to appeal to what their potential audiences immediately and unavoidably do experience as "what breaks with their habitual perception of reality": to start with those particular (and almost always distinctively individualized) divine Signs that are so unambiguous and overwhelming that they immediately compel a deeper response and more lastingly effective kind of motivation. Yet the immediately ensuing paradox and practical challenge is that the effective teacher must then find some lasting way to convey the complex *universality* of those deeper operative spiritual principles that were illuminated by that initially illuminating breakthrough—and which ultimately apply intimately to every area of our existence. That absolutely essential further integration of spiritual experience and active intelligence is of course extremely difficult to carry out, and it is normally something that—certainly in traditional Islamic contexts, and most likely in other civilizational settings as well—has been explored and actualized in a range of constantly evolving social and institutional arrangements, operative contexts which are only feebly and very inadequately reflected in any sort of strictly literary sources. Moreover, and well in keeping with the same initial paradox, we normally find, throughout history, that any of the older, more outwardly visible institutional arrangements constructed for this purpose themselves inevitably undergo the same confluence of corrupting reductive influences already mentioned, in ways that are again only too readily identifiable. So how could—and does—Ibn 'Arabī respond to that profoundly paradoxical challenge?

At the risk of oversimplification, one can indicate at least four major ways that he attempts to overcome those obstacles—while constantly striving at the same time, as we have seen repeatedly illustrated throughout the preceding Chapters, to construct a remarkably effective web of literary mirrors for catching and evoking those revelatory and initially "wondrous" spiritual states and experiences. Taken alone, each of those possible approaches to effective intelligent contextualization of our spiritual life has its own immediately obvious shortcomings and pitfalls, which had already been highlighted by any number of earlier Muslim spiritual teachers—and by their often vehement critics as well. In that respect, one of the distinctive features of Ibn 'Arabī's own unique language,[1] which makes it hard for his readers and students to become too dangerously locked into any of those perennial dangers, is the way that he—like his own inspired sources, especially the Qur'an—constantly combines and shifts between each of these possible responses, indeed often within the same sentence. That characteristically shifting, protean language of his is particularly obvious when his own works are compared with those of his commentators and their critics alike—all of whom, with rare exceptions, tended to exclusively favor one or the other of these different ways forward.

The most familiar and celebrated approach in his works is of course his systematic development and constantly repeated reminders of the universal metaphysical perspectives of the Qur'an. That particularly pervasive approach—which actually constitutes the historical figure of Ibn 'Arabī usually imagined by those many fervent partisans and critics who, through the centuries, have based their judgments on his *Fuṣūṣ al-Hikam* and its elaborate philosophical and theological commentaries—has now been studied and amply illustrated in a range of definitive scholarly works in Western languages, so that there should be no need to elaborate it here.[2]

The other three possible responses, each designed to help his readers break through the unconscious inner veils obstructing a deeper awareness of the inherent spiritual dimensions and challenges of their existence, are briefly discussed in the remainder of this section, with reference to further detailed studies in each case. The first of those other approaches is Ibn 'Arabī's ongoing subversive de-construction of his readers' common religious language, designed to restore a more direct awareness of the actual, immediate references of those symbols and allusions. The second response, particularly well illustrated in the selections from chapter 366 below, involves Ibn 'Arabī's Socratic tools for highlighting, in memorably pointed and politically sensitive ways, the fundamental differences between culturally prevailing ungrounded beliefs (potently masquerading as religious knowledge and claims of divine authority) and the radically different domain of actual spiritual awareness and illuminated intelligence. And the final, particularly pervasive and substantial, literary method has to do with his remarkable use of multivalent individual examples to illustrate, and simultaneously question or qualify, each of his arguments—an aspect of his writing as yet relatively un-studied, but which remains (for reasons discussed below) one of the keys to its lasting success and spiritual effective-ness.

One revealing way of approaching the fundamental para-dox that we began with—of the inherent tensions involved in any effort to speak or write about the actual realities and process of spiritual intelligence—is to start with the diffi-culties that are already so apparent when we simply com-pare the semantic resources of English and of Ibn 'Arabī's own Qur'anic language. In English, "discernment" seems to come closer than any other potential synonym for this complex process because it still retains a relatively active (not entirely reified or abstract conceptual) sense, and above all because it conveys simultaneously the multiple, inte-grally related meanings of an ongoing inner faculty of true perception and penetrating insight; deep understanding; good judgment expressed in action; and sound discrimina-tion—both between facets of understanding, and between the possible active expressions of our right understanding.

In addition, and perhaps most importantly of all, it is still universally applicable to all facets of human experi-ence: intellectual, ethical, practical, and especially the vast domain of our aesthetic realities and judgments. As we have already seen in the preceding Chapter Three, with re-gard to the comprehensive and culminating spiritual virtue of *ihsān* (in the hadith of Gabriel), in Ibn 'Arabī's Arabic, just as in English, one of the greatest veils to accurate spiri-tual perception was overcoming the normal, socially engrained tendency to separate and compartmentalize those relevant expressions of our intrinsic natural capacity—in

187

all those outwardly different domains—for what is actually spiritual contemplation, perception and judgment.

Yet if Ibn 'Arabī's own language for those multiple aspects of spiritual intelligence has its own problems, to which he turns our attention again and again, one has only to align his own underlying Arabic expressions with their normal English translated equivalents to perceive the phenomenologically far richer and more fitting resources of the Qur'anic language—a persistent contrast that constantly bedevils all translators and serious students of his writing.[3] Thus in English, we are frequently forced to resort to familiar abstract nouns such as wisdom, knowledge, integrity, good judgment, insight, recollection, and so on—almost all of which have Arabic "originals" (in the *masdar* or participial forms) meant to convey an active, ongoing, process-linked, "verbal" reality that can only be approximated in English by systematically substituting, in ways that are often painfully forced or artificial, gerundive forms like knowing, being aware, recollecting, and so on. Even more frustratingly, the richly evocative and multi-faceted Qur'anic language applied to all these common dimensions of spiritual intelligence—that is, to all human efforts at deciphering and responding appropriately to the infinite divine Signs—are often expressed in distinctive "reflexive" Arabic verbal forms that manage to convey explicitly with a single word, in ways that would properly require whole sentences in English, the intrinsic *inter-active dimensions* of simultaneous receptivity, internal activity, and external expression which are such a characteristic feature of most human spiritual activity.[4]

Moreover, some of the most fundamental Arabic roots for referring to the processes of spiritual intelligence already contain and express a particularly well-adapted broad family of multiple aptly related meanings and connotations, expressed across a range of visibly related grammatical and verbal forms, that defies any English translation. For example, the key word *hikma* and its related forms often refer simultaneously to wisdom (both theoretical and practical), to wise practical judgment, to its further effects (*hukm*), and to the lasting intrinsic solidity of those wise results. Much the same breadth also applies to the most common root for intelligence, again both theoretical and practical, and to its expression in all the moral and spiritual virtues (*'aql*). Finally, in every Arabic discussion of these realities, Ibn 'Arabī can rely on his readers' intuitive awareness of the immediate, unmediated metaphysical correspondences embedded in the intrinsic linkage of most of these key Arabic expressions with their corresponding "spiritual roots" in the constantly repeated divine Names of the Qur'an. In other words, his underlying metaphysics of theophanies or divine Self-manifestations, which can appear so contrived or artificially imposed—after all the necessary philosophical and conceptual explanations required in any Western language—is in fact far more immediately, linguistically embedded in the deepest structures of its original language.

As a result, Ibn 'Arabī's distinctive treatment of the language of the Qur'an (and its further reflections and exemplifications in the hadith) typically has a relatively clear—if to Western readers rather unfamiliar—underlying intention. Unlike most spiritual writers, in any tradition, who are faced with the creative challenges of forging their own phenomenologically adequate language for expressing their spiritual experience and insight,[5] his efforts are usually focused instead on restoring his readers to a deeper, spiritually authentic apprehension and renewed, consciously ex-

189

istential awareness of the already incomparably powerful and spiritually appropriate language and symbolism of the Qur'an. Most often this involves simultaneously exposing and subtly subverting or deconstructing the complex of unconscious veils—of assumed meanings, beliefs, paradigms and assumptions—constituted by the intersection of each reader's personal history and psychic predilections with the particular accumulated religious, social and cultural traditions of their milieu.

Now this brief summary description of his rhetorical methods might sound outwardly like what was always required or attempted by each of the earlier commentators and critics who fabricated those familiar interpretive traditions of the Islamic religious sciences in the first place. But it leaves out what is precisely most fundamental and unique (and apparently inimitable, to judge by the lack of any even remotely equivalent subsequent figures) about Ibn 'Arabī's own approach. That is his mysterious rhetorical ability to bring about this "undermining" of unconscious interpretations not by openly criticizing or even replacing them, but by somehow effectively evoking the inner connection, within each particular reader, between the actual Qur'anic words and the corresponding unique Signs (āyāt) in each reader's own experience. Those efforts have been increasingly studied, analyzed and illuminated by the most recent generation of his interpreters and translators,[6] but one must turn to a handful of literary geniuses who worked in several other Islamicate languages, yet equally inspired by the same formative Qur'anic models and structures, to find any equivalent of this strange power to so effectively elicit such immediately revelatory and transforming states of awareness.

190

SELF-DECEPTION AND UNCONSCIOUS "BELIEF"

As any teacher of religious studies at the university level still quickly discovers, nothing could be a greater veil to the serious understanding and penetration of classical religious texts and spiritual traditions than what beginning students have been socially conditioned to think of as "religious"—and it does not seem to matter much whether the attitude toward those initially unconscious restrictive assumptions happens to be positive or the opposite, or what particular cultural forms and contents are involved. Not surprisingly, then, one constant theme and approach throughout all of Ibn 'Arabī's writings intended for the religiously learned audiences of his day is his ongoing, persistently probing and subtly provocative efforts to raise to consciousness (and thereby call into question) the unexamined assumptions, implicit beliefs and guiding attitudes of those learned scholars, in many very different religious and scientific/philosophical disciplines of his time, who naturally tended to consider their own forms of learning as unimpeachable and certain knowledge.

Here it is important to point out that Ibn 'Arabī's works, including above all the *Meccan Illuminations*—unlike the writings of most Muslim authors traditionally identified (at least in Western translations and studies) as "Sufis," "mystics" and the like—were paradoxically directed primarily to that wider body of learned Muslim scholars. Thus his works often presuppose throughout an extraordinarily wide acquaintance with the most diverse fields of religious knowledge, and simultaneously with the most advanced stages of spiritual practice and accomplishment. The remarkably far-reaching vision and intentions underlying that peculiar, but consistent rhetorical approach and choice of highly learned

191

Muslim audiences have been highlighted in a series of on-going interpretive studies, including an earlier study of the Shaykh's political and legal philosophy (partially drawing on the same chapter 366 discussed below), and a more comprehensive forthcoming book outlining the broader development of those insights throughout the *Futūhāt*.[7]

Once again, what is essential and sufficient for this Chapter is to note that in this case, as in the preceding one, Ibn 'Arabī's distinctive critical approach to his original audience of learned religious authorities seems to stand almost alone—although its deeper spiritual intentions are clearly and so vividly paralleled, in vernacular Muslim literatures, in the more openly critical and popularly accessible language of masterful spiritual poets like Hafez, Rumi, or Yunus Emre. Just as with his constant deconstruction of fossilized forms of traditional religious language and institutions, Ibn 'Arabī's pervasive Socratic criticism with regard to the adherents of traditional fields of learning cannot honestly be attached to or confused with some particular, already existing ostensible alternative to what had previously passed for real knowledge or authority in each case. Instead, his penetratingly subversive questioning and critical rhetoric are all carefully designed in such a particular way—most familiar to Western audiences in the classic forms of theater, or in Plato's dramatic dialogues—so as to prick the conscience of the individual learned reader, to awaken each individual's poignant awareness, wherever the necessary aptitude exists, of their own contrasting experience of the actual realities of spiritual intelligence and awareness, in ways that will naturally be translated back into correspondingly appropriate manifestations of wisdom (the fruits of *ihsān*) in all their own domains of active life and responsibility.[8] This approach is repeatedly illustrated throughout the selections from chapter 366 translated below, perhaps most dramatically in his moving evocation there of one of his personal acquaintances, an outwardly unexceptionable judge of Ceuta who *alone*, he tells us, was able to carry out his functions in a spiritually acceptable and truly appropriate fashion.

THE AMBIGUITIES OF EXAMPLE

The case of this uniquely qualified judge brings us to one of the Shaykh's most intriguing forms of spiritual rhetoric: his highly complex use of individual human examplars. Within most related Islamic literary traditions, including the Sufi ones often apparently closest to Ibn 'Arabī's own interests and background, audiences were abundantly familiar with all sorts of rhetorical devices involving references to particular individuals and anecdotes, whether scriptural and literary or more recent, usually presented as memorable illustrations and (often hyperbolic) paragons of this or that particular spiritual virtue or vice. Here again, the Shaykh's abundant use of such anecdotal references (whether legendary, biographical, or often autobiographical) can rarely be reduced to such often simplistic literary forms of exemplification. Instead, his own chosen stories and examples—as is so powerfully illustrated in the case of the archetypal figure of "the Mahdī" in the chapter that concerns us here—typically function as problematically and challengingly as spiritual stories and illustrations taken from real life, whatever their original provenance.

To take what is probably the most accessible example for Western audiences, his anecdotal account of meaningful personal encounters with many of his youthful spiritual acquaintances and teachers in Andalusia and North Africa, partially translated as *Sufis of Andalusia*,[9] is radically different from the considerable surviving literatures, in Arabic or even other Islamic languages, that are ordinarily termed "hagiographies" or *malfūzāt* (notes of a spiritual guide's oral teaching), precisely in its overall governing intention. While it also teaches particular spiritual lessons, like those other familiar Islamic literatures, what is more important here is the author's actual guiding insistence on the fact that all of these very different, outwardly often quite ordinary people and their stories, carefully drawn from every gender, class, age, and walk of life—are not only real, but pointedly representative of the wider surrounding world of spiritual realities, tests, lessons, guides, and meaningful experiences in which we all live and participate. Or to put it a bit more pointedly, as Ibn 'Arabī himself forcefully and repeatedly stresses in the long and as yet largely untranslated opening sections of his book from which those stories were extracted: these examples are meant to instruct us not about "Sufis"—if that is understood as a specially spiritual group somehow set apart from the ordinary Muslims of his homeland—but precisely about the intrinsic spiritual situations and opportunities encountered by *all* human beings. They are meant to have the same illuminating, potentially transforming consequences as spiritually effective films do in our contemporary world.

The same essential observation applies at least equally to Ibn 'Arabī's use of anecdotes and references to exemplary individuals throughout the *Meccan Illuminations*, as practiced readers of that work quickly discover. And in that respect, of course, modern readers unfamiliar with Islamic history and traditions need to be reminded (by translators and interpreters) or else to constantly remind themselves of the pervasive presence throughout this work of the constant background of unnamed, implicit references to related illustrations, stories and spiritually significant incidents from the lives of those spiritual exemplars who were normally assumed and shared by Ibn 'Arabī and his original Muslim audiences. Most important in this respect, of course, is their assumed acquaintance with traditional accounts of the life of the Prophet and his Companions and the early Muslim community, but also with other significant prophetic figures from the Qur'an and related traditional Islamic sources (where the underlying stories rarely coincide exactly with same figures in canonical Christian and Jewish traditions). In relation to this book's overall theme of spiritual intelligence, it is particularly revealing to keep in mind that virtually all the unquestioned exemplars of those realized spiritual virtues, for Ibn 'Arabī and his original audiences, were figures who were above all actively, effectively and responsibly involved in all the constantly testing demands of political and social life "in the world": the Prophet Muhammad and his Companions, Abraham, Jacob, Joseph, Moses, David, Solomon, and so on. Ibn 'Arabī's characteristic insistence on the discovery, practice and perfection of all the principles of spiritual intelligence within the crucible of everyday human existence should not seem nearly so unfamiliar or problematic if we can simply keep the real lives, responsibilities and accomplishments of those particular spiritual exemplars clearly in mind.

But like the effective spiritual teachers in every religious tradition, he was nonetheless forced to work very hard to remind his thoughtful readers that those spiritual exemplars were not—as pious believers everywhere do tend to assume— simply "super-men" of an entirely unrelated species, but real people who had nonetheless passed through the same transforming tests and Fires as other mortals. In this respect, it is especially revealing to observe and reflect on the distinctive ways that Ibn 'Arabī typically juxtaposes his allusions to those more historically distant figures, whether from Islamic tradition or earlier Sufism, with more detailed firsthand accounts of related experiences and stories involving himself or (as in *Sufis of Andalusia*) real people he has personally known.

II. THE MAHDĪ'S HELPERS AND THE IMAM OF THE AGE

Chapter 366 of the *Meccan Illuminations*, which begins by quoting a number of long accounts from the hadith concerning the Islamic messianic figure of the Mahdī, the "Rightly Guided One" who will come to restore the true Religion and purify and guide humanity at the end of time, has often been read and studied apart from the rest of that immense work—although any attempt to understand and interpret it without reference to all the demanding preceding preparation Ibn 'Arabī had provided and surely intended is likely to be rather misleading. Reflecting the richness of this enigmatic, multi-faceted text, I have already published two other interpretive studies dealing respectively with its illumination of Ibn 'Arabī's unique political and legal philosophy, and with the ways it illustrates his consistent theme of the inalienable ethical, political and spiritual responsibility of each human being.[10]

Those two earlier themes intersect, of course, around the crucial question (in each of those different domains) of the roots and nature of true spiritual and religious authority. So here our interpretive focus is concentrated instead on the key central section of that same chapter, which deals explicitly, but in a very concise and relatively accessible form, with the basic sources and active expressions of spiritual intelligence. These same topics are of course elaborated throughout thousands of other pages of the *Futūhāt*, but the special advantage of this section is that here all these different practical facets of spiritual discernment are spelled out clearly in a single brief passage, so that it is possible to see something of the overall forest as well as the individually fascinating trees. At the same time, this passage offers a most effective illustration of Ibn 'Arabī's own distinctive language and forms of spiritual communication that we have just discussed.

BECOMING "RIGHTLY-GUIDED"

To summarize the conclusion of those earlier studies, it is highly likely that the figure called *al-mahdī*, the "rightly guided one" mentioned in Ibn 'Arabī's title for this chapter 366, far from referring uniquely to some particularly effective and powerful warrior chieftain in some distant time, is also meant to represent precisely—if only potentially at first—each properly prepared reader who begins to realize that ever-present divine Guidance in action. That is, the rightly guided person is whoever, by actualizing that divine inspiration, can also begin to become the *Imām al-waqt*, that "Guide-of-the-present instant," as Ibn 'Arabī actually describes that mysterious figure throughout the central sections of this chapter, largely abandoning his earlier appellation as *al-mahdī*.

If that is so, then these emblematic personalities, with their apparently familiar messianic titles and stories, are actually translated here—as is often the case with each earlier prophet and his initial supporters, in many other passages of Ibn 'Arabī—into the archetypal facets or stages of a single repeated process of spiritual transformation. For actually realizing the spiritual qualities of this Mahdī's "Guides" and "Ministers"—as Ibn 'Arabī goes on to describe them here in detail—necessarily does begins to make us more rightly guided, while by the same token it also makes us a more effective living guide and model (the literal meaning of *imām al-waqt* and *al-imām al-mahdī*) for all those with whom we interact. Indeed we have only to look at Ibn 'Arabī's own life and the eventual impact of his work—with its still ongoing and fascinatingly far-reaching influences—to see precisely how that wider process really works. And in fact, as he constantly points out, we can only ever see as much of that eschatological process as we have already begun to realize for ourselves.

Yet this is a process, as Ibn 'Arabī and the Qur'an alike insist, that ultimately engages every human being. Without the active discernment of that universal divine guidance—which is what alone makes us truly human (the theomorphic spiritual reality of *insān*)—each person (each *bashar* or "human-animal," that is) is necessarily "guided" instead by a constantly shifting combination of their inner impulses and fears, together with their even more unstable surrounding milieu of social and cultural programming. Within the individual and in larger social groupings alike, both those unavoidable sorts of purported guidance are in constant, never-ending conflict, disorder and states of repetitive change. Yet it is precisely those providentially arranged perpetual conflicts, with their distinctive inner and outer "fires," which eventually lead people to seek out and discover—and then to creatively translate into practice—that genuinely divine guidance which moves them toward the perception and eventual realization of a wholly different kind of order.[11]

Seen from that perspective, this entire chapter 366 thus turns out to be a kind of epitome of the entire *Futūhāt*—or rather, the decisive point at which each responsible reader

198

is openly challenged to begin to translate that work's central practical spiritual teachings, so carefully summarized here, into the kind of effectively and appropriately realized practice that is itself, in Ibn 'Arabī's perspective, the constantly repeated "end of time." For each instant of inspired awareness of that true spiritual guidance takes place quite literally "beyond (earthly) time" and simultaneously returns to that trans-temporal realm as the lasting spiritual fruits—in the central Qur'anic symbolism—of our purified intention and all the rightly guided actions flowing from that enlightened awareness and discernment.

INTRODUCING THE HELPERS

The key enigmatic figures of the Mahdī's "Helpers" or "Ministers" in Ibn 'Arabī's account are not actually a part of the standard hadith accounts of the Mahdī. So following the opening long quotation of those traditional accounts, punctuated by Ibn 'Arabī's significantly repeated insistence that this mysterious personage follows the reality of Muhammad in every respect, these figures suddenly appear out of nowhere, with the following detailed description of their functions and even their native language:[12]

> He will have divine men upholding his call (to the true Religion) and aiding him in his victory; they are the Helpers. They will bear the burdens of (his) government and help him to carry out all the details of what God has imposed on him....
>
> God will appoint as his Helpers a group (of people) whom He has kept hidden for him in the secret recesses of His Unseen (spiritual world). God has acquainted (these Helpers), through unveiling and immediate witnessing, with the realities and the

199

contents of God's Command concerning His servants. So the Mahdī makes his decisions and judgments on the basis of consultation with them, since they are the true Knowers who really know what is There....

Among the secrets of the knowledge of the Mahdī's Helpers whom God has appointed as ministers for him is His saying: *The victorious support of the people of faith is obligatory for Us* (30:47), for they follow in the footsteps of those among the Companions (of the Prophet) who sincerely fulfilled what they had pledged to God. These Helpers are from the non-Arab peoples;[13] none of them is Arab, although they speak only Arabic.... So his Helpers are the guides (*al-hudāt*), while he is the rightly-guided one (*al-mahdī*). And this is the extent of what the Mahdī attains of the knowledge of God, with the aid of his Helpers.

Then Ibn 'Arabī goes on to describe the core spiritual qualities, accomplishments and forms of inspired knowing associated with this particular spiritual stage, connecting his hesitant numbering of those distinctive spiritual virtues with the purposefully vague number of the Helpers, in an apparent allusion to the mysterious Qur'anic account of the disputed number of Sleepers and the years of their sleep, in the narrative of the corresponding Sura of the Cave (18:22, 25-26):[14]

....Now I *do* know what (spiritual qualities) are needed by the Mahdī's Helper. So if there is only one Helper, then everything he needs is united in that one person; and if they are more than one, then there are not more than nine of them.... And the

200

totality of what he needs to have performed for him by his Helpers are nine things; there is not a tenth, nor can they be any fewer.

THE SPIRITUAL QUALITIES OF THE IMĀM

Ibn ʿArabī then briefly enumerates the nine distinctive spiritual characteristics of these Helpers (described in detail in the following two sections below), and again insists that all nine of these qualities are required by these guiding figures, no matter what their exact number may be. However, these guiding Helpers themselves (like their Mahdī) are not even mentioned again in the rest of this chapter, where these different spiritual attributes are instead attributed directly to the "Imām," "Imām of the Age," "Rightly-guided Imām," and so on—or else more generally to the accomplished spiritual Knowers and Friends of God. Perhaps especially important here is his insistence, at the very end of this long discussion, that these particular spiritual qualities and abilities normally can only become manifest, at least in their completely adequate form, in various different individuals: in other words, that the full realization and earthly manifestation of these equally essential spiritual qualities is perhaps necessarily collective or *co-operative* by its very nature:

> Now these nine things are not combined all together for any Imām among the leaders of Religion and the vice-regents of God and His Prophet until the Day of the Rising, except for this Rightly-guided Imām....

201

III. DISCERNMENT AND SPIRITUAL RECEPTIVITY

It quickly becomes clear that the nine distinctive spiritual qualities of these Helpers (or rather of "the Imām") discussed in detail in this central section of chapter 366[15] all have to do either with (a) the proper reception and comprehension of divine guidance (the first three qualities); or else (b) with the further translation of that guidance into effective action and responsible spiritual communication and guidance of others (the last six). Thus, far from being unique to a single future Mahdī and his putative advisors, all nine of those spiritual qualities are clearly illustrated, at the very least, in what each reader will already know of the lives and teachings of many of the prophets and saints, whatever the religious tradition and sacred history in question.

But before we begin to explore Ibn 'Arabī's description of each of those distinctive spiritual qualities, let us stop and notice something much more important: what he has, rather surreptitiously, actually arranged for his attentive readers at this point. For his approach to these qualities is neither a personal interpretation of Islamic scriptural (or other Sufi) sources; nor is it a personal teaching about these particular qualities in themselves. What he has in fact done for each reader in this section is to set up a very complex, peculiarly interactive (indeed positively probing) mirror for the actual state of their own spiritual life and experiences—including all the different planes and sources and decisive verifications of those experiences—precisely insofar as each one of these nine essential qualities has already been partially actualized, intimated, or at least foreshadowed in their own uniquely individual experience, or in the lives of persons they may have personally encountered.

As we have seen in the preceding Chapters, this sort of powerfully probing mirroring takes place throughout the *Futūhāt*, but rarely do we find such far-reaching, spiritually essential issues so openly at stake and so carefully and sometimes passionately described as in this chapter 366. Since any detailed discussion of Ibn ʿArabī's often tightly condensed formulae here could easily become a book of its own, here I have simply translated (along with necessary explanations) the essential parts of these phenomenological accounts, leaving it to each reader, as Ibn ʿArabī surely intended, to provide their own indispensable concrete exemplifications of each of these spiritual qualities.

These short selections are striking illustrations of Ibn ʿArabī's typical rhetorical methods for suggesting, highlighting and gradually awakening the corresponding sorts of spiritual awareness. In each case, he first presents his readers with a scriptural phrase or allusion that seems to apply only to the great prophets, saints and some far-off future paragons of each distinctive spiritual ability. But that seemingly familiar verse or hadith is eventually followed, in each instance, by a kind of unexpected metaphysical punch-line which suddenly forces his readers to reconsider and reflect much more deeply on all the previously hidden (or as yet unconceived) ways in which that particular scriptural allusion or spiritual realization might actually apply to themselves and to their own circumstances.

"Penetrating Spiritual Vision"

As for penetrating spiritual vision, that is so that his praying[16] to God may be *with (clear) inner vision* (12:108) concerning what he requests in his prayer, not of Him to whom the prayer is addressed. So he regards the inner essence of each (divine Reality or Name) to Whom he is praying[17] and sees what is possible for (Him) to do in response to his prayer; then he prays to Him for that, even if it be by way of special pleading.[18]

As for those things where he sees that (God) will not (favorably) respond to his prayer, then he prays to Him, without any special pleading, to carry out the divine Argument (*hujja*) in this special case,[19] since the Mahdī is God's Argument for the people of his time, and that (i.e., his special function as divine *hujja*) is part of the rank of the prophets and participates in that rank. God said: [*Say: "This is my path:*] *I pray to God with inward vision, I and whoever follows me."* (12:108). (God) reported that (to us) through His Prophet, and the Mahdī is among those who follow him, because the Prophet does not err in his praying to God, nor does the person who (truly) follows him,[20] since he follows the trace of (the Prophet's) footsteps. And that is what appears in the (hadith) report describing the Mahdī, that the prophet said: "He follows in the trace of my footsteps, and he does not err."[21] This is the (inner state of) immunity from error in praying to God, and it is attained by many of the *Friends* (*of God*), or indeed by all of them.[22]

Among the attributes of this penetrating vision are that the person possessing it sees the luminous and fiery spirits (i.e., the angels and the jinn) without those spirits themselves wanting to appear or take on a form (for that person).

204

But if this key spiritual quality might at first seem impossibly difficult and remote, Ibn ʿArabī goes on to describe other manifestations of that same penetrating vision which are clearly inseparable from far more familiar levels of everyone's spiritual insight and awareness,[23] for which many readers can supply their own dramatic personal examples, from spiritual dreams and decisive intuitions to all the manifestations of what he elsewhere describes (Chapter Five below) as the ever-deepening recognition of all of existence as a mysterious divine "shadow-Play":

> Likewise (as a result of this spiritual insight) they perceive the people of the Unseen,[24] even when they want to be veiled and not to appear to (ordinary human) vision. And it is also (characteristic) of this penetrating vision that if the spiritual realities (*maʿānī*) take on bodily form, then they recognize (the underlying realities) in those very forms, and they know without any hesitation which spiritual meaning it is that became embodied (in that particular form).[25]

"UNDERSTANDING THE DIVINE ADDRESS
WHEN IT IS DELIVERED"

The next distinctive form of spiritual receptivity Ibn ʿArabī mentions begins with a well-known verse of the Qur'an which was normally understood—at least by certain theologians[26]—to speak of the highest and rarest forms of theophany, reserved for each of the great prophets. But in radical contrast to that view, he quickly makes clear here that his central concern is those personal veils—and corresponding unveilings and forms of guiding spiritual intuition, perception, and inspiration—which are far more intimate

205

and familiar to each of us than we might at first want to admit:

> Now as for understanding the divine address when it is delivered,[27] this is (summarized) in His saying: *And it was not for any ordinary man (bashar) that God should speak to him except through inspiration or from behind a veil or He sends a messenger* (42:51).
>
> So as for the divine address through inspiration,[28] that is what He delivers to their *hearts* as something newly reported (to them),[29] so that through this they gain knowledge of some particular matter—i.e., of what is contained in that new (inspired) report. But if it does not happen in that way (as something newly received from outside oneself), then it is not a (divine) inspiration or address. For instance, some people (may) find in their hearts the knowledge of something of the necessary forms of knowledge among people in general.[30] That is genuine knowledge, but it is not obtained from a (particular divine) address, and our discussion is only concerned with that form of divine address which is called "inspiration." [...][31]
>
> And as for His saying *or from behind a veil*, that is a divine address delivered to the (person's) *hearing* and not to the heart, so that the person to whom it is delivered perceives it and then understands from that what was intended by the One Who caused him to hear it. Sometimes that happens through the forms of theophany, in which case that (particular) divine form addresses the person, and that form itself is the veil. Then (the person having this condition of spiritual insight) understands from that divine ad-

dress the knowledge of what it indicates, and he knows that (this theophanic form) is a veil and that the Speaker (i.e., God) is behind that veil.

Yet again this is followed by the sudden punch-line, the sort of metaphysical formula designed to leave each reader reflecting, recalling, and re-examining so many dimensions of even our most mundane experience of the world and its infinite Signs:

> Of course not everyone who perceives a form of the divine theophany realizes that that form *is* God. For the person possessing this state (of spiritual insight) is only distinguished from other people by the fact that he recognizes that that form, although it is a "veil," is itself precisely the Truly Real's theophany for him.[32]
>
> And as for His saying *or He sends a messenger*, that is (the divine address) He sends down with an angel or that is brought to us by the mortal human messenger when either sort of messenger conveys *God's Speaking* in this particular way (i.e., perceived as an individual address coming from God)....[33] But if either sort of messenger (simply) conveys or gives expression to knowledge that he found (already) in his soul (and not as a distinct message given him by God), then that is not *divine* Speaking.
>
> Now it may happen that the messenger and the form (of the message) occur together, as in the very act of writing (the revealed Book). For the Book is a messenger, and it is also the veil over the Speaker (i.e., God), so that it causes you to understand what It/He brought. But that (i.e., the divinely revealed nature of the Book) would not be so if the messen-

ger wrote on the basis of his own knowledge: it is only the case if the messenger wrote on the basis of a (divine) new-Speaking (*hadīth*) addressed to him in those very words he writes down. So when it is not like that, then it is not (divine) new-Speaking. This is the general rule....

So all of this (i.e., all three of these forms of theophanic perception) is part of the divine address directed to the person who possesses this (spiritual) station.[34]

"KNOWING HOW TO TRANSLATE FROM GOD"

In contrast, the third quality of spiritual receptivity and proper responsiveness (*adab*) introduced here is unambiguously described in such terms that everyone who has ever "created," whatever the form of art or performance in question, will immediately recognize the sort of inspiration to which Ibn 'Arabī is referring:

As for the knowledge of how to translate from God, that belongs to every person to whom God speaks through inspiration or the inspired delivery (of a particular divine address, *ilqā'*), since (in such cases) the translator is the one who creates the forms of the spoken or written letters he brings into existence, while the *spirit* of those forms is God's Speaking and nothing else.[35] But if someone translates (into word or form) from (their own, non-inspired) knowledge, then they are inevitably not a "translator" (in this particular spiritual sense)....

Ibn 'Arabī then goes on here (at IV, 333.1-10) to distinguish carefully between this state of inspired vision which is typical of the perception of the Friends of God and the people of spiritual unveiling, on the one hand, and the purely theoretical references, by those religious scholars "who are learned in the outward forms (of the revelation),"[36] to the "language of states"—a term they employ in their standard theological interpretations of the frequent Qur'anic references to the "speech" of what we ordinarily call inanimate objects or lower creatures. The former group, those true Knowers who directly experience the living, theophanic nature of all beings, are able to see directly for themselves that "everything other than God really *is* alive and speaking, in the very nature of things," while the latter group "are veiled by the thickest of veils." Then there follows, so typical of Ibn 'Arabī's method of writing, the sort of sudden, peremptory concluding imperative that is really a book in itself:

> ... *Thus there is nothing in the world but Translator,*[37] *if it is translated from divine Speaking. So understand!*

IV. Spiritual Discernment and Right Action

With regard to the six remaining more active, creative qualities of spiritual intelligence needed by "the Imām"—a term which Ibn 'Arabī directly identifies elsewhere in the *Futūhāt* with every responsible human being[38]—once again the same rhetorical procedure governs Ibn 'Arabī's presentation. At first, just as with the messianic figure of the Mahdī, the unprepared reader's immediate reaction here is that Ibn 'Arabī, in describing this new authoritative figure, must be only giving the idealized qualities of an almost mythical being, presenting a sort of perfection and divinely inspired wisdom that exists only in the tales of the prophets and

209

saints, sometime safely after their death or in the far-distant future. But then other parts of this same description gradually oblige his attentive readers to begin reflecting, at the very least, on the extraordinary spectrum of degrees of approximation to (and corresponding distance from) each of these ideal spiritual qualities which actually do exist in other real people we do know—and even perhaps in our own experience. For it is clear that something like this inspired practical wisdom actually does exist, if only from those unforgettable situations, as we have all also experienced, when such inspiration and divine guidance, which we ordinarily took for granted, has turned out to be so terribly and painfully lacking.

Then, at the ensuing stage of realization, Ibn 'Arabī's thoughtful reader necessarily begins to reflect on the possible source and conditions of such inspiration and practical wisdom that is already visible in each of these domains— especially when and as we actually do begin to discover in ourselves (and simultaneously encounter in others) at least the seeds and memorable expressions of each of these distinctive forms of spiritual intelligence.

"Appointing the Ranks of the Holders of Authority"

This is one of the spiritual qualities of the Helpers/Imām which is most immediately and obviously comparable to those more familiar phenomena of our spiritual life, in every domain—beginning with parenting, family life, and all the wider forms of "management" required in every area of our social existence—which depend upon our spiritual discernment, especially our often inexplicable intuitive awareness (or lack thereof) of the inner states, capacities and limitations of all those with whom we daily interact:

As for appointing the ranks of the holders of authority, that is the knowledge of what each rank rightfully requires (in order to assure the) kinds of welfare for which it was created. The person possessing this knowledge looks at the soul of the person whom he wants to place in a position of authority and weighs the appropriateness of that person for that rank. If he sees that there is the right equilibrium between the person and the post, without any excess or deficiency, then he gives him that authority; and if the person is over-qualified there is no harm in that. But if the person is inadequate to the position, he does not entrust him with that authority, because he lacks the knowledge that would qualify him for that rank, so that he would inevitably commit injustice.

At this point, Ibn 'Arabī suddenly—but with no outward emphasis or warning—points to one of the most essential elements and manifestations of spiritual intelligence: our mysterious, but absolutely essential, shared spiritual dimensions of conscience and our inner intuitive awareness of what is spiritually right and appropriate behavior (and the opposite). Like so many other fundamental dimensions of spiritual intelligence, this essential human capacity usually operates without much direct awareness, and only becomes partly conscious in difficult testing situations where there is no apparent external precedent and guidance—or, as Ibn 'Arabī pointedly highlights here, in those constantly repeated (and usually quite memorable) learning situations where the inner absence of that active spiritual awareness is so dramatically absent:

For this (inner ignorance of the true reality of the divine revelation) is the root of all injustice in the holders of authority, since we hold it to be impossible that someone could (truly) know (a particular divine command) and then deviate from the judgment (required by) his knowledge all at once. This is something that is considered possible by those learned in the external forms,[39] although we ourselves consider that this "possible" thing never actually occurs in reality. It is indeed a difficult question.

Now it is because of this (inner knowledge of people's souls and of the truly divine commands) that the Mahdī "fills the world with justice and equity," just as "it was filled with injustice and oppression."[40] *Because in our view (true spiritual) knowing necessarily and inevitably implies action (in accordance with it)*; so if it does not do so, then it is not really knowledge, even if it appears in the (outward) form of knowledge.[41]

Ibn 'Arabī then goes on to discuss at some length the importance for the Mahdī—as for any wise ruler—to appoint judges and authorities who not only have the right formal knowledge of the appropriate provisions of the divinely revealed Pathway, but in whom that inner knowing also fully controls their own personal prejudices,[42] so that they will always act according to their knowing, and will not—like "those learned in the outward forms" of religion—instead twist their learning to gratify their own and others' particular worldly interests.[43]

"Compassion in Anger"

The next spiritual quality Ibn 'Arabī mentions is particularly distinctive, in that it focuses on a subtle, but critically important practical dimension of spiritual intelligence that every responsible parent—and ideally, all those in any other positions of authority—must unavoidably recognize, learn and practice on repeated occasions:

> As for "compassion in anger," that is only in the *divinely* prescribed penalties and punishment, since in everything else (i.e., in merely human judgments) there is anger without any compassion at all.... For if a human being gets angry of his own accord, his anger does not contain compassion in any respect. But if one becomes angry for God's sake, then one's anger is God's Anger—and God's Anger is never free from being mixed with the divine Compassion. Because (God's) Compassion, since it preceded (His) Anger,[44] entirely covers all the creatures and *encompasses every thing* (7:156). [...]
>
> Therefore this Mahdī does not become angry except for God's sake, so that his anger does not go beyond (what is required in) upholding *God's limits*[45] that He has prescribed; this is just the opposite of the (ordinary) person who becomes angry because of his own desires or (something happening) contrary to his own personal aims. And likewise the person who becomes angry (only) for God's sake can only be just and equitable, not tyrannical and unjust.
>
> Now a sign of whoever (rightfully) lays claim to this spiritual station is that if he becomes angry for God's sake while acting in judgment and up-

holding the (divinely prescribed) penalty against the
person with whom he is angry, then his anger dis-
appears once he has finished fulfilling (that religious
duty). (This even happens to the extent that) sometimes he may even go up to the (condemned) person and embrace him and be friendly with him, saying to him "Praise be to God Who has purified you!"
and openly showing his happiness and pleasure with
him. And sometimes (the condemned man) also
becomes friendly with (his judge) after that, for this
(inner fulfillment and realization of the divine commands) is God's Scale (of Justice), and all of (God's)
Compassion comes back to that condemned man.[46]

Ibn 'Arabī then proceeds to illustrate this phenomenon with
the memorable story (at III, 334.2-8) of a personal acquaintance who frequented the same masters of hadith in the city
of Ceuta, a highly respected and unusually modest religious
judge who was famous for his rare charismatic gift (*bāraka*)
of being able to establish peace among feuding parties or
tribes—an ability Ibn 'Arabī attributes to his extreme conscientiousness and concern for maintaining only a disinter-
ested, "divine point of view" in his inner relation to his legal duties. This leads him to take up several other essential
dimensions of spiritual intelligence: our mysterious inner
awareness of the broader divine standards of judgment regarding all of our actions, especially their inner spiritual
aspect, and the ways that awareness is only discovered and
refined in the process of life's ongoing, providential and
divinely arranged "tests."

This (necessary attention to the spiritual sources and
repercussions of all our actions) is also (expressed)
in God's saying: ...*and then We test your records*

214

(of your actions) (47:31). For first of all He tests
(people) with regard to the obligations He has imposed on them [i.e., according to the first half of the
same verse: *And surely we test you all until we know
those of you who make every effort and are perse-
vering...*]. And if they have acted (in accordance
with those divine commands), then their actions are
tested as to whether they have acted for the sake of
the Truly Real (*al-Haqq*), or instead for some other
end.

Likewise it is this (inner spiritual judgment that
is expressed) in God's saying: *On the Day when the
innermost selves are tested* (86:9). For the people
of inner unveiling hold this (judgment of each soul's
innermost being, the *sarīra*) to be *God's Scale* (of
Justice: 42:17, 57:25). Therefore the judge,[47] whenever he is carrying out the (divine) penalties, must
not forget to examine his own soul in order to guard
against the feelings of vengeance and aggression that
happen to souls (in such situations).

Here Ibn 'Arabī continues to explain how his friend, the
above-mentioned qadi in Ceuta, was always careful to examine his conscience in this way, even when his momentary emotions of anger or vengeance did not derive directly
from the case actually before him. In fact, he concludes,
the moral and spiritual factors involved in each case are so
complex that the responsibility of spiritual judgment—in
the ultimate, all-inclusive sense of that term—can only belong to God or those extremely rare individuals divinely
appointed for this role.[48]

Here again Ibn 'Arabī begins with apparently distant,
impossibly elevated examples, such as the Prophet, but dis-

cusses the underlying spiritual principles in ways that eventually make it clear he is pointing to basic dilemmas we all actually encounter in every situation requiring some form of effective spiritual communication. Nothing could be more explicit than his final all-encompassing comment at this point:

> So you must know that God has not appointed anyone but the judge to carry out the penalty against (the guilty person). Therefore no one (else) should be angry with the person who transgresses God's limits, since that (responsibility of anger in imposing the divine penalties) only belongs to the judges in particular, and to God's Messenger insofar as he is judge.
>
> For if (the Messenger) were only communicating (the divine Message)[49] and not judging, then he would not carry out the (divine) Anger against those who reject his call. That matter (i.e., whether or not people actually follow his call) does not involve him at all, and *he is not responsible for their being rightly guided* (2:272).
>
> Thus God says to the Messenger concerning this matter: *You are only responsible for communicating* (the divine Message) (42:48; etc.). So (the Prophet) communicated, and *God caused whomever He wished to listen* (cf. 8:23; etc.) and *caused whomever He wished to be deaf* (cf. 47:23), and they— that is, the prophets—are the most self-restrained of all people.[50] For (even) if the (prophetic) caller were (fully) revealed to the person whom God has made deaf to his call, that person would still not hear the call and would not be changed because of that. And if the (messenger who is) calling out

216

brought together those thus deafened, so that they knew that they did not hear his cry, that would still not help him (to convince them), and he would acknowledge their excuse.

Therefore if the Messenger acted as judge (*hakim*), that was (only because) he was made specifically responsible for the judgment that God had specified for him in that case. And this is a sublime knowledge required by everyone on earth who has authority over (this) world![51]

"THE FORMS OF (SPIRITUAL) SUSTENANCE NEEDED BY THE RULER"

Students of Ibn 'Arabī's works, especially of the *Meccan Illuminations*, gradually discover that he often embeds his most important, or most open and explicitly universal, formulations of central spiritual principles there in relatively hidden or unexpected places—just as, here in chapter 366, these decisive discussions of spiritual discernment and intelligence come after the opening long and tedious citation of traditional accounts of the Mahdī, and as this key chapter itself comes two-thirds of the way through this immense book. So we should not be surprised to encounter some of the Shaykh's most explicit and memorably autobiographical illustrations of the underlying realities of spiritual life at this rather unexpected point (unexpected, at least, in terms of the ostensible subject quoted as our heading here), exactly two-thirds of the way through this enumeration of these nine fundamental dimensions of spiritual intelligence.

Likewise, it is striking that Ibn 'Arabī's treatment of this subject of our proper relations with divine "Sustenance" (*rizq*)—an expression that his readers would ordinarily as-

217

sociate immediately with the material goods of this world—turns out to be almost entirely devoted to the apparently quite different practical question of the proper forms of spiritual aptitude, receptivity, and active response. Here again, it is important to keep in mind what Ibn 'Arabī makes clear elsewhere about *each* human being's essential responsibilities as the true ruler and "Imām" of everything that is in any way under our own control and influence:

> As for the forms of (spiritual) sustenance (*arzāq*) needed by the ruler,[52] this (requires) that he know the kinds of worlds, which are only two—i.e., by "world" I mean the worlds in which this Imām's influence is effective, which are the world of (physical) forms and the world of the souls[53] governing those forms with regard to their physical movements and activities. As for what is beyond those two kinds (i.e., the worlds of the angelic spirits and the jinn), he has no influence over them except for those, such as (individuals in) the world of the jinn, who may wish for him to have influence over their souls.[54]
>
> But as for the luminous world (of the angelic spirits),[55] they are beyond this mortal human world's having any authority over them, for each individual among them has a *known station* (37:163) determined for him by his Lord, so that he does not *descend* (to this earth) *except with the permission of his Lord* (cf. 97:4). Thus whoever wants one of them to be sent down to him must turn to his Lord (in praying) for that, and his Lord (may) order (that angel) and give him permission to do that, in compliance with that person's request—or He may send down an angel of His own accord.

As for the "travelers" among the angels, their *station is known* (37:163), since they are constantly traveling around seeking the sessions of *dhikr*.[56] So "when they find the people of *dhikr*"—who are the people of the Qur'an, those who are (truly) recalling the Qur'an[57]—they do not give precedence to anyone from the sessions of *dhikr* of those who are recalling (something) other than the Qur'an. But if they do not find people recalling the Qur'an and they do find people recalling God—not just reciting—then they come to sit with them and (in the words of the hadith): "they call out to each other: 'Come quickly to what you all desire!',", because that (remembrance of God) is their sustenance. Through it they flourish and in it they have their life.

Now since the Imām knows that, he always keeps a group of people *reciting the Signs*[58] *of God throughout the night* (3:113) and the day. And we ourselves, when we were in Fez in the lands of the Maghrib, used to follow this practice, thanks to the agreement of companions favored by God, who listened to us and readily followed our counsel. But when we no longer had them (with us), we thereby lost this pure (spiritual) work, which is the noblest and most sublime of the forms of (spiritual) sustenance.

So when we no longer had (companions) like those men, we began to take up the diffusion of knowledge,[59] because of those (angelic) spirits whose food is (spiritual) knowledge. And we saw that there was not a single thing we set forth that did not spring from this Source that is sought by this spiritual kind (of angels), which is the Qur'an.

Hence everything about which we speak, both in my (teaching) sessions and in my writings, comes only from the presence of the Qur'an and Its treasures.[60] I was given the keys of Its understanding and divine support from It—all of this so that we might not swerve from It.[61]

For this is the loftiest (spiritual knowledge) that can be bestowed on one, and no one can know its full worth except for the person who has actually tasted it in experience and directly witnessed its rank as a (spiritual) state within himself, the person to whom the Truly Real (*al-Haqq*) has spoken it in his innermost being (*sirr*). For when it is the Truly Real Who speaks to His servant in his innermost being—after all the intermediaries have been lifted away[62]—then the understanding is immediate and inseparable from His speaking to you, so that the (divine) speaking itself is identical with your understanding of it. The understanding does not follow after it—and if it does come after it, then that is not *God's* speaking.

Thus whoever does not find this (immediate spiritual understanding within himself) does not have real knowing of God's speaking to His servants. And if God should speak to him through the veil of a form—whether with the tongue of a prophet or whoever else in the world He may wish—then the understanding of that (divine) speech may accompany it or it may come later.[63] So this is the difference between the two (i.e., between immediate divine inspiration and the more complex processes of ordinary spiritual understanding).

Ibn 'Arabī then goes on to explain, far more briefly, that the role of the Mahdī—or rather of the "Imām of the Time"[64]—with regard to "the sensible forms of divine sustenance" concerns his unique, divinely inspired ability (resembling that of the Prophet) to decide what material goods of this world should rightfully belong to each person of faith, since individual human beings can only be at best the temporary owners (or more properly speaking, the "custodians") of all such earthly goods.

> Since everything in the world is divine sustenance and part of *What God has left*,[65] the Imām judges with regard to (allocating) it in accordance with the judgment God sends down to him concerning it.

In the meanwhile, Ibn 'Arabī advises, we should act in all those worldly matters "according to the commandment which the divinely revealed Pathway has conveyed to us," while abstaining from passing judgment in all other cases.

"KNOWLEDGE OF THE INTERPENETRATION OF THINGS"

This is one of the longest and best-known sections in this famous chapter, no doubt because Ibn 'Arabī here so vehemently and unambiguously contrasts the divinely inspired, personally revealed spiritual knowing of the Mahdī, the true Knowers and the Friends of God, with the familiar pretensions of the traditionally learned scholars (*'ulamā' al-rusūm*)—especially with the so-called "understanding" (*fiqh*) of the powerful jurists of his own time and culture.[66] In the context of the discussion here, it is essential above all to grasp that Ibn 'Arabī's fundamental contrast between truly inspired knowing and our normal—and in many ways often unavoidable—reliance on socially and historically constructed forms of belief and persuasion is something truly essential and inescapably bound up with the human (earthly) condition as such, by no means limited to the particular illustrations and situations he happens to provides from his own cultural milieu. He starts here by highlighting the practical universality and unavoidable centrality of this inspired awareness of the "interpenetration" of spiritual realities and their more visible outward forms and expressions—a situation which corresponds precisely to the fundamental inner problematic underlying every form of spiritual intelligence:

> As for the knowledge of the interpenetration of things,[67] that (reality) inwardly penetrates and informs all the practical and intellectual crafts. Therefore if the Imām knows this, he will not be bothered by doubt and uncertainty in his judgments. For this (precise inner awareness of the interpenetration of spiritual and manifest reality) is *the Balance* (of divine justice: cf. 42:17, 59:25, etc.) in the world, both in sensible things and in the inner spiritual meanings. So the rational, responsible person[68] behaves according to that *Balance* in both worlds—and indeed in every matter where he has control over his actions.
>
> So as for those who judge in accordance with the divine inspiration that (God) has sent down, those to whom (that inspiration) has been delivered[69] among the (prophetic) Messengers and those like them (i.e., the Friends of God), they did not depart from (their inner awareness of) this interpenetration (of spiritual and material being). Thus God made them the receptacle (of revelation) for that part of His judgment concerning His servants which He delivered to them, (as) He said: *The Faithful Spirit*

brought down (the revelation) upon your heart (26:193-194), and *He sends down the angels with the Spirit from His Command upon whomever He wishes among His servants* (16:2).

Therefore every judgment concerning the world that is made manifest through a (divine) messenger is the outcome of a "spiritual marriage."[70] This (essential spiritual inspiration underlying the resulting sound judgment) is not in the (outward) textual indications and it is not in those who judge on the basis of presumed analogy.[71] Hence it is incumbent on the Imām that he know what is (truly the revealed judgment) through its being sent down by God (through divine inspiration), and what is (ordinarily supposed) through analogy. However the Mahdī does not know this—I mean the (latter) knowledge acquired by analogy—in order to pass judgment according to it, but only so that he can *avoid* it! For the Mahdī only judges according to what the angel delivers to him *from what is with God* (2:89; etc.), (the inspiration) God has sent him in order to guide him rightly.

So that is the true "Muhammadan" revealed Pathway[72]—the one such that Muhammad, if he were alive (now on earth) and that particular case were presented to him, would pass judgment on it in exactly the same way as this Imām. For God will teach him (by inspiration) that this is the Muhammadan revealed Pathway and will therefore forbid him (to follow judgments arrived at by) analogical reasoning, despite the existence of the textual indications[73] God has bestowed on him. And this is why God's Messenger said, in describing the Mahdī, that

223

"He follows in the trace of *my* footsteps, and he makes no mistake."

Through this he informed us that he is a follower (of the Prophet), not one who is followed [i.e., not a messenger with a new revealed scripture], and that he is (divinely) protected from error[74]—since the only (possible) meaning of someone's being protected from error is that they do not make mistakes. Thus if the Messenger pronounced a judgment (in some matter), no mistake is ascribed to him, since *he does not speak from passion, but it is only an inspiration inspired in him* (53:3-4). And likewise analogical reasoning is not permissible in a place where the Messenger is to be found.

Here there follows a succinct and representative sample of Ibn 'Arabī's most uncharacteristically direct speech in this particular section, which portrays his own viewpoint with remarkable openness:

Now the Prophet *does* exist and *is* to be found (here and now) with the people of spiritual unveiling, and therefore they only take their (inspired understanding of the appropriate, truly divine) judgment directly from him. This is the reason why the truthful and sincere *faqīr*[75] doesn't depend on any school (of scriptural interpretation): he is with the Messenger (i.e., Muhammad) alone, whom he directly witnesses, just as the Messenger is with the divine inspiration that is sent down to him. Thus the (divine) notification of the (appropriate) judgment concerning the particular events and cases is sent down from God to the hearts of the truthful and sincere spiritual Knowers, (informing them) that this is the judgment of the (same) revealed Pathway that was sent with the Messenger of God.

But those adhering to knowledge of the external forms (of traditional religious learning) do not have this (spiritual) rank, because of their having devoted themselves to their love for (prominent social) position, the domination of others, (furthering) their precedence over *God's (purely devoted) servants*[76] and (insuring that) the common people need them. Hence *they do not prosper* (16:116) with regard to their souls,[77] nor shall anyone prosper through (following) them. This is the (inner) condition of the jurists (*fuqahā'*) of (our) time, those who desire to be appointed to posts as judges, notaries, inspectors or professors.

Quite characteristically, though—as highlighted in the earlier discussion in this Chapter of Ibn 'Arabī's complex use of examples—he immediately turns from the scholars and jurists of his own time to a powerful portrait of similar inner spiritual blinders and veils in certain parasitic pseudo-Sufis or hypocritical ascetics of that period. The intended effect, of course, is to turn his readers (in any age and circumstance) away from any thoughtlessly reflexive sort of externalized social or political criticism toward a closer, ongoing examination of their own inner spiritual state, motives and true inner sincerity (*sidq*):

As for those of them who cunningly hide themselves in (the guise of) Religion—those who hunch their shoulders and look at people furtively, with a pretense of humility; who move their lips as though in *dhikr*,[78] so that the person looking at them will know they are performing *dhikr*; who speak obscurely and in an affected manner—they are dominated by the

225

weaknesses of their domineering self (*nafs*) and "their hearts are the hearts of wolves," (so that) *God does not [speak to them nor] look at them* (3:77-78).[79]

This is the condition of those among them who (simply) make a show of Religion—not those (more actively misguiding religious figures) who are *the companions of Satan* (cf. 4:38; 43:36). Those (more dangerous religious hypocrites) are "dressed up for the people in the skins of gentle sheep":[80] (they are) brothers outwardly, and enemies inwardly and secretly. But God will examine them and *take them by their forelocks* (cf. 55:41; 96:15-16) to that (purifying "Fire" of Gehenna) which contains their happiness.[81]

Thus when the Mahdī comes forth (to establish justice in the world) he has no *open enemy* (2:188; etc.) except for the jurists in particular. For then they will no longer have any power of domination and will not be distinguished from the mass of common people, and they will only keep a slight knowledge of the (divine) commandment, since the differences concerning the commandments will be eliminated in this world because of the existence of this Imām.

However, if the Mahdī did not have the sword (of worldly authority) in his hand, then the jurists would all deliver legal opinions (demanding) that he be killed. But instead (as stated in the hadith) "God will bring him forth with the sword and noble character," and they will be greedy (for his support) and fearful, so that they will (outwardly) accept his judgment without having any faith in it; indeed they will grudgingly conceal their disagreement, just as do (the two legal schools of) the Hanafites and Shafiites concerning those matters where they disagree. For in fact it has been reported to us that the followers of these two schools in the lands of the non-Arabs (i.e., Iran and Transoxiana) are constantly fighting one another and that a great many people of both groups have died—that (they go to such extremes that) they even break the fast during the month of Ramadan in order to be stronger for their battles.[82]

So people like this, if the Imām-Mahdī did not conquer with the sword, would not pay any attention to him and would not obey him (even) in their outward actions, just as they do not obey him in their hearts. In fact what they (really) believe about him, if he makes a judgment involving them that is contrary to their school, is that he has gone astray with regard to that judgment, because they believe that the period of the people of *ijtihād*[83] has ended (long ago), that there remains no (authoritative) *mujtahid* in the world and that after the death of their (founding) imams God has not brought anyone into existence in the world with the rank of *ijtihād*.

So as for the person (i.e., among the true Knowers and Friends of God) who claims to be divinely informed about the judgments prescribed by the revealed Pathway, for (these jurists) such a person is a madman whose imagination has gone wild, and they would pay no attention to him. But if such a person happens to possess wealth and worldly power (like the prophesied Mahdī), then they will

227

submit to him outwardly because of their coveting his wealth and their fear of his power, although inwardly they have no faith in him at all.

"STRIVING TO ONE'S UTMOST ...
TO SATISFY THE NEEDS OF MANKIND"

The eighth spiritual quality of these Helpers, their absolute loving compassion (*rahma*) and unhindered devotion to the spiritual welfare of all the creatures, is the single theme to which Ibn 'Arabī devotes perhaps the greatest emphasis throughout all of his writings, above all whenever he is discussing the highest stages of spiritual perfection, the station of the "solitary ones" (the *afrād*):

> Now as for striving to one's utmost and going to any length to satisfy the needs of mankind, that is especially incumbent upon the Imām in particular, even more than (it is) for the rest of the people. For God only gave him precedence over His (other) creatures and appointed him as their Imām so that he could strive to achieve what is beneficial for them. This striving and what results from it are both prodigious....

In the intervening passage (III, 336.16-25) Ibn 'Arabī then illustrates the essential characteristic of this particular *intentional* dimension of spiritual intelligence—that it is above all through striving for the welfare of others, in the midst of the responsibilities of ordinary life, and not by seeking to obtain what one imagines to be special powers or experiences for oneself, that the individual may eventually reach the highest spiritual stages[84]—by referring to the Qur'anic account (at 28:29 ff.) of how Moses unintentionally dis-

228

covered God, without consciously looking for Him, precisely in the theophanic form of the burning bush that he
was only seeking in order to warm his family. For Ibn
'Arabī, who repeatedly insists on the fact that Moses was
only seeking to fulfill the immediate needs of his family,
"this verse constitutes an admonition from God (*tanbīh min
al-Haqq*) concerning the value of this (spiritual virtue) with
God."[85] Both his stories here, of Moses and of Khadir, beautifully illustrate our earlier discussion of the complex spiritual function of such examples in the *Futūhāt*.

> Now the activities of all of the just Imāms are only
> for the sake of others, not for their own sake. Hence
> if you see a ruler busying himself with something
> other than his subjects and their needs, then you
> should know that his (high) rank has cut him off
> from this activity (of divinely inspired guidance),
> so that there is no (intrinsic) difference between him
> and the mass of common people....[86]
>
> And Khadir[87]... was also like this. He was in an
> army, and the commander of the army sent him to
> explore for water for them, since they were in need
> of water. That was how he fell into the Fountain of
> Life and drank from it, so that he has remained liv-
> ing up until now, for he was not aware (before set-
> ting out on this search) of that Life through which
> God distinguishes the person who drinks of that
> Water...,[88] since this Fountain of Life (is that) Wa-
> ter through which God distinguishes with (spiritual)
> Life the person who drinks that Water.
>
> Then he returned to his companions and told
> them about that water, and all the people rushed off
> toward that place in order to drink from it. But God

turned their sight away from it so that they were not capable of (attaining) it. And this is what resulted for him from his striving for the sake of others.

... Thus no one knows what is their[89] rank with God, because absolutely all of their actions are for the sake of God, not for their own sake, since they prefer God to what their (bodily and psychic) nature demands.

"POSSESSING THE KNOWLEDGE OF THE UNSEEN REQUIRED FOR (RIGHTLY RULING) THIS WORLD..."

This concluding discussion of the different facets of spiritual intelligence starts off in a direction that seems completely distant from our ordinary experience and exercise of that faculty—but concludes, for those who reflect on its implications, with a far-reaching and fundamental insight. Since the language in which Ibn 'Arabī expresses this conclusion here is bound up in the unfamiliar (for many modern readers) technical vocabulary and categories of traditional Islamic religious learning and jurisprudence, it may be helpful to begin with a more direct explanation of the absolutely essential and universal point he is making. Put as simply as possible, people who are unaware of the deeper nature and intrinsic conditions of the recurrent human situations of spiritual testing and learning often naturally imagine that there must be a general "system" or formulaic code of teachable, codifiable spiritual principles or formulae that could somehow be learned, taught, and uncontroversially applied in a single unambiguous way to all possible human situations involving each of those principles. As Ibn 'Arabī's account below illustrates, that particular presumption was, and for some people still is today, expressed in the immense

230

project of attempting to codify a single complex imaginary external set of judgments or criteria supposedly pretending to formulate the relative spiritual status—on a spectrum stretching from "absolutely forbidden" to "absolutely obligatory"—of every conceivable form of outward action (since inner actions by definition still escape the visibility assumed by that project).

Of course on a more metaphysical level, which Ibn 'Arabī has already developed in his two immediately preceding sections highlighting the spiritual "interpenetration of all things," such a project requires an almost unfathomable total blindness to the actual spiritual dimensions of human beings and all of creation. But in this concluding section Ibn 'Arabī is not really seeking to point out the intrinsic blindnesses of such individuals or the resulting folly of their projects and presumptive claims to universal authority over everyone else (*taqlīd*)—something which he had already done very emphatically and unmistakably in the immediately preceding points—but rather to highlight a much wider, more universally applicable observation that actually ties together all his earlier points, since this last observation forcefully sends his readers back into the ever-renewed, unique challenges of their own spiritual life and experience, into their own unavoidable personal exploration of the carefully designed and providentially managed "Crucible" and unavoidable Fires of earthly life itself—the subject of Chapter Five below.

In short, his conclusion here that the vast majority of spiritually challenging situations and decisions that people actually encounter have not ever been subject to an unambiguous revealed divine judgment—and that they are therefore outwardly neutral or "openly permissible" (*mubāh*), in the technical language of the jurists—simply means that

231

each individual facing such situations, as we all constantly do, must in fact turn to their own practical capacities of discernment and spiritual intelligence, to their own gradual discovery and unveiling of authentically divine inspiration and guidance, in order to discover what is in fact the spiritually right response and appropriate "divine judgment" in that uniquely particular learning situation. In making this point, which he does again and again in every chapter of these *Futūhāt*, Ibn 'Arabī constantly engages in a kind of spiritual wrestling—briefly mentioned in section I above—with his readers' commonly accepted, socially and traditionally embedded understandings of a host of key religious and scriptural terms. The explanation of that particular wrestling-match, for a modern audience, accounts for the voluminous annotation required here. Indeed most of the key points the Shaykh is actually making here only become fully apparent—in an existentially effective, and not merely conceptual way, at least—to those of his readers who come to this chapter 366 after extensive reflection on many earlier sections of this immense book:

> As for possessing the knowledge of the Unseen (*'ilm al-ghayb*) that he requires for (rightly governing) this engendered world in particular during a particular period of time, this is the ninth matter which the Imām requires for his leadership, and there are no (others) besides these.
>
> This is because God informed (us) concerning Himself that *every Day He is in an affair* (55:29); and that *affair*[90] is whatever the state of the world is that day. Now obviously when that "affair" becomes manifest in (external) existence, (everyone) recognizes that it is known by whoever witnesses it.

But this Imām, because of this matter (i.e., his inspired foreknowledge of events), is well-informed by the Truly Real concerning those affairs which He wishes to bring into temporal being *before* they actually occur in (external) existence. For he is informed about that affair on the "Day" before it occurs. So if that affair contains something beneficial for his subjects, he thanks God and remains silent about it. But if it contains a punishment (in the form of) the sending down of some widespread affliction or one aimed at certain specific persons, then he implores God on their behalf, intercedes (with Him) and begs (Him). So God, in His Mercy and Bounty, averts that affliction from them (before it actually happens) and answers (the Mahdī's) prayer and petition.

This is why God (first of all) informs him about (each event) before it occurs to his fellows in actual existence. Then after that God informs him, with regard to those "affairs," about the (particular) events that will occur to (specific) individuals. And He specifies for him those individuals with all their outward particularities, so that if he should see those individuals (in the material world) he would not doubt that they were exactly the ones he saw (in this inspired vision). And finally, God informs him about the divinely prescribed judgment appropriate for that event, the (same standard of) judgment which God prescribed for His Prophet Muhammad to apply in judging that event.[91] Hence he only judges according to that (divinely inspired) judgment, so that (in the words of the hadith about the Mahdī) "he never makes a mistake."

233

The following long passage then develops the real core of Ibn 'Arabī's argument here, as was already highlighted at the beginning of the preceding passage:

> Thus if God does not show (the Imām/Mahdī) the judgment regarding certain events, and he does not experience any unveiling (of that divine judgment), then God's aim was to include those cases in the judgment of what is (religiously) permissible,[92] so that he knows from the absence of any (divine) specification (of a particular judgment) that this is the judgment of the divine prescription concerning that event. Thus he is divinely protected (*ma'sūm*) from resorting to personal opinion (*ra'y*) and analogy (*qiyās*) in Religion.
>
> For (the use of) analogy (to extend the revealed Pathway beyond God's explicit commandments), by whoever is not a prophet, amounts to passing judgment on God concerning *the Religion of God* (3:83; etc.)[93] on the basis of something that person simply does not know. This is because analogy (involves) extending a (hypothetical) "reason" [underlying a particular judgment to all other "analogous" cases].[94] *But what makes you know?—perhaps* (80:3)[95] God does not want to extend that reason!
>
> For if He had wanted to do that He would have clearly stated it through the voice of His Messenger and would have ordered this extension, if indeed the (underlying) "reason" were among what was specifically ordained by the divine prescription in a particular (legal) case. So what do you suppose (is the validity) of the "reason" that the jurist extracts (from an action or saying of the Prophet) all by him-

self and through his own reasoning, without its having been mentioned by the divinely prescribed Pathway in any specific textual stipulation concerning that? (Or about the jurist who) then, having deduced this "reason," then extends it generally (to whatever he arbitrarily assumes to be the "analogous" cases)? Indeed this is one arbitrary judgment on top of another arbitrary judgment, concerning a "divine stipulation" *of which God is unaware* (52:21)![96]

So this is what prevents the Mahdī from speaking on the basis of (this sort of factitious) analogy[97] concerning the *Religion of God*—all the more so because he also knows that the intention of the Prophet was to lighten the burden of (religious) obligation on this community.[98] That was why the Prophet used to say "Leave me alone (i.e., without requesting any further religious precepts) so long as I leave you alone,"[99] and why he used to dislike being questioned about religion, out of fear of (unnecessarily) increasing the (divine) commandments.

Therefore in everything about which nothing is said to him (by God) and concerning which he is not informed (by God) about a specific, definite judgment, he establishes the (divine) judgment concerning it, in natural consequence, (to be) the primordial judgment.[100] And every (judgment) of which God informs him through inner unveiling and (an inspired) "notification" (*ta'rīf*) is the judgment of the (eternal) Muhammadan revealed Pathway concerning that matter.

… Therefore the Mahdī is a (divine instrument of) Compassion, just as God's Messenger was a

235

Compassion, (as) God said: *And We only sent you
as a (vehicle of) Compassion to the worlds* (21:107).

Now since this *mahdī*, as we have already learned, is none
other than each human being (each *"imām"*) who has begun to discover and actualize through spiritual intelligence
all the forms and expressions of divine guidance, it is important to make the concrete connections between Ibn
'Arabī's final sentence here and its further practical exemplifications in all those actual instruments of God's Compassion—the divinely deputized "firemen" we have already
encountered in the hadith of the Intercession at the very
end of Chapter Three, who will become our primary subject in the following Chapter Five. If we can view his concluding sentence in that light, the ways it sums up all the
lessons of this enigmatic and challenging chapter, and all
our ensuing responsibilities, will become crystal clear.

V. FROM EXAMPLE TO INSIGHT

Ibn 'Arabī's descriptions of our soul's awakening to the
omnipresence of divine inspiration and to the active responsibilities of right action and creation which flow from that
gradual awakening are intentionally complex, difficult, and
challenging. For their actual meaning and implications only
unfold through a long (indeed never-ending), dialectical
effort of reflection on their actual—and necessarily unique
and individual—reference-points in our own life experience
of the spirit's alchemical transformation. Before moving
on to other discussions of that topic in the following Chapter, it is important to note that the final major section of
chapter 366, enumerating a long and fascinating series of
descriptions of the distinctive sorts of inspired knowing
which are inherent in this spiritual waystation,[101] gives some

powerful hints of certain ways in which each person is granted the occasional tastes of that particular deeper spiritual knowing which is the unitary subject of this chapter, in ways which can then suddenly come to define their path by so powerfully revealing some illuminating intimation of its ultimate Goal.

In each of the often equally enigmatic chapters (270-383) in this larger "Section on the Spiritual Waystations" of the *Futūhāt*, these puzzling lists of very different spiritual insights (often alluding to aspects of the corresponding Qur'anic Sura 18) given at the end of each chapter constitute a kind of dialectical springboard and effective cognitive touchstone that each reader can employ—through a complex process of careful inner comparison with what we think we have come to understand from the earlier sections of that same chapter—to help verify and illuminate (or equally to re-think and re-contextualize) the fruits of those preceding discussions. Typically, each reader has been granted, however briefly, some taste of at least a few of these further inspirations that Ibn 'Arabī describes in these concluding sections; and such revelatory moments are never truly forgotten. For each of us, in the long run, that dramatic initial tasting becomes inseparable from those further tasks of spiritual insight and creativity it so indelibly reveals.

The first of those decisive insights—and the short selections translated here are neither exhaustive nor in their exact original order—is the observation already placed as an epigraph to this Chapter:

This stage also includes knowledge of what God has placed in the world as (an object for) wonder— and the "wondrous" (as people usually understand

237

it) is only what breaks with the habitual (course of things).[102] But for those who comprehend things from the divine perspective, every thing in this "habitual" course is itself an object of marvel. But the people of habits only wonder at what departs from that habitual course.

The second, much longer observation included here is a remarkable autobiographical illustration of the earlier section on "penetrating spiritual vision" that apparently alludes to Ibn 'Arabī's spiritual encounter—long before he met him in real life—with the famous Persian Sufi Awhad al-Dīn al-Kirmānī. But at the same time, this story should evoke all sorts of more common, if not in fact universal, experiences of pre-cognition, dreams, intuitions and other more familiar forms of our gradual discovery of the guided order, purposefulness, and providentially arranged nature of each soul's spiritual "private lessons":

...And in this stage there is a kind of knowledge among the things known (only) by inner unveiling. This is that the person experiencing this "unveiling" knows that every person or group, however large or small, inevitably has with them one of the people of the Unseen[103] whenever they are speaking. Then that individual (among the people of the Unseen) spreads reports about those persons in the rest of the world so that people discover those things in their own souls, (for example) when a group is gathered together in (spiritual) retreat or when a man says something to himself that (presumably) only God knows. Then that man or that group (who have discovered these reports in this mysterious fashion) go out and tell people about it so that (soon) people are all talking about it.

Ibn 'Arabī goes on, in a long autobiographical passage illustrating this phenomenon, to cite two related personal experiences. The first (in the year 590)[104] was when he ran into a man in Seville who recited to him several verses that Ibn 'Arabī himself had composed, but never committed to writing, at a particular place in Tunis one night several months before. Not knowing Ibn 'Arabī's identity, the man went on to explain that he had learned the poem in a Sufi gathering outside Seville, on the very night Ibn 'Arabī had composed them, from a mysterious stranger "whom we did not know, as though he were one of the 'Travelers'."[105] After teaching his companions those verses, the mysterious stranger went on to tell them the full name of the author and even to give them the name and exact location of the particular quarter in Tunis where he had heard them—which was precisely where Ibn 'Arabī had actually been staying that same night.

On the second occasion, also in Seville, Ibn 'Arabī was listening to a Sufi friend praising "one of the greatest of the people of the path, whom he had met in Khorasan" (in Persia), when he noticed a stranger nearby who remained invisible to the rest of the group and who said to him: "I am that very person whom this man who met with us in Khorasan is describing to you!" Then Ibn 'Arabī began describing this otherwise invisible stranger—who continued to sit there beside them—to his Spanish friend, who confirmed the exactitude of his description of that distant Persian master.

Ibn 'Arabī's following observation, as most people consciously involved in spiritual work quickly discover, is of the utmost practical importance, since it relates to the kind of discernment needed to know when it is useful and mutually helpful to discuss or share the actual realities and fruits of that work, and when on the other hand it is (in any number of possible ways) essentially useless or even quite counterproductive:

> And this stage includes the knowledge of what sort of arguing (concerning the practice and principles of religion) is praiseworthy and what sort is to be condemned.[106] Someone who has (truly) surrendered (to God) among those who depend on God[107] should not argue except concerning what he has had confirmed and realized (through God) by way of inner unveiling, not on the basis of (his own) thinking and inquiry. So if he has actually witnessed (as direct inspiration from God) that about which they are arguing, then in that event it is incumbent on him to argue about it *using that which is better/more beautiful* (29:46)[108]
>
> But if he does not have a divine command to do so, then the choice is up to him. So if the task of helping the other person (by convincing him of) that (spiritual insight) has been assigned to him (by God), then he has been entrusted with that mission for him. But if he despairs of his listeners' ever accepting what he has to say, then he should shut up and not argue. For if he should argue (with no serious hope of affecting his listeners), then he is (actually) striving to bring about their perdition with God.[109]

The final point to mention here, which we have already encountered in Chapter Two above, relates to two of the most foundational principles, and most basic discoveries, that are themselves intrinsic to the process and practice of spiritual intelligence. First, he alludes to the central role of what we ordinarily think of as "aesthetic" perceptions and judgment in our immediate spiritual perception of the world. And at the same time he highlights the corresponding centrality of discerning the true source of all ugliness and—since this Arabic root (*q-b-h*) is the exact opposite of that central virtue of knowing and expressing the "good-and-beautiful" (*ihsān*) we have just explored in the preceding Chapter Three—of all wrong and evil in the divine creation:

> And in this stage is the knowing that what God has made manifest to vision in the bodies is an adornment for those bodies; (the knowing) of why it is that some of what is manifest seems ugly to a particular person when they regard it as ugly; and (the knowing) of which eye it is that a person sees with when they see the whole world as beautiful—when they do see it—so that they respond to it spontaneously with beautiful actions. Now this knowing is one of the most beautiful (or "best") and most beneficial forms of knowing about the world.

Those readers who have grasped these two points, he suggests, will already recognize the real location and significance of all the interrelated eschatological symbols of the Qur'an, of that divine "shadow-Play" which is the subject of our next, concluding Chapter. For that Fire is only recognizable as such through its contrast with a very different reality:

> In this (spiritual stage) there is a knowing which removes the burden of anguish from the soul of the person who knows it.[110] For when one looks at what is ordinarily the case with souls, the way that all the

241

things happening to them cause them such anguish and distress, (it is enough) to make a person want to kill himself because of what he sees.[111] This knowing is called the "knowledge of blissful repose," because it is the knowledge of the People of the Garden (of Paradise) in particular.

So whenever God reveals this knowledge to one of the people of this world (already) in this world, that person has received in advance the blissful repose of eternity—although the person with this quality (in this world) still continues to respect the appropriate courtesy (towards God)[112] concerning the commandment of what is right and the prohibition of what is wrong, according to his rank.

RETURNING

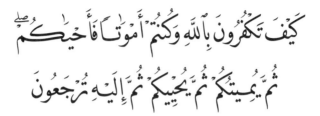

How do you all deny God, and you were dead, but He brought you all to life?! Then He causes you all to die; then He brings you all to life; then unto Him you are all made to return.

Sūrat al-Baqara, 2:28

كَيْفَ تَكْفُرُونَ بِٱللَّهِ وَكُنتُمْ أَمْوَٰتاً فَأَحْيَٰكُمْ

ثُمَّ يُمِيتُكُمْ ثُمَّ يُحْيِيكُمْ ثُمَّ إِلَيْهِ تُرْجَعُونَ

وَإِنَّهَا لَكَبِيرَةٌ إِلَّا عَلَى ٱلْخَٰشِعِينَ

ٱلَّذِينَ يَظُنُّونَ أَنَّهُم مُّلَٰقُواْ رَبِّهِمْ وَأَنَّهُمْ إِلَيْهِ رَٰجِعُونَ

… Certainly it is an enormous thing, except for those who are humble, those who know that they are encountering their Sustainer, and that to Him they are returning.

Sūrat al-Baqara, 2:45-46

CHAPTER FIVE

RETURNING:
EXPLORING THE DIVINE SHADOW-PLAY

... "Surely we are God's, and to Him we are returning!"

Sūrat al-Baqara, 2:156[1]

Readers who have followed Ibn 'Arabī to this point will surely have noticed the recurrence of eschatological language and imagery as a favored means for expressing so many of his essential insights into the universal processes of realization and spiritual intelligence. That is certainly no accident, nor is it a peculiarly personal characteristic of this author. The purpose of this concluding Chapter is to introduce and properly contextualize some of the most fundamental features—both metaphysical and spiritually practical—of this teacher's comprehensive vision of the soul's twofold "Returning," in order to open up the wider perspectives of spiritual realization that orient all of his writing and teaching. These far-reaching insights should provide the basic hermeneutical tools and assumptions that can help to ease the eventual transition from these selective, highly contextualized thematic studies of the *Meccan Illuminations* to the difficult, but rewarding, challenges of a more direct encounter with the steadily increasing number of integral translations of longer sections from that immense work.[2]

244

This chapter opens with Ibn 'Arabī's own comprehensive image of the divine "Shadow-Theater" of human existence, reflecting on both its metaphysical implications and the spiritually central dramatic mysteries of mortality, transience and suffering. Sections II and III move on first to the abstract epistemological dimensions of that image of the universal "Return," and then to the corresponding practical dialectic of spiritual intelligence and realization. Then section IV outlines the characteristic features of Ibn 'Arabī's own highly distinctive rhetoric of realization in this eschatological context, and the ways that intentionally multifaceted language is designed to elicit successive stages and perspectives within the broader spectrum of spiritual realization. Section V moves on from the metaphysical implications of this shadow-Play to its unavoidable practical implications, "from map to voyaging." And that movement naturally leads on, in sections VI and VII, to the introduction of a few of Ibn 'Arabī's indispensable keys to the ongoing challenges of spiritual orientation and navigation—the task of "seeing through the shadows" of this Play—as those insights are introduced in a series of revealing eschatological passages from different chapters of the *Futūḥāt*.

Finally, recapitulating the concluding section of each earlier Chapter, we come back again to the enlightened perspectives, and the ongoing responsibilities, of the final—but unceasing—earthly movement of this divine concert of Return. Paradoxically, for Ibn 'Arabī that concluding movement is not found in some all-encompassing metaphysical abstraction, but in the ineffable mystery of each heart's everrenewed acts of Presence: in the uniquely individual, transforming compassion and empathy of those realized spiritual Knowers—those whom the Qur'an calls the "Friends of God" (the *awliyā' Allāh*)—who are already and always "returning back" from the Day of Visit and their theophanic vision of the Real (already introduced in Chapter Three above) to their creative sharing and mirroring of that vision in the transforming works of beauty and true service that are the spontaneous expression of *ihsān.* So we conclude here with those mysterious "firemen," in the long hadith of the Intercession, who are sent back into the Fire again and again to help awaken each soul from all the sufferings and endless forms of heedlessness that do prepare us to learn.

WIDER CONTEXTS: THE CENTRALITY OF ESCHATOLOGY IN THE QUR'AN:

As background for the following discussions, given the unfamiliarity for modern audiences of many of the basic religious and cultural assumptions shared by Ibn 'Arabī and his original audiences, it is important to observe that the centrality of eschatological symbolism and teaching in the Qur'an simply cannot be exaggerated, as its pre-eminent role there is unparalleled in the scriptures of any of the other world religions. The fact that at least half the verses of the entire Qur'an, equally from both the Meccan and Medinan periods, deal directly with a single, highly complex and re-markably systematic set of eschatological themes means that there is no domain of Islamic thought (or of Ibn 'Arabī's own wide-ranging writing) which is not in reality inseparably interconnected with our understanding and interpretation of that eschatological language. This judgment is equally true, for example, of cosmology and cosmogony, in all their metaphysical and proto-scientific dimensions;[3] of theology and our understanding of the complex Qur'anic articulation of the divine Names and Attributes; of those historically later legal systems claiming to articulate the

246

religious status of human actions, rituals and prohibitions; of the perpetually conflicting claims of religio-political authority; of the most fundamental aesthetic standards, symbols and categories reflected in the infinite riches of Islamic poetry, music, architecture and the visual arts; and of the deepest ethical and spiritual forms of practice, teaching and devotional life eventually elaborated in the manifold traditions broadly associated with Sufism and *'irfān*. For Ibn 'Arabī, the essential key to the adequate understanding and proper utilization of each of those fundamental dimensions of religious life, in terms of their truly divine aims and their ultimate ends, lies precisely in the uniquely intimate human process of each individual's spiritual realization.

Now Ibn 'Arabī's discussion of the eschatological language of the Qur'an, woven throughout the *Meccan Illuminations*, constantly draws on all of those different dimensions of Islamic tradition and religious learning as they had developed over the preceding six centuries. And the intellectual, spiritual, and aesthetic richness, breadth and depth of his development of those questions was such that his teachings (often passed along in more popularly accessible forms) quickly imposed themselves as authoritative—or at the very least, unavoidable—for the most thoughtful and lastingly influential Muslim thinkers, artists, creators and spiritual teachers down to our own day.

In this Chapter, moreover, the particular subject of the interconnections of spiritual realization and eschatology has one additional distinct advantage. Although Ibn 'Arabī's scriptural and traditional symbolic language may well be unfamiliar to most readers, the actual existential challenges of eschatology, and the spectrum of possible human responses, are inherently universal and therefore practically ineluctable. The fundamental underlying questions of our ultimate destiny, of the interrelations of our uniquely particular spiritual circumstances, "tests" (learning situations), actions and their wider consequences, are not optional subjects, and they are not restricted to any particular religious or cultural situation. Nor is their resolution some abstract, elite philosophical or theological pastime. Every human being, he constantly reminds us, begins this journey with equal access to the twin divine "Books"—*on the horizons and in their souls* (41:53)—of all creation.

This characteristically insistent universality, which Ibn 'Arabī so strikingly shares with his own original Qur'anic Source, also suggests a wider spectrum of helpful contexts and comparisons which can bridge the distances between Ibn 'Arabī's time and culture and our own. It was certainly no accident that the first extensive study of his *Meccan Illuminations* in a Western language was Asin-Palacios' pioneering and provocative comparison of Ibn 'Arabī's themes with Dante's nearly contemporary *Divine Comedy*.[4] For whenever we explore Ibn 'Arabī's approaches, we quickly recognize recurrent allusions to equally classical developments of these same subjects in Plato, Rumi, Hafez, Goethe, the *I Ching*, and many others: allusions that can help ensure that no reader becomes too mystified or feels unfairly constrained by the unfamiliarity and complexity of Ibn 'Arabī's characteristically dense Qur'anic language, symbolism and technical vocabulary. Over the years, for example, I have found that certain cinematic masterworks are particularly effective in suggesting more concretely the essential existential connections between Ibn 'Arabī's teachings and the corresponding phenomenology of spiritual life, in terms more familiar in our own lives and contemporary surroundings.[5]

I. INTRODUCING THE SHADOW-THEATER

Chapter 317 of the *Meccan Illuminations* contains some of the most succinct and vivid allusions to Ibn 'Arabī's understanding of the universal "Divine Comedy" and its ultimate significance for each human being. Like most chapters of that work, it is a sort of extended commentary on a single brief Qur'anic passage (68:1-2): *Blessed be He... Who created death and life in order to test you all, which of you is best/most beautiful in action.* Its main subject—already foreshadowing later passages in this Chapter on Ibn 'Arabī's understanding of the Fire, Gehenna and the earthly "school of suffering"—is that ongoing spiritual education (or "testing," in the language of the Qur'an) which is the ultimate purpose of human earthly existence.[6]

This late chapter begins by recapitulating, in a rapid poetic enumeration, the host of quintessential metaphysical and theological questions raised by all the repeated Qur'anic allusions to God's omnipotence and "testing" of human beings. As is often the case with the Shaykh's unique and densely metaphysical poetry that opens each chapter of the *Futūḥāt*, each line of this poetry must be read on at least two levels, as a reference to the entire manifest universe (here the divine "Abode" of the Spirit), and to the existential situation of each individual human being. On the first level, his rhetorical dilemmas seem to call for a purely abstract theodicy; but as those same issues actually arise in each person's life they necessarily raise the more unavoidable question of the ultimate ends and meaning of our very existence—and of its far more particular challenges and suffering. The same constant ambiguous interplay of shifting perspectives between macrocosm and microcosm, between the universal realization of the Perfect Human

Being and the difficult path of each imperfect soul, underlies all the facets of spiritual intelligence and the pathways
of realization discussed in each of the preceding chapters:

I was astonished at the abode that He had *built and formed:*[7]
   He housed a noble Spirit there and then He tested It.

Then He destroyed it like someone who doesn't sustain it.
   So who can put it all together for me? Who can make it last?

From the start He knew quite well what He had established:
   Would that *I* knew now what He knew then!

Why didn't He build it and sustain it from the first—
   in a permanent way, forever its Source of Life?

What did it do? What made it deserving of ruin?
   What had exalted it? And what made it forsaken?

The Hand of tribulation toyed with us and with it;
   and after a time He restored it, then raised it high.

And restored that Spirit to it, then *mounted*
   on its *Throne*[8] as King, and immortalized its inhabitants,

Bequeathing them (the gardens of) Eden and Eternity,
lodging them in Firdaws and Ma'wā,[9] out of His loving concern.

Ibn 'Arabī's own comprehensive conception of that complex metaphysical situation—remarkably paralleling in so
many ways Plato's equally complex imagery of the Sun-
line-cave section at the heart of the *Republic*—is beautifully summarized in the concluding section of that same

chapter, in the Shaykh's archetypal image of the children's shadow-theater of this world:[10]

> Whoever wants to know the inner reality of what we have alluded to concerning this question [i.e., of the deeper reasons for death, suffering, ignorance and wrongdoing in this transient world] should reflect on the Image/Imagination[11] of the screen and the forms (of this cosmic shadow-Play). Who is the Speaker, for the little children who are far from the veil of the screen set up between them and the person playing with those characters and speaking through them?
>
> Now that is just how it is with the forms of the world: most people are those little children we just mentioned—so you should know how it is that happened to them! The little ones at that show are happily playing and having great fun: (and likewise) *the heedless ones consider* (this life only) *an amusement and pastime.*[12]
>
> But as for those who truly know, they reflect and see more deeply: so they realize that God has only established all this as a symbol/likeness (*mathal*).
>
> That is why at the beginning of the show a person comes out who is called the "Describer." He delivers a speech in which he glorifies God and praises Him. Then he talks in turn about every sort of form that will emerge behind that screen after him, and he informs the audience that God has established all this as a likeness for His servants, so that they can reflect on it and come to know that the world, in relation to God, is like these shadow-forms with the person who is moving them—and that this

251

veil is the mystery of Destiny (*sirr al-qadar*) governing the creatures.

Yet despite all this, the heedless ones take it to be an amusement and pastime, as in God's saying: *those who have taken their religion to be an amusement and pastime [and have been deluded by the life of this world... They forgot the meeting (with God) this Day and denied Our Signs]* (7:51).

The rest of this Chapter can be seen as an extended commentary on this particular all-encompassing image: its aim is simply to explore how Ibn 'Arabī suggests that we are all gradually moved from the state of these heedless children to that of spiritually mature adults, through the interactions of the Play itself—and through the profound, but initially invisible, transforming influence of the prophetic "Describers."

To begin to penetrate this image, of course, one needs to recognize initially that the "Describers" mentioned here are all the messengers, prophets, Friends and other divinely inspired guides (most of them historically invisible in their own earthly lifetimes); and that all the forms of this divine Image and Imagination—of both the audience and the drama alike—are simultaneously parts of this single, unique presentation, both "in front of" and (as Spirit) also "behind" the screen of our spatio-temporal separations. But once we have acknowledged those two premises, this single cinematic image beautifully conveys one of the most basic Qur'anic principles of Ibn 'Arabī's teaching: the holographic nature of the divine "Book"—or "Speaking," or creative "Breath" and Spirit—as equally manifest in all the three homologously corresponding forms of (1) revealed "Scripture" (including, as throughout the Qur'an, all of the ever-present spiritual realities (*rūhāniyyāt*) of the prophets and messengers, and not only, or even primarily, the fragments of historically surviving written texts); (2) the "World" or cosmos (*al-'ālam*, which for Ibn 'Arabī extends to all the levels and forms of creation and divine Self-manifestation brought into being through the creative Breath); and (3) the Spirit, including each individual human spirit (*rūh*) and the intrinsically divine dimensions of each human "soul-breath" (*nafs*).

Ibn 'Arabī's fertile image of this universal "divine comedy" immediately suggests as well the particular role of his own writings within that larger process. For within that perspective, every human being already brings the specific capacities and depths of their spirit. And—given enough time—most human beings will eventually participate in and witness enough of this Play to begin to realize for themselves the deeper meanings, directions and guidance already, and repeatedly, indicated by each of the inspired Describers. Those are the most obviously indispensable elements, the very starting points of the larger process of realization.

Against that backdrop, it becomes clear that Ibn 'Arabī's own writings are intended essentially as a kind of spiritual catalyst or actively illuminating agent whose role is to help his students to apply the broad directive guidance of the Describers (and their prophetic Books) in what are the requisite spiritually effective and creative ways. In other words, these writings are all carefully crafted "director's notes" designed to help us to make the indispensable revelatory connections between our own particular experiences and trials—the infinite divine *Signs in their souls and on the horizons* (41:53) that constitute this Play—and the particular deeper lessons that are illustrated by each of those potentially theophanic experiences. One of the significant terms Ibn 'Arabī himself most frequently uses for that ongoing mediating spiritual function is that of "Translator" (*tarjumān*). And indeed the decisive evidence of the genuinely effective use of his work is whenever Ibn 'Arabī's words actually do help bring about one of these actually illuminating spiritual "openings" which provide the title, inspiration, and ongoing subject of this immense work.

That unmistakable opening effect is beautifully described at the very beginning of his Introduction to these *Meccan Illuminations*, where he points out the immediate recognition and unshakeable positive certainty that can be occasioned by even the most allusive and indirect statement of an actually experienced spiritual reality:

> For you are necessarily in a state of immediate "unveiling" (*kashf*) concerning that, even if you aren't aware of it. There's no other way: for the heart is not gladdened except by what it knows for sure to be real (*haqq*). And the intellect can't enter in here, because this kind of knowing (through spiritual intuition or "tasting") is not within its grasp.

In fact Ibn 'Arabī carefully sets forth all the basic elements of this dramatic process of spiritual realization in that same Introduction, at the very beginning of the *Futūhāt*.[13] Indeed, what he says there about the various essential "levels" of belief and knowledge is interesting not only as it illuminates his own writings, but also for what it may suggest about the presuppositions and actual workings of cognate spiritual writings and forms of teaching from many other religious traditions and paths of spiritual realization.

II. Deciphering the Divine Signs:
the Epistemological Dimensions

Those students of Ibn 'Arabī who have primarily worked with his famous *Bezels of Wisdom* (*Fuṣūs al-Hikam*) or its long line of commentaries will already be helpfully acquainted with his recurrent basic distinction between three different groups of people whose perceptions of all reality, including God, are primarily dominated and determined either by (1) their conditioned, usually unconscious "beliefs" (*i'tiqād* and *taqlīd*); (2) by their restricted individual "intellect" (*'aql*); or (3) by inspired spiritual "knowing" (*ma'rifa*) and divine "informing" (*ta'rīf*). While that basic three-fold epistemological distinction continues to operate throughout all of Ibn 'Arabī's writings, his remarks here in his Introduction to the *Meccan Illuminations* are considerably more nuanced, and they highlight more clearly the extraordinary complexity of the aims and functions of his rhetoric throughout this immense work. Specifically, Ibn 'Arabī explicitly adds here a fourth distinct form of awareness—the immediate knowing of our experiential states, spiritual and otherwise—which in fact has the effect of revealing the existentially fundamental question of *discernment* as the essential key to every form and operative expression of spiritual intelligence, as the central common aim of all these exemplary spiritual "openings."

Taken in isolation, of course, such abstract epistemological distinctions are often not particularly illuminating, since it is precisely their detailed concrete phenomenology, their actual practical significance in the real processes of spiritual life and growth, that is gradually brought to life throughout these *Futūhāt*. Within that intended phenomenological context of realization, however, their significance as indispensable keys to Ibn 'Arabī's distinctive language and intentions can be summarized in the following five fundamental points.

• First, all four of these levels or forms of cognition are at least potentially—and usually actively—alive and accessible to some extent (if only potentially) in the broader experience of each human being. Correspondingly, perhaps the most obvious initial purpose of the *Futūhāt* is therefore to open up our awareness of those higher dimensions of spiritual understanding which have remained either unconscious or not significantly actualized. For it is precisely those experiential spiritual openings which are both the occasion—through the unexpected wider perspectives they reveal—and the partial foundation for all subsequent spiritual work and reflection.

• Secondly, there are critically important distinctions—either between what is true and false, or more commonly, between what is real and what is illusory or misunderstood—that actually operate *within* each level or dimension of knowing. This is what discernment, or spiritual intelligence, is all about. To take only one example, at the most basic level of beliefs, the movement from purely unconscious and habitual conditioning to greater conscious awareness of each previously unconscious, yet determinant, belief-structure is a familiar, essential initial step in every spiritual path or discipline.

• Thirdly, the traditional language of levels of awareness used here should not delude us into imagining either that particular individuals are somehow

256

exclusively localized in only one particular condition, or that our (entirely relative) opening to higher levels of knowing implies some kind of total abandonment or practical superseding of the preceding forms of awareness. On the contrary, Ibn 'Arabī's writing throughout the *Futūhāt* is carefully designed to raise his readers toward an all-encompassing vision of the Whole of the divine action and purpose in the vast crucible of human transformation. And that wholistic vision, like the practical spiritual intelligence and enlightened right-and-beautiful action (*ihsān*) that flows from it, depends decisively on an intimate awareness of the indispensable concrete spiritual roles of every existing level of spiritual realization.

• Fourthly, Ibn 'Arabī constantly reminds his readers—with an intensity and richness that increases in direct proportion to their own level of increasing spiritual awareness and intelligence—that true communication and right action in this world depend decisively on the most deeply accurate and empathic awareness of the actual potential for realization within each particular individual with whom we are communicating and interacting.

• Finally, once Ibn 'Arabī's reader has become more fully cognizant of these four broad levels of awareness and realization, it becomes relatively easier to perceive the many subtle ways in which each chapter of his work constantly shifts—often with an intentionally shocking abruptness—between radically different rhetorical forms. For example, to list only a few: abstractly metaphysical poems; pointed allusions or enigmatic analyses of short pas-

257

sages from the Qur'an or hadith; direct anecdotal
recounting of his own or others' revealing spiritual
experiences; allusions to (or partial elaborations of)
spiritual parallels and implications of many different rational and religious sciences of his day; significant stories of familiar historical and religious
figures; and so on. Most revealingly, we find powerful reflections of the same constantly shifting rhetorical resources and metaphysical perspectives, of
course, throughout Rumi's similarly complex—and
likewise superficially discontinuous—construction
of his equally unique and far-reaching contemporary *"Spiritual Epic"* (the famous *Masnavī-yi
ma'navī*).

In almost every such case, with Ibn 'Arabī, the particular
literary form in question can potentially be grasped and received—subject above all to the actual receptivity and spiritual preparedness of each particular reader—as operating
initially at any of these four basic levels: i.e., in relation to
belief (whether conscious or more often unconscious); intellectual conceptualization; experientially grounded symbol (the Qur'anic "Signs"); and actual reality. Likewise,
with each of these literary forms, Ibn 'Arabī typically adds
a distinctive unexpected spin or peculiar rhetorical device
designed potentially to confuse, disorient, or short-circuit
each reader's normal, habitual, unconscious way of receiving that particular lesson. In doing so, he continuously clears
the way for—or at the very least, reminds us of—the basic
pre-condition of inner openness, wonder and profound bewilderment (*hayra*) required for receiving any new spiritual opening or deeper realization. These intentionally un-
settling, disorienting literary devices, many of them already

familiar from his *Fusūs al-Hikam*, include a host of complex forms of paradox, etymological reminders, puzzles,
problematic allusions, and so on.

Now the possible cumulative effects of all those distinctive rhetorical devices, together with the receptive states
of puzzling bewilderment they intentionally engender, are
meant to confront his readers, at almost each step, with three
simultaneous possibilities: either (1) to let go and be carried to or inwardly reminded of a higher, more adequate
spiritual level of realization intended by that remark;[14] or
(2) to try to work out (whether with one's intellect or within
one's currently available beliefs) a satisfactorily reasonable
conceptual solution to the bewildering problem in question;
or (3) to abandon further reading and reflection, for the time
being, in response to the normal reactions of boredom, frustration and irritation such puzzling rhetorical devices typically engender in unprepared readers. Practiced readers of
the *Meccan Illuminations*, including all the selections translated in this book, will notice that one dramatic result of
this distinctive rhetoric—if it is integrally combined, as intended, with each reader's own ongoing process of practical realization—is that over time the same familiar passages
from this work will typically take on entirely different meanings and coloration with each renewed reading, as they are
perceived from a different experiential perspective. Another
common, even more dramatically memorable effect of these
"Openings" is that attentive readers, actively engaged in
the process of realization, will often find to their surprise
that the apparently extraordinary spiritual phenomena so
richly described in certain passages almost simultaneously
actually do occur, as if by magic, quite concretely in the
context of their own lives and dream-work.

III. Getting Started: The Dialectic
of Spiritual Intelligence

As we follow Ibn 'Arabī's own guidelines in his Introduction, briefly summarized in the previous section, his language in these *Meccan Illuminations* is carefully constructed to set up a constantly shifting set of spiritual mirrors designed to reveal to each of his readers and interpreters those particular dimensions of their being and understanding which are momentarily determined by their own unique operative nexus of all the possible levels of belief, conceptual understanding, immediate experience, and active spiritual intelligence. In reality, that intentionally mirroring effect of his writing is now beautifully illustrated by the considerable spectrum of critical and interpretive literatures about Ibn 'Arabī (primarily referring to his *Fusūs al-Hikam*) already available in Western languages. For there it is immediately apparent that the particular cognitive level at which each interpreter primarily encounters and describes their experience of the Shaykh's writing is usually unmistakably (sometimes even embarrassingly) obvious, particularly when writers indulge in polemics against other interpreters who happen to have focused on other different dimensions of the Shaykh's teaching and intentions.[15] Unfortunately, since simply the bare intellectual comprehension of the *Meccan Illuminations* today (just as with reading Dante or Plato) normally requires the presentation of an elaborate explanatory and contextual background once implicitly familiar to the author's original audiences, the result is that it is all too easy for many modern readers to assume that Ibn 'Arabī was primarily writing this book as a purely intellectual composition, accessible only to a handful of specialized scholars.

With regard to Ibn 'Arabī's own potential and intended audiences, at least, nothing could be farther from the truth. As anyone working in the field of religious studies quickly discovers, the distribution of particular spiritual gifts, insights, capacities, and degrees and forms of spiritual intelligence and sensitivity to be found among human beings has nothing at all to do, in its roots, with the outwardly visible accidents of age, culture and upbringing. Instead, the gifts of those wide-ranging spiritual capacities and receptivities fortunately appear to be considerably more broadly distributed than corresponding intellectual powers. For that substantial number of potential spiritually apt readers, then, it is especially important to know that the recurrent spiritually autobiographical portions of these *Meccan Illuminations* together constitute what is surely the most extensive "phenomenology of spiritual experience" to be found throughout the Islamic tradition, and perhaps even in all world literature. As a result, curious readers approaching the *Futūhāt* within its intended context of active spiritual realization are in fact likely to find many of Ibn 'Arabī's particular illuminations to be readily identifiable and immediately, intuitively accessible in precisely the sort of way that—as we have already indicated—he describes and encourages at the very beginning of his Introduction:

> Therefore you should know that if this (report of the inspired "knowing of spiritual secrets") seems good to you, and you accept it and have faith in it— then rejoice! For you are necessarily in a state of immediate unveiling concerning that, even if you aren't consciously aware of that. There's no other way: for the heart is not gladdened except by what it knows for sure to be real.

261

Again, in highlighting the fundamental role of trusting our own intuitions as both the starting point and the ultimate touchstone in any spiritual effective reading of these *Futūhāt*, it is essential to keep in mind that Ibn ʿArabī's guiding intention is precisely the gradual unfolding of each reader's own spiritual intelligence, of our uniquely human capacity to perceive the whole world and all our experience directly as "divine new-speaking" (*hadīth ilāhī*). And then, flowing from that enlightened awareness, to encourage the appropriate practical application and unfolding of that ever-present Guidance. This is the spirit in which he encourages his most apt and properly prepared readers, at the very beginning of this book, to pay attention to each of those indispensable, intimate, and uniquely personal forms through which we alone can begin to "read" each of the three divine Books—of the cosmos, the souls, and the revealed scriptures—in order to discover the intended meanings and purpose of this shadow-Play:

> But they (the true Knowers)—may God be pleased with them!—only bring secrets and wisdom concerning the secrets/inner meanings (*asrār*) of the revealed Pathway, about that which is beyond the power of discursive thinking and intellectual acquisition, secrets which are never ever attained in any way except through direct witnessing and (divinely inspired) confirmation and other paths like those.
>
> Do you not see that if someone brought you (these inspirations) as if they were a dream he had seen—wouldn't you try to interpret them and figure out what they really mean? So likewise, take whatever this Sufi brings you, and let yourself be rightly guided by it for a little while. And open up your place (of your heart) for what he has brought

262

you, so that their inner meanings can become manifest to *you*.

What actually happens whenever one actually practices this
simple advice, whenever we begin to pay careful attention
to such apparently random intuitions, to follow and act on
the subtle threads of divine guidance and spiritual discernment they always provide, is intimately familiar to everyone consciously engaged in that process of realization pro-
fusely illustrated in each of the preceding Chapters.[16]

The relation of Ibn 'Arabī's writing to the different facets of that process can at least be described consecutively,
even though in reality their interrelation typically takes place
through a continual kind of ongoing inner dialogue involving every relevant dimension of our experience. That dialectic begins by the awakening of our awareness of what
we truly do "know" (in the essential sense of that distinctively spiritual knowing, or *ma'rifa*, which forms the explicit title-subject of almost all of this book's 560 chapters); and by simultaneously revealing, with unavoidable
intensity, the immensity of our corresponding, ordinarily
unconscious, spiritual ignorance. Secondly, Ibn 'Arabī constantly provides a vast spectrum of reminders or guidelines
(both symbolic and intellectual) concerning the particular
spiritual realities, practices, intentions and principles that
we need to actualize in order to begin to move from that
momentarily awakened awareness of our spiritual ignorance
to a deeper actual knowing of the Real. Usually these operative spiritual principles are drawn first from the Qur'an
and hadith, combined with his own and other knowers' more
persuasively direct and detailed experiential accounts.

Next, the combination and motivating existential effects
of these two first stages oblige his engaged readers to turn
their attention to the necessary forms of right action and

other previously neglected spiritual resources—always with a newly refined intention, seriousness, and clearer awareness of the actual goals of those essential actions and experiences, even where those same readers were already engaged in various outward forms of practice. And finally, he constantly impels all of his readers to recall, ponder and reflect upon the actual lessons and meanings to be drawn from their own necessarily unique, gradually unfolding personal experience of each of those three preceding elements. Once we keep these four equally essential dimensions of realization in mind, the guiding purposes behind almost all of Ibn 'Arabī's often strange, sometimes apparently incoherent forms of writing quickly begin to come into perspective.

INTEGRATING SPIRITUAL REALIZATION:
THE CHALLENGE OF ESOTERICISM

As soon as we have clearly recognized what is actually involved in the process of spiritual realization, however, we cannot help but encounter one absolutely central, unavoidable problem of communication and interpretation—a problem so central that Ibn 'Arabī actually begins and ends his Introduction to the *Meccan Illuminations* by alluding to this challenge and the particular dilemmas it poses. This problem, in its simplest form, is that it is simply impossible to speak or write about many fundamental dimensions of spiritual experience, insight and reflection without generating some form of confusion, misunderstanding, or even potentially more dangerous consequences in listeners or readers who have not yet shared in the experiential premises of that discussion. Equally importantly, on the other hand, all those who have actually shared in the particular forms of spiritual realization in question will immediately recognize references to those realities in the most unfamiliar languages, cultures, and symbolic forms of expression. (This is one reason why masterpieces of spiritual cinema are so quickly becoming an such extraordinarily effective cross-cultural means of spiritual communication and teaching throughout the contemporary world, as music has always been.)

For example, to take one simple, but dramatic illustration particularly relevant to Ibn 'Arabī's teachings, every beginning student of any of his writings is familiar with his characteristic insistence on the "ever-renewed creation" (*tajdīd al-khalq*), on our direct experience of the unmediated emergence of all manifestation from its one Source at every instant (or with each divine "Breath," *nafas*, to use his most common expression for this reality). Reading about this fundamental metaphysical thesis, and then understanding its conceptual role in the wider philosophical or theological framework of Ibn 'Arabī's teaching, is a relatively straightforward and communicable matter in the classroom. But no one who has actually experienced what Ibn 'Arabī was really talking about will ever have any trouble recalling precisely where, when, and for how long that particular knowing was bestowed on them—nor just why Ibn 'Arabī uses that particularly appropriate language to describe the reality in question.

In other words, given the very different levels of belief and awareness involved at every stage in the larger process of human realization, it should be clear that most of us are normally and understandably still in many respects like the children in Ibn 'Arabī's image of the divine shadow-play: i.e., unconsciously ruled by the limiting forms of belief, distracting attachments and illusions which make it difficult for us to read and perceive any of the divine Books— whether of creation or in our souls—"as they really are."[17]

So it should not be too surprising, then, that Ibn 'Arabī immediately follows his initial allusion to these different levels of spiritual knowing, at the very beginning of his Introduction to the *Futūhāt*, by quoting in succession three impassioned, highly revealing declarations making precisely that same point, which are drawn from three of the most highly respected Companions of the Prophet and transmitters of his teachings: Abū Hurayra, Ibn 'Abbās, and Imām 'Alī.

Each of those three highlighted statements explicitly emphasizes the existence of centrally significant elements of revealed spiritual teaching that Muhammad (and by implication, many other prophetic teachers) had not publicly disseminated—but had instead reserved for oral, symbolic communication to those who were spiritually prepared to receive it—because those particular teachings would so shock or undermine most people, restricted as they are within their accepted forms of belief, that they might immediately kill anyone who attempted the wider public dissemination of those teachings.[18] Ibn 'Arabī's dramatic citation of these three successive authoritative statements takes on added special significance in light of what he then goes on to say again twice, in the middle and at the very end of this same Introduction, about his own intentional scattering throughout the *Futūhāt* of his most fundamental teachings, those reserved for the "quintessence of the spiritual elite":

> But as for presenting the creed of the quintessence (of the spiritual elite), I have not given it in detail in any one place, because of the profundities it contains. Rather, I have given it scattered throughout the chapters of this book, exhaustively and clearly explained—but in different places, as we have men-

tioned. So those on whom God has bestowed the understanding of these things will recognize them and distinguish them from other matters.

For this is the Knowing of the Truly Real (al-Haqq) and the Truthful Saying, and there is no goal beyond It. "The blind and the truly seeing" are alike in Its regard![19] It brings together things most far and most near, and conjoins the most high and most low.

What is practically most important for any student of the Futūhāt to keep in mind, in reflecting on Ibn 'Arabī's citation of these thrice-repeated opening cautions about the Prophet's oral teachings, is a very simple and familiar reality—one we can all observe repeatedly, for example, in the relations between parents and children, or between experts in a particular discipline and novices or curious outsiders. The fact is that no one can really explain or teach any particular spiritual phenomenon or direct experience of reality (i.e., the actual results of the existential process of spiritual intelligence and realization) to someone who has not yet actually "been there" and experienced that same reality for themselves. The results of any attempt at premature communication of these teachings, as we all soon learn, are inevitable misunderstandings and often grotesque misrepresentation: unintended results which may be comic or—as Ibn 'Arabī has just powerfully emphasized in his own opening cautions—memorably tragic, depending on the particular surrounding circumstances. The possibilities of resulting misunderstandings—and the corresponding challenges of effective spiritual teaching—are especially dramatic and kaleidoscopic when, as in the case of those different key epistemological dimensions of belief and knowing Ibn 'Arabī outlines in his Introduction, the various levels involved are not really successive at all, but more like integral and inseparable aspects of spiritual intelligence: dimensions of a single living whole which are potentially explosive and dangerously misleading if any one of those very partial elements (belief, critical intellect, inspired experience, etc.) is considered in isolation from the larger Reality it so inadequately reflects.

IV. THE RHETORIC OF REALIZATION

Ibn 'Arabī's corresponding, endlessly fascinating rhetorical response to that unavoidable and distinctively human situation—inspired on almost every point by fundamental features of the uniquely revealing discourse of the Qur'an—is twofold. First, he seeks above all to provoke and bring to conscious awareness all the internal contradictions, limitations and metaphorical short-sightedness of each of his readers insofar as they may be locked into any particular lower or more partial form of perception (whether of belief, intellectual reasoning, inspiration, etc.). At the same time, he is equally devoted to highlighting and probing that characteristic inner cognitive dissonance which exists whenever our conscious self is caught or torn between two very different levels of knowing. This is especially visible, for example, in the familiar processes by which we gradually discover the deeper meanings of our dreams, inspirations, intuitions and so many other forms of spiritual experience, precisely through ongoing reflection on their meaningful interactions with all the relevant particular dimensions of our experience, memory, and events constituting our particular destiny.[20]

Fortunately, on a more practical, interpersonal level, most people have already encountered certain practical spiritual equivalents of many of Ibn 'Arabī's essential literary and rhetorical methods in their corresponding experiences, beginning in childhood, with explicitly oral teaching: i.e., with their own effective teachers, therapists, counselors, and spiritual guides and mentors. So it is critically important to keep all our relevant personal experiences in those domains in mind whenever we approach the *Meccan Illuminations*—so much of which must be studied, if we are approaching it within the intended framework of realization, precisely in light of those uniquely specific dreams, visions, and other telling coincidences and experiences that fortuitously happen to arise in conjunction with our actual process of reading, study and reflection on this work.

THE PLAY OF PERSPECTIVES:

It is interesting to note how differently Ibn 'Arabī's cosmic image of the divine shadow-Play—and the actual realities suggested by the corresponding eschatological symbols—are perceived when we look at them from the different partial perspectives (perhaps a more accurate term than stages or levels) that are dramatized here by each of the active participants whom he mentions in this account. How does each of those actors and their corresponding viewpoints eventually contribute to the overall process of spiritual realization?

- To begin with, from the perspective of the usual human state of (primarily unconscious) beliefs, that of the "heedless children" of all ages in Ibn 'Arabī's shadow-theater, several important points may be immediately observed. Most obviously, people in that condition do not even notice the actual existence or immediate relevance of the realms of the ultimate life (*al-ākhira*), of the spiritual realities "behind the screen" of earthly appearances, multiplicity and changes. That is because they normally imagine the corresponding scriptural symbols of those unseen spiritual realms to refer to a kind of horizontal, progressive time-line of *as yet distant* "places" and "events"—all imagined as being basically comparable in their sequential temporality, materiality, and so on to those familiar, apparently obvious realms of spatio-temporal, material existence that we normally take to be the whole of reality.

• On the other hand, those whose perceptions and actions are strictly limited by such beliefs are also often intensely focused on a fixed, strictly limited set of particular visible ethical or ritual preparations which they believe will somehow uniquely determine their eventual conditions in those various future events that they imagine to occur only after their bodily death. Since the constantly changing particulars of this *"lower* [or 'nearer'] *life"* (*al-hayāt al-dunyā*) are the only dimension of the divine shadow-Play that they can normally see, they naturally tend to interpret the prophetic "Descriptions" entirely from this imagined uni-dimensional perspective, focusing on fragmentary this-worldly political, legal, ethical and ritualistic dimensions of those teachings. Thus they are essentially dismissing—in reality, that is, although not perhaps verbally—all those wider metaphysical and spiritual contexts and essential finalities of this drama that were actually so poignantly and insistently highlighted by each of the prophetic Describers.

• On the other hand, to take the second possible perspective, whenever this shadow-Play is viewed

270

primarily or solely through the lenses of the conceptualizing, discursive intellect,[21] the usual result, as Ibn 'Arabī constantly points out, is a quarrelling diversity of mutually exclusive descriptions or "critical reviews" of that drama. Whether we call such quarrelling intellectual drama-critics theologians or philosophers—and Ibn 'Arabī himself rarely distinguishes between those two groups, focusing instead on their common, shared restriction by the inherent spiritual limitations of their reliance on discursive reasoning—their typical practical focus, both in their conceptions of right action and in their operative interpretations of the prophetic Describers, is understandably on the necessity of a properly coherent intellectual grasp of what they can actually see of the Play, necessarily "in front of the Veil." In other words, those determined by their individual intellect commonly focus on arriving at the "right reading" of their own particular versions of the scenario, script or libretto—and not on the unique, necessarily individual spiritual lessons constantly emerging within the actual, ongoing divine Play itself. This limiting intellectual perspective seems absolutely self-evident to such theological observers and critics[22]—while to almost everyone else, it may well seem like preferring the menu to the meal.

Thus when it comes to the central eschatological symbolism of the divine Books and Describers, such restrictively intellectual observers tend to move directly from the imagined "horizontal," linear time-line assumed by the people of unconscious beliefs, to the different kinds of "vertical," abstract metaphysical symbolism that do emerge from almost any intellectually coherent consideration of the deeper recurrent visible patterns of this divine Play. In other words, they carefully map out the corresponding degrees of being and knowing implied by this ongoing drama and its relation to the One divine Agent, using the familiar philosophical and religious parallelism between the ontological (or cosmological) and epistemological (or eschatological) symbolism of the creatures' "Origin and Return" that traditionally structures almost all the serious classical Islamic intellectual versions of the Qur'anic teaching. And in fact most of Ibn 'Arabī's later generations of philosophically minded Muslim interpreters—almost all focusing on his *Fusūs al-Hikam*—were predominantly rooted in just this type of primarily intellectual perspective and approach.

However, from the comprehensive perspective of spiritual realization, as Ibn 'Arabī never ceases to remind his readers, maps are certainly not the same as the journey. So the discursive intellect alone (like the earlier starting point of informed belief) provides only one further, albeit quite essential, key to the much wider process of spiritual learning. Indeed often, for Ibn 'Arabī, the seeker's intellect is initially useful precisely for the contradictions and disturbing dead-ends it so naturally creates: for such theological and philosophical puzzlements are often indispensable practical hints suggesting further essential, but as yet unseen, spiritual dimensions of reality that must first be discovered and explored by other means.

- In particular, within this shadow-Play the conceptual and analytical powers of the intellect alone are only as useful as our relevant fields of perception and their input, with which the properly informed intelligence can then work. Indeed, as we

272

have just noted in the preceding section, the process of spiritual realization itself is a kind of ongoing, ascending dialogue between the intellect and our actually expanding spiritual perceptions. For most people, therefore, the end of their childlike heedlessness begins—not surprisingly—with some quite unexpected momentary glimpse "behind the curtain." That is to say, with those unforgettable epiphanies of the One Player and the realities that actually lie behind the shadow-Play's "veil of Destiny": this is the experience of what Ibn 'Arabī's technical vocabulary quite appropriately describes as the many forms of—always partial, and therefore problematic—spiritual unveiling or immediate witnessing (*kashf* and *shuhūd*). At the beginning, of course, such momentarily illuminating experiences or intuitions are like a vast unfamiliar nocturnal landscape suddenly revealed by lightning-flashes: dramatically striking, memorable (even unforgettable)—but also typically puzzling, extremely partial, incomplete, and constantly subject to misinterpretation through our own deceptive imagination, speculation and misconstrual.[23]

But what is equally obvious, as again one discovers over time, is that such memorable revelatory incidents, no matter how transforming and motivating they may often be, are not in any way self-sufficient; indeed they may often act like spiritual drugs or intoxicants, giving rise to various kinds of addictive or self-deluding "magical thinking." In other words, as so many classical Sufi writers have long pointed out (based on ample practical experience), such unusual "spiritual experiences," when taken in isolation, can even become dangerous pitfalls or unconscious idols, if they are mistakenly taken as ends in themselves or are misunderstood in countless other destructive or time-wasting ways. For the most part, as Ibn 'Arabī's image of the shadow-Play quite intentionally highlights, such initial, momentary "back-stage glimpses" are not unlike a small child being placed at the controls of an airliner or some immensely complex and advanced laboratory: in itself, such raw partial "seeing," however vivid or prolonged, has little to do with the lasting, realized integration of real knowing. And those initially dazzled or entranced by even a few such revelatory moments of eschatological unveiling will of course tend to see in all the prophetic Describers and their teachings only the reflection of those first fragmentary but impressive personal insights—although at the same time they may also become more highly motivated, as a result, to begin to explore and seek more deeply.

• Finally, for Ibn 'Arabī's primary intended audience in the *Meccan Illuminations*, those seekers who have already been long engaged in the actual spiritual work and processes of realization, their focus of interest shifts above all to the actual Play, to the concretely ongoing, carefully prepared "private lessons" uniquely contained in their own actual, immediate and specifically individual drama and their own interactions with the Real Player behind the screen. As they gradually learn how to "take direction," they also slowly learn to focus on the wider co-operative, interactive dimensions of spiritual realization—and on the resulting divine gifts of that ongoing "increase in knowing" which lies at the very heart of all of Ibn 'Arabī's thought, writing and intention.[24]

In the end, what alchemically transforms each person's distinctive apprehension of the Describers' efforts into that long gradual process of spiritual maturation and realization can only be referred to obliquely as the additional indispensable discovery of Grace, right Guidance, and the humanly decisive role of our innermost spiritual intentions. But clearly such richly allusive words—like the rest of the Describers' symbolic indications—are themselves not even adequate descriptions of that mysterious transformational catalyst, much less of the corresponding spiritual realities and experiences.

EXPLORING THE SHADOW-PLAY: CONTRAST AND DISCOVERY

Returning to Ibn 'Arabī's outwardly simple image of the cosmic shadow-theater—in which all human beings are simultaneously both the outwardly apparent actors and the audience—the following brief observations may help to suggest the complexity, richness, and overlapping complementarity of the host of spiritually practical, theological, metaphysical, and aesthetic (poetic, visual, and musical) perspectives and approaches which are in fact conveyed by these particular images. To begin with, the Qur'anic symbols and hadith accounts of eschatology underlying Ibn 'Arabī's imagery here focus consistently on the essential inner connections between human actions—in every dimension, including above all the central role of our inner intentions—and their ultimate consequences. The actual spiritual laws governing those connections, as explained and illustrated throughout the Qur'an, are to be discovered (and eventually, more adequately applied) precisely through those ongoing lessons or "tests" that constitute the Play of our earthly existence. For some, of course, those deeper laws and their regularly occurring consequences are already palpably visible and familiar.

For most of us though, like the children in Ibn 'Arabī's theater, those spiritual principles—and their goal of realized loving Compassion and all the other Most-beautiful Names that constitute the *fully* human being (*insān*)—must still be actualized in practice through all the individually appropriate learning-situations and transforming experiences of this drama. Against the wider backdrop of Islamic tradition, Ibn 'Arabī's single poignant image of the shadow-Play is intended to suggest and evoke the whole process of spiritual education encompassing a multitude of contrasting stages of transformation that gradually emerge as we move between the heedless state of the restless children (or of carping, quarreling "critics") and the inspired, all-encompassing vision of the prophetic Describers. As we have already seen concretely in each of the preceding Chapters, the whole process of learning necessarily unfolds through the experienced contrasts between the poles of that spectrum of different states and perspectives—contrasts which Ibn 'Arabī most commonly refers to through the Qur'anic language of the contrasting divine Names of Beauty and Majesty, or of immanence and transcendence: those Names being in reality the spectrum of humanly experienced qualities that together express all the spiritual dimensions of existence.

Each of the resulting dramatic contrasts briefly enumerated here has much more elaborate symbolic, intellectual and practical equivalents—all of them constantly assumed by Ibn 'Arabī and his original audiences—in the Qur'an, hadith, and later complex Islamic intellectual and spiritual traditions. But for readers interested in the Play itself, rather than past commentaries, performances, and critical reviews, the complexity and unfamiliarity of those earlier traditions can sometimes obscure at least as much as it may help to reveal.

On a more practical level, two essential observations stand out. The first is the essential complementarity and practical significance of each of these contrasting perspectives in the larger process of spiritual realization. The most obvious practical consequences of failing to respect that deeper complementarity of perspectives and practical realities are the endless confusions, quarrels, and misunderstandings which inevitably arise whenever we approach the reality of this shadow-Play simply through the words of its theological and intellectual critics—words which may well be outwardly borrowed from the divine Describers, but which so palpably have none of their original transforming and awakening effects. The second, and also profoundly Qur'anic, lesson is the constant recurrence, in every domain of existence, of a spectrum of polarities or contrary conditions which are in themselves inconceivable and profoundly unknowable without our actually passing through the whole requisite spectrum of underlying educational experiences, through the Play itself.[25]

Here, then, is a brief summary reminder of only some of the real spiritual processes and transformations that are actually embedded in Ibn 'Arabī's single image of the divine shadow-Play.[26] It is also helpful to keep in mind that the culminating realization of each of these many pairs can be summed up in the single Arabic expression that Ibn 'Arabī himself repeatedly uses to describe the ultimate human aim of this drama: *kamāl*—a term that can only be approximated as perfection, wholeness, comprehensiveness, integration, plenitude, fulfillment, and so on:

- From children (in their heedlessness) to spiritually mature adults.

- From shadows to the Light.

- From confusion or blindness to clarity and spiritual insight (Chapter 3 above).

- From plurality (people as infinitesimal parts) to wholeness or Unicity (or *ahadiyya* and *tawhīd*).

- From causal, cyclically repetitive existence to its meta-causal Ground (from *khalq* to *Haqq*)—and hence to true freedom.

- from continuous, homogenous serial time to the trans-temporal Now (from the illusions of *zamān* to the divine *dahr* and only real Instant, *waqt*).

- From beliefs (or illusion and hypocrisy) to true knowing.

- From apparent chaos or randomness to order.

- From dreaming (or sleepwalking) to awakening.

- From the near-animal ego to realized Spirit: from *bashar* to *insān.*

- From separation to reunion (and all the integrally related Qur'anic themes of divine covenant and promise).

- From distance (or exile) to divine proximity (*qurba* and *walāya*).

- From the outward (*zāhir*) to the inner (*bātin*).

- From wandering to being rightly guided (the Straight Path).

- From reaction or passion to right action (*ihsān*: Chapter Three above).

- From distraction to intention and clear focus.

- From manipulation, acquisition, and defensiveness to creation and co-operation.

- From rebellion or resistance to loving-service (*'ubūdiyya*).

- From dissonance to harmony, cacaphony to music (Chapter Two above).

- From determination or slavery to actualized freedom, rational choice, and moral responsibility.

- From speaking-deafness to real listening (*samā'*, at the end of Chapter Two).

- From effortful journeying to "being-carried" (Chapter One above).

V. FROM MAP TO VOYAGING: NAVIGATING THE OCEAN OF SIGNS

While there are several reasons for providing this intentionally dizzying, yet still highly abridged list of subjects and lessons suggested by Ibn 'Arabī's single outwardly simple image of the shadow-Play, one of the most important is simply to suggest something of the actual experience of reading his works, and more particularly the *Meccan Illuminations*. For such intense density and deceptive simplicity of expression, mystifying allusiveness, and rushing alternation of different spiritual and metaphysical perspectives are among the truly defining characteristics of his dis-

279

tinctive rhetoric and its immediate effects on attentive and active readers.[27]

Incidentally, none of those characteristic rhetorical effects—intended to re-create that receptive spiritual condition Ibn 'Arabī often calls *hayra*, or spiritual bewilderment—are particularly attenuated or remedied by greater familiarity with Ibn 'Arabī, or by greater depth of background and relevant experience. Instead, just as with Hafez's even more compressed lyrical equivalents of these rhetorical devices in his incomparable songs, precisely the opposite is more often the case. For everything a reader is able to bring to these enigmatic symbolic expressions only deepens their allusiveness, resonating intensity, and the expanding webs of significance they continue to open up. One very important result, as each of his serious readers usually discovers fairly rapidly, is that Ibn 'Arabī's writing was certainly never constructed—like most modern prose—to be read through quickly, while attempting to assimilate rapidly a few key guiding ideas or new intellectual insights and observations. Instead, works like the *Meccan Illuminations* are meant to be read—and only begin to reveal their secrets—when we approach them in an appropriate spirit. And what that actually means, in practical terms, is not that difficult to grasp. One very traditional way to start, that we have already encountered in Chapter One of this book, is with the classical metaphor of the spiritual journey that is implied—and existentially demanded—by each of those contrasting poles of spiritual conditions we have just briefly evoked.

Returning to the four constitutive elements of the process of realization, and the different corresponding perspectives on the divine shadow-play, which were outlined in the three preceding sections, the severe limitations of each of those first three possibilities are all equally apparent. If the above accounts were too abstract, those corresponding practical options are beautifully dramatized, for anyone to see, in the all too familiar comic figures of those memorably self-satisfied "bird-souls" who open *'Attār*'s famous *Mantiq al-Tayr* ("The Language of the Birds"), with their familiar litany of compelling reasons for staying safely at home in their own familiar psychic territories.[28]

Thus resting in the apparent safety of belief or unthinking conformity to any external authority (the inner state of *taqlīd*) has the signal, quite visible advantages of comfort, safety and ample reassuring social reinforcement. By its very nature, that facile option implies—or even demands—little real forward motion, an absence of clear direction, and at best the slow ritual accumulation of religious merit, a process whose eventual spiritual results are far from immediately visible, and which is also open to many historically obvious forms of deviation or self-delusion. The second option of relying instead on the restricted discursive intellect, as intellectuals themselves know best, naturally tends to turn one's attention and efforts away from the journey—or the Play itself—to the endless circular elaboration of ever more refined "maps" or forms of theatrical and scriptural criticism. And finally, the option of reliance on the accidental, intermittent occurrences of random moments of memorable inspiration or unveiling has its own abundant—albeit often highly educational—spiritual dangers: those recurrent pitfalls are amply illustrated throughout the remainder of 'Attar's parable of this spiritual journey, and are thoroughly analyzed in many sections of Ibn 'Arabī's own writings. For the lightning-flashes of illumination often accompany devastating storms.

281

If we stop to think, then, of what is most practically important for the actual voyaging of spiritual realization, beyond those three familiar starting positions, the most basic needs are immediately apparent—and all of them are already powerfully expressed in key symbols from the Qur'an and Islamic tradition. They include close attention to, and eventually discernment of, the different transporting "winds" (a symbol sharing the root-meanings of both "spirit" and "soul-breath," *rūh* and *nafs*), and of the treacherous hidden currents of the basharic ego-self. Secondly, an intimate knowledge of the changes and guiding functions of the stars, planets, moon, as well as the times defined by the sun—that is, of all the scripturally central reference-points of guidance (the standard Qur'anic symbols of prophecy and sainthood or *walāya*). And finally, the accompaniment of a fully experienced guide or a master-navigator—or "Director" of this Play—who can also teach us to undertake our own navigating.

Now this brief catalogue of the would-be spiritual voyager's basic needs happens to coincide precisely with the essential aims and intentions of all of Ibn 'Arabī's works, and especially of the *Meccan Illuminations*—where we have already encountered his development of many of these navigational aids in each earlier Chapter. But this last-mentioned point also suggests what is precisely most unusual and distinctive about his own work and characteristic spiritual approach, when we compare it to the many early and contemporary Islamic traditions of spiritual guidance on which he constantly draws.[29]

What, then, can concretely move this drama's childish audience from the safety, distractions and intermittent excitement of the three preceding stages into active, spiritually effective participation in the Play itself, into the actual process of spiritual realization? One essential hint lies in Ibn 'Arabī's telling explanation, as he elaborates his image of the shadow-theater of existence, that the veil that screens most of its heedless viewers from the Player represents the mystery or inner reality of the divine determination of all things, and especially of each person's own individual destiny: *sirr al-qadar*.[30] On the level of the intellect and religious beliefs, this phrase is commonly understood to refer to all the abstract challenges of theodicy: that is, to the ultimate theological explanation of all the apparent injustices, undeserved sufferings, inexplicable misfortunes and other metaphysical complaints endemic to human existence. At that strictly intellectual level, the range of possible theological and philosophical responses are familiar in every civilization and had already been well-explored throughout earlier Islamic traditions, in ways that basically parallel the limited set of possibilities in any monotheistic religious setting.

VI. The Alchemy of Earthly Existence

In striking contrast to those earlier abstract, purely intellectual approaches, what Ibn 'Arabī himself is directing his readers to through this rich image of the divine shadow-Play is something far more direct and existential: it is each individual human being's unavoidable—and inherently unique and personal—quest for the meaning, ultimate purpose, and deeper causal processes underlying his own personally inescapable "Fire-like" experiences of suffering, injustice and imperfection. As the mysterious prophet Idrīs had already indicated, near the very beginning of the *Futūhāt*,[31] there is a more straightforward reason why human beings' earthly path and spiritual development—if not their spirit's origin—begins with the all the attractions and pitfalls of the Fire: for most novices, such educational experiences are far more effective and lastingly motivating than the subtle fragrances and distant promises of the Gardens.[32] What Idrīs unfolds there provides a particularly dramatic illustration of the reasons for paying closer attention to those prophetic "Describers" who play such a mysterious role in Ibn 'Arabī's ongoing account of this Divine Comedy.

THE REFINING FIRE: FROM THE DIVINE "BREATHS" TO TRUE SERVANTHOOD

Idrīs's revealing teaching first appears at the heart of one of Ibn 'Arabī's first extended discussions of eschatology in the *Meccan Illuminations*, chapter 15 (out of 560), entitled "Concerning the Inner Knowing of the (divine) Breaths and the Knowing of Their Poles Who Realize the Breaths, and of Their Secrets." The "Breaths" here, as Ibn 'Arabī soon explains, following a famous hadith, "are the fragrant scents of the divine Proximity." The spiritual "Pole" in question at this point is the central spiritual reality of the prophet Idrīs (or Ilyās/Elias, as he is called in the corresponding chapter of the *Fuṣūs al-Hikam*): "the Healer of Wounds," "the Pole among the Knowers of the divine Breaths, the axis around which their sphere revolves and the Leader (*Imām*) through which their kingdom subsists."[33]

This early chapter—which dramatically foreshadows Ibn 'Arabī's most fundamental eschatological teachings—opens with a poem expressing the Shaykh's own urgent pleading to the divine "Gatekeeper" to reveal the deeper reason for the apparently arbitrary and undeserved sufferings and vicissitudes all human beings necessarily experience in this world, due to the conflicting divine influences transmitted by the "watchmen" of the planetary spheres and their governing angelic "spiritual realities."[34] Significantly, what Ibn 'Arabī is really asking for here is precisely a revelatory glimpse "behind the curtain" of the divine shadow-Play:

I said to the gatekeeper, when he noticed (me):
    "What is it I am suffering from the watchmen?"

He said:"What do you desire, O my son?"
    I said:"Closeness to the Master, the Wise-Healer (*Hakīm*):

Who (will be) my intercessor with the Leader (*Imām*)?
    Perhaps he will give thought to one who steals a glance?"

(The gatekeeper) said: "He does not give of His knowing
    to someone self-sufficient, not experienced in suffering!"

Now "the first secret" revealed by this mysterious "Healer of Wounds" has to do with that quintessential spiritual alchemy which constitutes the very purpose of human beings' earthly existence. Ibn 'Arabi explains that this spiritual transformation sought and communicated by Idrīs[35] has to do with the mysterious fiery conversion of the symbolic "iron" of our terrestrial school into the "silver" and "gold" of beautiful action and realized spiritual knowing:

> He does not seek this (transformation) out of any desire for wealth, but rather out of a desire for a good-and-beautiful ultimate Goal, so that he might reach through it the stage of Perfection (*kamāl*), which is only acquired through (this world of) engendering-and-change (*takwīn*).

In other words, the whole manifest universe, symbolized by the seven heavenly spheres, is in reality, by its very design and formative Intention, what Ibn 'Arabī goes on to describe here as a cosmic "mine" or fiery "crucible" whose ultimate aim is the achievement of that golden Perfection constituted by and through each accomplished, fully human being (*insān*):

> ...and everything engendered in that mine is seeking its goal which is Perfection, the "golden" state. But while in the mine, there occur to it illnesses and diseases, by way of an imbalance of its elements and humors.... So this (cosmic spiritual) Physician/ Wise-Man (*hakīm*) was given the knowledge of the remedies and medicines, the use of which removes these incidental illnesses that had overcome the personality of this seeker of the stage of Perfection.

Ibn 'Arabi immediately goes on to specify that the "Perfection" (or Wholeness, Plenitude, Completion: *kamāl*) sought here has nothing to do with bodily health, nor with the accidental absence of any distracting bodily imbalances: "The Purpose (of our earthly existence) is nothing but the rank of human Perfection in Servanthood (*'ubūdiyya*)."

Among the other special knowings connected with this central prophetic Healer are the "secrets of revivifying the dead," and of the ways that the entire cosmos—the entire divine shadow-theater—is spiritually a single "Great Human Being" (*insān kabīr*) whose infinite realities are all paradoxically contained and potentially accessible in the single infinitesimal "Point" (*nuqta*) of the human spirit, in the illumined Heart:

> For God entrusted all Knowing in the (heavenly) spheres, and He made the fully human being (*insān*)

the total sum of the "subtle-spiritual-connections" (*raqā'iq*) of the entire cosmos. So there exists a spiritual connection extending from the human being to every thing in the cosmos, in such a way that through it the human being has those "commands" which God entrusted in those things, that they might deliver them to this human being. It is through this subtle connection that the human being who is a Knower actually moves that thing when he wants to.

So there is nothing in the universe that does not have an influence on the human being, and on which the human being does not also have an influence. For this (spiritual Pole, Idrīs as the "Healer of Wounds") had the unveiling and inner awareness of those spiritual connections, which are like rays of light.

At the conclusion of this remarkable brief chapter, recounting a fascinating story "reported to me by that Spirit from whom I have taken all that I have confided in this book," Ibn 'Arabī has Idrīs repeat, this time in even more compressed language, that same central eschatological secret of the indispensable refining, educational role of the Fire of our earthly existence, with all its inescapable suffering and loss, in the ultimate attainment of human spiritual perfection. This telling story is an account of Idrīs's private "last testament" (*wasiya*) to his earthly disciples, just prior to his being divinely *raised up* to his *lofty place* (19:56-57), as he sums up all his healing wisdom and understanding of this infinite shadow-Play in the form of a single mysterious riddle:

...The Real is the Real, while the path is the path!

So—[Ibn 'Arabī then interprets]—the Garden (of Paradise) and this lower-world were combined in the adobe and in the building (of Adam-*insān*, the fully human being), even though one of them is made from clay and straw, and the other from gold and silver.

This is an enormous question which he gave us as a riddle and then went away. Whoever knows its (meaning) will be happy and rested![36]

THE BRIDGE THROUGH THE FIRE TO THE GARDENS

As for the way out through this Fire, the Qur'anic eschatological symbolism underlying much of Ibn 'Arabī's initial outline of the human spirit's ascension or Rising (*qiyāma*) is developed systematically throughout chapters 61-65 in the initial larger Section of his *Meccan Illuminations*, an extremely complex discussion to which I have devoted a separate forthcoming book. So here one can only provide an indicative selection of a few of Ibn 'Arabī's most central and indispensable guidelines—an approach that is certainly much easier for the reader than slowly working through those elaborate symbolic discussions, but which also tends to short-circuit all the more challenging original spiritual processes and rhetorical intentions discussed earlier in this chapter.

In any case, if the very title of his opening chapter 61 on Gehenna—stating quite explicitly that "*most of the creatures are (already) in It, with regard to their suffering*"— was not a sufficiently explicit allusion to the unavoidable starting point for this ascending journey, we begin here with an even more unambiguous indication. This short passage also helps to make explicit the direct connection between the complex, scattered symbolic allusions of the Qur'an and the simpler, unforgettable dramatic portrayal of this cosmic process in the almost cinematic "hadith of the Intercession" (translated in full at the very end of Chapter Three above). In a relatively hidden "appendix" (*wasl*) at the end of chapter 64, Ibn 'Arabī begins to speak of that path across the Fire of Gehenna: *"which is (already) here spiritually and in reality,"* even though it appears in the hadith dramaturgy of the Last Day in more sensible form, as a kind of Bridge leading across the Fire of Gehenna to the gates of Paradise:

> And the group (of most human beings) who do not remain everlastingly in the Fire are only seized and questioned and chastised upon the Bridge (or Path: *al-sirāt*). The Bridge is upon the surface of Gehenna, disappearing from sight into It. And it is with the hooks in (that Bridge, mentioned in the hadith) that God seizes those (who are traveling) upon it.
>
> Now since that Bridge is in the Fire—for there is no Way to the Garden except upon it—, God said: *And there is no one among you all, but that he is entering It (the Fire): That was absolutely decreed (as incumbent) upon your Lord!* (19:71) So whoever truly knows the real inner meaning of this (divine) Saying knows where is the *place* of Gehenna.[37]

So once we have grasped where we already are—and where our own Rising always begins—a great many other puzzles and allusions in these eschatological chapters begin to come into clearer perspective, especially since each of Ibn 'Arabī's readers already naturally brings to this subject a considerable body of uniquely firsthand experience of the particular sorts of hooks, fires, and powerfully illuminating tests in question. Indeed, as these *Openings* continue to unfold,

289

Ibn 'Arabī's allusions to the clarifying implications of this "voluntary dying" or spiritual awakening of each soul's "first death" gradually become more explicit in later passages, as in the following key autobiographical remark from chapter 351, which points directly to the indispensable role of his own experience expressed in and illuminating these earlier chapters:[38]

> The voluntary return to God is something for which the servant [i.e., Ibn 'Arabī himself] is most thankful. God said: *The whole affair is returned to Him* (11:123). So since you know that, return to Him willingly and you will not be returned to Him by compulsion. ...For He meets you in (the form of) your attributes, nothing else but that—so examine your self, my friend! (As the Prophet) said: "Whoever loves to meet God, God loves to meet him; and whoever is averse to meeting God, God is averse to meeting him."[39]
>
> Now since we knew that our meeting with God can only be through death,[40] and because we knew the inner reality of death, we sought to bring it about sooner, in the life of this world. Hence we died, in the very Source of our life, to all of our concerns and activities and desires, so that when death overcame us in the midst of that Life which never passes from us, ...we met God and He met us.
>
> ...Hence when there comes what is commonly known as death, and *the veil* of this body *is removed from* us (50:22), our state will not change and our certainty will not be any greater than what we already experience now. For we *tasted no death but the first death*, which we died during our life in this world, because our Lord *protected us from the tor-*

290

ment of Gehenna, as a bounty from your Lord: that is the Supreme Achievement (44:56-57).

So the person who returns to God in this way is among the blessed and does not even feel the inevitable, compulsory return (at bodily death), because it only comes to him when he is already there with God.... And their condition when they are raised up will be just like that: it will not change insofar as their being with God is concerned, nor with regard to what God gives them at every instant.

Of course the gradual accumulation of many such short revelatory passages eventually suggests that Ibn 'Arabī—like the earlier prophetic Describers—is attempting to convey in this work a sense of the spiritual reality of the entire cosmic drama of the human "Rising-up" (*al-qiyāma*) as viewed almost "from the outside," from the macrocosmic perspective of its Goal and conclusion, in which the actual roles and underlying realities of each spiritual element and stage can be more clearly perceived and specified.

CONSTRUCTING THE CRUCIBLE: THE ELEMENTS OF TESTING

We are all aware, in matters great and small, of the often miraculous ways our discovery of the ultimate purpose or "final cause" of an outwardly chaotic situation can entirely, often quite suddenly, transform our awareness and experience of that situation. Indeed, it may well be that the gradual disclosure of that element of finality may in itself be one of the great dramatic—and spiritually effective—secrets of the larger divine Comedy that is Ibn 'Arabī's subject, just as it is in all the poetic and literary mirrorings of that same story.[41] If we return to Idrīs's earlier terse revelation (in chapter 15) of that Goal of the fiery crucible of earthly existence and

291

suffering as Perfection, or the active realization of fully human being (*kāmil al-insān*), that chapter now provides us with a kind of connecting thread that can help us to gradually assemble a single, intellectually coherent meaningful picture of the many eschatological realities Ibn 'Arabī alludes to in chapters 60-65 of these *Meccan Illuminations*.

Accordingly, Ibn 'Arabī devotes the preliminary chapter 60 to an elaborate preparatory cosmological depiction of the immense stage and outer framework of this shadow-Play, in which all the elements of creation, of the Qur'anic *"heavens and the earth"*—especially its hidden spiritual, angelic dimensions—are all carefully orchestrated toward the ultimate divine Purpose of human perfection. He sums up that situation, near the end of that chapter (IV, 358), in a corresponding Qur'anic verse: *And He has subjected to you all whatever is in the heavens and in the earth, altogether from Him: Surely in that is a Sign for a people who think and reflect!* (45:13), as well as in a famous divine saying "sent down in the Torah": *O son of Adam, I created the things for your sake; and I created you for My sake!* Or as Ibn 'Arabī himself puts it even more succinctly there: "So the Whole (of the cosmos) is subjected (by God) for our sake, since we are the Goal of the universe."

Thus it is no surprise that Ibn 'Arabī's opening poem in the immediately following chapter (61) on Gehenna immediately introduces three of the most essential elements of this eschatological drama of the human spirit's Rising and Return—"Act 2" of this elaborate eschatological process, which eventually recapitulates the over-arching cosmological Act 1 of the divine creative Descent and Self-manifestation that he had already detailed in so many earlier chapters of the *Futūhāt*. The first key element, beginning that opening poem, is his still enigmatic assertion of the aim and omnipresence of divine Justice (*'adl*) justifying and explaining the entire drama. For all the eschatological events of the spirit's Rising and Return, beginning with the Qur'anic eschatological image of the "rolling up" of the dome of heaven, are

...so that the Upholder of its earth may do Justice to you:
    For upon Him stood Its support and its construction.[42]

The next lines introduce the other two foundational parts in this drama: the indispensable Mephistophelean testing role of Iblīs (and hence of all the "*Satans among the humans and jinn*") in this most familiar abode of Gehenna—and, in contrast, the radically different and more complex transformational nature of human being (of Adam, as the archetype of human being, *insān*):

Thus the creature of God with the most intense pains in it (Iblīs)
    was not created from (the earth). So as for its/His heaven:

The garments of (Iblīs's) Fire shroud him from (God's) Light!
    Therefore the test (of the Fire) is immense in the souls.

Not only do these introductory lines remind us openly of the peculiarly infernal, delusive qualities represented here by the Qur'anic figure of Iblīs: i.e., a purely illusory "light" whose eventually experienced reality is actually anger, rage and pure pain and—ultimately the same thing—a smoky "curtain" entirely obscuring the infinite heavenly Lights of all the divine Self-manifestations. At the same time, by implication, these opening lines highlight above all the correspondingly much greater complexity of the uniquely free, responsible, and potentially theomorphic Adamic nature. For that nature was uniquely created, as the Qur'an constantly reminds us, from the entire spectrum of Being: from

293

the life-giving "Breath" of the divine Spirit to the earthly "Clay" indispensable to that divine Spirit's Self-manifestation, ongoing mirroring, and ultimate acknowledgement in the accomplished reality of *insān*.

Simply as an important excursus here—briefly interrupting Ibn 'Arabī's own introduction to these "rules of the game"—it is important to stop and notice how the eventual deciphering of the deeper message and intended meaning of these short opening lines of poetry entirely depends on each reader's active provision of two further, initially only implicit elements. First, recalling the corresponding symbolic web of hundreds of related passages from the Qur'an and hadith (and their subsequent Islamic elaborations). And secondly, filling in the picture of what is openly said—i.e., the brief allusions to God's Justice and especially to Iblīs/ Shaytān's essential fiery nature and testing role—with what is thereby implied about the wider network of connected realities (in this case, the corresponding human experiences of suffering). It is important to stress the reader's own key role here, because almost every line in these chapters of the *Futūhāt* is carefully constructed to reveal its most important meanings precisely through that same actively participatory process, in which what is not openly mentioned— but indubitably intended and implied—is typically a kind of careful pointer to far more extensive and more important corresponding realities.

As one particularly important illustration of this repeated rhetorical process of indirect allusion, we eventually come to realize that almost everything that Ibn 'Arabī says in his chapters largely focusing on the cosmic theater of Gehenna and its Fires (60–64), regarding its distinctive qualities and what keeps its rare "true inhabitants" on its manifold tempting "descending stairs" (*darak*), also has an infinitely greater existential and spiritual significance in actually pointing to the corresponding ascending *ways out*: to all the qualities and phenomenological interactions of the different kinds of Gardens (of "merits," "inheritance," "actions" and "Vision") which he only very sketchily outlines in this particular section. Thus in this rich opening poem of chapter 61, for example, there is only one passing word about Iblīs's veiling from "*(God's) Light*"—and yet absolutely everything in these first eschatological chapters, when we read them more closely, continues to turn on the central contrast between our own personal veiling and the transforming spiritual Vision of God made possible through that Light—the central themes already elaborated in Chapter Three above.

Returning to chapter 61 of the *Futūhāt*—and confirming and elucidating Ibn 'Arabī's remarkably open indication, in his very title and in the immediately preceding chapter, as to where this "Gehenna" is and how it operates—he goes on to explain that this is simply the world perceived as Iblīs (or the shadow-Play's initially heedless children) perceive it, without any deeper awareness of its Ground or purpose or true dimensions. As the Shaykh puts it, quoting as always the pertinent Qur'anic verses, this Gehenna:

> ... is an abode...with no live coals but the children of Adam and those "*stones*" they have taken as their gods; and the jinn (like Iblīs) are Its *flames*. [As God] said: [...*a Fire*] *whose fuel is people and the stones*... (2:24; 66:6). And He said: *Surely you all, and whatever you worship/serve other than God, are the firewood of Gehenna!* (21:98).

Within that entirely closed and futile, despairingly cyclical perspective, everything seems to fan the infernal flames of desire, frustration, corruption and hopelessness:

Thus the instruments (of their chastisement/suffering) are newly-generated in (Gehenna) through the arrival of the actions of *the jinn and the humans* (7:179; etc.) who are actually entering it![43]

VII. From the Fire to the Light

Almost immediately, in chapter 61, Ibn 'Arabī turns to his deeper subject, the secret of the Rising (*qiyāma*) and the soul's transforming way out of this Crucible, which he finds dramatically exemplified, in all its existential essentials, in one of the most familiar of the divine sayings, usually called the "hadith of the Questioning," since its story—closely paralleling a nearly identical eschatological passage at the end of Matthew (25:31–46)—recounts God's revelatory questioning of an archetypal human soul at the Rising, who has signally failed to recognize and respond appropriately to God's earthly Self-manifestations in all the infinite human forms of suffering, longing and need.[44] Of course readers of the Qur'an are well aware that in its underlying symbolism, merely physical hunger, thirst and illness are, among human beings, the tiniest tip of the iceberg of that immense realm of suffering and needfulness.

The particular metaphysical language Ibn 'Arabī uses in this discussion, referring to the contrasting human manifestations of the divine Attributes of Compassion or Lovingmercy (*rahma*) and of Anger (*ghadab*), is characteristic of all his writing, and so all his readers are meant to understand that ultimately—as foreshadowed in various well-known divine sayings that he cites repeatedly—God's "Compassion encompasses all things," since *My Compassion has precedence over My Anger.* Equally important, the contrast of these two key divine Attributes is meant to contain and refer implicitly to all the intrinsic oppositions or polarities of so many of the other divine Names (for example, the contrasting Names of Beauty and awesome Majesty, of *jamāl* and *jalāl*), paired Names whose direct experiential knowing—as highlighted in the repeated central Qur'anic accounts of Adam's uniquely theomorphic "knowing of the Names"—is uniquely accessible through the inherent extremes of the human condition.

THE WAY OUT—THE HADITH OF THE QUESTIONING

The underlying human problem, of course, is that we all start out in life—wherever we happen to start, including Gehenna—as naïve, unconscious dualists, somehow anthropomorphically supposing that these two divine qualities, the Fire of anger and the life-giving Water of Love and Compassion, are strict opposites, entirely incompatible. And yet as Ibn 'Arabī carefully points out here, echoing Idrīs's earlier lessons in chapter 15, it is precisely the dynamic interaction of these contrasting qualities within the Crucible that actually reveals and highlights the Iblīs-like, satanic qualities of Anger and distorted, "one-eyed" materialistic vision as the indispensable precursors—indeed as essential engines and instruments—in bringing to birth the "silver and gold" of the full manifestation and appreciation of the depths of divine *Rahma*, both in our purified acts of beauty and in immediate inspired knowing:

> Thus God created (Gehenna) from the Self-manifestation (the theophany, *tajalli*) of His Saying—in the hadith (recorded by) Muslim: "*I was hungry, yet you didn't feed Me! And I was thirsty, yet you didn't give Me to drink! And I was sick, yet you didn't visit Me!*" This is the most immense of the descents through which the Real has descended to His servants in His Gracious-Kindness with them.

297

Therefore Gehenna—may God preserve us and you all from It!—was created from this Reality. And because of that, It has dominated over *the domineering ones* (14:15-17) and shattered *the arrogant ones* (16:29; etc.).

...So all that is created in (Gehenna), of the pains which are found by those who enter It, is from (the manifestations of) the attribute of the divine Anger. But that (purifying suffering) only comes to be through the entering into (Gehenna) of the creatures, among *the jinn and the humans* (7:179, etc.) when they have entered It. ... Gehenna is only a place for them, while they are the ones descending-to-lodge in It. So they are the place-of-settling of the Anger, while it is what descends to lodge through them. So the Anger, here, is precisely the pain itself!

Yet as Ibn 'Arabī soon goes on to explain, the ultimate significance of all the suffering and destruction inherent in that infernal condition of Anger is not in its outward results, in its more immediately visible revealing and eventual destruction of all the "Iblīs-like" forms of human pride, pretence, anger and self-aggrandizement—but rather in the inner, quite literal divine "Com-passion" that is ultimately brought about precisely through those manifestations of Anger: in the mysteriously transforming opening-up of the human Heart to those distinctively divine attributes and realities of divine Love and Compassion (*rahma*) which people cannot help but seek whenever they are caught up in that apparently hopeless condition:

For the descending of God, the Truly Real, to (Gehenna) with His *Compassion that encompasses*

every thing (40:7) and with His *Tender Sympathy*
(19:13), opens up the space, for this One Who does
so beautifully for It this (divine) act-of-good-and-
beauty (*ihsān*), by which He can manifest (His Compassion), through *the calling out* (for God's Help
by those suffering in Gehenna) (21:11-15), as well
as through Its corrective-authority over whoever was
(formerly) domineering.

[All this happens because of people's having to
pass through Gehenna], together with the totality of
what It does for the (former) "rejecters (of God)"
that is part of (their eventual) gratefulness toward
the Bestower of blessings, through (His) bestowing
blessings upon It.[45] Thus (Gehenna) does not truly
know and recognize of Him—may He be glori-
fied!—anything but Absolute Blessing, untouched
by anything contrary to that.[46]

Significantly, Ibn 'Arabī returns again to highlight the spiritually central practical importance of this same far-reaching insight into the aim and deeper meaning of the shadow-
Play at the very beginning and end of chapter 62, on "the
people of the Fire":

Now God says to Iblīs, out of His Generosity and
the all-inclusiveness of His Loving Compassion,
when (Iblīs) said to Him [after witnessing the creation of the theomorphic Adam and the angels' obe-
dient prostration before him as God's "stand-in"
(*khalīfa*, at 17:61)]:
    "*Do You see, You, this (thing of clay) that You
have honored above me!? Surely if You put off until
the Day of Rising, I will most certainly take over his
progeny, except for a few!*" /

299

(God) said: *"Go! For whoever follows you among them, Gehenna is surely the recompense for you all, an abundant recompense! / And try to incite whomever of them you are able to with your voice; and draw up against them with your horses and footmen; and be their partner in (their) possessions and children; and promise them!"* [—*for Satan does not promise them anything but delusion...*] (17:62-64).

Hence Iblīs did not come (to tempt and test human beings) except by the Command of God. For it is a *divine* Command, including a promise and a threat, and it was an intense testing (*ibtilā'*: 89:15-16, etc.) concerning our right/reality/truth (*haqq*), so that God might show (Iblīs) that among (Adam's) progeny are *those over whom Iblīs has no control* (17:65) and no power.

For the paradoxical "hidden secret" of Iblīs/Shaytān—which Ibn 'Arabī reveals elsewhere, pleading that he only dares to do so because Iblis never stops to look back at the actual long-term consequences of his angry and destructive efforts[47]—is that all his testing, like the crucible of the Fire more generally, ultimately results (in all but a relative handful of cases) in *tawba*, in the human soul's "turning back" to God in repentance, and in its consequent discovery of the spiritual Guidance and domains of realization lying beyond and above the pains of this lastingly memorable starting point. At the very end of this same chapter on the people of the Fire, Ibn 'Arabī pointedly, and with rare explicitness, highlights the fundamental role of all these subtle "educational allusions" (*tanbīhāt*) in helping us to recognize the essential interactions of these uniquely individual tests and their consequences in our own development of spiritual intelligence, as we slowly develop the judgment and discernment needed to recognize both the tests themselves, and above all the lastingly meaningful lessons to be drawn from their proper consequences:

> Now we have pointedly hinted at certain situations, from this book of mine, where the inquiring regard (*nazar*) of the inquiring-and-observant person should roam, including the verses which we brought to witness in this chapter, at its very beginning, about God's commanding Iblīs (to do) what He mentioned to him (17:62-64).

Or as the Shaykh sums it up it even more bluntly:

> *So there is no chastisement/suffering more intense, for (human) spirits, than ignorance. For it is stupidity and neglect, all of it!*

INSIGHT AND INTERCESSION

Each time human beings eventually succeed in truly turning away from the Fire and the sufferings of spiritual ignorance, it is always toward—and often together with—those various "firemen," the effective instruments and vehicles of the divine loving-Compassion, whose actions and intercession are so memorably described in the famous hadith of the Intercession (translated at the end of Chapter Three above): that is, the angels, divine messengers, prophets, all the protecting Friends of God (*awliyā'*), and the rare "people of true faith" (*mu'minūn*) who are already, all of them, "in the Gardens." Phenomenologically speaking, the actual, individually operative forms and manifestations of that divine Love and Guidance are truly infinite. Indeed the key passages of the *Futūhāt* we have just quoted—like their extraordinary classical "film versions" already men-

301

tioned above—paradoxically highlight precisely the indispensable role of all the manifestations of Iblīs in that larger process.

But we can only perceive and respond appropriately to the particular manifestations of that always-available Intercession and Guidance when we are—to adapt Rumi's famous poetic adaptation of this same Qur'anic language—"fully cooked" (spiritually mature) and thus adequately prepared to listen, see and act appropriately. Within that larger process of spiritual realization, so beautifully illustrated in those many key passages brought together in the four preceding Chapters here, insight and intercession are in fact inseparable. Each uniquely individual "lesser Rising" (*al-qiyāmat al-sughrā*) is all about their synergy: about the spiraling interaction of "intercession" (in all the mysterious forms of Grace); receptivity and insight; action, consequences, and reflection.

Now without any doubt, the "Describer"—and intercessor and fireman—who is the constant, undivided focus of all of Ibn 'Arabī's own spiritual pedagogy and attention is that prophetic Messenger whose reality and intentions are outwardly approached through the historical forms of the Qur'an and certain hadith. But most importantly, Ibn 'Arabī's focus remains there not because of some autobiographical accident of history, culture or personal predilection, but because of his own uniquely informed assurance of the universality and all-inclusiveness of the Reality conveyed through those particular scriptural forms. Without entering into all the relevant autobiographical dimensions of Ibn 'Arabī's characteristic focus and assurance, which have been discussed in many other studies, the range of ongoing interest in his work by spiritual students from every imaginable religious and cultural tradition is already

302

one very visible sign that the Shaykh's universal perspectives here might not be entirely unfounded.

In any event, the real and constantly ongoing practical
problem in this Play, as we have already noted, is that even
the most effective and accurate of descriptions and describers can only too easily be profoundly misunderstood, mis-
interpreted and mis-applied by the denizens of the Fire. So
it is surely no accident that in his initial chapter on Gehenna,
while describing his own divinely granted vision of the constant quarrelsome disputatiousness (and their underlying,
blindly driving will to dominate) of the inhabitants—or
"owners" (ashāb)—of the Fire, Ibn 'Arabī parenthetically
remarks that:

> ...Indeed their way of quarrelling (in the Fire, as I
> saw it in my vision) did not resemble anything more
> than the "people of (theological and juridical) dif-
> ferences" in their public disputations, whenever one
> of them uses his debating-evidence (to convince oth-
> ers of his own position).

In telling contrast, the immediately following line beautifully encapsulates that spirit which is indispensable for the
fruitful reading of the Shakyh's works, or those of any of
the divine Describers:

> Now when I saw that, I was reminded of the state
> that God had made me cognizant of, so I saw that
> (God's) Loving Compassion, all of it, lies in inner
> surrendering and willing receptivity to prophecy, and
> in halting-in-openness in the presence of the (di-
> vine) Book and the Teaching (of the Prophet).[48]
>
> ...So for us, the *only* thing is to be in a state of
> inner readiness to receive whatever of the speech of
> prophecy newly-arrives through the "transmitter-of-

speaking," without disputing[49]—and to do so whether that new-speaking is in response to a question or spontaneous speech. So halting-in-openness in the presence of (the Prophet's inspired) speech is obligatory—whether that is occasioned by a question or by something sent down.[50]

At first, this indispensable profound spiritual receptivity might seem to be the unique possession of the accomplished saints, masters and Friends of God. But normally some effective and prolonged experience of spiritual work and realization does suffice to begin to reveal—as we have already seen in Chapter Four above—how much most of us are in fact constantly relying upon the intuitive, previously acquired and integrated fruits of precisely this process, gradually obtained throughout the everyday tests and spiritual learning experiences of life. After a long discussion of these indispensable conditions for true listening and spiritual receptivity, Ibn 'Arabī concludes with the following beautiful description of this indispensable "get-out-of-jail" card, to be used whenever we find ourselves in the "prison" (as he repeatedly and explicitly calls it) of Gehenna:

> ...Therefore it is incumbent on the person with practical intelligence and true faith, who *"gives good-counsel to his own soul,"*[51] whenever he hears someone saying "God said" or "the Messenger of God said," to listen attentively; to pay close attention; to try to find the proper courtesy (the *adab* required for applying it in that particular spiritual situation); and to seek to understand what God said or what His Messenger said. For God says: *When the Qur'an is read, then you all (should) listen to It attentively and pay close attention, so that perhaps*

304

you all may receive (God's) Loving Compassion!
(7:204) So He made our expectantly hoping (for
God's loving *rahma*) dependent on this attribute (of
listening attentively and humbly)...

Eventually, almost all of the scattered—initially often apparently random or unrelated—anecdotes and stories recounted in these eschatological chapters can be clearly understood as further pointed reminders (*tanbīhāt*) highlighting the indispensable role of this transforming element of
inspired insight (*basīra*) and spiritual intelligence, if we are
ever to begin to recognize the "firemen," all the constantly
varying forms and instruments of divine guidance, instruction and providence, who are constantly working both in
front of and behind the curtain within this Play.[52] And beyond that, needless to say, those elements are always required if we are to begin to discover our own unique personal responsibilities for bringing other human beings out
of that same Fire.

Thus in chapter 61, Ibn 'Arabī's longest, elaborate discussion of that decisive saving role of spiritual insight takes
the peculiar outward form of a long, at first apparently parenthetical, discussion of the different astronomical causes
of "eclipses"—an account that the reader only slowly comes
to realize must be pointing in fact to all the corresponding
(inner and outward) causes of spiritual "veiling." This critically important "aside" is then immediately followed by an
even more apparently incongruous and unexpected discussion—in the midst of a chapter supposedly about the people
of the Fire—of the people of "spiritual cautiousness" (*wara'*)
and their inspired ability to perceive directly the inner states
of certain things which are in reality—but not outwardly
and obviously—illicit:[53]

305

Now most of what illustrates this (intuitive unveiling of hidden realities) belongs to the people of spiritual cautiousness.[54] Thus the possessor of spiritual cautiousness who is (divinely) protected sees the (outwardly) licit food as pork or as excrement, and (the outwardly licit) drink as wine,[55] and he does not at all doubt what he actually sees.

Ah, if only people knew who truly possesses "sound (spiritual) senses," and who really has (only delusive) imagination![56] Is it the one who perceives the divinely prescribed judgment in a (visible) form, or the person who habitually perceives the sensible form (only) according to its (outward) state!?

The deeper lesson Ibn 'Arabī is conveying here has to do with our constant need, in the process of spiritual realization, for effective spiritual discernment of *all* the divine tests, lessons and responsibilities inherent in each given situation, tests which only become more complex and demanding at each level of our ascent. Here in the same passage he goes on to discuss that central spiritual faculty—and daily challenge—of discernment in terms of the enlightened perception of spiritual laws (and corresponding rights and wrongs, and rewards and penalties) which often go beyond those outward norms immediately given by our everyday, socially reinforced practical intellect:

However, it is not in the power of the human-animal (*bashar*), regarding most things, to perceive (accurately) either the reprehensible or the good in things. So if the Real has caused us to truly know them, then we do recognize them. For among them are things whose reprehensible (quality) is perceived by the intellect, in our customary usage, such as ly-

306

ing and being ungrateful toward someone who benefits us; and those whose good is (also perceived) by the intellect, such as truthfulness and being grateful to someone who benefits us.

But life, he continues, also brings up many conflicting, more challenging situations in which those initially simple, commonly accepted rules do not apply, such as the following illustration:

> But as for the (spiritual) "penalty"[57] connected with certain kinds of truthfulness, or the (spiritual) "reward" connected with certain kinds of lying—that is up to God. He grants that compensation, according to whatever He wishes, according to the (actually) reprehensible or good (quality of that particular action). (For example) the truly human being (*insān*) is (spiritually) rewarded for lying in order to save a person of faith from destruction, even though lying is reprehensible in its essence. And the truly human being is (spiritually) penalized for (some kinds of) truthtelling, such as calumny and slander, even though truthtelling is good in its essence. So those (ultimate spiritual rewards and penalties) are something pertaining to divine prescribing (*amr shar'ī*).

Here again, all of Ibn 'Arabī's "openings"—in this book and his many others—can be seen as repeatedly renewed efforts to awaken, as far as possible, each reader's essential, transforming insight into the universal reality (*haqīqa*) intended by each of the authentic divine prescriptions. So it is certainly no accident if the set of much longer chapters immediately following these openly eschatological ones—

chapters 66-71—are entirely devoted to the immense, and phenomenologically utterly universal, realm of spiritual "mysteries" or inner meanings potentially conveyed and unveiled by the detailed particular features of each of the obligatory prescribed forms of worship, the *'ibādāt*.

Nor should it be any surprise if one of Ibn 'Arabī's most explicit statements in this regard comes in that same almost hidden passage (near the end of chapter 64) where he so explicitly pointed to the true places of the Fire and Gehenna. Having pointed out just where that saving Bridge—which is itself the "divinely revealed Path" (*al-sirāt al-mashrū'*)— is actually, practically situated, he then goes on to explain its description, in the words of the original hadith of the Intercession, as being "finer than a hair, and sharper than a sword." Those essential spiritual qualities of subtle insightfulness and saving discernment, which make all the difference between the safe Pathway (to the divine Water of Life) and the Fire, he continues, correspond to the dilemmas of our

> ...knowledge of the divinely revealed Pathway (*'ilm al-sharī'a*) in this lower life. For (without true spiritual guidance and inspiration) the actual aspect of Right/Truth/Obligation with God (*wajh al-haqq 'inda Allāh*) applying to that particular problematic situation is not known. Nor do we know which of those (jurists) striving to understand that has rightfully succeeded in reaching that (real and applicable meaning) in itself. So because of that we are (misleadingly) led to worship merely according to the predominance of their suppositions (*tu'ubbidnā bi ghalabāt al-zunūn*)!

This constantly recurring spiritual dilemma, Ibn 'Arabī continues, can never be resolved simply on the basis of the outward authenticity and relative accuracy of the transmission of those teachings: even at their best and most accurate, those traditional external approaches "can only give us the *form of words* of the (Prophetic) saying," by "knowing that the Messenger…said this or did that (in some earlier circumstance)." For the essential inspiration of *the pertinent divine intention* actually pertaining to each new existential situation we encounter is simply not accessible in terms of this world at all:

> For what we are (really) seeking is *to know what should be understood from that* (earlier Prophetic) saying or action, in order to apply its (relevant) judgment to this (new) problematic situation, with absolute certainty.

In matters of this material world, of course, the lack of such authentic spiritual intelligence and inspired higher direction often might not seem so serious. But understandably, the actual presence of this razor-sharp, hair-thin Bridge—and the unmistakably familiar smoke and heat of those fires over which the soul's path is always suspended—may suggest a profoundly different situation and response. So for those consciously involved in the tasks of spiritual realization and actively participating in this Play, such dramatic images are not a mere abstract description—neither a passing game nor "mere cinema." Real fires always concentrate our attention.

VIII. THE PERSPECTIVE OF THE WHOLE: SEEING THROUGH THE SHADOWS

Already near the end of his initial account of the events of the Rising, at the end of chapter 64, Ibn 'Arabī had signaled this unveiled secret of the divine shadow-Play—and the far wider tasks, perspectives and clarified intentions which flow from that realized spiritual intelligence:

> It is precisely the human being's "dying" that is his Rising—but only the "lesser Rising" (*al-qiyāmat al-sughrā*), as the Prophet says: "Whoever dies, his Rising has already begun." And the "Gathering" [i.e., the "*greater* Rising"] is the coming together of *all* the particular souls in the Universal Soul....

Allusive references to this "*greater* Rising" (and "greater" Gathering, Imām and many other symbolic eschatological terms likewise reflecting other aspects of this larger cosmic Whole) are scattered throughout the *Meccan Illuminations*, like so many seeds ready to grow and expand into other Gardens, if only....

And it turns out that the same secret of the twofold Return, the same comprehensive Vision, also lies at the very heart of each of those long eschatological hadith—translated in full at the end of Chapter Three above—that have accompanied us throughout this volume. In the nearly identical opening passage of both the two final hadith,[58] the omnipresent divine reality underlying that theophanic vision is already clearly suggested in the Prophet's paradoxical allusion—even though his interlocutors do not immediately remark it—to the already present phenomena, and the corresponding theophanic symbolism, of our relative vision of the Sun, moon, stars and planets, including his careful indication of the passing obstacles of clouds, veils and blinding sun-light. In the first of those two, the hadith of God's "transformation through the forms," that thinly veiled secret of the shadow-Play—as Ibn 'Arabī so often points out—is re-enacted in the unenlightened souls' repeated paradoxical failure to recognize what is already (and always) before us: those divine Signs and Presences that are quite literally everywhere, shining through every created form. While in the second hadith of the Intercession, what is dramatized is our even more puzzling failure to recognize and acknowledge the equally omnipresent reality of all the saving forms and loving instruments of Grace, Guidance and divine Compassion.

Even more concretely, in the unforgettable intensity of the hadith of the Questioning (at the Last Day)—what my students have often called the "hadith of God in the subway"—the lack of realized spiritual vision becomes far more personal, as that story highlights each person's extraordinary, if usually untapped, innate spiritual capacity to perceive the inner realities, suffering and longings of other human beings, often at levels that few of us can ever even begin to articulate, even when we do act out of that intuition.

At the same time, that hadith also shines a spotlight on the unspoken, but immense and uniquely personal panoply of unconscious excuses, fears, blinders and distractions that somehow keep each of us from more fully exercising that depth of unacknowledged spiritual awareness. Incidentally, that failure of vision—or perhaps more often, of concretely acting upon our inchoate vision—is often even more egregious with regard to our own hidden states of hunger, thirst, and illness, at least as compared to the more obvious needs and demands of those around us.

Finally, two other, even more famous shorter hadith already discussed throughout Chapter Three above, the hadith of Gabriel (on *ihsān* and *dīn*) and the hadith of the supererogatory works, carefully outline the essential practical steps toward actually achieving that beatific vision—steps which, like most of practical spirituality, are remarkably

311

the same everywhere, in every revealed tradition. However, at the very end of both those hadith we also find revealing allusions to the further, post-graduate secrets of that group of spiritual firemen Ibn 'Arabī often calls simply "those who return back (from the realized vision of God)" (the *rāji'ūn*): i.e., all those mediating Guardians or Friends of God (*awliyā' Allāh*) who are perhaps the most central, recurrent human subject of his interest throughout these *Meccan Illuminations*.

In both those latter hadith, the allusions in question are almost identical. And in each case, the goal and the highest stage of realization begins with our vision of the Real, with our illumined spiritual hearing and sight. But immediately, indeed intrinsically, those concluding statements move on to the inseparable translation of that enlightened vision into *action*, into the equally transformed instruments of those "hands" and "feet" that are now carrying out, actually manifesting, the corresponding transformational acts of true good-and-beauty, of *ihsān*.

As always, of course, this map alone is not yet the journey. And as Ibn 'Arabī's account of that "second Returning," from the Divine Presence back to all our companions in this Play, so boldly and unmistakably suggests, in this life we ourselves are far more likely to be moved and transformed not by any descriptive or scriptural account, but by each unforgettable encounter with one of those rare compassionate souls who are *already* returning from the Day of the Visit, with those Friends whose inner radiance—as the hadith of the Visit so beautifully describes—is already illuminating and reflecting off the faces of whoever encounters them.

Some of Ibn 'Arabī's most pertinent remarks about the distinctive levels of spiritual vision—and resulting transforming ways and aims of life—of those accomplished Knowers and Friends who are in these highest ranks on the Day of the Visit (with God) are to be found in chapter 73 of the *Futūhāt*, where his discussions are often directly adapted from his own memorable visionary experiences of these eschatological realities, first recorded in his book *al-Tanazzulāt al-Mawsiliyya* ("The Divine Inspirations Received at Mosul"). Here is a small taste of that illumination, hopefully sufficient for us to begin to reflect on how these bare scriptural descriptions might actually apply to ourselves and those around us:

> ... Now the full explanation of this matter is that the vision (of God) on the Day of the Visit is according to (each individual's) beliefs in this world. Thus the person who believes concerning his Lord what was given to him by intellectual reflection (*nazar*), and by immediate unveiling (*kashf*), and by careful imitation of his Messenger (*taqlīd*), sees his Lord in the form of the aspect of each belief he held concerning Him. So such a person receives three theophanies, with three "eyes," at the same instant. And similarly with the condition of the person (who follows) solely intellectual inquiry, or the person (who follows) only immediate unveiling, or the person (who follows) only imitation. But... *the Friends of God... who are not governed by any* (limited spiritual) *station* (33:13) ...are distinguished from all of (the ordinary believers) by their integral relationship to their Lord.
>
> However, the people of intellectual reasoning among them are in a rank lower than the people of spiritual unveiling, because in their (intellectual)

vision the veil of their thinking stands between them and the Truly Real (*al-Haqq*). Whenever they want to lift that veil (of thinking), they are unable to do so. And likewise the followers of the prophets (by way of outward imitation, *taqlīd*), however much they may desire to raise the veils of the prophets from themselves so that they can see God without that intermediary, are still unable to do so.

Therefore absolutely pure and flawless (spiritual) vision belongs in particular only to the Messengers among the prophets... and to the people of immediate unveiling. So whoever happens to attain this station...still participates in this (Vision) to the extent of what they have realized—even if they be on (any of) a thousand paths!

This key passage concludes with a description that could itself be taken as a kind of "spiritual motto" (*hijjīr*) for all those drawn to the study of religion:

So as for those fully human beings who concur with the belief held by each individual, with regard to what led that person to that belief, taught it to them and confirmed them in it: on the Day of the Visit such people see their Lord with the eye of *every* belief. Hence whoever strives to do well by their soul must necessarily seek out, during their (stay in) this world, all the things that are professed concerning that (ultimate Reality), and must come to know why each individual professing a position affirms what they profess....

For the gaze of the person who (truly) looks never leaves God, nor is it even possible for it to do so.... But this group (among the Friends of God),

314

who have this special kind of (comprehensive) knowledge of God, are in a separate row on the Day of the Visit. So when the (ordinary believers) return from the Visit, every one of them who holds a (particular) belief imagines that (this Friend) belongs to them (alone), because they see that the (Friend's) form of belief during the Visit is like their own form (of belief). *So the person who is like this* (i.e., who realizes the underlying Reality mirrored in every individual's unique inner forms of belief) *is beloved by all the groups—and it was (already) that way in this world* !

Now what we have just mentioned is only truly understood by the most outstanding and accomplished representatives of the people of unveiling and "finding-true-being" (*wujūd*). As for the people of only intellectual inquiry, they have not caught even a whiff of its fragrance. So pay heed to what we have just mentioned, and act accordingly!

Give the Divinity its rightful due, so that ...you may come to know for yourself the universality of the felicity of all God's creation and the vast extent of that (divine) *Loving-Compassion which encompasses every thing* (40:7).

One final closing parenthesis: these last words, beyond their metaphysical and spiritual intentions, have even more visibly practical and far-reaching political and social implications. One does not have to look far to discover such unique "firemen" at work. For Ibn 'Arabī's thought and teachings, and the implicit political philosophy and comprehensive religious understanding which is inherent in those spiritual principles illuminated throughout this volume, have continued for almost eight centuries to play a central historical

315

role in the elaboration of ever-renewed, locally adapted forms of the Islamic humanities that together helped bring about the creative development of richly diverse forms of Islam as a truly world religion, harmoniously and creatively co-existing with many other religions and cultures, in a vast range of cultural, linguistic and civilizational settings.

So today these concluding words of Ibn 'Arabī here, immediately before the "descending Return" of the Friends of God from their Vision of the Real, point to the essential practical pre-conditions for the quintessentially human pursuit of realized spiritual intelligence in any age: individual freedom and moral responsibility; the fundamentally human responsibility of inspired creativity (the opposite of *taqlīd*); and the equally inseparable practical consequences, whenever people exercise those defining spiritual responsibilities, of ever-increasing diversity and of tolerance—or more accurately, of conscious spiritual co-operation.[59]

But all that, understandably, is the subject for another book.

NOTES

1. See the detailed explanation of the significance of these issues in the recent study of "Ibn 'Arabī's Rhetoric of Realisation: Keys to Reading and 'Translating' the *Meccan Illuminations*," *Journal of the Muhyiddīn Ibn 'Arabī Society* [*JMIAS*], XXXIII (2003), pp. 54–99 [Part I]; XXXIV (2004), pp. 103–145 [Part II]

2. In this volume I shall normally refer either to the *Meccan Illuminations*, as this work is now most commonly known in Western languages, or simply to the *Futūhāt* (an abridged version of the original Arabic title, *al-Futūhāt al-Makkiyya*, literally "The Meccan Spiritual-Openings"). The Bibliography at the end of this volume includes, in addition to the translations and studies cited in these footnotes, a broad selection of the translations, biographies of the author, and major analytical studies now available in English.

3. The specifically Qur'anic significance of the "Heart" (*qalb*) and the different aspects of its "polishing" and purification are the primary subject of Chapter Two, although the same themes are also extensively developed in each of the other Chapters below.

4. Given the immensity of this work, which would probably require at least forty large volumes in an adequately annotated English translation, the following introductory studies, in the first three Chapters below, are primarily based on Ibn 'Arabī's developments within the large opening section (*Fasl al-Ma'ārif*, the "Section of [Foundational Spiritual] Knowledge"), chapters 1–73 of the 560 chapters included in the entire work. The first of six such sections making up the *Futūhāt*, this *Fasl* takes up more than a quarter of the total pages. For a more detailed explanation of this overall structure of the work, see my Introduction to *Ibn 'Arabī: The Meccan Revelations*, vol. I (New York, Pir Press, 2002). [In subsequent notes, this important anthology of translations (co-authored with W. Chittick) is referred to simply as *Meccan Revelations*.]

5. For a careful account of the challenges that task would involve, for translators and readers alike, see "Ibn 'Arabī's Rhetoric of Realisation…" (n. 1 above).

6. Many of these complementary forms of spiritual teaching are particularly illustrated at length in the massive concluding chapter (560) of the *Futūhāt*, which is often reprinted as a separate large Arabic volume. As discussed in more detail at a number of places below, the great extent of the openly autobiographical dimensions of Ibn 'Arabī's teaching, especially notable in the very title of this immense work which he completed and revised over several decades, were a relatively unusual innovation in comparison with the traditional literary expressions of Islamic spirituality, especially in learned Arabic writings normally intended for the elite of educated religious scholars.

7. This is the case because those recurrent questions of proper spiritual practice and understanding are intrinsically embedded in and arise spontaneously from any conscious experience of the deeper spiritual laws and realities in question. (The same phenomenon can be readily observed in the similarly remarkable pedagogical usefulness and immediate cross-cultural accessibility and effectiveness of contemporary spiritual films and related works of art.) In Chapters 4 and 5 below, which take up more explicitly the distinctive rhetorical and artistic methods and assumptions of Ibn 'Arabī's teaching, there are a number of allusions to parallel or analogous developments in other well-known representatives of the Islamic humanities.

8. This particular inter-active dimension of the mature development of spiritual intelligence is the primary subject of Chapters 3–5 below, after the preliminary familiarization with a number of constitutive elements of that process in the first two Chapters.

9. See the broad introduction to those different historical strands of interpretation and utilization of Ibn 'Arabī's teachings, both throughout Islamic history and in his more recent assimilation in various ways in the West, in "Ibn 'Arabī and His Interpreters," in the *Journal of the American Oriental Society* [*JAOS*], 106 (1986), pp. 539–551 and pp. 733–756; and 107 (1987), pp. 101–119. That initial survey has been continued and updated in several recent studies, especially "Ibn 'Arabī in the 'Far West': Visible and Invisible Influences," *JMIAS*, XXIX (2001), pp. 87–122; and "'*Except His Face...*': The Political and Aesthetic Dimensions of Ibn 'Arabī's Legacy," *JMIAS*, XXIII (1998), pp. 1–13.

10. The complex symbolism of the Prophet's "Night-Journey" (*isrā'*), together with Ibn 'Arabī's own more autobiographical development of his own related spiritual experiences and insights (especially

318

in chapter 367 of the *Futūhāt*), are introduced and translated in "The Spiritual Ascension: Ibn 'Arabī and the *Mi'rāj*," *JAOS*, 107 (1987), pp. 629–652, and 108 (1988), pp. 63–77. Most of that same translation and discussion is also included in the recent anthology volume, *The Meccan Revelations* (n. 4 above).

CHAPTER ONE
JOURNEYING: WANDERING AND ASCENT

1. *Kitāb al-Isfār 'an Natā'ij al-Asfār*, now available in the critical edition and French translation, with an indispensable Introduction, by Prof. Denis Gril: *Le Livre de dévoilement des fruits du voyage, d'Ibn 'Arabī*, (Combas, 1994).

2. To bring these diverse sources to a wider audience, I am preparing a separate volume of translations and studies relating to Ibn 'Arabī's treatment of the spiritual journey, consisting of a complete annotated English translation of the *Kitāb al-Isfār* and of all the related discussions scattered through these opening volumes of the *Futūhāt*.

3. See the famous autobiographical passages in chapter 1 (and the Prologue) of this work, which have been discussed by most writers on Ibn 'Arabī, conveniently summarized in chapter 8 of C. Addas' biography: *Quest for the Red Sulphur: The Life of Ibn 'Arabī* (Cambridge, Islamic Texts Society, 1993). For Ibn 'Arabī's complex understanding of the rituals of the Hajj (as elaborated in chapter 72 of the *Futūhāt*) as a symbolic representation of the entire initiatic journey of the soul, readers without access to the Arabic can consult the summary of that chapter in C.-A. Gilis, *La Doctrine initiatique du Pèlerinage à la Maison d'Allāh*, (Paris, les Éditions de l'Oeuvre, 1982). Also intentionally excluded from this discussion here in Chapter One is Ibn 'Arabī's extensive treatment throughout the *Futūhāt* of the related theme of *ziyāra* (alluding to verse 102:2 and many related hadith on this theme), of "*visiting* the tombs"—of the Friends of God, and by extension, of life in this world more generally.

4. The other four verses mentioning this Arabic root instead involve related meanings (in eschatological contexts) of "shining" or "glowing" and of "disclosing" or "unveiling"—all related root-meanings that Ibn 'Arabī often has in mind when he uses those terms, as in the title of his *Risālat al-Isfār* (at n. 1 above).

319

5. Interestingly enough, the same classical Arabic expression is now commonly used in modern times to refer to the phenomena we call "tourism." Lane (IV, p. 1482), quoting the *Lisān al-'Arab*, mentions the primary meaning as "journeying through the earth for the purpose of devoting oneself to religious services or exercises." The notions of relative isolation and of avoiding settled areas and communal social activities are also assumed in this primary meaning. The same Arabic expression was also used for the life-style and practices of ascetic hermits and solitaries (the original "monastics," in the root sense of that term) in early Christian tradition, and those characteristic ascetic practices were still a visible part of the immediate social world of Ibn 'Arabī and at least his Andalusian contemporaries.

6. Again, as mentioned at n. 3 above, we have had to set aside in this Chapter the closely related theme of the Hajj and other important Islamic forms of religious pilgrimage.

7. See R. W. J. Austin (translator), *Sufis of Andalusia* (London, Allen & Unwin, 1971); as well as the partial translation of other key parts of the Introduction and concluding sections of that work—not included in Austin's volume—by R. Boase and F. Sahnoun, "Excerpts from the Epistle on the Spirit of Holiness (*Risālah Rūh al-Quds*)," in *Muhyiddin Ibn 'Arabī: A Commemorative Volume*, ed. Hirtenstein and Tiernan, pp. 44–72.

8. Ibn 'Arabī identifies this figure as one of the four *Awtād* ("Supports") at the summit of the spiritual hierarchy—or rather, as the contemporary earthly "representative" (*nā'ib*) of that spiritual rank; there are other indications as well that this particular figure is the earthly representative of Jesus. See the details of Ibn 'Arabī's understanding of the spiritual hierarchy, including these key figures, in chapter 3 of the translation of M. Chodkiewicz' *Seal of the Saints: Prophethood and Sainthood in the Doctrine of Ibn 'Arabī* (Cambridge, Islamic Texts Society, 1993).

9. Bukhārī 97:15, 97:50, Muslim 48:22, and Ibn Māja 33:48; see also the variants and detailed textual discussions of this famous *hadīth qudsī* in W. Graham, *Divine Word and Prophetic Word in Early Islam*, pp. 127–129 and 175–176. Ibn 'Arabī's discussions of this topic here (and wherever it arises in the *Futūhāt*) also allude to the even more famous divine saying that emphasizes the ultimate result of this realized proximity: "...My servant continues to come nearer Me through the acts of piety, until I love him. And when I love him, I am his hear-

ing with which he hears, his sight with which he sees, his tongue with which he speaks, his hand with which he grasps, and his foot on which he walks."

10. Which is devoted to the lofty spiritual station of the *afrād*, the "hidden saints" who are among the highest ranks of spiritual realization: see M. Chodkiewicz, *Seal of the Saints*, index references under *afrād*.

11. Following up on this last remark, Ibn 'Arabī goes on to point out the ways in which these other, non-human companions—not least of them the jinn or spirits—can eventually be just as distracting, or even as spiritually dangerous, as the human society these solitary wanderers had originally fled.

12. As indicated by the many parenthetical additions in this translation, this extraordinarily rich Arabic phrase alludes to a number of interrelated ideas which are based on the famous hadith that "the Heart of the person of faith is the Throne of the All-Compassionate." At the same time, the symbol of the divine Throne is typically taken to encompass the entire world of creation, or even all the domains of Manifestation of the divine Names, including the apparent opposition between the Names of divine "Beauty" (*jamāl*) and those Names of divine "Majesty" or Severity (*jalāl*)—which, as Ibn 'Arabī stresses here, we are normally quite unable to experience as manifestations of God's Love and Compassion.

13. The reference here, to verse 17:110, assumes the reader's knowledge of the beginning of this verse: *Say: "Call upon God (Allāh) or call upon the All-Compassionate (al-Rahmān)": By whatsoever (Name) you all call,....*

14. Again, the larger Qur'anic context (25: 59–67) of this question in verse 25:60 is assumed here: *And when it was said to them, "Bow down to al-Rahmān!," they said: "And who is al-Rahmān?! Are we to bow down to whatever you order us?!" And it (only) increased them in aversion....*

15. That is, *Allāh*, the "all-inclusive divine Name" which is understood to represent the *totality* of the divine Names and their manifestations, including all their oppositions and complementarities.

16. Which may or may not be something sacred and true or spiritually appropriate: Ibn 'Arabī is alluding here to the Prophet's famous hadith (given at the very beginning of Bukhārī's *Sahīh*), in specific reference to those who perform the Hajj for social or commercial mo-

tives (rather than serving God), that "actions are only (judged by God) according to their intentions...."

17. All of these points were already elaborated at some length in the opening passages of Ibn 'Arabī's earlier *Risālat al-Isfār* (see n. 1 above).

18. See Ibn 'Arabī's detailed development of this theme in the key passages from the *Futūhāt* (especially chapter 367) translated in "The Spiritual Ascension: Ibn 'Arabī and the *Mi'rāj*," in the *JAOS*, 107 (1987), pp. 629–652, and 108 (1988), pp. 63–77, as well as the additional works of Ibn 'Arabī on this theme discussed in the closing chapter of M. Chodkiewicz' *Seal of the Saints*. Most of this long *JAOS* study and the accompanying translation of chapter 367 is also included in the *Meccan Revelations* anthology, volume I.

19. Chapter 173, II, pp. 293–294; chapter 175, II, pp. 294–295 in the standard Beirut edition of the *Futūhāt*.

20. Throughout this section Ibn 'Arabī plays in untranslatable ways with the twofold meanings of two opposing Arabic roots: *wahsha* (which can mean both "wild"—including "wild animals"—and "painfully lonely" and estranged); and *uns*, which refers explicitly to "companionship," comfortableness and "feeling at home" (with other people), and then by an association of Arabic roots, to "human beings" (*ins* or *insān*). The aesthetic and spiritual theme of the paradoxical "comfort of loneliness" that Ibn 'Arabī develops here also has important roots in key aspects of the pre-Islamic traditions of Arabic poetry, profoundly familiar to the Shaykh and his original readers, which provide an important implicit backdrop to all of his discussions of spiritual journeying.

21. The theme of God's metaphysical "Jealousy" (*ghayra*) toward all conscious or unconscious human pretensions of divinity is a recurrent one throughout Ibn 'Arabī's writings, as well as earlier Sufi tradition. As in this case, his allusions to this subject almost always presuppose a famous hadith in which the Prophet refers to one of his companions: *"He is jealous, I am more jealous than him, and God is more jealous than I...."* (Bukhārī, *tawhīd*, 20; Muslim, *li'ān*, 17).

22. Or "cause him to journey" (*asfara*): this pun on the two possible meanings of this same Arabic root is likewise presupposed in the title of Ibn 'Arabī's *Risālat al-Isfār* (n. 1 above).

23. Alluding to the famous verse: *...Wherever you all may turn, there is the Face of God* (2:115).

CHAPTER TWO
LISTENING: CONTEMPLATION AND THE PURIFIED HEART

1. To limit the number of footnotes, references to the many Arabic passages from the *Futūhāt* translated here in Chapter Two are usually given (in parentheses) together with the actual translation and have been restricted to the chapter number and, in parentheses, the volume and page numbers of the translated passage in the modern O. Yahya Cairo critical edition. Certain recurrent key Arabic terms (*adab, hāl, nafs,* etc.) without any suitable English equivalent have been explained in a footnote at their first occurrence and are then used in italics without any further explanation.

2. To cite only two of the more explicit statements of this perspective in the *Futūhāt*: "...Now the Truly Real (*al-Haqq*) is the Vision (*basar*) of the world, and He is the Seer (*al-Rā'ī*) (in the 'mirror' of all created things), ...and everything that appears is a sign pointing to the Seer, Who is the Truly Real. So reflect—and know who you really are!" (chapter 371, III [Beirut ed.], p. 443). "Therefore the gaze of (every) person who looks never leaves God, nor is it even possible for it to do so...." (chapter 73, question 67).

3. For other verses (besides 50:37) connecting the Heart with *dhikr* or Remembrance of God, see 8:2, 13:28, 18:28, 39: 22–23; for divine strengthening and support or harmonization of Hearts, see verses 2:97, 3:103, 8:11, 8:63, 18:14, 28:10, 57:27, 64:11; for the beatific "tranquility" (*itmi'nān al-qalb*) of the Hearts of those with pure faith, see verses 3:126, 5:113, 8:10, 13:28–29, 16:106, and 48:4 (on the *sakīna*).

4. Among the verses on purification of the Heart (either by God or by the individual), see 5:41, 8:11, 26:89, 33:53, 37:84; and for the "humbling" or "softening" of the "sound" and "mindful" heart, verses 8:2, 22:32, 22:35, 22:54, 50:33, 57:16.

5. The image of "rusting" in this connection refers back to the following verse in the Qur'an: ...*and what they were acquiring has rusted on their Hearts* (83:14).

6. See the translation and discussion of his own explanation of his intentions, audiences and corresponding rhetorical and compositional procedures, from his Introduction to the *Futūhāt*, in the earlier essay "How to Study the *Futūhāt*: Ibn 'Arabī's Own Advice," in *Muhyiddin*

Ibn 'Arabī, A Commemorative Volume, (Shaftesbury, Element Books, 1993), pp. 73–89.

7. Not surprisingly, given the author's repeatedly avowed inspiration and intentions, the experience of studying the *Futūhāt*—despite the more obvious outward differences in structure and rhetoric—is remarkably similar to the ongoing process of reading the Qur'an. Most obviously, no one can ever seriously claim to have "finished" reading any part of that book: in light of the reader's own changing spiritual experiences and learning situations, each chapter continually reveals new facets and new thematic connections and complexities at each encounter. Likewise it is certainly not surprising, for anyone who has spent much time studying this book, that no one (to the best of my knowledge) has ever attempted either a stylistic imitation of its unique rhetoric and structure or a comprehensive commentary of the kind so frequently attached to the *Fusūs al-Hikam*.

8. This alludes to the various questionings regarding our earthly stewardship of God's Blessings (*al-na'īm*, etc.) mentioned in both the Qur'an and related hadith accounts of the events of the Rising.

9. Or divine "Temple" (*bayt Allāh*): the Kaaba of the divine Presence, the "Heart of Being" (*qalb al-wujūd*).

10. Directly alluding to the famous divine saying discussed in section I above.

11. I.e., the appropriate inner spiritual attitude and its expression in right action at each moment. (The transliterated Arabic term is often used alone in subsequent occurrences.)

12. This passage explicitly recalls the specific imagery of Ibn 'Arabī's opening autobiographical poem quoted above. See also the longer discussion of the heart as the "Doorway" (or "Gate," *bāb*) connecting God and the soul, in the translated selections on prayer from chapter 41 below.

13. This very important passage of chapter 68 (V, pp. 354–56), regarding God's ultimate "duping" (*makar*) of Iblīs, is discussed and partially translated near the end of section IV below. The crucial passage of the same chapter on the non-dualism ultimately required by true monotheism (at V, 363–67) is also an important explanation of the profound significance of the Shaykh's pointed allusion to the "*two* Right Hands" here.

14. I.e., from the "auspicious" or "fortunate" or "right" Source—the spiritual "Homeland" (*mawtin*) of all souls. There is an intentional

pun here on the root meanings of the Arabic term *al-yaman*. While the centrality of the image of this "Breath of the All-Merciful" mentioned by the Prophet in a famous hadith is familiar to all readers of Ibn 'Arabī's *Fusūs*, it is worth mentioning that these particular hadith (and their related wider metaphysical implications) also underlie the complex imagery of the "morning breezes" and other significant "garden-winds" that are one of the recurrent sets of eschatological symbols throughout later Islamicate mystical poetry, in Persian, Turkish , Urdu, etc.

15. The words for "reciting" in this passage are all drawn from the Arabic term (*tilāwa*) usually limited to the recitation of the Qur'an itself (the divine "Book" and "Speech" mentioned below), which is a central element in the traditional form of Islamic ritual prayer (*salāt*): that standard recitation of certain Qur'anic verses during the prayer is assumed as the background for this section's divine reversal of the usual visible—or audible—roles in prayer.

16. The imagery here alludes to the following famous divine saying that forms the background for the entire preceding passage: "Our Lord descends every night to the heaven of this world when the last third of the night remains, and then He says: *'I am the King! Whoever calls on Me, I answer them. Whoever asks (something) of Me, I give to them. Whoever requests My forgiveness, I forgive them.'*" This divine saying is included in Ibn 'Arabī's own collection, the *Mishkāt al-Anwār* (no. 56, pp. 86–87 in the French translation by M. Vālsan), and is recorded in almost all the canonical Sunni hadith collections.

Here it may also help to recall that in chapter 34 (III, 320–332), the Shaykh had already explained that the *"Night,"* in this hadith, *"is the place of the descent in time of God and His Attribute"* (of creative Loving-mercy and Compassion, *rahma*), and that this "last third of the night"—which, he insists there, *lasts forever*—is therefore the "Complete Human Being" (*al-insān al-kāmil*), with the first two "thirds" being respectively the Qur'anic *"the heavens and the earth,"* the human being's ontological "two parents."

17. The term Ibn 'Arabī employs here (*'isma*) was more commonly reserved for heated theological debates about the purported "sinlessness" or infallibility of the prophets (and for Shiites, of the Imāms). The Shaykh's usage of it here and elsewhere in the *Futūhāt* is distinctively personal and meant to be intentionally troubling, de-constructing the current mental categories and implicit theological assumptions that presupposed radical, even humanly incomprehensible, distances between the conditions of the prophets and those of ordinary human souls.

18. See the further discussion of the centrality and radical distinctiveness of this *explicitly universal* spiritual perspective of Ibn 'Arabī—which he constantly and very self-consciously highlights as demarcating his outlook from what was then (as now) often popularly considered as "Sufism"—in "Situating Islamic 'Mysticism': Between Written Traditions and Popular Spirituality," pp. 293–334 in *Mystics of the Book: Themes, Topics and Typologies*, ed. R. Herrera, (New York/Berlin, Peter Lang, 1993).

19. I.e., the *Fasl al-Ma'ārif*, or "First Section, Concerning the (fundamental) Forms of Spiritual Knowing" (I, 75–83 in Ibn 'Arabī's *Fihrist* or Table of Contents), comprising chapters 1–73 (of 560 in all). This section is the first of a total of six such major divisions, but covers considerably more than a quarter of the total length of the book. See details on these basic overall divisions of the *Futūhāt* in our Introduction to *The Meccan Illuminations* (NY, Pir Press, 2002), volumes I and II.

20. Literally, the divine "restaurants" or "places for tasting" (*matā'im*) this inspired spiritual knowing.

21. An allusion to the well known hadith repeatedly cited in the *Futūhāt*: "take on as your qualities of character the moral qualities of God."

22. See the translation and analysis of that key section from the Introduction to the *Futūhāt* in the article cited in n. 6 above.

23. *Bāb*: Ibn 'Arabī normally reserves this term for the 560 chapters of the *Meccan Illuminations*, and he uses a number of other different terms to describe and set apart the various subsections (sometimes quite numerous) within the individual chapters of the *Futūhāt*. It is therefore very striking that he uses the identical term (*bāb*) to describe this short—but extremely unusual—sub-section within chapter 68. In other words, since this is clearly not another chapter, it seemingly points the reader toward the other sense of this term as "Door."

24. This quality of being equally true and applicable to the elite and unenlightened alike is also one of the distinctive characteristics of the special wisdom of the "elite of the elite" identified in the key passages of Ibn 'Arabī's Introduction translated and discussed in the "How to Study the *Futūhāt*" (n. 6 above).

25. Following the Yahya edition's readings; however, the adjective here might also be construed (with the shift of a single dot) as "innate" or inherent, instinctive knowledge—a reading that may better fit the sense of the passage.

CHAPTER THREE
SEEING: SPIRITUAL VISION AND THE MYSTERIES OF *Ihsān*

1. *Kulliyāt-i Shams-i Tabrīz*, ed. B. Furūzānfar (Tehran, 1341 h.s.), p. 64 (no. 11) of the *Rubāʿiyyāt* section.

2. Claude Addas's lengthy study of Ibn ʿArabī's life and wider social and intellectual milieu (*Ibn ʿArabī, ou la quête du soufre rouge*, Paris, Gallimard, 1988; English translation at Chapter 1, n. 3 above) has underlined the relative anonymity—or at least the lack of any widespread public following and notoriety—of Ibn ʿArabī's writing and teaching during his own lifetime, a fact which only highlights the paradox of his constantly widening and deepening influence in later centuries, including the remarkable spread of his writings in the West in this century. For the broad outlines of those subsequent historical influences, see the historical overview in "Ibn ʿArabī and His Interpreters" (*JAOS*, 1986 and 1987), along with the more recent survey articles also cited at the Introduction, n. 9 above. This initial historical survey has been continuously updated by several dozen other detailed historical studies and reviews of related subsequent publications, all of which are now directly available for downloading (in .pdf format) at the website of the Ibn ʿArabī Society : *www.ibnarabisociety.org/IbnArabi* .

3. The *Meccan Illuminations* and Ibn ʿArabī's other writings contain a number of autobiographical allusions to the inspired roots of those distinctive qualities in the Shaykh's own decisive youthful experience of his spiritual identity with both the Qurʾan and the Muhammadan Reality. See the translation of several such key passages from chapter 366 (and 367) of the *Futūhāt*, in *The Meccan Revelations* anthology, chapter II. For example: "I and the Qurʾan are brothers...," and "...everything about which we speak, both in my (teaching) sessions and in my writings, comes only from the presence of the Qurʾan and Its treasures; I was given the keys of Its understanding and divine support from It...."

For further explanation, see the related biographical discussions in C. Addas, *Ibn ʿArabī, ou la quête du soufre rouge*, Paris, Gallimard, 1988; the detailed illustrations of Qurʾanic influences given throughout M. Chodkiewicz, *Un Océan sans rivage: Ibn ʿArabī, le livre et la loi*, Paris, Seuil, 1992; and the closely related discussions of Ibn ʿArabī's self-conception as "Seal of Muhammadan Sainthood" in M. Chodkiewicz, *Le sceau des saints: Prophétie et sainteté dans la doc-*

trine d'Ibn 'Arabī, Paris, Gallimard, 1986. (Details of English translations in Bibliography below.)

4. Much closer to Ibn 'Arabī's own Andalusian cultural roots, although in an outwardly different form, the nearly contemporary *Zohar* exhibits in its distinctive approach to earlier scripture—as well as its extraordinarily pervasive eventual influences—many of the same underlying rhetorical methods and metaphysical assumptions of the *Futūhāt*.

5. All these problems of reading, interpretation and translation are outlined in the opening sections of Chapters Four and Five (Returning) below, and discussed in more detail in "Ibn 'Arabī's Rhetoric of Realisation" (details at Introduction, n.1 above).

6. See the translation of that critical section of his Introduction in "How to Study the *Futūhāt*..." (Chapter 2, n. 6 above). Some of the wider political and practical spiritual implications of that Introduction—and related passages throughout the *Futūhāt*—are developed in an earlier article on "Ibn 'Arabī's 'Esotericism': The Problem of Spiritual Authority," pp. 37–64 in *Studia Islamica*, LXXI (1990).

7. The *'ibādāt*: purification and prayer, charity, fasting and pilgrimage, chapters 67–72; the length and relative importance of these particular chapters within the opening Section (*fasl al-ma'ārif*) of the work as a whole is suggested by the fact that they alone comprise most of volumes V–XII in O. Yahya's (incomplete) critical edition of the *Futūhāt*.

8. Or "*its* face," as this particular Qur'anic verse is sometimes read by Ibn 'Arabī and others, a reading that is grammatically allowable and quite meaningful in itself, given the sense of *wajh* as "essence" and the eschatological context of this particular verse (which concludes "... *His is the judgment, and to Him you are all returned*"), as well as the many verses mentioned below which clearly use "face" to refer to the essential, surviving aspect of *souls* in the other world.

9. For the positive usage, see verses 2:112, 3:20 (applied to Muhammad), 4:125 (of *one who is best/most beautiful in Religion, man ahsana dīn^{an}*, and who truly follows Abraham), and 31:22. The contrasting state of inwardly "facing away" from God is described at 22:11 and 67:22.

10. Given the pervasiveness of this usage in these eschatological contexts, it is quite possible that the Arabic term (*wajh*) here is being used to refer to the substance or soul or essential spiritual being of each

person in the other world, as Ibn 'Arabī often seems to presume (see the relevant selections translated in sections III–V below). Passages where the "faces" of the *blessed* in paradise are referred to include 10:26–27, 20:111, 48:29 (on "the marks of prayer"), 75:22, 80:38–39, 83:24, and 88:8–16. There are more than twenty corresponding descriptions of the "faces" of those suffering torments, often in immediately contrasting sections of the same Qur'anic passages just cited.

11. This "first section, concerning the (fundamental) forms of (divine spiritual) Knowing" (*fasl al-ma'ārif*: I, 75–83 in the author's own *fihrist* or Table of Contents), including chapters 1–73 (of 560 in all), is the longest of the six major subdivisions of the entire book; it comprises volumes I–XIII in the new critical edition, and all of volume I and almost a quarter of volume II in the older four-volume lithographed editions of the *Futūhāt*.

12. This is particularly true of the hadith of Gabriel on *ihsān* and the three dimensions of Religion (commonly used as a sort of catechism in popular religious teaching throughout the Islamic world) and, for Ibn 'Arabī's own metaphysical teachings, of the "hadith of the supererogatory works" and the hadith of God's "transformation through the forms." See the more detailed references and full translations in the concluding section of translated hadith at the end of this Chapter Three.

13. For references to other chapters of the *Futūhāt* (outside the focus of this study) where Ibn 'Arabī also discusses this hadith in some detail, see the notes to the translation of this particular hadith included at the end of this Chapter.

14. *Hijāb*, in the singular: the term is probably to be understood here in the context of the much wider symbolic imagery of the divine Court, referring to the complex series of curtains and dividers, and corresponding ranks of courtiers and nobility, normally setting off different degrees of access and intimacy to the "King" and His "Throne." This, in any case, is the context assumed in Ibn 'Arabī's own amplified discussion of the divine "Visit" and beatific "Listening" of the blessed in chapter 65 (partly translated in section V) below.

15. *al-nawāfil* is a later technical legal term referring to the supplementary, personally chosen acts of devotion, often mentioned in the Qur'an and described at length in the hadith, which were constantly practiced by the Prophet and his close Companions, especially in the early Meccan period, but which were not made incumbent on the wider body of Muslims in Medina and by later legal schools. Those devo-

tions would normally include longer and more numerous prayers, especially at night, much more frequent fasting, spiritual retreats during Ramadan (and some other times), a wide range of invocations (*dhikr*), and more specific devotional vows or covenants (*nadhr*). See additional references in the translation and notes to this hadith included in the final section of this Chapter.

16. I.e., "And *if you are not*, then you *do* see Him...," as explained in several translated passages from the *Futūhāt* (and related notes) in section IV below.

17. For some of Ibn 'Arabī's own interpretations of these details, see the important eschatological passages from chapter 73 of the *Futūhāt* included among the translations in the recent *Meccan Revelations* anthology.

18. See the references to this long hadith and Ibn 'Arabī's use of it in other contexts in the translations included at the very end of this Chapter.

19. See the translation and discussion of the key passages from his Introduction to the *Futūhāt* included in "How to Study the *Futūhāt*..." (Chapter 2, n. 6 above).

20. In her pioneering study of the Shaykh's development of a phenomenologically revelatory Arabic language, *Ibn 'Arabī wa Mawlid Lugha Jadīda*, Beirut, Dandara, 1411/1991, pp. 59–90.

21. *Risālat al-Mubashshirāt*: the title of this treatise alludes to a famous hadith where the Prophet explains that these "good tidings...are the dream of the *muslim*, either what that person sees or what is shown to them, which is one of the parts of prophecy." The following translation is based on the text of this short work included in Yūsuf al-Nabhānī's *Sa'ādat al-Dārayn fī al-Salāt 'alā Sayyid al-Kawnayn* (Beirut, n.d.), pp. 472–478 (photocopy kindly provided by Prof. Denis Gril). This *Epistle* is No. 485 in O. Yahya's *Histoire et Classification de l'œuvre d'Ibn 'Arabī* (Damascus, 1964), II, p. 394, where it is noted that the work is mentioned in both Ibn 'Arabī's *Fihris* (no. 71) and his later *Ijāza* (no. 76). This particular formula of *dhikr* certainly contains an implicit allusion to the famous Prophetic prayer in the hadith : "O my God, cause me to see things as they really are."

22. Volume I, p. 73. Unless otherwise specified, this and all subsequent references in this Chapter to chapters 1–73 of the *Futūhāt* are to the ongoing recent critical edition (Cairo, 1971 onward) by O. Yahya, with the volume number in Roman numerals followed by the page num-

bers of the translated or summarized passage. As in the preceding Chapters here, references to chapters of the *Futūhāt* not available in that more recent edition are to the older, frequently reprinted four-volume Beirut lithographed (Dār Sādir) version which is most commonly cited in recent translations and scholarly studies of the *Futūhāt*.

23. *al-'ayn*: Ibn 'Arabī's untranslatable pun here—and at many other passages translated in this Chapter—on the multiple meanings of this key Arabī term, which also means "essence," "source," "concrete reality," etc., is repeated many times in the *Futūhāt, Fusūs al-Hikam* and all of his poetry. In all of those settings—and certainly here—he is consciously intending all of those meanings, which occasionally are partially suggested by the corresponding English pun between "I" and "eye."

Ibn 'Arabī's intended reference here to the subsuming of his individual ego in the ultimate Reality of the one "See-er" (and Seen) is vividly portrayed in his more extensive autobiographical account of this transforming experience of union (or "annihilation" of the ego, *fanā'*) in chapter 367 of the *Futūhāt*. See my annotated translation of that account, and an earlier parallel passage in his more immediately autobiographical *Kitāb al-Isrā'*, in the article on "The Spiritual Ascension: Ibn 'Arabī and the *Mi'rāj*," *JAOS*, 108 (1988), pp. 63–77, as well as further details in C. Addas' biography, *Ibn 'Arabī, ou la quête du soufre rouge*, Paris, Gallimard, 1988, chapter 3. Most of that translated passage from chapter 367 is now available in *The Meccan Revelations* anthology, volume I.

The phrase *"the Splendors of His Face"* in this line of the opening poem alludes literally to the end of the famous hadith on the "70,000 veils" of light and darkness (see full translation at the end of this Chapter), where that divine Gaze is said to "burn up" any creature who would behold the divine Face.

24. I.e., that one divine "Eye" and ultimate Subject/Object (*'ayn*: see preceding note) which is the knowable, manifest dimension of *al-Haqq*. The last half-line of poetry includes a complex pun drawn from the key concluding line of the hadith of *Ihsān* explained in the following sections (IV–V), an understanding which is critical to Ibn Arabī's own conception of the mystery of theophany.

25. At III, 362: the immediate context of this confession is Ibn 'Arabī's explanation of the way his own spiritual path involved the successive revelation or "opening" of the spiritual stations associated

with Jesus, Moses, Hud, "all the prophets," and finally Muhammad—
allusions which are apparently amplified in his account of his own spiritual Ascension in the *Kitāb al-Isrā'* and chapter 367 of the *Futūhāt* (see
references to available translations in n. 23 to this Chapter).

26. Chapter 366 (on the spiritual station of the "Mahdi's Helpers"), further discussed and partly translated in Chapter Four below.
The short passage translated here is from volume III (Beirut edition),
pp. 338–339. More complete translations from this major chapter of
the *Futūhāt* are also included in the recent anthology volume, *The
Meccan Revelations,* vol. I.

27. "Burden of anguish" = *haraj*, referring here to the inner state
of constraint, oppression, anxiety, distress, etc. that usually accompanies and underlies (whether consciously or not) much of our everyday
psychic and outward activity. A number of Qur'anic verses stress that
there is *no haraj for you in Religion* (22:78; etc.) or *in the Book sent
down* from God (7:2), and that this state of inner distress is a sign of
those wandering astray, while it is removed from those *whom God
guides rightly* and *who inwardly surrender* to Him (6:125).

28. This phrase could also be translated as "to kill one's *nafs*" (the
ego or "domineering self" responsible for this sense of oppression and
anxiety), in the hope of eliminating this inner torment.

29. Or "good" or "virtuous" actions: the Arabic root *hasan* (translated here with forms of "beautiful") covers much the same semantic
range as the Greek *kalos*; it is the same root of the expression *ihsān*
discussed throughout this Chapter. The phrase immediately preceding
this note could also be understood, with equal justification, taking *God*
as the subject: "...for He comes to meet (the true seer), by His very
Essence, with beautiful Actions." Both meanings are clearly relevant
to Ibn 'Arabī's description of this theophanic state and of the actions of
ihsān which are its necessary consequence and sign.

30. Another explicit indication that all the eschatological states
discussed in greater detail below (sections V–VI) are also clearly understood as symbolizing levels of spiritual realization or the lack
thereof—points that are further developed throughout Chapter Five
below.

31. *Qalb al-insān*: as always in Ibn 'Arabī—again closely based
on Qur'anic usage and related hadith sources—the Heart here has the
extended sense of the (necessarily metaphysical) locus of all experi-

332

ence and perception, of whatever sort. See the extended explanations given in the preceding Chapter Two (Listening).

32. The *locus classicus* for Ibn 'Arabī's discussion of the Heart in this sense is the famous chapter XII (on the prophet Shu'ayb/Jethro) in his *Fusūs al-Hikam*; pp. 147–155 in the translation by R. Austin: *The Bezels of Wisdom*, (NY, Paulist Press, 1980).

33. *al-khitāb al-shar'ī al-mahmūd*: this typically dense expression, which would require many lines for a more adequate translation, is especially revealing of Ibn 'Arabī's typical, profoundly etymological understanding of the reality of the divine *shar'* (and related key terms like *sharī'a* and *shāri'*) as a universal, ongoing metaphysical process or relation between the human heart and its divine Source, a kind of spiritually indispensable *"opening of the Way"* always linking the divine "Subject" and all Its theophanic manifestations.

While Ibn 'Arabī certainly aims for his peculiar use of these key religious expressions to transform or illuminate the accepted popular usages for properly receptive readers, the frequent Western translation of these particular terms as "Law," "lawgiving," "revelation" and the like—while partially reflecting their common *contemporary* usage in more familiar legal, political and ideological contexts—cannot possibly begin to convey to uninitiated readers their actual meanings and their deeper, often profoundly deconstructive, intentions in the Shaykh's own writings. See the more detailed development of this point, drawn from chapter 366 of the *Futūhāt*, in the final two sections of Chapter Four below.

34. The immediate references are to the following verses: *We have placed veils over their hearts* (6:25, 17:46, 18:57, 41:5); ... *or are there locks on their hearts?!* (47:24); *It is not their eyes that are blind, but blind are the hearts in their breasts* (22:46), along with many other Qur'anic references to spiritual "blindness" (and "deafness," etc.); and *Indeed, what they were acquiring has rusted over their hearts!* (83:14).

35. *al-'ulamā' bi-llāh*: Ibn 'Arabī's technical usage of this expression here refers to those rare, fully enlightened souls who are able to perceive the divine Presence in all things, for whom all experience is realized theophany, because they perceive "with" and "through" (*bi*) God. *Allāh* is being used here in the technical theological and metaphysical sense of the "Comprehensive Name" that encompasses all the manifest divine Attributes.

36. One of the most dramatic illustrations of this basic spiritual principle in Ibn 'Arabī's writings is in Moses' explanation to him, during his description of his own spiritual Ascension recounted in chapter 367 (III, 342) of the *Futūhāt*, of how he accidentally discovered the Burning Bush while seeking fire to warm his family (alluding to the Qur'anic account at 28:29). In chapter 366 of the *Futūhāt* (III, 336), Ibn 'Arabī discusses in this connection both Moses and the case of al-Khadir—who is also said to have discovered the Water of Life while searching for a drink for his fellow soldiers—explaining that this principle is realized by "all of the righteous leaders (Imāms)." See our translations of both of these key passages in *The Meccan Revelations* anthology, volume I.

37. In the opening longer story of his important autobiographical work *Rūh al-Quds* (p. 66 in R. Austin's translation, *Sufis of Andalusia*), Ibn 'Arabī attributes this saying to the earlier Spanish Sufi teacher Ibn al-'Arīf (d. 1141).

38. *Kun*: i.e., the imperative divine Command that continually brings all creation into being, referred to eight times (2:117, etc.) in the celebrated Qur'anic expression *...He only says to it "Be!", and it is.*

39. "Complex" because Ibn 'Arabī's particular reading here, as applied to the highest spiritual state of the true Knowers, continues to presuppose the applicability of the ordinary, unenlightened reading of that same description to the state of most individuals' understanding and application of *ihsān*. It is also important to keep in mind that for Ibn 'Arabī the first, necessarily practical part of the Prophet's description—"that you worship/serve God *as though you saw Him*"—remains equally applicable to everyone, even as the actual meaning of this "as though" is itself inwardly transformed throughout each ascending stage of spiritual growth and realization.

40. *Kitāb al-Fanā' fī al-Mushāhada*, in *Rasā'il Ibn 'Arabī* (Hyderabad, 1367/1948), I, pp. 2–9; that short work is now available in an English translation by S. Hirtenstein and L. Shamash, pp. 1–17 in the *JMIAS*, IX (1991). The discussion of this hadith and this consciously unusual reading occurs at the very end of that treatise, which more clearly stresses the ongoing, real ontological distinction between the contempla*tor*, even in this state of "ego-annihilation," and the ultimate divine Reality or Essence which can never be entirely grasped: what is "seen" even in this deep contemplative state, the Shaykh concludes, is precisely, and necessarily, only a particular divine "Face."

41. III, 320–24, "concerning the inner knowing of the 'Jesus-like' Friends…" (*al-'īsawiyyūn*). In this chapter of the *Futūhāt*, as in many parts of the *Fusūs al-Hikam*, Ibn 'Arabī's interpretation of this metaphysical "as though" is connected especially to the fundamental role of "(divine) Imagination" (*khiyāl*) in making possible all manifest creation and spiritual experience. See also the translations of key related discussions (from chapter 63 of the *Futūhāt* on the *Barzakh*) in our study of "Spiritual Imagination and the 'Liminal' World: Ibn 'Arabī on the *Barzakh*," in *POSTDATA* (Madrid), 15, no. 2 (1995), pp. 42–49 and 104–109.

42. This is the same elite group of realized Knowers which he elsewhere calls the *Malāmiyya* or "the people who reproach (their domineering souls)." For a detailed explanation of Ibn 'Arabī's understanding of both of these spiritual groups, drawn from discussions throughout the *Futūhāt*, see the index references for both terms in Michel Chodkiewicz, *Le sceau des saints: Prophétie et sainteté dans la doctrine d'Ibn Arabī*, Paris, Gallimard, 1986. (See Bibliography for the recent English translation of this work.)

43. This important hadith is included, with minor variations, in the canonical collections of Tirmidhī, Ibn Māja, and Ibn Hanbal. See the complete text of this hadith (which further emphasizes the hiddenness and lack of public notoriety of these saints) and additional explanations in W.A. Graham, *Divine Word*, pp. 120–121.

44. *Musawwad al-wajh*: an Arabic idiom suggesting their social anonymity and invisibility, with possibly a note of non-conformity or opprobrium going beyond the kind of simple, humble life suggested by the other descriptions of the hadith itself.

45. *Al-sadaqa burhān*: this is the second half of a frequently quoted hadith which begins with the phrase—also discussed later in this same passage from the *Futūhāt*—that *"Prayer is a Light* (from God)" (*al-salāt nūr*). (It is included in most of the canonical hadith collections: see Wensinck, *Concordance*, I, 177, which cites versions in Muslim, al-Nisā'ī, Ibn Māja, Ibn Hanbal and al-Dārimī.) The notion of the divine Proof (*burhān*) is Qur'anic, and the point of the hadith turns on the contrast between *zakāt*, as the general duty of religiously obligatory charity or almsgiving; and *sadaqa* as further voluntary, "supererogatory" giving and sacrifice—symbolizing the same extraordinary inner spiritual state described in the famous hadith of the *nawāfil* (see full translation at the end of this Chapter) or other well known hadith stress-

ing the comparable spiritual significance of the *spontaneous* inner desire for prayer (*tatawwu'*).

46. Throughout this passage the Arabic term *tabī'a* and its derived forms (translated as "natural," etc.) are used according to their common technical sense in much Sufi literature, to refer specifically and narrowly *only* to the carnal, animal (basharic) "nature" and inclinations within human beings—not to "human nature" in any wider sense (as is the case in the Arabic philosophic tradition and with the usual English associations of the term).

47. Or "self-abnegation," *sabr*: i.e., the same divinely bestowed ability to transcend our animal, basharic nature that is manifested in the voluntary or supererogatory acts of charity (*sadaqāt*) discussed in the immediately preceding passage.

48. *al-da'wā*: i.e., a kind of self-deifying inner egoism, according to the technical usage of Ibn 'Arabī and earlier Sufi tradition; see his further discussion of this key concept in the passage from chapter 69 (VI, 351) translated at the beginning of section VI below. The same term is more commonly used for a legal "complaint" or grounds for a lawsuit, and as such is central to the (negative) protagonist found throughout classical Sufi poetry (most notably in Hafez), of the *muddā'ī*, the unconscious, hypocritical "critic" or "plaintiff" against God. Ibn 'Arabī's remarks translated above (in section III, from chapters 36 and 366 of the *Futūhāt*), describing the extraordinary lack of any inner complaint or quarrel with God in those who have experienced true enlightenment and theophanic vision, help to highlight the widespread inner spiritual condition he is pointing to here.

49. *Ghadab*: there is no good English equivalent, since "anger" or "wrath" are far too inadequate and anthropomorphic in this context; the essential point is that this attribute encompasses every manifestation of the apparent "opposite" or lack or negation of the divine *Rahma*, God's all-encompassing, creative Compassion and Lovingmercy.

50. *al-sirāt*, a key symbol which is described in a number of central eschatological hadith, including the final two long hadith translated at the end of this Chapter below.

51. Ibn 'Arabī's allusion here presupposes the remainder of these two Qur'anic verses, with their forceful contrast between physical "eyesight" (*basar*) and inner spiritual "insight" (*basīra*): ...*but He encompasses (all their) seeing (al-absār), and He is the Most-Subtle, the All-Aware. There have already come to you spiritual insights (basā'ir) from your Lord, so whoever has seen, that is for the good of his soul,*

336

and whoever was blind, that is against it—and I am not a keeper over you! (part of Arabic epigraph preceding this Chapter.)

52. At the end of the famous "hadith of the supererogatory works" (*hadīth al-nawāfil*) translated in full at the end of this Chapter below.

53. This is apparently Ibn 'Arabī's first explicit citation and discussion of this key verse in the *Futūhāt*. See the detailed discussion of its meaning and importance in our Introduction to *Orientations: Islamic Thought in a World Civilisation* (London, Archetype, 2004).

54. *Taswīr kull shay:* here Ibn 'Arabī employs the same Arabic term that is commonly applied to painting and could easily be extended, in this context, to sculpture, filmmaking, literature and each of the creative arts.

55. From this point on, throughout the rest of this passage (unless otherwise indicated) Ibn 'Arabī actually uses the Arabic *al-Haqq* ("The Truly Real" or "Absolute Reality"), a favorite expression of his which more accurately conveys the full universality of this process, but tends to sound very stilted (and more abstractly un-theological than is actually the case with the Arabic term) when used repeatedly in this sort of setting in English.

56. *Al-hajaba*: here that rank of courtly protocol could be translated more literally as the divine "Veil-keepers."

57. *Yasrī*: a powerful Qur'anic expression, from the same root as *isrā'*, the "nocturnal" spiritual journey of the Prophet, which Ibn 'Arabī often uses to suggest the secret and "invisible" inner relationship between the Creator (or the divine Spirit-Breath, *rūh*) and the manifest universe.

58. *Mawāqif al-qiyāma*: see the longer discussion of this hadith and Ibn 'Arabī's uses of it in the *Futūhāt* and his *Mishkāt al-Anwār* in the translation section at the end of this Chapter.

59. V, pp. 78–80: the selections translated here are restricted to passages directly bearing on this Chapter's theme of the Vision of God's Face; the entire highly poetic passage, with lengthy references to eschatological imagery from the Qur'an and hadith, is more than twice as long as these short excerpts.

60. The same verbal construction is used repeatedly in the Qur'an (e.g., at 7:143, 38:24, 12:100, etc.) to describe the reaction of the prophets (and angels and others) to the direct experience—or recognition—of a particular theophany.

61. *Bi-mushāhadatī*: Ibn 'Arabī frequently stresses, in other contexts in the *Futūhāt*, that this technical Sufi expression in fact extends to *all* possible forms of spiritual awareness, including all the spiritual

senses (hearing, smell, taste, etc.) as well as normal inner or external 'sight'.

62. *Kun*: referring to the repeated Qur'anic expression ...*He only says to it "Be!," and it is* (2:117, etc.). Here the reference may allude more specifically to the famous divine Words of the primordial Covenant, addressed to all human souls at 7:172: *alastu bi-rabbikum, "Am I not your Lord?!".*

63. In addition to the complete version of that hadith included in the translation section at the end of this Chapter, see our translation of several related passages describing Ibn 'Arabī's interpretation of the inner meaning of some of those images and ranks of spiritual vision, from chapter 73 of the *Futūhāt*, included in *The Meccan Revelations* anthology, volume I.

64. Ibn 'Arabī's characteristic insistence on the uniqueness and ongoing transformations of each soul's individual path (*tarīq*) to and with God is well illustrated in the following excerpt from his own conversation with the prophet Yahyā (John the Baptist) included in his account of his own spiritual ascension in chapter 367 of the *Futūhāt* (full translation and study in *The Meccan Revelations* anthology, volume I):

I said to (Yahyā): "I didn't see you on my path: is there some other path there?"
And he replied: "*Each person has a path that no one else but they travel.*"
So I said: "Then where are they, these (different) paths?"
And he answered: "*They come to be through the traveling itself.*"

65. This passage clearly alludes to such memorable Qur'anic descriptions of the "*faces*" of the blessed on the Day of the Rising or in the Gardens (see section I above) as *shining white* (3:106); *glowing radiantly, gazing upon their Lord* (75:22); *blissful and contented with their striving* (88:8); or *shining forth, laughing and joyful* (80:38).

66. See the short, but accessible development of this theme in his *Risālat al-Anwār* ("Treatise of the Lights," in *Rasā'il Ibn 'Arabī*, Hyderabad, 1367/1948, II, no. 12, pp. 1–19), translated as *Journey to the Lord of Power*, R.T. Harris, (London, Inner Traditions, 1981); and especially the detailed commentary (with extensive cross-references to related sections of the *Futūhāt* and other works) and French translation by M. Chodkiewicz, *Le Sceau des saints: prophétie et sainteté dans la doctrine d'Ibn 'Arabī*, Paris, 1986, pp. 181–221.

67. Directed by Percy Adlon, 1988.

68. See Ibn 'Arabī's more phenomenological description of this distinctive "knowledge of the People of the Garden," from the conclusion of chapter 366 of the *Futūhāt*, translated at the beginning of section III above.

69. *Ghayra* is ordinarily used, in human situations, to describe positively the virtue of being righteously "jealous" in defense of one's rightful honor and self-respect. Even on the purely human plane, not to mention its use as a divine Attribute, this particular expression does not have many of the negative connotations almost universally associated with "jealousy" in English (which are expressed by other, different Arabic terms).

70. *Al-muddā'ī*: see the earlier note on the hidden spiritual illness of *da'wā* and the related passages translated above (at the end of section IV) on the spiritual veils normally constituted by this ordinarily unconscious human "pretension" (*da'wā*) to judge and criticize God by our own egoistic standards and interests, implicitly raised to the level of divinity. This naturally self-destructive egoistic claim to divine Lordship (*rubūbīya*) is of course the exact opposite of the ultimate human qualities of "servanthood" (*'ubūdiyya*) which Ibn 'Arabī views as the essential practical keys to theophanic vision, as he makes clear in the remaining passages included in this section.

71. Qur'an 58:7. The remainder of the verse, alluding to what Ibn 'Arabī often calls the mystery of the divine "with-ness" (*ma'aīya*), is clearly assumed here: *...nor of five but that He is their sixth, nor of more or less, but that **He is with them wherever they may be**. Then He informs them of what they did, on the Day of the Rising....*

72. *Al-Ruk'a al-ilāhīya*, where the three stages of the cycle of ritual prayer are taken to symbolize the whole Origin and Goal of human destiny, in the three cosmic "movements" of God's "descent" and "prosternation"—both described in this divine saying—and the third culminating stage of the "rising" (*qiyāma*: the same term ordinarily applied to the eschatological "Rising," as briefly described in section V above). The image here of "God as Imām"—i.e., standing immediately in front of the person praying—directly recalls the injunction in the hadith on *ihsān*, to "worship/serve God *as though you see Him*."

73. This passage is alluding explicitly to the famous hadith: "*take on as your own character the qualities of God.*"

74. III, 350.20–32: see our more complete translation and analysis of this key autobiographical document, as well as the corresponding

and earlier account of the same experience from his *Kitāb al-Isrā'*, in the concluding section of "The Spiritual Ascension: Ibn 'Arabī and the Mi'rāj," *JAOS*, 108 (1988), pp. 63–77, as well as the related discussions in Claude Addas' biography, *Ibn 'Arabī, ou la quête du soufre rouge*, Paris, Gallimard, 1988. This and other translated sections from chapter 367 are now readily available in *The Meccan Revelations* anthology, vol. I.

75. I.e., what he elsewhere calls the cosmic "Tree of Existence," *shajarat al-Kawn*, the "universal Human Being" with its roots in heaven and its "branches" and "fruits" manifest here on earth, "which is all of it divine Imagination" (*khiyāl*). This *sidrat al-muntahā* (where the Prophet *saw Him in another descent*) is part of a longer, classic Qur'anic description (at 53:2–18) of two extraordinary occasions of revelation to Muhammad. See also the translations of the closely related cosmological treatise often mis-attributed to Ibn 'Arabī, the "Tree of Existence" (*Shajarat al-Kawn*), by A. Jeffery, "Ibn 'Arabī's *Shajarat al-Kawn*," in *Studia Islamica*, X, pp. 43–78 and XI, pp. 113–160; and by M. Gloton, *L'Arbre du Monde*, Paris, 1982. The same cosmological symbolism is developed in more detail in Ibn 'Arabī's early—and authentic—*Risālat al-Ittihād al-Kawnī*, translated by D. Gril as *Le Livre de l'Arbre et des Quatre Oiseaux*, Paris, 1984.

76. I.e., comprising all the same planes of being (*nash'a*) contained within the universal "Complete Human Being" (*al-insān al-kāmil*), both spiritual and bodily or material. The metaphysical and spiritual equivalencies that this implies, especially the essential correspondence between the Universal Human Being and the Reality of Muhammad, are elaborated in Ibn 'Arabī's works mentioned in the preceding note. In another register, readers will immediately recognize here the extraordinary echoing of this same archetypal symbolism in one of Wallace Stevens' last poems, "Of Pure Being."

77. W.B. Yeats, final lines of the late poem "Among School Children."

78. See Wensinck, *Concordance*, I, 464 (mentioning versions in the hadith collections of Muslim, Ibn Māja, and Ibn Hanbal). This celebrated hadith is usually given according to the version recorded in Ibn Māja, I, 44. (Muslim, *īmān*, 293 cites a similar hadith which mentions simply "a veil of Light," without any specific number.) Ibn 'Arabī interprets this hadith in greater detail in chapter 426 of the *Futūhāt* (IV, 38–39), focusing on the question of how light can be a "veil"; in ch. 73,

question 115 (II,110; end of vol. XII of the new critical edition), on the meaning of the "Splendors of God's Face"; and in his *Kitāb al-Tajalliyāt* (ed. O. Yahya, Beirut, 1967), VI, 728. Other discussions, usually mentioning the different versions of this hadith, can be found in the *Futūhāt* at II, 80, 460, 488, 542, 554; III, 212, 216, 289; and IV, 72.

79. When Ibn 'Arabī discusses or paraphrases this hadith, including the passages cited in the preceding note, he usually adds here the additional phrase "of the (human) creatures (or 'of creation': *al-khalq*)": it is not clear whether he is simply paraphrasing (and personally qualifying) the hadith, or actually quoting it in another slightly longer version.

80. *Hadīth al-nawāfil*: this classical *hadīth qudsī* is one of the best-known and most influential of the divine sayings, since it so clearly states the essential inner link between religious action and spiritual realization (*'ilm* and *'amal*) and its deeper ontological underpinnings. It is the ninety-first divine saying included in Ibn 'Arabī's own *Mishkāt al-Anwār* (see the translation by M. Vālsan, *La Niche des Lumières*, pp. 118–121). For a full discussion of the canonical sources (including Bukhārī's *Sahīh*) and variants, as well as the special prominence of this hadith throughout the major Sufi writings from earliest times, see W. Graham, *Divine Word*, pp. 173–74 and related notes.

81. From the same root as *farīda*, the technical term for the obligatory religious duties (the daily ritual prayers, fasting in Ramadan, charity, etc.) in later schools of Islamic jurisprudence.

82. *Al-nawāfil* in later Islamic tradition becomes a technical legal term referring to the supplementary acts of personal devotion, often mentioned in the Qur'an and described at length in the hadith, which were constantly practiced by the Prophet and his close Companions, especially in the early Meccan period, but which were not made incumbent on the wider body of Muslims in Medina and in later legal schools. These devotions would normally include longer and more numerous prayers, especially at night, much more frequent fasting, spiritual retreats during Ramadan (and some other times), a wide range of invocations (*dhikr*), and more specific devotional vows (*nadhr*). Probably even more relevant, from Ibn 'Arabī's own practical spiritual point of view, is the earlier, more basic Arabic root meaning of simply "what comes next" (i.e., after the obligatory forms of worship), originally referring to the end of a caravan.

83. The special Arabic root for "love" (*hubb*) used here, as in the Qur'an, refers to the individual, particularized and reciprocal divine

Response to the special devotion of the Friends of God. That personal relationship is always discussed there in terms quite distinct from the universal, creative divine Lovingmercy or absolute Compassion (*rahma*) that "*encompasses all things.*"

84. Literally: "(already) *was*," a metaphysical dimension of this saying that is often very important in Ibn 'Arabī's own interpretations. The Arabic conditional used here grammatically requires the past tense, but it can be translated in the past, present or future, according to the context and sense.

85. Translated here according to the version attributed to Abū Hurayra, recorded by Muslim, *birr*, 43, which is the source for the same hadith (no. 98) in Ibn 'Arabī's own *Mishkāt al-Anwār*. See Graham, *Divine Word*, pp. 179–180. Wensinck, *Concordance*, VI, 198, mentions another version in Ibn Hanbal (*wasāyā*, 7).

86. This literal translation seems to accord with the intentional reference to the eschatological context here—in which the souls of those being judged are themselves understood to be suffering terribly from the spiritual "hunger" and "thirst" often mentioned in those contexts in the Qur'an and the eschatological hadith.

87. Reported by Abū Hurayra, from the *Sahīh* of al-Bukhārī, Book II (*īmān*), 37, which is the shortest (and therefore probably the earliest) version of this famous story. Wensinck, *Concordance*, I, 467 notes the multiple versions in Bukhārī, Muslim, al-Dārimī, Ibn Māja and al-Tirmidhī. Ibn 'Arabī was certainly aware of those differences (which, however, do not affect the central definition of *ihsān*), since he sometimes mentions the different ways Muhammad refers to Gabriel and the purpose of his visit in those various versions of this hadith.

88. All of these points are frequently included in Qur'anic enumerations of the objects of faith (e.g., at 2:285), although the Qur'an even more frequently mentions simply "*Faith in God and the Last Day (Rising)*" (at 2:8, etc.).

89. Here, as in some of the later passages in the Qur'an and in a number of hadith, the root *islām* has taken on a narrower, specific association with basic social-ritual practices typifying Muhammad's nascent religious community. It is important to keep in mind, however, that the primary Qur'anic sense of this term—much closer to the Arabic root—refers to the highest spiritual condition of total inner surrender to God's will, in which meaning it is often applied in the Qur'an to pre-"Islamic" prophets, messengers and people of exemplary faith.

90. Or "purifying acts of charity" (*zakāt*): the meaning of this Arabic root—originally referring to "purification" (of the soul)—in the

Qur'an itself remains closely linked to acts of charity and the root sense of spiritual purification in general: cf. 2:177, 261, 267; 9:60. In the hadith and later forms of Islamic jurisprudence the same term was more often applied to the forms of annually prescribed charitable giving begun during the Medinan period, as opposed to other more voluntary forms of charity (the *sadaqa* already discussed in section IV of this Chapter above).

91. This version in Bukhārī (unlike the more elaborate variant in Muslim's *Sahīh*) does not mention the Pilgrimage (*Hajj*) specifically. Muslim's version, reported by *'Umar* instead of Abū Hurayra, also discusses *islām* before *īmān*, adds faith in "the decreeing of good and evil alike" (a later theological issue), and includes more description of the mysterious stranger: each of those additions is a likely indicator of a later literary and theological reworking of this simpler version recorded by Bukhārī.

92. Literally (although the definition given here is far more appropriate to its particular Qur'anic usage): "to do what is both good and beautiful or noble." The reference in the hadith is certainly to the Qur'anic usage of the term, where "those who do *ihsān*" (*al-muhsinūn*) are referred to frequently (25 times) with the highest praise, promised the highest paradise, associated with the prophets and messengers, connected with the central spiritual virtues, etc. Even more strikingly, the Qur'an insists that *Verily God is with those who act in awareness of Him and the muhsinūn* (16:128; again at 29:69); *Perform ihsān, verily God loves the muhsinūn* (2:195). The restriction of God's profoundest Love (*hubb*) to them is repeated similarly at 3:134, 3:148, 5:13, 5:93; and *God's Lovingmercy* (*rahma*) *is near to the muhsinūn* (7:56).

93. This particular hadith, quoting Abū Hurayra's account of his conversation with the Prophet, is recorded in essentially the same version by al-Tirmidhī (*sifāt al-janna*, 15, 25; *birr*, 54) and Ibn Māja (*zuhd*, 39)—from which the quotations are taken here—as well as by al-Dārimī (*riqāq*, 116) and in a number of places by Ahmad ibn Hanbal; see the full references in Wensinck, *Concordance*, V, 542–543. Most notably, this particular long hadith comes at the very end of Ibn Māja's entire hadith collection, and is therefore clearly understood there to concern the ultimate ends and finality of all human actions.

94. That is, *yawm al-jum'a*, or Friday; but the reference is essentially to the fact that all the people of Paradise, whatever their rank, are brought together on this "Day." The vague phrase *fī miqdār* underlies the very different nature of whatever time is appropriate in this context.

95. Ibn 'Arabī's own interpretations of the different ranks of the spiritual Vision of the prophets, Friends and others alluded to in this hadith are detailed in his responses to the spiritual "test-questions" of Hakīm al-Tirmidhī in chapter 73 of the *Futūhāt* (questions 67–72; II, 84–86 in the older Beirut ed.; vol. XII of O. Yahya's newer critical edition). English translations of his interpretations in questions 67 and 71 are included among the eschatological selections from the *Futūhāt* we have translated and commented in *The Meccan Revelations* anthology, volume I.

96. This same divine description of "what God has prepared" in the Garden occurs separately, in almost the same words (adding only "of mortals" [*bashar*] at the end), as an even more famous *hadīth qudsī* that Ibn 'Arabī includes as no. 21 in his *Mishkāt al-Anwār*. That short divine saying is included in all the canonical hadith collections, and echoes I Corinthians 2:9, Isaiah 64:4, and even more literally the *Gospel of Thomas*, saying no. 17 (tr. T. Lamdin, in *The Nag Hammadi Library*, ed. Robinson, p. 128). See the detailed discussion of the variants and sources in W. Graham, op. cit., 117–119.

97. Literally: "is imaged" or "its likeness appears": the Arabic root (*m-th-l*) is that of all the Qur'anic "likenesses," and this particular verbal form of that root is specifically used in the Qur'an to describe all the forms of perception of the blessed in the Gardens.

98. Or "our spiritual twins": alluding to the celestial counterparts or serving companions ("houris" and "young men") mentioned in several Qur'anic verses concerning the divine Court in Paradise.

99. For this transformation (*inqilāb* and *taqallub*) or "turning inside-out" in the resurrected state, see the Qur'an 84:9; 7:165; 26:50 and 227; 43:14. The first part of this sentence could also be translated: "And He obliged us to…" or "authorized us to…."

100. *Al-tahawwul* or *al-taqallub fī al-suwar*: translated here from the *Sahīh* of Muslim, *īmān*, 81. This hadīth and the immediately following one (in Muslim) are both recorded in almost identical terms near the end of Bukhārī's *Sahīh* (*tawhīd*, 23 and 24; repeated in the chapter on *riqāq*, 52); see additional references in W. Graham, *Divine Word*, pp. 134–135 (for the *hadīth qudsī* section only) and Wensinck, *Concordance*, I, 348 (versions also recorded by Ibn Māja, al-Tirmidhī, al-Dārimī and Ibn Hanbal). This hadith is obviously very similar in meaning and structure to the following "Hadith of the Intercession," although Ibn 'Arabī tends to cite the opening section of both versions

(concerning the hypocrites and their inability to perceive what surpasses their beliefs) independently of the rest of the hadith.

101. *Tawaffā*: the root of this untranslatable term—which the Qur'an also uses several times to describe the angels' *"receiving and greeting"* each human soul at the moment of death—also has equally important connotations of (1) giving satisfaction, completion and fulfillment; (2) giving someone their due, fully requiting or compensating them; (3) fulfilling and keeping faith with a vow or promise; and (4) restoring wholeness, perfection, abundance and completion.

102. Or "dreaming": the root of *manām* can refer to both states.

103. "Sends (back?)": the verb used here (*arsala*) is actually the same used to refer to the divine "sending" of the Messengers (*rusul*), a term which in the Qur'an normally refers to the bearers of scriptural revelations among the prophets (*anbiyā'*), as well as to angelic emissaries.

104. This Qur'anic phrase has two closely related meanings: in its ordinary, extended usage it would mean something like "They did not value/appreciate/esteem/rank Him properly/truly." But three more literal and concrete senses of this verb and *masdar* from the Arabic root (*q-d-r*) are even more relevant to the hadīth in Muslim. *Qadr*, as an active participle form, is frequently used in the Qur'an to refer to (1) the divine "determination" or "specification" of all manifest existence (e.g., in *Laylat al-Qadr*, Sura 97). (2) The same root—especially in the divine Name *al-Qadīr*, the All-Capable, "Omni-potent"—has the common sense of ability, capacity, or possibility (of doing something). And (3) *qadr* commonly refers to the size or extent, amount, degree, or measure of something (whether qualitatively or quantitatively). This following hadīth well illustrates the failure of ordinary human "estimation" (*taqdīr*) of the ultimate Reality in respect to all three of these meanings of *qadr*.

105. All of what follows becomes clearer if one keeps in mind that the expression *Rabb* ("lord," "sustainer," "provider," etc.) here is always used by speakers in the Qur'an to refer to their most undeniable, ultimate *concrete, personal and intimate awareness* of the Truly Real, the particular "Face of God" that is most powerfully and undeniably real to them.

106. Literally, both here and in the following question: *"Does it give you pain to... ?"*—a sense which suggests other key interpretive dimensions of the contrast here (with complex echoes of Qur'anic sym-

345

bolism) between our direct vision of the moon and (only for an instant) of the sun.

107. The verb in this reply, as in the original question, is in the ongoing *present imperfect* (as with most of the eschatological language in the Qur'an), here with a further intensive suffix indicated absolute certainty and affirmation. Although such verb forms can also be understood as English future tenses, it would be very easy (and common) to add a special unambiguously future prefix ruling out any uncertainty, had that actually been desired.

108. *al-nās*: the vague, indefinite plural used in the Qur'an as an approximate, loosely pejorative equivalent to the English "most people"—typically in explicit contrast to those realized individuals whose spiritual senses (heart, inner vision, etc.) have been awakened.

109. A mysterious, recurrent Qur'anic term referring to all the illusory objects of desire and attraction that lead people toward the "shadows" of illusion and obscure the "Light" of the divine Presence.

110. Or "*protect* (them)" (*sallim, sallim*). The translation here omits a few words describing the Hooks that seize those crossing this Bridge.

111. As is often the case in the Qur'an, these references to the Rising, as described from the divine perspective, are all in the past "perfect," *already accomplished* tense.

112. *Sujūd*: literally, their "bowing down" in (true, spontaneous) prayer. The word translated broadly as "effect" here could also refer to a more visible mark or trace, like that left on the forehead after frequently repeated prostrations.

113. This hadith, a somewhat different version of the preceding one narrated this time by the Abū Saʿīd al-Khudrī who corrects Abū Hurayra at the end of the preceding hadith, comes immediately after that hadith in both Bukhārī's and Muslim's *Saḥīḥ*. Ibn ʿArabī himself quotes the central, divine saying section of this hadith, from the collection of Muslim, in his *Mishkāt al-Anwār*, no. 26; this is the version he also tends to cite when discussing the actual wording (rather than the general theme) in the *Futūḥāt*. In chapter 64 of the *Futūḥāt* (IV, 458–462), Ibn ʿArabī quotes another lengthy "hadith of intercession"—without mentioning any particular source or chain of transmission—that coincides with this version of the hadith only at the very end (IV, 461–62).

114. Usually translated as "(religious) community." But here—as often in the Qur'an, where the same expression is applied to other crea-

tures—the term may well be understood in a much more complex and less strictly historicist sense.

115. The term here is *al-nās*, here in the openly pejorative sense of what they take to be ordinary or sinful people (including those of other socio-religious communities).

116. *Al-dunyā*: i.e., the earthly, material world (since this story has now placed them in the "other" world, *al-ākhira*).

117. The hadith here presupposes quite literally the situation in the rest of this Qur'anic passage (68:42–43): *... and they are called to bow down (in prayer), but they are not able, their eyes abased, humiliation overcoming them—although they used to be calling (others) to pray, when they were whole and sound!* (Many hadith, like these eschatological ones, frequently include or presuppose long quotations or detailed allusions to related Qur'anic passages.)

118. The phrase mentioned here (*sallim, sallim*) is exactly the same as in the previous hadith's account of the Intercession, except that the "they" here are not yet specifically identified: these words could be taken either as the cry of the various intercessors (see below) pleading with God for *others*, or more generally as expressing the inner state of *all* the souls terrified (for *themselves*) by the events of the Judgment and the visible sight of Gehenna.

119. An extremely tiny, feather-weight gold coin. The version of this same hadith given in Bukhārī (see references above) substitutes "faith" (*īmān*) in each case where this version has "good."

120. Alluding to a well known Qur'anic passage at 99:7 (and several related verses, including the one at 4:40 which Abū Sa'īd al-Khudrī goes on to quote just below).

121. *Al-nabīyūn*: the all-inclusive Qur'anic term for many of the pre-Islamic Messengers, Friends, and sages.

122. *Arham al-rāhimīn*: alluding especially here to the verse 12:92, although the same divine Name or attribute is also cited at 7:151, 12:64, and 21:83.

123. *Ridwānī*: alluding to such Qur'anic verses as 57:20, 5:16, 9:21, etc. (mentioned 13 times, in addition to related uses of the root *r-d-y*); this term is often translated as divine "Satisfaction" or "Contentment," but obviously such approximate English expressions are utterly inadequate in this context.

124. *Mawāqif al-qiyāma*: Ibn 'Arabī also frequently refers to this hadith as the "hadith of al-Naqqāsh," using the name of one of its intermediate transmitters.

125. The *Mishkāt al-Anwār*, Ibn 'Arabī's personal collection of 101 divine sayings, includes eight selections (numbers 49, 53, 55, 60, 66, 69, 78 and the concluding 101st) drawn from this single hadith, and the specific conditions in which he learned it (at Mecca in 599 A.H., the same year the *Mishkāt* was itself composed) are described at the very end. These particular divine sayings are basically parts of the same long hadith recorded in full in chapter 65 of the *Futūhāt* and partially translated in section V above. See the translation (with facing Arabic text) by M. Valsān, *La Niche des Lumières*, Paris, 1983—and the English translation and critical edition by S. Hirtenstein and M. Tiernan, Oxford, Anqa publishers, 2004.

126. This is clearly intended as an allusion (given the total of fifty Stations) to the famous Qur'anic description of the *Rising of the angels and the Spirit* in *a Day whose extent is fifty thousand years* (70:4).

CHAPTER FOUR
DISCERNING: LEARNING TO TRANSLATE FROM GOD

1. Whatever the underlying reasons, it is interesting that the distinctive rhetoric of Ibn 'Arabī's *Futūhāt* was never seriously imitated by his followers and interpreters—who at most adapted only a few of its individual features. However, its underlying intentions and re-creation of essential deeper Qur'anic structures and forms were beautifully and successfully mirrored in subsequent Persian poetic traditions, above all throughout the incomparable lyric poems of Hafez and the equally effective and complex structures of Rumi's *Masnavī*. (Further volumes devoted to elucidating those parallels are in preparation.)

2. See especially the extensive works of William Chittick (for the *Futūhāt*) and Toshihiko Izutsu (for the *Fusūs al-Hikam*), among many other relevant studies cited in the Bibliography below.

3. See especially *Ibn 'Arabī's Rhetoric of Realisation* (details at n. 1 to Chapter 1 above).

4. Thus, in regard to the recurrent Qur'anic emphasis on the processes connected with our deciphering and applying and interpreting the divine Signs, a few such key expressions include *'aql, dhikr, tadhakkur, tadabbur, tafakkur, 'ibra, faqaha, hikma* (and related forms in many of these cases).

5. Of course this is something that Ibn 'Arabī himself was also readily capable of doing—most obviously in his unusual, recondite

metaphysical poetry throughout the *Futūhāt* and in many other works, or in the striking symbolic language typical of many of his earlier youthful writings.

6. See numerous illustrations in the Bibliography below, including especially the related studies by Chittick, Sells, and Chodkiewicz.

7. See "Ibn 'Arabī's 'Esotericism': The Problem of Spiritual Authority," *Studia Islamica*, LXXI (1990), pp. 37–64; the long volume currently in preparation is tentatively entitled *Many Paths to the Real: Freedom, Creativity, Diversity and Tolerance in Ibn 'Arabī's Political Philosophy*.

8. See in particular the detailed development of this theme in *Orientations: Islamic Thought in a World Civilisation* (London, Archetype, 2004), especially chapter 2 which is devoted specifically to Ibn 'Arabī.

9. See n. 7 to Chapter 1 above for details on this volume (tr. Austin) and another related translation from Ibn 'Arabī's famous *Rūh al-Quds*.

10. See "Ibn 'Arabī's 'Esotericism': The Problem of Spiritual Authority," in *Studia Islamica*, LXXI (1990), pp. 37–64; and chapter 2 of *Orientations: Islamic Thought in a World Civilisation* (London, Archetype, 2004). More extensive translations of much of chapter 366 are also included in the recent anthology, *The Meccan Revelations,* vol. I.

11. See the fuller development of this theme, in terms of Ibn 'Arabī's favored eschatological symbolism, throughout Chapter Five below.

12. The brief selections given in this Chapter are greatly abridged from my longer, fully annotated version in the anthology of translaations, *The Meccan Revelations* (section on "The End of Time"), vol. I.

13. *'Ajam*: the same term could also refer more particularly to "the Persians."

14. As originally noted publicly by M. Chodkiewicz, in his seminal *The Seal of the Saints*, each of the chapters 270–383 in the long *Fasl al-Manāzil* ("Section on the Spiritual Waystations") in the *Futūhāt* corresponds consecutively—counting from the end of the Qur'an—in manifold ways to a specific Sura of the Qur'an (in this case of chapter 366, to *Sūrat al-Kahf*, 18).

15. III (Beirut edition), 331.34–338.2; see also the more complete translations and commentary included in *The Meccan Revelations* anthology.

16. Or "calling" or "requesting": the Arabic root *d-'-w*, translated here by forms of "pray," refers not to the obligatory, daily ritual divine

service (*salāt*), but to an individual's personal prayers to God, often—as is clearly the case here—with the added sense of a specific petitionary call or request for some particular divine action or response. The subject remains unspecified here, as in the original Arabic, since the spiritual condition described here ultimately turns out to apply not only to the Mahdī or his Helpers, but potentially to each person participating in this spiritual state, as Ibn 'Arabī states more explicitly later in these discussions.

17. Ibn 'Arabī's expression here apparently refers to his characteristic understanding that each individual's inner strivings or petitions to God (i.e., "prayer" in the broadest possible sense, whether or not consciously and appropriately formulated) necessarily are directed toward one or another specific aspects of the overall divine Reality, expressed in Qur'anic terms by the many divine Names (*Exalted, King, All-Compassionate*, etc.), that variously constitute the deeper ontological "lords" of that individual.

18. *ilhāh*, a term that implies not only urgency and insistence, but also a sort of specific, determined pleading, close to an open demand. Ibn 'Arabī goes on to explain that this sort of attitude—evidently inappropriate in our ordinary relationship with God—is apparently permitted to the Mahdī as part of the divine Proof (*hujja*) of his special, quasi-prophetic function (following note).

19. I.e., to realize this otherwise impossible request as one of the unique miracles (*mu'jizāt*) performed by the prophetic messengers that constitute part of the decisive divine Argument or Proof (*hujja*) of their special mission.

20. In fact, Ibn 'Arabī is apparently alluding here more broadly to his understanding of his own status as the preeminent "follower of Muhammad" (see Chodkiewicz, *Seal*)—and by extension, to the similar position of all the (fully accomplished) "Muhammadan saints," which he brings out more explicitly at the end of this passage and in the rest of his discussion here in chapter 366. For the deeper grounds of this special status of the Friends in relation to the universal spiritual "heritage of Muhammad" (which ultimately encompasses the metaphysical realities of all the other prophets and messengers), see the extended references in Chodkiewicz, *Seal*, chapters IV-V.

21. This hadith was quoted in full among the many traditions concerning the characteristics of the Mahdī cited at the beginning of chapter 366 (not translated here), and Ibn 'Arabī repeats this phrase whenever the question of *'isma* (see following note) arises in the following sections.

22. See the excellent, more complete discussion of Ibn 'Arabī's distinctive understanding of this inner spiritual state of *'isma*—which is far more profound and universal, in its metaphysical and spiritual dimensions, than the more familiar treatments of this subject in kalam theology (where it is primarily limited to discussion of the special exalted spiritual station of the prophets and Imāms)—in Hakīm, *Mu'jam*, pp. 806–810.

23. Ibn 'Arabī goes on here to illustrate this particular ability with a story about Ibn 'Abbās and Aisha, who both saw a stranger conversing with the Prophet and subsequently learned that they had actually seen the angel Gabriel—the kind of partial spiritual perception (in which people see the divine manifestation or veil, but do not yet understand its actual reality or meaning) that is equally illustrated in a number of other hadith, including the famous hadith of Gabriel translated and discussed in Chapter Three above.

24. *Rijāl al-ghayb*: this technical Sufi expression refers to Friends of high spiritual rank (especially the *abdāl*) or other spiritual beings (angels, etc.) who may receive a divine mission to become invisible or take on a human form in another place. As an illustration of this phenomenon, see Ibn 'Arabī's own firsthand account (from this same chapter 366) of two personal experiences with such "mysterious strangers," including an unnamed Iranian Sufi master, which are summarized at the end of this Chapter (section V below).

25. Ibn 'Arabī frequently interprets in this light the many symbols mentioned in the visions of the Prophet (e.g., during his *Mi'rāj*, as explained in chapter 367 [III, 340–354]); see the translation and detailed study of this key chapter included in *The Meccan Revelations* anthology, vol. I. One of his favorite illustrations of the phenomena referred to here is the Prophet's immediate recognition of the milk offered him by an angel in a vision (according to a famous hadith) as a symbol of spiritual knowledge.

Chapter 311 of the *Futūhāt* (III, 41–44) is entirely devoted to these phenomena of "manifestations" or "projections"—both by Sufi saints and by angels, etc.—in various sensible and imaginal forms. Ibn 'Arabī gives there a number of fascinating anecdotes concerning such incidents, analyzes their metaphysical underpinnings (in the Presence of the divine Imagination, *khiyāl*) and discusses the special unerring ability of the Prophet to perceive the spiritual realities (*ma'ānī*) underlying such common spiritual phenomena. (See the translations from that chapter by W. Chittick in *The Meccan Revelations*, vol. I.)

26. The earlier theological (*'ilm al-kalām*) issue here—which Ibn 'Arabī boldly ignores (in keeping with the more obvious sense of the verse)—turns on many later Muslim theologians' restriction of the Qur'anic term *wahy* (in all its grammatical forms) to the scriptural and other revelations specially reserved for the prophetic messengers (*rasūl*). (For those accepting such theological restrictions, it was customary to use the broader term *ilhām* to refer to other, more widely accessible forms of spiritual "inspiration.") Throughout the translations here, however, the generic English term "inspiration" (and related forms) is used to refer to *wahy*, in keeping with Ibn 'Arabī's own intentionally inclusive approach at this point.

27. Ibn 'Arabī's technical vocabulary for describing the many facets of divine communication and its human reception, which combines a profound concern for the subtleties of Qur'anic expression with close attention to the diverse phenomena of spiritual experience and their complex metaphysical foundations, is so extraordinarily rich that any English equivalents of the key terms can only be very approximate.

Here the divine "address" (*al-khitāb al-ilāhī*) or "discourse" is the divine "Speech" (*kalām*; or *hadīth*, "New-Speaking") specifically as it is directed toward and received by a particular person. Its "personal delivery" or transmission (*ilqā'*: literally "projection") into the heart (or hearing or any other spiritual senses) of the person thus addressed may take any of the forms described below—since ultimately (for Ibn 'Arabī, but relying on many passages of the Qur'an) all Being is nothing but divine "Speech," an insight that he boldly amplifies in the immediately following point. For an excellent presentation of these and related technical terms in their broader context in the Shaykh's writings (as well as a helpful reminder of the complexities of their actual Qur'anic usage), see Hakīm, *Mu'jam*, pp. 400–405 (*al-Khitāb al-Ilāhī*) and 1182–1191 (*al-Wahy al-Ilāhī*), together with the careful attention to such recurrent technical vocabulary in W. Chittick's recent volumes of translations from the *Futūhāt*.

28. *Wahy*, again. As just noted, Ibn 'Arabī himself understands and employs this key expression (and related forms of the same root) to convey an extremely wide range of meanings, which—as shown by S. al-Hakīm (*Mu'jam*, pp. 1182–1191)—closely reflect the broader dimensions and subtleties of the original Qur'anic usage. In particular, readers familiar with the usual discussions of *wahy* (as the uniquely prophetic form of "revelation") in Islamic theological and philosophical literature (as well as in more apologetically oriented Sufi texts) should

take careful note of the very different parameters and intentions of Ibn 'Arabī's complex usage of this key epistemological term here and elsewhere in his writings. The critical problem of the relation of the *wahy* of each prophet to that of those Friends of God and spiritual Knowers who are his true "inheritors" is clarified in Chapter 14 (On "the Secrets of the Prophets among the Friends..."), O.Y. II, 357–362 (Beirut ed. I, 149–152).

29. *'alā jihat al-hadīth*: here the emphasis implied by this term is on both the (relative) novelty of information conveyed and the fact that it is perceived as a message coming from outside the person to whom it is delivered—not so much on the usual meaning of verbal "speaking," since this kind of inspiration is perceived by the heart and not by the physical sense of hearing (again, see his detailed explanations in Chapter 14, O.Y. II, 357-360). Here and in the other examples described in this section, Ibn 'Arabī wants to emphasize the specific kind of divine "address" or inspiration in which there is a conscious awareness of this particular message as something clearly received or "projected" into the person's awareness from a higher, divine Source, and not as the product or expression of his personal thinking (*nazar*) or previously acquired knowledge.

This fundamental aspect of genuine inspiration is also brought out in the continuation of the Qur'anic verse opening this section: *And likewise We inspired in you a spirit from Our Command. You did not know what was the Book nor the Faith...*.(42:52). The decisive importance of the Heart (*qalb*: see Hakīm, *Mu'jam*, pp. 916–921) as the instrument of this direct inspiration (following the Qur'anic usage of *wayh*), and thus of its immediate spiritual apprehension without any sensible "veil," becomes clearer only in contrast to Ibn 'Arabī's immediately following discussion of the auditory and other "veiled" forms of the divine Speech addressed to particular individuals.

30. The "necessary sciences" or forms of knowledge (*'ulūm darūriyya*), used here in the accepted sense of that term in Islamic philosophy and theology, are the abstract universal premises (prior to sense-perception) of all thought (including logic, mathematics, etc.), which therefore underlie all communication and ordinary, non-revealed knowledge. These premises are innately shared by all human beings and cannot be doubted or questioned, although because of their universality they are not always (or even usually) consciously formulated. For Ibn 'Arabī's own distinctive conception of the necessary forms of knowledge, in the broader context of his spiritual epistemology, see chapter 19 (O.Y. ed. III, 78–87).

31. Here Ibn 'Arabī goes on to reiterate that although our awareness of various forms of knowledge within ourselves may often strike
us as a new discovery, this familiar experience does not ordinarily share
the other essential characteristics of this particular form of *divine inspiration*—i.e., it is not perceived by the heart as a divine Speech freshly
"delivered" to us from a higher source outside ourselves.

32. *'ayn tajalli al-Haqq*: i.e., the theophany or Self-manifestation
of the ultimate divine Reality, the absolutely Real (*al-Haqq*). As we
have already seen in the preceding Chapters, this ambiguous status of
all phenomena, which can be either "veils" or "theophanies" depending on the inner perceptivity of the person experiencing them, is one of
the central themes of all of Ibn 'Arabī's writing. It is frequently expressed, for example, in his typical ontological (and etymological) understanding of *kufr*, *kafara*, etc.—usually mistranslated as "unbelief"—
as "covering up" or "veiling" the infinite Signs of God's Presence. For
further references, see Hakīm, *Mu'jam*, pp. 265–269 (theophany, etc.)
and 313–318 (veil, etc.).

33. This "particular," individual modality of the divine Speech
(*Kalām Allāh*) here is illustrated by Ibn 'Arabī with the citation of three
Qur'anic verses (9:6, 19:52, 27:8) among those where God is referred
to as speaking directly and openly to particular individuals (especially
to Moses, popularly known as *Kalīm Allāh*). Again he is stressing the
essential phenomenological distinction between this kind of specific,
individual divine "address" and the more universal manifestations of
the divine Speech.

34. It is important to note that Ibn 'Arabī clearly sees all of these
forms of revelation or inspiration as applying to the case of the Prophet
and the Mahdī's Helpers, and by extension to all those inspired Knowers
who share in this particular spiritual station (*maqām*)—and that he is
not using these distinctions to justify a particular theological ranking
of prophets (or of prophets and Friends). Instead, this concluding allusion points the discerning reader toward the more essential problem of
developing one's own awareness and understanding of that "divine
address" (in all its dimensions) that is delivered personally to each of
us. See again the more detailed treatment of these basic epistemological questions in Chapter 14 of the *Futūhāt*, O.Y. ed. II, 357–362 (=
Cairo ed. I, 150).

35. Perhaps the most pertinent illustration in Ibn 'Arabī's own
writing of this sort of "translation" (*tarjama*) of a divine inspiration—
in this case received from the hand of the Prophet—into human lan-

guage is his famous book *Fuṣūs al-Hikam*. In his Prologue to that work, he explicitly sets forth his claim (or wish) to be the Prophet's faithful "translator" (*mutarjim*).

It should be noted that this much more widespread and inclusive form of divine inspiration is clearly differentiated here from the direct angelic dictation of the actual words of the revealed Book (as described in the immediately preceding passage), which evidently constitutes one of the unique attributes of the Qur'an. Ultimately, for Ibn 'Arabī, every form of human knowing is based on divine inspirations and individual theophanies, although most often those relying on their own reasoning and inquiry (*naẓar*) are unaware of this or simply take it for granted: see, for example, *Futūhāt*, chapter 19, O.Y. ed. III, 81–82.

36. *'ulamā' al-rusūm*—a group he continues to criticize pointedly throughout the rest of this section, and indeed throughout the *Futūhāt*: see many related illustrations drawn from a number of other chapters of *Futūhāt* in my earlier study of "Ibn 'Arabī's 'Esotericism'...," *Studia Islamica*, LXXI (1990), pp. 37–64.

37. *mutarjim*: though this phrase may sound strange in English (and even in the original Arabic), since we would more naturally expect to see the world referred to as a *translation* of the divine Speech, it does express in a simple and memorable formula the very essence of Ibn 'Arabī's central insight into the theophanic, continually recreated nature of all Being and the transcendent, paradoxical unity of the "subject" and "object" of that Whole, as it unfolds in the realized vision of the "people of unveiling," in the Heart of the Fully Human Being.

38. See the different translated selections on this theme, drawn from other earlier chapters of the *Futūhāt*, included in *Orientations: Islamic Thought in a World Civilisation* (London, Archetype, 2004), chapter 2.

39. *'ulamā' al-rusum*: here this term (used more broadly in the previous section) refers specifically to the formal "knowledge" of the external traces of the Prophetic heritage typical of the mass of legal scholars (*fuqahā'*) popularly known as the "learned" (*'ulamā'*). The roots of Ibn 'Arabī's radically differing point of view—which at first seems to contradict his own discussion here of those individuals whose formal legal "knowledge" is apparently overcome by their passions— are explained more openly throughout the immediately following passages. Again, see the related illustrations from throughout the *Futūhāt* included in "Ibn 'Arabī's 'Esotericism': The Problem of Spiritual Authority."

It should be stressed that this particular epithet, for Ibn 'Arabī, is primarily used here in an essentially descriptive (and not necessarily pejorative) sense, since many of the famous spiritual Knowers and Sufis—including, for example, the pious judge Ibn 'Arabī describes immediately below—were also notable representatives of this same category of the religiously learned '*ulamā*'. See his discussion of the complementary functions of "those who preserve (the outward literal) *forms* of the divine judgment" as expressed by the prophet and "those who preserve (the Prophet's spiritual) *states and secrets*" in Chapter 14, O.Y. II, 361–362 (= Cairo ed., I, 151), along with the more detailed discussions and references in the article ("Ibn 'Arabī's 'Esotericism'...") just cited.

40. This is a short quotation from the classical hadith accounts of the characteristics of the Mahdī which are given in full at the opening of this chapter 366 (not translated here).

41. I.e., Ibn 'Arabī is not specifically pointing to some outwardly reformable defect in the teaching and transmission of the revelation in his time, nor to the fraudulent pretensions or moral defects of particular individuals (although that latter subject does come up below). Rather he is primarily alluding here (and even more clearly in the following sections) to the fundamental—and in our present circumstances, humanly inescapable—problem that the just, appropriate application and interpretation of the traditional sources concerning the divine commands and their historical application by the Prophet usually require a far deeper understanding of both their ultimate contexts and intentions and the relevant factors in each particular case than can be expected of any but the rarest individuals, those whose every action is divinely inspired and protected from error. As he remarks more openly in the following sections, those truly qualified authorities (the true *wulāt*) in any age, whether or not they outwardly rule, are none other than the divinely guided Friends of God—i.e., the *awliyā'* (a term drawn from the same Arabic root as the words translated as "authority" in these passages, and having explicit connotations of spiritual authority [*wilāya*] that are not readily conveyed by the term "saint" in Western languages).

42. I.e., what Ibn 'Arabī calls their "passion" (*shahwa*), referring to all the various ways in which their personal emotions may run contrary to their knowledge of the spiritually correct judgment. The person exhibiting this moral capacity of rational self-control is called "judicious" ('*āqil*), an expression which Ibn 'Arabī derives from the Arabic root sense of binding or hindering (one's personal emotions, in this

case), but which is closely related to our wider theme of spiritual intelligence, in all its dimensions.

43. See the more elaborate and widespread illustrations of this point, drawn from throughout the *Futūhāt*, included in "Ibn 'Arabī's 'Esotericism': The Problem of Spiritual Authority."

44. This refers to a famous divine saying ("My Compassion has precedence over My Anger") which is constantly cited by Ibn 'Arabī.

45. *hudūd Allāh*, a Qur'anic concept which originally includes both the divine "statutes" and commandments—which can of course be understood in a more spiritual and universal as well as a more exoteric and legalistic sense—and the earthly punishments and penalties applied for offenses against them in the various later historical systems of Islamic jurisprudence.

46. I.e., to the one who has realized within himself the fundamental justice of the divine Command and has carried out the process of inner repentance and recourse to God's Mercy that has spiritually purified him and enabled him to avoid the further consequences of his offense (in this world or the next). Ibn 'Arabī goes on to make clear that his point here actually applies to the inner spiritual situation of every individual with regard to the infinite range of the divine commands or "limits" more generally understood (see preceding note), not just those infractions that happen to involve particular criminal actions and the external forms of the revealed Pathway. He thereby suggests a similar extension from legal, official "punishments" to a deeper consideration of the realities and functions related to the much larger interrelated questions of "infringing" spiritual laws and of the purifying consequences of such situations.

47. *al-hākim*: although translated throughout as "judge" (in the more familiar legal sense), this multi-faceted term—which shares the identical root with the central divine Name "*the All-Wise*" or "*Just Judge*" (*al-Hakīm*)—can also be understood in an extended (and more exact) sense as anyone who seeks to ascertain and apply the *divine* "judgment" or "commandment" (*hukm*) appropriate to a given action or situation—a grave responsibility if viewed from the broader spiritual perspective that Ibn 'Arabī gradually unfolds here and in the following sections.

48. Ibn 'Arabī's conception of the unique qualifications of the accomplished Friends of God (*awliyā'*) in this regard is developed in greater detail in the following sections. But at the very end of chapter 366 (in a remark quoted in section V below) he places severe restric-

tions on the situations in which they should even attempt to argue with others on the basis of their revealed insights—i.e., only when they actually receive a divine *order* to do so.

A revealing illustration of the complex responsibilities involved in the position of human, worldly judgeship is Ibn 'Arabī's remark at this point (III, 334.13) that "In my opinion none of the questions concerning the religiously prescribed legal judgments is more difficult than *zinā'* (i.e., adultery and other forbidden sexual relations) in particular; even if the punishment is carried out, after that there still remain other claims (against those responsible) on the part of the persons injured."

49. An allusion to the many Qur'anic verses repeatedly insisting that *the Messenger is only responsible for the clear communication* (*balāgh*) (24:54; 29:18; etc.) of God's Word, not for the particular reactions of his listeners. Those differing responses are discussed in the many other verses alluded to here stressing God's role, as well as the listeners' individual responsibilities, in those contrasting reactions and degrees of receptivity.

50. *a'qal al-nās* (which could also be translated as "*the most intelligent* of people"), translated here in accordance with Ibn 'Arabī's earlier discussion of the *'āqil*, in this ethical and juridical context, as the person whose spiritual knowledge is in full control of his egoistic passions. Clearly the exceptional degree of spiritual intelligence ideally required here—to the extent of refraining from judging others (even inwardly), based on a full recognition of the inner necessity of their actions—could be expected only of the prophets and the most accomplished Knowers.

For Ibn 'Arabī's understanding of the "prophets" (*anbiyā'*, sing. *nabī*) in general as a group far larger than the small number of "messengers" specifically charged with communicating a specific divine legislation (i.e., a *rasūl* or *shāri'*)—and his related understanding of the Friends (*awliyā'*) as "the *anbiyā'* of the Muslim Community"—, see the many references in Chodkiewicz, *Seal*, chapter III; Hakīm, *Mu'jam*, pp. 1058–1053; and chapter 14 of the *Futūhāt*, O.Y. II, pp. 356 and following.

51. The "sublime knowledge" referred to here appears to be the divine inspiration of the appropriate "judgment" (*hukm*) that, as Ibn 'Arabī goes on to explain, is shared with the prophets by the "people of unveiling," the Knowers and the Friends of God. But it may also refer more specifically here to the prophet's awareness of the inner states of those whom God has made insensitive to the divine message, as dis-

cussed in the immediately preceding paragraphs. As already noted above, the term used for "having authority" here (*wāl^(in)*) is etymologically very close to the familiar Qur'anic expression usually translated as "saint" or "Friend of God" (*walī*)—no doubt alluding to Ibn 'Arabī's understanding of the truly inspired authorities developed more openly in the immediately following passages.

52. The Qur'anic notion of *rizq*, for Ibn 'Arabī, ultimately extends to all the physical and metaphysical forms of divine "sustenance" or "nourishment" by which the world and its creatures are given life and being: see the discussion of his usage of this and related terms in Hakīm, *Mu'jam*, pp. 531–534. Thus—as in his initial enumeration of the qualities of the Helpers earlier in this same chapter—he commonly distinguishes between the spiritual or noetic (*ma'nawiyya* or *ma'qūla*) forms of this divine sustenance, which are discussed at the beginning of this passage, and the visible material blessings that are so briefly mentioned at the very end.

53. Here Ibn 'Arabī is emphasizing the considerable limits on the realm directly subject to the temporal functions of the Mahdī. The Arabic term *nufus* (translated here as "souls") refers specifically in this context only to that very limited lower aspect of the individual's soul which controls our physical body in this material, "mortal human" (*basharī*) realm, not to the infinitely wider dimensions of the "spirit" (*rūh*) which ultimately constitutes the fully human *insān*.

54. Or simply "themselves" (*anfusihim*). This final qualification alludes to the insistence throughout Islamic tradition (including the schools of jurisprudence) on the existence of both disbelieving and believing individuals among the jinn, the latter category being followers of one or another of the human prophetic messengers: see the references to Ibn 'Arabī's discussions of the jinn—a term he uses elsewhere in several other, different senses—in Hakīm, *Mu'jam*, pp. 279–281.

55. I.e., the spiritual beings who were created from "light" (*nūr*), just as the jinn (according to Islamic tradition) were created from the lower, purely physical element of fire (*nār*).

56. This particular group of angels (*al-sā'ihūn*), who "travel around the roads (*turuq*) seeking out the people of *dhikr*," are mentioned in a long hadith—cited in the *Sahīh* collections of both Bukhārī and Muslim, as well as in the *Musnad* of Ahmad ibn Hanbal—that Ibn 'Arabī included as number 84 in his personal collection of divine sayings, the famous *Mishkāt al-Anwār* (p. 110 in the French translation, with facing Arabic text, by M. Valsan, *La Niche des Lumieres*, Paris, 1983; new

English translation cited in Bibliography below.) The passages included in full quotation marks here are an approximate quotation from that hadith. These angelic "travelers" are mentioned again at the end of chapter 366 of the *Futūhāt*, in the strange story concerning the "people of the Unseen" (*rijāl al-ghayb*), summarized below at the end of this Chapter.

57. I.e., as he explains later in this sentence, the *dhākirūn* (those who do actually "recall" its true spiritual reality), not necessarily all those who are merely reciting the Arabic words. The reference here to "sessions" (*majālis*) of *dhikr* seems to imply specifically Sufi gatherings; this is clearly the case in his reference to a particular experience involving these angelic "travelers" in the anecdote summarized at the end of this Chapter below. For Ibn 'Arabī's own personal preference, in that practical spiritual context, for *dhikr* of the Qur'an as opposed to the other (primarily musical) forms of *dhikr* already popular in Eastern Sufi circles of his time, see chapter 182 of the *Futūhāt*, "Concerning Inner Knowing of the Station of *Samā'* and Its Secrets," II, 366–368.

58. *āyāt*: i.e., the verses of the Qur'an.

59. *bathth al-'ilm*: the term implies the unfolding or opening up of what was concealed—apparently in reference to Ibn 'Arabī's increasing literary production (and his provision of many of his works with an *ijāza 'āmma*, a "general permission" for their reading and propagation), pedagogical activities which may have coincided with his growing realization of his unique personal role as "Seal of the Muhammadan Saints." See Chodkiewicz, *Seal*, and the biographical studies listed in the Bibliography below.

60. This echoes Ibn 'Arabī's earlier statement (in a passage of chapter 366 not translated here) that "he (i.e., as the 'Seal of Muhammadan Sainthood') and the Qur'an are brothers," along with other references there concerning his distinctive personal understanding of what is really meant by that term (*al-Qur'ān*). Ibn 'Arabī's decisive personal realization of the universal Reality of the Qur'an and the corresponding comprehensive spiritual "Station of Muhammad" is described in detail in his *Kitāb al-Isrā'*, written in Fez in 594 a.h., or roughly during the Moroccan period alluded to here. See the translation and commentary of a key autobiographical passage from the *K. al-Isrā'* in my article on "The Spiritual Ascension: Ibn 'Arabī and the *Mi'rāj*," along with related sections describing the culminating stage of his own spiritual Ascension in chapter 367 of the *Futūhāt* (III, 340–354), now available in *The Meccan Revelations* anthology, volume I.

61. The striking usage of the first person plural here—unlike the case with the preceding sentences, where it may be only a polite form of "I"—appears to be a clear allusion to Ibn 'Arabī's self-conception of his particular individual spiritual role as the "Seal of the Muhammadan saints" (see Chodkiewicz, *Seal*) responsible for the ongoing spiritual guidance of the entire Community. Likewise, just as the Seal reflects the total Reality of Muhammad (who at that cosmic level *is* the Qur'an, for Ibn 'Arabī), so the expression "I was given the keys of Its understanding" echoes a fundamental hadith of the Prophet, cited repeatedly throughout the Shaykh's writings, that begins: "I was given the totality of the (divine) Words..." (*jawāmi' al-kilam*).

62. The "intermediaries" (*wasā'it*), in this immediate context (and judging from the earlier analysis of the divine discourse), appear to be all the "veils" of the particular "forms"—whether angelic or human prophetic messengers, or perhaps the infinite variety of theophanies in general—through which the divine inspiration is more often perceived. But elsewhere in the *Futūhāt* Ibn 'Arabī applies this same term more specifically to the learned public transmitters of the external forms and traces of the Prophetic heritage; see chapter 14, O.Y. II, 358: "...the intermediaries—I mean the *fuqahā'* and the *'ulamā' al-rusūm.*"

63. An important reminder—underlying Ibn 'Arabī's already noted complementary understanding of the proper relations between the "guardians of the (divine) commandments" and the "guardians of the (spiritual) states"—of the fundamental fact that mere access to the external forms of a prophet's speech and activity, no matter how perfect and exact, is not the decisive (or even sufficient) factor in coming to understand properly their actual meaning and currently applicable intentions.

64. *Imām al-Waqt*: i.e., the "Pole" (*qutb*) or "Lord of the Age." For the different meanings of this term (and at least eight other common synonyms in Ibn 'Arabī's technical vocabulary),see Hakīm, *Mu'jam*, pp. 678–683 and Chodkiewicz, *Seal*, chapter VI. It is significant that instead of actually referring to the Mahdī here, Ibn 'Arabī uses this highly ambiguous expression three times (and other forms of "Imām" four additional times) in the space of this relatively short section (III, 335.2–17), clearly implying that this responsibility for the just apportionment of the world's material goods is in some sense a perennial spiritual function. The potential political sensitivity of this expression in his own historical context is suggested by the fate of several

prominent Andalusian and Maghrebi Sufis of his time who were at least accused of claiming the "Imamate" in this more overtly political sense.

65. *baqiyat Allāh*: a reference to the verse 11:86, *What God has left is better for you all, if you are among the faithful....* Much of this section stresses the extreme relativity of our judgments concerning the individual possession (*mulk*) of what is actually God's, and for which we are at best only temporary stewards or custodians in this world.

66. Those extremely important passages, in their wider context in the *Futūhāt* and Islamic thought, have been analyzed in the articles already cited above. See also the discussions of the peculiar role played by Ibn 'Arabī's writings, in the article on "Situating Islamic 'Mysticism': Between Written Traditions and Popular Spirituality," pp. 293–334 in *Mystics of the Book: Themes, Topics and Typologies*, ed. R. Herrera (New York/Berlin, Peter Lang, 1993).

67. That is, of the all-encompassing penetration of spiritual realities, sources and meanings in everything that we normally or unconsciously take to be self-subsistently material, earthly or natural.

68. *al-'āqil*: i.e., the "spiritually intelligent" person whose reason and knowledge restrain the demands of his passions.

69. *ahl al-ilqā'*: see Ibn 'Arabī's discussion of the various modalities of this delivery or "projection" (*ilqā'*) of the divine Speech in the preceding section.

70. *nikāh ma'nawī*: i.e., of the divine Source (the Spirit) and its human receptacle, and more broadly, of all the spiritual, noetic realities and principles manifested in each material event.

71. *Qiyās*. Here "textual indications" translates *nusūs*, a technical term which evidently refers in this context to the outward, literal forms of the scriptures and hadith collections—or rather to the complex of specific divine "stipulations" which they are usually understood to contain, and from which are then extrapolated all the later systems of Islamic jurisprudence. Together, such materials form the ostensible basis for the vast system of analogies or inferences—in fact based on certain influential jurists' reasoned suppositions concerning the presumed purposes underlying the various textual indications in those scriptural records—that constitute the various schools of Islamic jurisprudence (*fiqh*). The roots of Ibn 'Arabī's fundamental criticism of the common practice of *qiyās* (legal inference based on analogy or implicitly analogical reasoning)—as opposed to the infallible divine inspiration characterizing the Mahdī and the Knowers who have reached this spiritual station—are detailed in the final point in this section.

The key issues of the proper conditions for a true understanding of the original intentions and meaning of hadith—which are the *sine qua non* of any truly living transmission of genuine spiritual knowledge—raised throughout the rest of this section are beautifully summarized in the conclusion of chapter 29 (I, 198; O.Y. ed. III, 240–242), concerning the true "people of the Prophet's House" (*Ahl al-Bayt*).

72. *al-shar' al-haqīqī al-muhammadī*: the key term *shar'* discussed throughout this section is ordinarily understood simply as the religious revelation or what was outwardly, historically revealed by the Prophet (and ultimately by God) as prescribed guidance for right human action. Here Ibn 'Arabī, as is often his practice, alludes to the original meaning of that Arabic root as the "opening" or establishment of the authentic "pathway to water" (i.e., to the Water of divine Life, as becomes clearer in the ensuing story of al-Khadir)—a sense which does not necessarily contradict the popular usage, but which does set it in a much larger, potentially transforming perspective.

73. *al-nusūs* : as at the explanatory note 71 just above. Ibn 'Arabī again stresses that he is not questioning the validity and necessity of the traditionally transmitted forms of earlier revelation as such, but rather the spirit and methods that are frequently applied—and by no means only in "legal" situations—to rediscover and realize their more profound truth and actual perennial intentions.

74. *ma'sūm*: Ibn 'Arabī's conception of *'isma*, divinely assured "immunity from error" in one's spiritual judgment and perception, as an essential concomitant of the divine inspiration of the Knowers as well as of the prophetic Messengers, was already developed in his first point in section III above (n. 22). The Mahdī's inspired condition of *'isma*—in contrast with the very fallible *ra'y* and *qiyās* of the ordinary jurists—is again repeatedly emphasized in Ibn 'Arabī's concluding point at the end of this section below.

75. *al-faqīr al-sādiq*: although the term *faqīr* (literally, anyone who is "poor" in relation to God, i.e., "the perfect servant") has often been a vague (and sometimes pejorative) popular synonym for "Sufi" in the broadest sense, here it is used quite specifically to indicate the rare spiritual state of pure openness and receptivity allowing the Knower or Friend of God who is inwardly "sincere" to receive the inspiration transmitted originally to the prophet-Messenger he faithfully "follows." A clearer sense of the deep-rooted psychic obstacles to this rare spiritual state of untarnished receptivity may be gathered from Ibn 'Arabī's telling enumeration of the corrupting inner motives of many of the reli-

gious scholars "learned in the outward forms (of religion)" in the following paragraphs.

76. This term could refer simply to Muslims in general, but more commonly in Ibn 'Arabī and other Sufi writers (following explicit indications in the Qur'an and hadith) it refers quite specifically to the far smaller group of the accomplished Friends of God and the prophets. The impassioned tone of this passage—combined with what we know of the martyrdom or persecution of many prominent Andalusian and Maghrebi Sufis of the time (Ibn Qasī, Ibn Barrajān and Ibn al-'Arīf)— strongly suggest that the latter sense is indeed intended here. The cases of these famous saints who were intimately involved with certain political events of their time (and some of whom may well have claimed the role of "Imām" in a more openly political sense) also indicate that Ibn 'Arabī's extended discussions of divine governance in this chapter are probably not purely academic: see the historical references concerning the three above-mentioned Andalusian Sufis in the corresponding articles (all by A. Faure) in the *EI²*, vol. III.

77. Although they may well outwardly succeed, Ibn 'Arabī implies, with regard to the things they do prize in this world. The full Qur'anic verses (at 16:116) alluded to in this sentence are especially important in understanding the biting critique of the *fuqahā'* that follows: *And do not say, regarding what your tongues describe (as divinely forbidden or commanded) the lie (that) "This is licit, and that is illicit," so that you make up lies against God. Surely those who make up lies against God do not prosper!* (the last phrase is repeated at verse 10:69). Ibn 'Arabī may also be alluding to verses 6:20–21, with their implicit contrast of the two approaches in question here: *Those to whom we have brought the Book recognize it as they recognize their own sons, (but) those who have lost their souls do not have faith. And who does more wrong than whoever makes up a lie about God and calls His Signs a lie? Surely those who do wrong shall not prosper.*

78. Here, "recollection" or remembrance (of God): the continuous invocation (whether silent or virtually inaudible) of certain prayer formulae or divine Names throughout the day's activities, often with the accompaniment of the *tasbīh* or *suhba* (prayer beads), a practice later frequently—though by no means exclusively—associated with adherence to a particular Sufi order. Ibn 'Arabī's criticism of this particular group's hypocritical pretense of Sufism already foreshadows the following Qur'anic allusion (to verses 3:77–78).

79. Again the full Qur'anic verse here is directly applicable to this psycho-spiritual type in a sense which clearly brings out Ibn 'Arabī's understanding of the immediate contemporary dimensions of the "Last Day" (the larger subject of Chapter Five below): *Surely those who buy a thing of little value with God's covenant and their faith, those people have no share in the next world, and God does not speak to them nor does He look at them on the Day of the Rising, and He does not purify them* [or: *'cause them to increase'*], *and theirs is an excruciating torment. And there is a group of them who twist the Book with their tongues, so that you might consider that (what they say) is from the Book, although it is not from the Book. And they say that (what they say) is from God, although it is not from God—and they say lies against God while they know (what they are doing).* See the following note 80 for the full dramatic hadith to which Ibn 'Arabī alludes, in the short passages placed in quotation marks here, at the beginning of this sentence.

80. The phrases in quotes here and in the sentence preceding the previous note are taken from the following saying of the Prophet recorded by Tirmidhī (from Abū Hurayra) and selected by Ibn 'Arabī in his personal collection of divine sayings, the *Mishkāt al-Anwār* (no. 35; pp. 64–65 in the translation by M. Valsan): "At the end of time people will appear who will dupe the world with (the pretense of) religion: they will dress up for the people in the skins of gentle sheep and their tongues will be sweeter than honey, but their hearts are the hearts of wolves. God will say: *'Are they completely deluded about me, or do they openly dare (to affront) me?! I swear by Myself that I shall surely send those people a trial* (or torment: *fitna) that will leave even the calmest of them completely dismayed!'*."

81. The last phrase, evoking the Qur'anic references to the fate of the inveterate, extreme "wrongdoers" (*mujrimūn*), is an allusion to Ibn 'Arabī's famous assumption that the people of Gehenna nonetheless do take a certain pleasure in precisely those particular addictions which—by distracting and veiling them from God—ultimately help constitute their personal punishment and torment: see, for example, the famous verses at the end of the chapter on Ismail in the *Fuṣūs al-Hikam* (I, 94; *Bezels*, pp. 109–110).

82. The vast extent of the bloody internecine conflicts between these and other legal and theological schools serving as rallying points for a wide variety of ethnic and social loyalties—and fueling civil wars, riots and repeated massacres which over more than a century effectively destroyed, even before the Mongol conquests, important parts of

the major Persian cities of Nishapur, Rayy and Isfahan—are surveyed in W. Madelung's (too modestly entitled) article "The Spread of Maturidism and the Turks," pp. 109–169 in his *Religious Schools and Sects in Medieval Islam* (London, 1985); Madelung also traces there the spread of these violent, ostensibly juridical and theological conflicts to those Ayyubid realms where Ibn 'Arabī spent much of the latter part of his life. The particularly dramatic role of this Hanafi-Shafi'i conflict (frequently cited by al-Ghazali) in the century-long self-destruction of Nishapur—strikingly similar to that of modern-day Beirut— is detailed in R. Bulliet's *The Patricians of Nīshābūr*, (Cambridge, Harvard U. Press, 1972).

83. I.e., the "imams" or founders of their particular legal schools (Shāfi'ī, Malik, etc.). In the long chapter 69 of the *Futūhāt* on ritual prayer (I, 386–546), Ibn 'Arabī, stressing the diversity of the evidence of hadith on particular details of religious practice, repeatedly criticizes the *fuqahā'* of his day for hypocritically and arrogantly denying the personal religious obligation and individual responsibility of *ijtihād* while simultaneously insisting that everyone else must follow only their own particular legal school. See, for example, his ironic remark at I, 494: "So the first (person) to deny them on the Day of Rising will be their (own) Imām!" For Ibn 'Arabī, in contrast (at I, 392), the perennial obligation of *ijtihād* for all people of faith (or at least for those individuals with the necessary practical qualifications to interpret the Qur'an and hadith for themselves) follows from the divine injunction: *And strive* (*jāhidū*) *for God with the striving due to Him. He picked you out and did not place any constriction* (*haraj*) *upon you in Religion....* (22:73).

84. I.e., the state of "pure servanthood" (*'ubūdiyya*) characterizing Ibn 'Arabī's typical conception of the spiritual superiority of the *afrād* (also termed *al-malāmiyya*, the "people of blame")—whose spiritual rank is often invisible to the outside world and whose lives frequently exhibit this same characteristic of extraordinary devotion to their "ordinary" responsibilities—as embodying the very summit of the spiritual path. The repeated references in this chapter to Khadir (one of the archetypal representatives of the *afrād*, for Ibn 'Arabī) point in the same direction. See the references from many other chapters of the *Futūhāt* to this "ultimate stage of *walāya*," which is one of the recurrent themes of his religious thought, in Chodkiewicz, *Seal*, chapter VII.

85. Ibn 'Arabī emphasizes the broader metaphysical significance of this story, that God becomes manifest (whether or not we are aware of it) in the form of each person's deepest desire, virtually every time he deals with the figure of Moses: see, e.g., the end of the chapter on Moses (25) in the *Fusūs al-Hikam* (= Affifi ed., I, 212–213), the beginning of the concluding chapter on Muhammad, and especially Ibn 'Arabī's own encounter with Moses during his autobiographical spiritual Ascension in chapter 367 of the *Futūhāt* (III, 439–440), included among our translations in *The Meccan Revelations* anthology, vol. I.

86. Ibn 'Arabī illustrates this point here (concerning the "external Imāms," those with a visible, public role in this world) with a brief story about the extreme conscientiousness of 'Umar ibn 'Abd al-'Azīz in regard to his public responsibilities.

87. Here Ibn 'Arabī mentions Khadir's puzzling "original," genealogical name (going back to Noah), as given by later Islamic tradition: see the article "al-Khadir" by Wensinck, summarizing the historical sources, in *EI²*, vol. IV. The underlying story of Khadir's discovery of the fountain of Life is apparently taken from the popular literature of the "Tales of the Prophets" (*qisas al-anbiyā'*), rather than from the standard hadith collections. For the broader role of Khadir in Ibn 'Arabī's thought (building on an extensive pre-existing body of Sufi tradition), see his description of his personal encounters with Khadir on three separate occasions in chapter 25 (I, 186–188; O.Y. ed. III, pp. 180–185); the numerous references in Chodkiewicz, *Seal*, Index s.v.; and the chapter focusing more specifically on Khadir's initiatic function in H. Corbin, *L'imagination créatrice*, pp. 43–54.

88. Here Ibn 'Arabī interrupts this story with a long aside (III, 336.32–337.5) describing his first personal encounter with Khadir, in the person of a stranger (during his youth in Seville) "who taught me to surrender to the spiritual masters and not to dispute with them (even when they are wrong)." It was Ibn 'Arabī's master at the time (one Abū al-'Abbās al-'Uraybī) who subsequently identified that mysterious individual as being Khadir. This anecdote itself (summarized in H. Corbin, *L'imagination creatrice...*, p. 51) is translated in the biographical study at the beginning of M. Asin-Palacios' *L'Islam christianisé* (French translation, Paris, 1983), p. 36. Another longer version of the same story—along with descriptions of Ibn 'Arabī's subsequent meetings with Khadir—is given in chapter 25 (I, 186–188; O.Y. ed. III, pp. 180–182), where it is also implied that the subject of this dispute was

the identity or name of the Mahdī (and that Khadir confirmed the validity of Ibn 'Arabī's own vision in that regard).

For water as one of Ibn 'Arabī's primary symbols—based on passages in the Qur'an and several key hadith—for the "Throne of divine Life" flowing through all things, see chapter 317 (III, 65–66) and further extensive references in Hakīm, *Mu'jam*, pp. 1071–1077.

89. It is not entirely clear whether the pronoun here refers to the "Imāms" discussed earlier in the chapter; to *those who have faith in God and the Last Day* (from the immediately preceding Qur'anic verse [58:22] not translated here); or—what is most probable, and could include the previous two categories—to the accomplished Friends of God (*awliyā'*) in general. This description again seems to allude to Ibn 'Arabī's conception of the *afrād* or *malāmiyya*, the usually unrecognized "true servants of God" who represent the highest stage of sainthood, as noted earlier.

90. *Sha'n* suggests an activity or occupation as well as a general state or condition. For Ibn 'Arabī, this verse is usually taken in reference to the universal process of theophany (*tajalliyāt*) through which the world (i.e., all that is the "other-than-God") is continuously re-created and made manifest: see the references in Hakīm, *Mu'jam*, pp. 639–643 (*al-sha'n al-ilāhī*).

91. *nāzila*, usually translated here as "event," could equally be translated, in this legal context, as "case"—i.e., in the broad sense of a unique event subject to a particular judgment, not necessarily as a generalizable legal type or precedent (=*qadiya*, also translated as "case" below).

As in earlier passages, *hukm* is usually translated here as "judgment" (and its verbal forms accordingly), although the actual meaning tends to vary in emphasis, according to the context, between the following: the timeless divine "commandment" or underlying principle of judgment; the particular inner aspect of the case or circumstance to which that divine standard actually applies; the human religio-legal statute, rule or precept (supposedly corresponding to the first two meanings); the actual activity of applying those standards to particular circumstances (whether or not in an explicitly legal context); and finally, the resulting verdict or conclusion.

92. *mubāh*: i.e., what is "permitted" in the sense of what is neither explicitly illicit (*harām*) nor positively prescribed by the divine Pathway (*shar'*). The usual translation of this term as "indifferent," while appropriate for its traditional legal usage as a specific category in Islamic jurisprudence, fails to convey the positive and much wider onto-

logical perception Ibn 'Arabī is pointing to here. Historically speaking—and this is the ground of Ibn 'Arabī's vehement protests in this chapter and in many other places—virtually all the schools of Islamic jurisprudence (both Sunni and Shiite) used some schema of extrapolated analogies (in the sense described here) to set up complex systems of graded categories of relative preference or prohibition extending, at least in theory, to include virtually every imaginable human action. The extremely limited meaning of *mubāh* in that legalistic context—where it implies at best a "neutral" value, and implicitly a rather dubious religious status in relation to the extensive positive and obligatory categories—is therefore radically different from what Ibn 'Arabī actually intends by that term here. For his own distinctively positive and more comprehensive usage, see especially the more complete discussion and references in "Ibn 'Arabī's 'Esotericism': The Problem of Spiritual Authority," pp. 37–64.

93. *Dīn Allāh*: this is only one of several related Qur'anic expressions—e.g., *al-Dīn* and *al-Dīn al-Khālis* (39:3), "the Pure Religion," both used in a similar sense at the very beginning of this chapter 366 (not translated here)—referring to the eternal, divine Reality that is the Source of the prophets' message, in contrast to the many religions of men. In a certain sense, all of Ibn 'Arabī's works constitute a sort of extended commentary on this fundamental distinction: see the extensive references and careful analysis of these key terms in Hakīm, *Mu'jam*, pp. 475–483, and especially Ibn 'Arabī's moving description of his own decisive realization of this fundamental insight in chapter 367 (III, 350: included in *The Meccan Revelations* anthology) and in his *K. al-Isrā'* (see references above).

94. The technical terms here are taken from the traditional learned discipline of *usūl al-fiqh* ("principles of jurisprudence": see the articles *usūl* in *SEI* and *fiqh* in *EI²*) which, from the third century (A.H.) onward, gradually elaborated the theoretical rationales underlying the practice of the earlier Islamic jurists (*fuqahā'*). In the practice of *qiyās*—upon which most of the influential historical forms of Islamic jurisprudence were largely dependent—the hypothetical "reason" (*'illa*) seen as underlying a particular commandment or decision (*hukm*) derived from the Qur'an, or more commonly from the many reported actions and sayings of the Prophet, was first extracted or deduced from that particular precedent and then extended to a wider range of supposedly analogous cases.

Ibn 'Arabī's personal criticisms of *qiyās*, here and elsewhere, specifically presuppose the continued spiritual presence of the Prophet (i.e.,
of His spiritual Reality) as realized among the accomplished Knowers
(the *ahl al-kashf* or "people of unveiling"), as he explained in the immediately preceding passage (III, 335). His conception of the proper
modalities and conditions of a living and truly authoritative understanding and transmission of hadith (by the inspired Knowers), based on the
same types of spiritual insight discussed here with regard to the Mahdī,
is more fully summarized in chapter 29 (O.Y. III, 240–241), on the *Ahl
al-Bayt* and Salmān (one of the archetypal Knowers in the Islamic tradition). As stressed by M. Chodkiewicz, "Ibn 'Arabī, la lettre et la loi,"
pp. 29–30 (in *Actes du colloque 'Mystique, culture et société,'* ed. M.
Meslin, Paris, 1983), Ibn 'Arabī—while forcefully rejecting *qiyās* (and
taqlīd, for reasons detailed at II, 165) for himself—does not necessarily reject the usage of *qiyās* by those who do not fulfill these (admit-
tedly rather rare) spiritual pre-conditions. Therefore his own spiritually based position should not be confused with the universal—if problematic—condemnation of *qiyās* typical of the Zahiri legal school and
some Shiite groups.

95. The Qur'anic passage (80:1-10) alluded to here is a particularly striking illustration of Ibn 'Arabī's argument that people—at least
in their ordinary, uninspired state—should not pretend to decipher the
essential reasons underlying God's specifically stated commands and
prohibitions, much less attempt to extend those principles beyond their
explicitly prescribed areas of application. In these verses the Prophet
is reproached for having distractedly turned away a poor blind man
who came asking about faith while he was talking with an important
Meccan notable—i.e., for judging on the basis of outward appearances—
and reminded that *perhaps (the blind man) will grow in purity or come
to remember (God)... .*

96. The full verse is again assumed in this powerful allusion: *Or
do they have partners who prescribe as law for them concerning Religion that about which God is unaware* [or: *"does not permit"*] *!?* This
paragraph therefore explains in detail the basic principles underlying
Ibn 'Arabī's earlier remarks (not all translated here) concerning the
inveterate hatred of the *fuqahā'* for the Mahdī, as well as his earlier
impassioned assertions that in fact even the most well-meaning of them
unconsciously *"make up lies about God."*

97. I.e., *qiyās*, in the legalistic sense—and above all with reference
to its intrinsic suppositions about the very nature of religion—described
in the preceding paragraphs.

98. *Taklīf*: hence the more profound justification of Ibn 'Arabī's earlier insistence that all that is not most explicitly commanded or forbidden is "permitted" (*mubāh*), in an unrestricted, essentially and spiritually positive sense very different from its usage in the legal categories of the *fuqahā'*. This is brought out more powerfully in the further allusions, translated in the final section of this Chapter, to the Knowers' theophanic perception of the religiously unrestricted—indeed intrinsically "paradisiac" and marvelous—nature of everything in the world not bound by the rare explicit divine indications to the contrary.

99. This particular hadith is mentioned by both Bukhārī (*I'tisām*, 2) and Muslim (*Hajj*, 411). As Ibn 'Arabī explains in his brief chapter 262 "On the Inner Knowing of the *Sharī'a*" (II, 561–562), the divinely prescribed Pathway includes both "the precepts God prescribed of His own accord" and "what was prescribed at the request of the community"—so that "if they had not requested it, then that (precept or commandment) would not have been sent down." The Prophet's saying was therefore intended to avoid the unnecessary proliferation of this latter category of additional religious prescriptions and the resulting burden of obligation on His community.

Elsewhere (II, 162–166; chapter 88, "On the Inner Knowing of the Secrets of the Principles of the Precepts of the *Shar'*"), Ibn 'Arabī points out the parallel between this hadith and the following Qur'anic injunction: *O those who have faith, do not ask about things which, if they were revealed to you, would harm you. And if you ask about them when the Qur'an is being sent down, they will be revealed to you.... For a people before you did ask (such) things, and after that they began to disbelieve in them.* (5:101-102). In the same section (II, 165) he explains in detail his conviction "that the bearer of revelation only wanted to *reduce* (the burden of religious prescriptions) of this Community." (See also the following note.)

100. *Hukm al-asl*: In chapter 88 (II, 165; see preceding note), Ibn 'Arabī clearly states that this primordial state of affairs is "that there is no *taklīf* (i.e., divinely imposed religious obligation) and that God created for us the totality of everything on earth...." In other words, as far as the divine revealed-prescribing is concerned, everything God has not expressly forbidden or made obligatory is implicitly permitted (*mubāh*) for our delight in His creation.

101. III, 338.3–340.12. The complete list at this point includes some fifty-four kinds of spiritual knowledge.

102. *kharq al-'āda*: this technical expression (again borrowed from kalam theology and used here in a radically different, quite concrete spiritual context) is used throughout this section as a sort of pun corresponding to two very different conceptions of the divine "habit" or "custom" (*'āda*). Ordinarily this term refers to the unenlightened perception of the usual course of affairs in the world, which the "people of habits" (*ashāb al-'awā'id*) heedlessly take for granted: hence the usual understanding of *kharq al-'āda* as some exceptional miracle, prodigy or otherwise "supernatural" event departing from that unconsciously assumed norm. But the true Knowers—those who are actually (in the words of a famous Prophetic prayer) "made to see things as they really are"—are of course profoundly aware of the genuinely miraculous re-creation of the world at every instant, of the marvelous, never-repeated theophany of Being in all Its infinite self-manifestations.

103. *rijāl al-ghayb*: the ability to perceive those mysterious spiritual beings "even when they do not wish to be seen" was earlier described (section III above) as one of the basic signs of the "penetrating (spiritual) vision" characterizing this particular spiritual waystation.

104. At this point (III, 339.21) Ibn 'Arabī also mentions that he is writing down this particular story in the year 635 a.h. (i.e., only three years before his death and shortly before the completion of his final recension of the *Futūhāt*); lacking a critical edition of this chapter 366, we do not know how much of chapter 366 in its present form may also have been added to the first version.

105. See Ibn 'Arabī's earlier discussion of this special group of angels who seek out the gatherings of all those who are remembering or invoking God (or the Qur'an).

106. Given Ibn 'Arabī's repeated claims, throughout the main body of this chapter 366, for the superior insight and spiritual authority of the accomplished Knowers and Friends—as opposed to the so-called *'ulamā'*—as the only fully qualified interpreters of the truly divine revelation, and as the authentic heirs of the larger body of religious tradition, this passage provides some extremely important guidelines for determining the degree to which the *walī* should directly attempt to communicate his spiritual inspirations beyond himself and those who voluntarily seek out his guidance. It also underlines another essential difference separating the scripture-bearing divine messenger (*rasūl* or *shāri'*) ordered to fulfill a universal mission from the much larger group of all the other prophets (*anbiyā'*), including the Friends of God (*awliyā' Allāh*). Perhaps even more important in this context are what these

particular criteria imply about the even more limited spiritual utility of any sort of disputing about religion for all those who would not even pretend to have reached this rare and lofty station.

107. I.e., the Friends of God (*awliyā'*) or accomplished Knowers, such as those having realized this high spiritual station. Again there is a typical ambiguity in the expression (*intamā ilā*) translated here as "depend on," which can also mean, especially in everyday speech, "belong to" in the sense of joining or adhering to a particular group. For Ibn 'Arabī used the same verb in just that sense earlier in this same chapter to allude to the unquestioning followers of the different schools of Islamic jurisprudence and kalam theology (and their founders). Here he clearly implies that there is no point in even raising this question with regard to such groups, since arguing or disputing (*jidāl*)—along with the underlying aim of somehow converting others or otherwise imposing their own opinions—is inherent in their very methods and presuppositions. For the same reasons, the expression here of "one who has truly surrendered to God" (*muslim*) would of course be understood rather differently by those groups.

108. This is the literal translation of this rich Qur'anic expression, which colloquially means simply "in a friendly or polite manner"— i.e., not, for example, using the methods followed by (among others) the supporters of those juridical and theological schools involved in the bloody sectarian disputes in Eastern Islamic lands that Ibn 'Arabī had alluded to earlier in this chapter.

109. I.e., he is really trying to establish his own self-righteousness and satisfy the cravings of his own egoistic *nafs* rather than actually carrying out the divine Will (as expressed in their current state of unreceptiveness). This section echoes Ibn 'Arabī's earlier remarks stressing the essential distinction between the general prophetic task of communicating the divine Message and the even more difficult responsibility of acting as a divinely-appointed "wise-judge" (*ḥākim*).

110. "Burden of anguish" translates the Qur'anic term *haraj*, referring here to the inner state of constraint, oppression, anxiety, distress, and the like that usually accompanies and underlies (whether consciously or not) much of our everyday psychic and outward activity. In connection with the subject of this chapter 366 and the special divine inspiration characterizing the Mahdī (or his Helpers), a number of Qur'anic verses stress that there is *no haraj for you in Religion* (*al-Dīn*: 22:78; etc.) or in the *Book sent down* from God (7:2), and that this chronic state of inner distress is a sign of those *wandering astray*, while

373

it is removed from those whom God *guides rightly* and *who inwardly surrender* to Him (6:125).

111. This phrase could also be translated literally as "to kill his *nafs*"—i.e., in Sufi psychology, the domineering self (*al-nafs al-ammāra*), directly responsible for this sense of oppression and anxiety—in the hope of eliminating this torment.

112. *adab*, the proper respect or principles of conduct regarding God in every aspect of one's spiritual life—a central spiritual virtue whose practical expression, as Ibn ʿArabī indicates here, obviously varies greatly according to one's inner spiritual state.

CHAPTER FIVE
RETURNING: EXPLORING THE DIVINE SHADOW-PLAY

1. The allusion here (too long to quote and explain in full as an epigraph) is in fact to the entire key Qurʾanic passage at 2:151–157.

2. See the recent article on "Ibn ʿArabī's Rhetoric of Realisation..." (n. 1 to Ch. 1 above), which more fully develops a number of points briefly alluded to in the opening sections of this Chapter.

3. See especially W. Chittick's volume of extensive translated selections on this general topic, in his recent *The Self-Disclosures of God* (and its forthcoming continuation): details in the Bibliography below.

4. Far more important than the much-debated question of possible "influences" on Dante is the vast field of historically parallel traditions, interpretations and alternative approaches—extending to almost every field of Western Christian religious and philosophical/scientific thought and expression—which is beautifully illustrated and summarized in Christian Heck's recent study, *L'échelle Céleste: une Histoire de la Quête du Ciel* (Paris, Flammarion, 1999). While there is no even remotely comparable survey work for the equivalent range of Islamic traditions, closely parallel developments are evident in almost every cognate discipline and artistic domain.

5 For the eschatological and metaphysical topics covered in this concluding Chapter, in addition to W. Wenders' *Wings of Desire* (*Der Himmel über Berlin*), both *Field of Dreams* and *Groundhog Day* provide especially effective and comprehensive illustrations of many of Ibn ʿArabī's central eschatological teachings.

6. III (Beirut ed.), pp. 65–68. This chapter is entitled "On the Inner Knowing of the Waystation of Testing (*ibtilāʾ*) and Its Blessings, which is the Waystation of the Imām Who is at the Left of the (spiritual) Pole."

Ibn 'Arabī's table of contents for the *Meccan Illuminations* (*fihrist*) adds that "the (present earthly) representative of this Imām is Abū Madyan." So the "Imām of the Left"—as he explains elsewhere (see Chodkiewicz, *Seal*)—is Jesus, and his appearance here alludes not only to the central question of human suffering and spiritual testing (as a fundamental expression of God's universal Compassion, *rahma*), but also to Jesus' recurrent role throughout Ibn 'Arabī's works, and to some extent even in the Qur'an, as a pre-eminent prophetic symbol and manifestation of the divine Spirit, *Rūh Allāh*.

7. While the immediate allusion here is to God's *building and rightforming* of *the (spiritual) Heavens* at 79:28 (and in slightly different terms, at 2:39), the same multifaceted Qur'anic term used here (*sawwā*) is also used in several metaphysically central passages (at 15:29, 32:9, 38:72, 91:8, etc.) to refer to the shared role of the divine Spirit (*rūh*) in the creation of the primordial human being (*insān/ādam*) and the inspiring of the human soul (*nafs*) with its theomorphic knowledge of good and evil. Thus the divine "Abode" (*dār*) that is the subject of this poem and chapter is clearly understood throughout as being simultaneously both of these macro- and microcosmic realities (the fully human being and the manifest creation).

8. See 7:54 and six other Qur'anic passages referring to God's "*Standing up*" (*istiwā'*) on the divine Throne—an expression semantically tied to the same key root of the divine "*rightly shaping*" (*sawwā*) of the world and the souls discussed in the preceding note.

9. While *Ma'wā* appears in the Qur'an occasionally (e.g., at 53:15) as one of the seven names of particular Gardens, it is used more generally (some twenty times) to refer more generally to the souls' ultimate abode, refuge, or dwellingplace, whether in the Fire or the Gardens. It is not entirely clear which of those meanings Ibn 'Arabī may intend here.

10. III, 68.18–27.

11. *Khiyāl*: as explained in Chapter 3 above, the term refers more generally to the imagination or its images, but in Ibn 'Arabī it usually refers specifically to the *barzakh* or vast realm of all manifestation constituted by the divine Imagination. See our translation of most of Ibn 'Arabī's key chapter 63 of the *Futūhāt* devoted to the *barzakh*, in "Spiritual Imagination and the 'Liminal' World: Ibn 'Arabī on the Barzakh," *POSTDATA* (Madrid), 15, no. 2 (1995), pp. 42–49 and 104–109—as well as further illustrations and discussions of this central theme in all the major analytical studies included in the Bibliography below.

12. See, for example, 30:7 (for "the heedless ones," *al-ghāfilūn*); and 6:70 and 7:51, on *those who consider their Religion an amusement and pastime, having been deluded by the life of this world.*

13. See the more complete translation and discussion in "How to Study the *Futūhāt*: Ibn 'Arabī's Own Advice," pp. 73–89 (Ch.2, n.6 above.)

14. Normally, one should add, this sort of intended illumination takes place either in relation to the synchronistic occurrence of an unexpected probative experience (a divine "Sign" or "Proof") or in the form of related spiritual dreams, visions, or the like. In either case, what is involved is a deeper experiential transformation, not a simply mental or intellectual conclusion—even if, as we can see throughout the selections assembled in this book, it is often quite possible to recognize and describe the characteristic insights, transformations, or spiritual laws after they have been experienced.

15. See the new web-based volume *Ibn 'Arabī and His Interpreters: Historical Contexts and Contemporary Perspectives*, which brings together ten earlier monographs and articles, and nearly thirty reviews, all devoted to contextualizing the work and influences of Ibn 'Arabī, and to situating the immense range of recent translations, interpretive studies, biographies and works by and about his later Muslim interpreters. Downloadable versions (in .pdf format) of all of those earlier publications, including the long, three-part review article on "Ibn 'Arabī and His Interpreters" (*JAOS*, 1986–87), are currently freely available at the website of the Ibn 'Arabī Society (*www.ibnarabisociety.org/IbnArabi*), until they can be brought together in published book form.

16. This process is of course beautifully described in a number of short hadith favored by Ibn 'Arabī and many other Sufi writers, including the "hadith of the supererogatory works" (*hadith al-nawāfil*) translated in the final section of Chapter Three above.

17. Alluding to a famous Prophetic prayer which Ibn 'Arabī cites repeatedly: "O my God, cause me to see things as they really are!"

18. O.Y. I, 142–144, fully translated in the article, "How to Study the *Futūhāt*...." See also the equally telling illustration later in this Chapter (section VI, from chapter 35 of *Futūhāt*) of the prophet Idrīs's final oral teachings to his close disciples, even then reserved for the moment of his earthly departure.

19. Here Ibn 'Arabī appears to be playing with the familiar, expected Qur'anic contrast or opposition of the blind and spiritually seeing (cf. 6:50, etc.): he thereby alludes to the particularly universal, metaphysical character of the accomplished wisdom in question here.

He emphasizes this same point again and much more powerfully in the concluding chapter 560 of this same work: the title of that long final chapter stresses that the diverse spiritual teachings and ethical advice included in its contents concern both the novice or aspiring seeker (*murīd*) and the fully accomplished Knower who has already arrived at the Goal (the *wāsil*).

20. As we shall see, one cannot overemphasize the key role throughout the *Futūhāt*—both in motivating each reader's continued seeking, and in providing the indispensable experiential raw data for the process of realization—of what Ibn 'Arabī and other Islamic spiritual teachers normally call "the secret/inner meaning of (one's own unique personal) destiny," *sirr al-qadr*. That same leitmotif of the *sirr al-qadr*—serving as a shorthand expression for the concrete determinant moments of each reader's unique process of realization—is highlighted in even more dramatic forms throughout Book I of Rumi's famous *Masnavī*.

21. *'aql*: another Arabic word whose root, as Ibn 'Arabī often points out, likewise significantly suggests "hobbling" and restrictive delimitation. (Ibn 'Arabī also often uses *nazar* in that same unduly restrictive sense.)

22. In Hafez's own dramatical poetic language, these recurrent "creation-critics"—who can be found within each of us, in every culture—are the familiar personae of the carping, self-righteous "plaintiff" (*muddā'ī*) and the public "censor" (*muhtasib*).

23. As Ibn 'Arabī argues very pointedly in a famous passage from chapter 63 (on the *barzakh*: translated in "Spiritual Imagination and the 'Liminal' World", n. 11 above) that applies to our dreams and waking life alike, it is never the Imagination *per se* and its images that are false, but rather our particular personal interpretations and partial understandings of those images.

24. This is an allusion to Ibn 'Arabī's characteristic repetition of that famous Prophetic prayer that is a kind of leitmotif for his own spiritual quest: "O my Lord, increase me in knowing!" (*rabbī zidnī 'ilmán*).

25. Again, this central Qur'anic teaching is beautifully communicated (following *Faust* and perhaps Goethe's own Islamic inspirations in Hafez) in Wenders' *Wings of Desire* (*Der Himmel über Berlin*) and its sequel, *Far Away, So Close*. For Ibn 'Arabī, that fundamental spiritual lesson—emblematically conveyed in the repeated central Qur'anic passages recounting Adam's inspired theomorphic spiritual awareness of those divine Names and the contrasting reactions of the angels and

Iblīs—is the very secret of the purpose and uniqueness of the truly human (*insānī*) condition.

26. A few significant Arabic equivalents and technical terms from Ibn 'Arabī (or related Sufi and Qur'anic sources) have been added to highlight the significance of these perspectives, for those familiar with those Islamic contexts.

27. Again, see the recent long study of "Ibn 'Arabī's Rhetoric of Realisation" (n. 1 to Ch. 1 above), as well as the initial brief discussions of these characteristic features already in Chapter Four above.

28. See the translations by D. Davis (or P. Avery), and my introductory study: "Reading 'Attār's *Conference of the Birds*," in *Approaches to the Asian Classics*, ed. Wm. Theodore de Bary and Irene Bloom (N.Y., Columbia University Press, 1990), pp. 77–85.

29. For example, only the very rarest Sufi writings (such as the poems of Hafez, and possibly Rumi's *Masnavī*) do not leave many of the most essential practical teachings and instructions to be developed and explained by an external guide and pīr. R. V. Holbrooke, in a series of important studies on the "Malāmī super-order" in Istanbul (*JMIAS*), has highlighted Ibn 'Arabī's later unique role as a kind of "shaykh for shaykhs" in Ottoman Turkey and even more recently. This relatively unique comprehensiveness—and undoubtedly extraordinary depth and breadth—of these *Meccan Illuminations* is also certainly intimately connected to Ibn 'Arabī's famous, if highly mysterious, self-conception of his own personal mission as the "seal of the (Muhammadan) saints": see Chodkiewicz, *Seal*.

30. This is the same key existential theme which, as already noted (n. 20 above), provides the essential dramatic leitmotif running throughout Book I of Rumi's *Masnavī*.

31. In the passages from chapter 15 which are translated and discussed in the immediately following sub-section below.

32. This point is especially well illustrated, in a painlessly abstract and humorous way, in the familiar images of *Groundhog Day*, a remarkably condensed and practical schematic vision of the entire path of the soul's twofold Returning.

33. The relevant features of Idrīs's spiritual role and central "solar" functions—related to his spiritual location as described in the different hadith of the Prophet's Ascension—are carefully outlined in Chodkiewicz, *Seal*; see also our translations of the parallel sections of chapter 367 from the *Futūhāt* and the important background explanations, now included in *The Meccan Revelations* anthology, volume I.

34. Again, the connection between these symbolic figures, including the *rūhāniyyāt* of each of the major prophets associated with specific planetary spheres, is initially developed in the hadith of the Prophet's *Mi'rāj*: see the preceding note for our translation and study of related sections of the *Futūhāt* (especially chapter 367).

Readers familiar with the imagery of the *Song of Songs* and its role in both Jewish and Christian spiritual traditions will immediately note the resonant parallels in Ibn 'Arabī's poetic imagery here.

35. In his cosmic role, as the spiritual Reality corresponding to the central heavenly sphere of the Sun, Idrīs here symbolizes the spiritual influences of the entire pleroma of divine Realities and spiritual intermediaries: see the further references indicated in the two preceding notes.

36. Clearly alluding to the remarkable selection from the end of chapter 366, on the beatific "knowledge of blissful repose," that concluded the preceding Chapter Four

37. Chapter 64, O.Y. ed. IV, p. 472.

38. Chapter 351 ("Concerning Inner Knowing of the Station of the Sharing of the Souls and Spirits in the (Divine) Attributes..."), ninth subsection (*wasl*); III (Beirut ed.), 223.8–10, 18–33.

39. See the versions of this hadith in Muslim (*dhikr*, no. 14, 16–18); Bukhārī (*riqāq*, no. 41); and the additional citations from Tirmidhī, Nisā'ī, Ibn Māja, Dārimī, and Ahmad Ibn Hanbal given in Wensinck, *Concordance*, VI, 140.

40. Referring to the famous hadith "Not one of you will see His Lord until he dies," recorded by Muslim (*fitan*, no. 95) and Tirmidhi (*fitan*, no. 56). The same idea is conveyed in another famous hadith recorded several times by Ahmad Ibn Hanbal (VI, 44, 55, 207, 232): "Death is before the meeting with God" (cf. Wensinck, VI, 140).

41. For this particular dimension of our Return, particularly helpful—and sometimes intense—"cinematic versions" include *Far Away, So Close* (the sequel to *Wings of Desire*), *Groundhog Day*, *The Shawshank Redemption*, *Jacob's Ladder*, and *After Life* (which actually takes place literally in the *barzakh*). As with the *Futūhāt* itself, each of these closely related shadow-plays must be seen and pondered a number of times in order to reveal its own remarkable inner cohesion and depths of meaning, not to mention the complex parallels to the even more elaborate eschatological symbolism and intentions of the Qur'an and hadith.

42. These ideas are of course strongly echoed in the opening poem of chapter 317 (beginning Ibn 'Arabī's account of the divine shadow-theater) that was translated at the very beginning of this Chapter, in section I above.

43. Ibn 'Arabī is alluding here particularly (among the eighteen Qur'anic verses associating *the jinn and humans*) to the famous verse 7:179, which most strongly emphasizes the ongoing, already existing reality of Gehenna: *And we have **already** winnowed/blown away to Gehenna a great many of the jinn and humans. They have hearts with which they do not understand, eyes with which they do not see, ears with which they do not hear: those are like livestock—indeed they are more misguided! Those, they are the heedless ones!*

44. See the full translated text of both these hadith included at the end of Chapter Three above, as well as Ibn 'Arabī's discussion of them in passages discussed throughout that Chapter.

45. To paraphrase Ibn 'Arabī's single lengthy and precise Arabic sentence here (which we have had to break into several shorter pieces to make it comprehensible in English): It is through the suffering of those human souls "in Gehenna"—unavoidably incurred because they were manifesting God's Anger to themselves and others—that they eventually come to "call out" in repentance to God and become receptive to, and ultimately fully grateful for, the infinite blessings of His Lovingmercy and Compassion. Thus Gehenna "Itself" can only recognize and see this *ultimate* outcome, the Absolute Blessing of God's all-encompassing Love and Compassion (*rahma*).

46. Cf. Ibn 'Arabī's comment, later in this same chapter, that "We only adduced that so that you should know this: Just as the divine Anger is specially connected with the pains of the *people* of Gehenna, so the very being (*wujūd*) of Gehenna itself is specially connected with the descending of the divine Lovingmercy."

47. Translated and discussed above in Chapter Two, section IV (from *Futūhāt* V [O.Y. ed.], p. 356).

48. The actual—highly distinctive and personal—meaning of each of the key terms here gradually emerges in the following passage (especially in Ibn 'Arabī's repeated forceful emphasis on the ongoing presence of the Prophet and God, among the Knowers and Friends of God), and above all through the ongoing cumulative example of all of Ibn 'Arabī's own writings. Profound misunderstanding and misrepresentation would be possible here if any of those quite distinctive special meanings are not clearly understood.

49. *Jidāl*: Ibn 'Arabī is alluding to some thirty key Qur'anic verses, most of them specifically referring to people's frequent reactions to divine Signs and revelations, repeatedly highlighting and criticizing the human tendency toward disputing and quarrelling about what they actually do not really understand. Throughout the *Futūhāt*, Ibn 'Arabī comes back frequently to those verses in order to highlight the dramatic visible differences between true spiritual understanding (*ma'rifa*, *'ilm*, etc.) and the infinite possible forms of misunderstanding, belief, supposition, etc.

50. Ibn 'Arabī's particular language here explicitly places this distinctive sort of "spiritual listening" (see Chapter Two above) directly in the *present*, as though one were actually there with the Prophet. In doing so, he highlights for his readers the wider question of our inner sensitivity, awareness and responsiveness to all the forms of divine "new-Speaking" and inspiration, which eventually emerge as the primary subject of this entire chapter 62—just as repentance or "turning" eventually emerges here as the entire purpose of Gehenna and its fires.

51. Ibn 'Arabī frequently uses this distinctive phrase to refer very specifically to the person who has become fully aware and conscious of the wiles and hidden inclinations and ruses of his lower, domineering "self" (*nafs*), and who is therefore able to effectively struggle and oppose them. While the verb here is Qur'anic, the allusion is more directly to a famous hadith referred to throughout Ibn 'Arabī's writing, stating that "*nasīha* ('good-counsel' or especially '*painfully critical* advice') is part of true faith...," going on to enumerate those to whom one should give such unwanted "good-counsel," including especially political leaders and authorities.

52. Here one cannot help but be reminded of that chiropractic angel who, at the very turning point of the film *Jacob's Ladder*, paraphrases Meister Eckhart, just after rescuing Jacob from the depths of this same place:

> The only thing that burns in hell is the part of you that won't let go of your life... of your memories, your attachments. They're burning them all away. They're not punishing you: they're freeing your soul. So if you're frightened of dying and you're holding on, you'll see devils tearing your life away.
>
> But if you've made your peace, then the devils are really angels freeing you from the earth. It's just a matter of how you look at it... So don't worry.

53. *Harām*: The type of situation actually in question here, as in much Sufi literature of this period, involves the moral difficulty of gifts to Sufis (or others) of food or money—often from rulers or military figures—that was actually acquired by unjust, illicit means. Such gifts were obviously not of an outwardly illicit nature, and often the ethical status of their original source or the moral qualities of the giver were sometimes not known to the recipients of that largesse.

54. For Ibn 'Arabī—as he carefully explains in detail in his *Book of Spiritual Advice* (*K. al-Nasīha*), and illustrates in certain striking stories included in his *Rūh al-Quds* (*Sufis of Andalusia*)—what is actually (divinely and spiritually) "illicit" (*harām*) goes far beyond outward forms, and includes particularly the moral character of the ways in which food or other property was originally acquired, or the spiritual appropriateness (or harmfulness) of one's companions, and so on. For his *K. al-Nasīha*, see the partial translation and study in "Introducing Ibn 'Arabī's '*Book of Spiritual Advice*'," *JMIAS*, XXVIII (2000), pp. 1–18.

55. Here it is important that "grape-wine" (*khamr*) is the particular form of alcoholic drink specifically declared illicit—along with various specific local forms of gambling, etc.—in the Qur'an (at 2:219 and 5:90–91).

56. Here Ibn 'Arabī is clearly alluding to popular stereotypes, even in his own day, contrasting the "wild imagination" of the Knowers with the "common-sense" religious formalism of respectably "sound" people.

57. *Ithm* is a frequent Qur'anic expression that is sometimes translated as a certain kind of "sin," but which is used at this point specifically—as it is in the Qur'an, for example, at 2:173—to indicate the negative inner, spiritual consequences of particular deeds, flowing from the actor's particular intentions, context, situation and other factors, which eventually enter into the individual's ultimate divine reckoning (*hisāb*). Likewise the common Qur'anic term *ajr* (used more than 60 times) is used in parallel here to refer more specifically to the corresponding divine (and, Ibn 'Arabī stresses, humanly unknowable) inner spiritual compensation or reward connected with certain *good* intentions and other individual factors.

58. Whose imagery is beautifully echoed and expanded, again and again, throughout the film *Bagdad Cafe* (dir. P. Adlon, 1988).

59. See the further development of these timely themes in my recent *Orientations: Islamic Thought in a World Civilisation* (London, Archetype, 2004); and in the longer volume now in preparation, tentatively entitled *Many Paths to the Real: Freedom, Creativity, Diversity and Tolerance in Ibn 'Arabī's Political Philosophy*.

BIBLIOGRAPHY AND FURTHER READING

1. This short list includes only full book-length volumes; many important shorter translations—along with dozens of key historical and contextual studies—have also appeared in article form, especially in recent decades, in the *Journal of the Muhyiddīn Ibn 'Arabī Society* and related publications (including the *Commemorative Volume* cited above). A list of translations from Ibn 'Arabī now available in French, including important sections of the *Meccan Illuminations* not available in English, would be almost as long as that given here, and there has also been a recent renewal (after Asin-Palacios' pioneering studies) in Spanish translations, editions and studies of his work, especially by P. Beneito and V. Palleja. In German, we now have an excellent wide-ranging selection of translations by Alma Giese in the recent volume: *Ibn 'Arabī—Urwolke und Welt: Mystische Texte des Größten Meisters* (Munich, C.H. Beck, 2002).

2. In addition to each of the major studies and translations from the *Futūhāt* (by Chittick, Chodkiewicz, and Morris) already listed above.

BIBLIOGRAPHY AND FURTHER READING

Because this work is intended for very different audiences, from scholars already familiar with Ibn 'Arabī's works and historical context and influences to other readers interested in spirituality and other areas of religious studies who may be encountering his writings for the first time, I have added to the following complete List of Works Cited several shorter lists of further readings, primarily in English, which might be especially useful for newer or even beginning students of his work. These are limited to a small number of volumes, almost entirely in English, that can provide helpful biographical and historical background, additional annotated translations or selections from several of Ibn 'Arabī's key writings, and some of the more comprehensive analytical and critical studies. Several of those longer analytical studies include more comprehensive bibliographies extending to many other languages.

Related films cited in the footnotes to Chapter Five have been listed here beginning with their *English title* (followed by original title in languages other than English), then director and year of first commercial appearance. Their screenwriter(s) and additional details for each work can be readily found at the comprehensive International Movie Database website: *www.imdb.com*. Translations of works by Ibn 'Arabī have been listed here both under the name Ibn 'Arabī, following the original Arabic title of the work in question, and also under the name of the original translator(s).

I. List of Works Cited

Addas, Claude. *Ibn 'Arabī, ou la quête du soufre rouge.* Paris, Gallimard, 1988. English translation (P. Kingsley), *Quest for the Red Sulphur: The Life of Ibn 'Arabī.* Cambridge, Islamic Texts Society, 1993.

————. *Ibn 'Arabī et le Voyage sans Retour.* Paris, Éditions du Seuil, 1996.

After Life (Wandarafu raifu), director H. Koreeda, 1998.

Asin-Palacios, M. *L'Islam christianisé* (French translation). Paris, 1983.

Austin, R.W.J. (transl. and intro.). *Ibn al'Arabi: The Bezels of Wisdom.* Ramsey, NJ, Paulist Press, 1980.

————. *Sufis of Andalusia* (partial translation of Ibn 'Arabī's *Rūh al-Quds*). London, Allen & Unwin, 1971.

Bagdad Cafe, directed by Percy Adlon, 1988.

Boase, R., and F. Sahnoun. "Excerpts from the Epistle on the Spirit of Holiness (*Risālah Rūh al-Quds*)." In *Muhyiddin Ibn 'Arabī: A Commemorative Volume*, ed. S. Hirtenstein and M. Tiernan, pp. 44-72. Shaftesbury, Element Books, 1993.

Bulliet, Richard. *The Patricians of Nīshābūr.* Cambridge, Harvard University Press, 1972.

Chittick, William C. (transl.). *The Self-Disclosure of God: Principles of Ibn al-'Arabī's Cosmology.* Albany, NY, SUNY Press, 1998.

————. *The Sufi Path of Knowledge: Ibn al-'Arabī's Meta-physics of Imagination*. Albany, NY, SUNY Press, 1989.

Chodkiewicz, Michel. *Un Océan Sans Rivage: Ibn 'Arabī, le livre et la loi*. Paris, Seuil, 1992. English translation (D. Streight), *An Ocean Without Shore: Ibn 'Arabī, the Book, and the Law*. Albany, NY, SUNY Press, 1993.

————. *Le Sceau des saints: Prophétie et sainteté dans la doctrine d'Ibn 'Arabī*. Paris, Gallimard, 1986. English translation (L. Sherrard), *Seal of the Saints: Prophethood and Sainthood in the Doctrine of Ibn 'Arabī*. Cambridge, Islamic Texts Society, 1993.

Chodkiewicz, M. (general editor), W.C. Chittick, C. Chodkiewicz, D. Gril, and J.W. Morris (translators). *Les Illuminations de la Mecque: Textes Choisis*. Paris, Sindbad, 1988.

Corbin, Henry. *Creative Imagination in the Sūfism of Ibn 'Arabī* [reprinted as "*Alone with the Alone*"]. Princeton, Princeton University Press, 1969.

EI² = *The Encyclopedia of Islam*, 2nd edition. Leiden, E.J. Brill.

Field of Dreams, director Phil A. Robinson, 1989.

Gilis, C.-A. *La Doctrine initiatique du Pèlerinage à la Maison d'Allāh* [partial translation of chapter 72 of the *Futūhāt*]. Paris, les Éditions de l'Oeuvre, 1982.

387

Gloton, Maurice (transl.). *L'Arbre du Monde* (translation of *Shajarat al-Kawn*). Paris, 1982.

Graham, William. *Divine Word and Prophetic Word in Early Islam.* Paris/the Hague, Mouton, 1977.

The Gospel of Thomas (transl. T. Lamdin). In *The Nag Hammadi Library in English* (3rd ed., J. Robinson), pp. 124-138. Leiden, E.J. Brill, 1988.

Gril, Denis (transl. and ed.). *Le dévoilement des fruits du voyage, d'Ibn 'Arabī.* Combas, Éditions de l'éclat, 1994.

———. *Le Livre de l'Arbre et des Quatre Oiseaux* (translation of Ibn 'Arabī, *Risālat al-Ittihād al-Kawnī*). Paris, 1984.

Groundhog Day, director H. Ramis, 1993.

al-Hakīm, Su'ād. *Ibn 'Arabī wa Mawlid Lugha Jadīda.* Beirut, Dandara, 1411/1991.

———. *al-Mu'jam al-Sūfī: al-Hikma fī Hudūd al-Kalima.* Beirut, Dandara, 1401/1981.

Harris, Rabia T. (transl.). *Journey to the Lord of Power* (translation and commentary of Ibn 'Arabī's *R. al-Anwār*). London/NY, Inner Traditions, 1981.

Heck, Christian. *L'Échelle Céleste: une Histoire de la Quête du Ciel.* Paris, Flammarion, 1999.

Hirtenstein, Stephen. *The Unlimited Mercifier: the spiritual life and thought of Ibn 'Arabī.* Oxford, Anqa Publishing, 1999.

————, and Michael Tiernan, editors. *Muhyiddīn Ibn 'Arabī: A Commemorative Volume.* Shaftesbury, Element, 1993.

Hirtenstein, Stephen, and Michael Tiernan, translators and eds. *Divine Sayings: The Mishkāt al-Anwār of Ibn 'Arabī.* Oxford, Anqa Publishing, 2004.

Holbrooke, Victoria R. "Ibn 'Arabi and Ottoman Dervish Traditions: The Melāmī Supra-Order," Part One and Part Two. *Journal of the Muhyiddīn Ibn 'Arabī Society*, IX (1991), pp. 18-35, and XII (1992), pp. 15-33.

Ibn 'Arabī. *Fusūs al-Hikam* (ed. A. 'Affīfī). Beirut, Dār al-Kitāb al-'Arabī, 1946. English translation: see Austin, *Bezels.*

————. *K. al-Futūhāt al-Makkīyya* (in 4 volumes). Beirut, Dār Sādir, n.d.

————. *K. al-Futūhāt al-Makkīyya*, ed. O. Yahya. Cairo, Bibliotheca Arabica, 1392/1972-present (14 volumes). See partial translations (in this List) under M. Chodkiewicz, W. Chittick, and J. Morris.

————. *al-Isfār 'an Natā'ij al-Asfār.* Edition and translation by Denis Gril. *Le dévoilement des fruits du voyage, d'Ibn 'Arabī.* Combas, Éditions de l'éclat, 1994.

————. *K. al-Isrā' ilā al-Maqām al-Asrā* [also in *Rasā'il*]. Ed. Su'ād al-Hakīm. Beirut, Dandara, 1988.

————. *Kitāb al-Fanā' fī al-Mushāhada*, in *Rasā'il Ibn 'Arabī* (Hyderabad, 1367/1948), I, pp. 2-9. *Le livre de l'extinction dans la contemplation*, translation by M. Valsān. Paris, Editions de l'Oeuvre, 1984. English translation by S. Hirtenstein and L. Shamash, *JMIAS*, IX (1991), pp. 1-17.

————. *Mishkāt al-Anwār*. See translation by M. Vâlsan (French), and critical edition and English translation by S. Hirtenstein and M. Tiernan.

————. *Rasā'il Ibn al-'Arabī* (2 volumes). Hyderabad, Dā'irat al-Ma'ārif al-'Uthmānīya, 1361.

————. *Risālat al-Anwār* ("Treatise of the Lights"). In *Rasā'il Ibn 'Arabī*, Hyderabad, 1367/1948, II, no. 12, pp. 1-19). Translated as *Journey to the Lord of Power*, R.T. Harris, (NY, Inner Traditions, 1981); major portions also translated in Chodkiewicz, *The Seal of the Saints*, concluding chapter.

————. *Risālat al-Ittihād al-Kawnī*. Translated and edited by D. Gril, *Le Livre de l'Arbre et des Quatre Oiseaux*, Paris, 1984.

————. *Risālat al-Mubashshirāt*. Printed in Yūsuf al-Nabhānī's *Sa'ādat al-Dārayn fī al-Salāt 'alā Sayyid al-Kawnayn* (Beirut, n.d.), pp. 472-478.

————. *Rūh al-Quds*. See partial translations under Austin and Boase/Sahnoun.

————. *al-Tajalliyāt al-Ilāhīya* [also in *Rasā'il*, above]. Ed. O. Yahya, Beirut, 1967.

———— [apocryphally attributed to]. *Shajarat al-Kawn.* Translations by A. Jeffery, "Ibn 'Arabī's *Shajarat al-Kawn*," *Studia Islamica* X, pp. 43-78 and XI, pp. 113-160; and by M. Gloton, *L'arbre du Monde*, Paris, 1982.

Jacob's Ladder, director Adrian Lyne, 1990.

Jeffery, Arthur. "Ibn 'Arabī's *Shajarat al-Kawn*." *Studia Islamica* X, pp. 43-78; XI, pp. 113-160.

Lane, E. J. *An Arabic-English Lexicon*... London, Williams and Norgate, 1863. (Reprinted Beirut, Librairie du Liban, 1980.)

Madelung, Wilferd. "The Spread of Maturidism and the Turks." In *Religious Schools and Sects in Medieval Islam*, pp. 109-169. London, 1985.

Morris, James Winston. "An Arab 'Machiavelli'? : Rhetoric, Philosophy and Politics in Ibn Khaldun's Critique of Sufism." Forthcoming in *Proceedings* of the Harvard Ibn Khaldun Conference, ed. Roy Mottahedeh, (date and publisher t.b.a).

————. "Body of Light: Ibn 'Arabi's Account of His Father's Death." *Newsletter* of the Muhyiddīn Ibn 'Arabī Society, 15 (1999), p. 4.

————. "Communication and Spiritual Pedagogy: Exploring the Methods of Investigation (*tahqīq*) in Classical Islamic Thought." Forthcoming in *Time, Space and Motion in Islam*, ed. H. Ahmed (date and publisher t.b.a.).

———. "The Continuing Relevance of Qaysarī's Thought: Divine Imagination and the Foundations of Natural Spirituality." In *Papers of the International Symposium on Islamic Thought in the XIII*[th] *and XIV*[th] *Centuries and Da'ūd al-Qaysarī*, ed. T. Koç, pp. 161-171. Kayseri (Turkey), 1998.

———. "Eschatology and Spiritual Realisation in Ibn 'Arabi's '*Meccan Illuminations*'." *Newsletter* of the Muhyiddīn Ibn 'Arabī Society, 19 (2003), pp. 8-10.

———. "'*Except His Face...*': The Political and Aesthetic Dimensions of Ibn 'Arabi's Legacy." *Journal of the Muhyiddīn Ibn 'Arabī Society*, XXIII (1998), pp. 1-13.

———. "'From the Heart to the Throne': The Spiritual Journey in a Nutshell (chapter 72 of *al-Futūhāt al-Makkīya*)." *Newsletter* of the Muhyiddin Ibn 'Arabi Society, 10 (1994), pp. 1-2.

———. "'*He moves you through the Land and Sea...*': Learning From the Earthly Journey." *Journal of the Muhyiddīn Ibn 'Arabī Society*, XVIII (1996), pp. 1-30.

———. "How to Study the *Futūhāt*: Ibn 'Arabī's Own Advice." In *Muhyiddīn Ibn 'Arabī: 750th Anniversary Commemoration Volume*, ed. S. Hirtenstein and M. Tiernan, pp. 73-89. Shaftesbury/ Rockport, Element Books, 1993.

———. "Ibn 'Arabī and His Interpreters." *Journal of the American Oriental Society*, 106 (1986), pp. 539-551 and pp. 733-756; 107 (1987), pp. 101-119.

———. *Ibn 'Arabī and His Interpreters: Historical Contexts and Contemporary Perspectives.* Web-based volume bringing together twenty previously published monographs, shorter studies and reviews all relating to the historical influences and contemporary interpretations of Ibn 'Arabī. Available in .pdf format on website of Ibn 'Arabī Society: *www.ibnarabisociety.org/IbnArabi* .

———. *Ibn 'Arabī: Les Illuminations de la Mecque* (co-author with M. Chodkiewicz, W. Chittick, D. Gril and C. Chodkiewicz). Paris, Sindbad, 1989.

———. "Ibn 'Arabī in the 'Far West': Visible and Invisible Influences." *Journal of the Muhyiddīn Ibn 'Arabī Society*, XXIX (2001), pp. 87-122.

———. *Ibn 'Arabī: The Meccan Revelations* (co-author with W. Chittick), vol. I. New York, Pir Press, 2002.

———. "Ibn 'Arabī's 'Esotericism': The Problem of Spiritual Authority." *Studia Islamica*, LXXI (1990), pp. 37-64.

———. "Ibn 'Arabī's Messianic Secret: From 'The Mahdī' to the Imamate of Every Soul." *Journal of the Muhyiddīn Ibn 'Arabī Society*, XXX (2001), pp. 1-19.

―――. "Ibn 'Arabī's Rhetoric of Realisation: Keys to Reading and 'Translating' the '*Meccan Illuminations*'." Part I, *Journal of the Muhyiddīn Ibn 'Arabī Society*, XXXIII (2003), pp. 54-99; Part II, XXXIV (2003), pp. 103-145.

―――. "Introducing Ibn 'Arabī's '*Book of Spiritual Advice*'." *Journal of the Muhyiddīn Ibn 'Arabī Society*, XXVIII (2000), pp. 1-18.

―――. "Listening For God: Prayer and the Heart in the *Futūhāt*." *Journal of the Muhyiddīn Ibn 'Arabī Society*, XIII (1993), pp. 19-53.

―――. *Many Paths to the Real: Freedom, Creativity, Diversity and Tolerance in Ibn 'Arabī's Political Philosophy*. [Volume currently in preparation.]

―――. *The Master and the Disciple: An Early Islamic Spiritual Dialogue*, Arabic critical edition and English translation and Introduction to Ja'far b. Mansūr al-Yaman's *Kitāb al-'ālim wa'l-ghulām*. London and New York, I. B. Tauris Publishers, 2001.

―――. *Orientations: Islamic Thought in a World Civilisation*. London, Archetype Press, 2004.

―――. "Reading 'Attār's *Conference of the Birds*." In *Approaches to the Asian Classics*, ed. Wm. Theodore de Bary and Irene Bloom, pp. 77-85. N.Y., Columbia University Press, 1990.

——. "Seeing Past the Shadows: Ibn 'Arabī's 'Divine Comedy'." *Journal of the Muhyiddīn Ibn 'Arabī Society*, XII (1993), pp. 50-69.

——. "'*Seeking God's Face...*': Ibn 'Arabī on Right Action and Theophanic Vision." *Journal of the Muhyiddīn Ibn 'Arabī Society*, XVI (1994), pp. 1-34, and XVII (1995), pp. 1-39.

——. "Situating Islamic 'Mysticism': Between Written Traditions and Popular Spirituality." In *Mystics of the Book: Themes, Topics and Typologies*, ed. R. Herrera, pp. 293-334. New York/Berlin, Peter Lang, 1993.

——. "Some Dreams of Ibn 'Arabī (from his *Risālat al-Mubashshirāt*)." *Newsletter* of the Muhyiddīn Ibn 'Arabī Society, 9 (1993), pp. 2-3.

——. "The Spiritual Ascension: Ibn 'Arabī and the *Mi'rāj*." *Journal of the American Oriental Society*, 107 (1987), pp. 629-652, and 108 (1988), pp. 63-77.

——. "Spiritual Imagination and the 'Liminal' World: Ibn 'Arabī on the *Barzakh*." *POSTDATA* (Madrid) 15, no. 2 (1995), pp. 42-49 and 104-109.

——. "Theophany or 'Pantheism'? : the Importance of Balyānī's *Risālat al-Ahadīya*," and "*la description de abū 'abdallāh balyānī par jāmī*." *Horizons Maghrébins* (Toulouse), special festschrift issue for Michel Chodkiewicz, 30 (1995), pp. 43-50 and 51-54.

395

————. *Understanding Religion and Inter-Religious Understanding: Four Classical Muslim Thinkers*. Kuala Lumpur, Center for Civilisational Dialogue, 2003.

————. *The Wisdom of the Throne: An Introduction to the Philosophy of Mulla Sadra*. Princeton, Princeton University Press, 1981.

Rumi, Jalāl al-Dīn. *Kulliyāt-i Shams-i Tabrīz*, ed. B. Furūzānfar. Tehran, Amīr Kabīr, 1341 h.s..

————. *Masnavī-yi Ma'navī* (ed. and transl. R. Nicholson, 8 volumes). Cambridge, E.J.W. Gibb Memorial Series, 1925-1940.

The Shawshank Redemption, director F. Darabont, 1994.

Vâlsan, M. (transl.) *La Niche des Lumières: 101 Saintes Paroles Prophétiques*. Paris, Les Éditions de l'Oeuvre, 1983.

Website of the M. Ibn 'Arabī Society: *www.ibnarabisociety.org*.

Wensinck, A.J., et. al. (eds.). *Concordance et Indices de la Tradition Musulmane* (8 volumes). Leiden, E. J. Brill, 1992.

Wings of Desire (*Der Himmel über Berlin*) and *Far Away, So Close*, director Wim Wenders, 1987 and 1993.

Yahia, Osman. *Histoire et Classification de l'Oeuvre d'Ibn 'Arabī: étude critique* (2 volumes). Damas, Institut Français de Damas, 1964.

II. Biography and Historical Context of Ibn ʿArabī

Addas, Claude. *Ibn ʿArabī, ou la quête du soufre rouge.* Paris, Gallimard, 1988. English translation (P. Kingsley), *Quest for the Red Sulphur: The Life of Ibn ʿArabī.* Cambridge, Islamic Texts Society, 1993.

———. *Ibn ʿArabī: The Voyage of No Return.* Cambridge, Islamic Texts Society, 2000.

Hirtenstein, Stephen. *The Unlimited Mercifier: the spiritual life and thought of Ibn ʿArabī.* Oxford, Anqa Publishing, 1999.

III. Representative Translations (English only)[1]

The Meccan Illuminations / al-Futūhāt al-Makkiyya (partial translations):

Chittick, William C. (transl.). *The Self-Disclosure of God: Principles of Ibn al-ʿArabī's Cosmology.* Albany, NY, SUNY Press, 1998.

———. *The Sufi Path of Knowledge: Ibn al-ʿArabī's Metaphysics of Imagination.* Albany, NY, SUNY Press, 1989.

Chodkiewicz, C. and D. Gril (translators); ed. M. Chodkiewicz. *The Meccan Revelations,* vol. II. New York, Pir Press, 2004.

Morris, J.W., and W. C. Chittick. *Ibn ʿArabī: The Meccan Revelations,* vol. I. New York, Pir Press, 2002.

Winkel, Eric. *Mysteries of Purity: Ibn al-'Arabī's **asrār al-tahārah***. Notre Dame, Cross Cultural Publications, 1995.

Fusūs al-Hikam:

Austin, R.W.J. (transl. and intro.). *Ibn al'Arabi: The Bezels of Wisdom*. Ramsey, NJ, Paulist Press, 1980.

Dagli, Caner K. (transl.). *The Ringstones of Wisdom (Fusūs al-Hikam)*. Chicago, Kazi Publications, 2004.

K. 'Anqā' Mughrib:

Elmore, G. *Islamic Sainthood in the Fulness of Time: Ibn al-'Arabī's "Book of the Fabulous Gryphon."* Leiden, Brill, 2000.

Mashāhid al-Asrār:

Twinch, C. and P. Beneito (translators). *Contemplation of the Holy Mysteries and Ascensions of the Divine Lights*. Oxford, Anqa, 2003.

Mishkāt al-Anwār:

Hirtenstein, S., and M. Tiernan, translators and eds. *Divine Sayings: The Mishkāt al-Anwār of Ibn 'Arabī*. Oxford, Anqa Publishing, 2004.

R. al-Anwār:

Harris, Rabia T. (transl.). *Journey to the Lord of Power*. London/NY, Inner Traditions, 1981.

Chodkiewicz, M. Concluding chapter of *Seal of the Saints: Prophethood and Sainthood in the Doctrine of Ibn 'Arabī*. Cambridge, Islamic Texts Society, 1993.

Rūh al-Quds:

Austin, R.W.J. (transl.). *Sufis of Andalusia*. London, Allen & Unwin, 1971.

Tarjumān al-Ashwāq:

Nicholson, R. (ed. and transl.). *The Tarjumān al-Ashwāq: A Collection of Mystical Odes*. London, Royal Asiatic Society, 1911.

Sells, M. *Stations of Desire: Love Elegies from Ibn 'Arabī*. Jerusalem, Ibis Press, 2000.

Wird (Awrād al-Usbūʿ):

Hirtenstein, S. and P. Beneito (transl.) *The Seven Days of the Heart*. Oxford, Anqa, 1999.

IV. Broad Analytical and Interpretive Studies[2]

Chodkiewicz, Michel. *Un Océan Sans Rivage: Ibn 'Arabī, le livre et la loi*. Paris, Seuil, 1992. English translation (D. Streight), *An Ocean Without Shore: Ibn 'Arabī, the Book, and the Law*. Albany, NY, SUNY Press, 1993.

————. *Le Sceau des saints: Prophétie et sainteté dans la doctrine d'Ibn 'Arabī*. Paris, Gallimard, 1986. English translation (L. Sherrard), *Seal of the Saints: Prophethood and Sainthood in the Doctrine of Ibn 'Arabī*. Cambridge, Islamic Texts Society, 1993.

Corbin, Henry. *Creative Imagination in the Sūfism of Ibn 'Arabī* [recently reprinted as "*Alone with the Alone*"]. Princeton, Princeton University Press, 1969.

Izutsu, Toshihiko. *Sufism and Taoism*. Berkeley, University of California Press, 1984.

Nettler, Ron. *Sufi Metaphysics and Qur'anic Prophets: Ibn 'Arabī's Thought and Method in the "Fusūs al-Hikam."* Cambridge, Islamic Texts Society, 2004.

Sells, Michael A. *Mystical Languages of Unsaying*. Chicago, University of Chicago Press, 1994.

INDEX

275, 276, 277, 284, 291,
302. *See also* prophet,
messenger, *awliyā'*
prophetic 270, 271, 274
destiny 248, 268, 377. *See also*
qadr
individual 283
mystery of 252
veil of 273
determination. *See also qadr*
divine 35, 283
devil 90, 91, 92, 93. *See also*
Iblīs, Shaytān, test
dhawq
tasting 27
dhikr 2, 23, 25, 70, 80, 123,
219, 225, 323, 330, 341,
348, 359, 360. *See also*
remembrance, recollection
Allāh 49
invocations 330
dialectic 263
dialogue
ascending 273
dīn 166, 312. *See also* Religion
al-Dīn 369
Dīn Allāh 369
al-Dīn al-Khālis 369
al-qayyim 111
discernment 67, 84, 86, 182,
187, 255, 256, 263, 301.
See also 'āqil, 'aql
spiritual 180, 197, 210, 306
Divine Comedy 248
divine saying 113, 325, 341. *See
also hadīth qudsī*
Door 59, 71, 72, 80, 96. *See
also bāb*, gate, Garden
God's 124, 143
of being-veiled 144

of the Garden 171
seven 143
to the awareness of God 146
drawn near to God 78. *See also*
angel
dreams 268. *See also* Imagination, Joseph
du'ā
petionary prayer 349
Dune
Hadith of the 152, 166
of Musk 118
of the beatific Vision 148
dying
voluntary 290

E

L'échelle Céleste 374
Eckhart, M. 381
eclipses
spiritual 305
Eden 250
elect 35. *See also* elite
Elias 284. *See also* Idrīs
elite 40, 96, 97, 326
of the elite 95, 326
spiritual 266
epistemology 353
Epistle
introductory 124
Epistle of Good Tidings 123
Essence 55, 81, 89, 94
exile 96
experience 3, 6, 27, 34, 55, 94,
97, 268. *See also dhawq,
shuhūd*, tasting, witnessing
Eye. *See also 'ayn, basīra*
divine 131
of the Real 124

416

tion) 128. *See also* Imagination, *khiyāl, takhayyul*
wahy 352. *See also* inspiration,
revelation, address
wajh 107
  al-Haqq 125
wakīl 43
walī 164, 359, 372. *See also*
  awliyā', Friend
walāya 278, 282, 367
wanderer 19, 21, 25. *See also*
  sā'ihūn, Travelers
  wandering 18, 19, 22, 24, 37,
  38, 39, 41, 42
wara' 72
  spiritual scrupulousness 24
wāridāt 58, 94
watchmen 284. *See also* Gate,
  bāb
Water 84, 229, 297, 308, 368
  of divine Life 170, 363. *See
  also Khadir, 'ayn*
Wenders, W. 374, 377, 379
wilāya 356. *See also walī,
  walāya,* Friend
wilderness 6
winds 282. *See also* Breath,
  nafahāt
Wings of Desire 374, 377, 379
wisdom 60, 75, 192
  inspired practical 210
Wise-Healer 285, 286. *See also*
  Idrīs, *hakīm*
witnessing 92, 129. *See also*
  shuhūd, kashf, experience,
  Knower
  direct 262
  immediate 273
wondrous 180
Words

of God 58

Y

Yahyā (John the Baptist) 338
Yahya, O. 330, 341
Yeats, W.B. 162, 340
Youth 56, 129. *See also fatā*
  eternal 127
Yunus Emre 192

Z

zāhir al-Dīn 75, 76
Zahiri 370
zakāt 158, 335, 343. *See also*
  charity, *sadaqa*
ziyāra 319. *See also* pilgrim
Zohar 328